Chance and the Text of Experience

BY THE SAME AUTHOR:

Reading Clarissa: *The Struggles of Interpretation*

CHANCE AND THE TEXT OF EXPERIENCE

Freud, Nietzsche, and Shakespeare's *Hamlet*

William Beatty Warner

Cornell University Press

ITHACA AND LONDON

First published 1986 by Cornell University Press.

International Standard Book Number 0-8014-1754-6
Library of Congress Catalog Card Number 86-6276
Printed in the United States of America
*Librarians: Library of Congress cataloging information
appears on the last page of the book.*

*The paper in this book is acid-free and meets the guidelines
for permanence and durability of the Committee on Production
Guidelines for Book Longevity of the Council on Library Resources.*

FOR MY PARENTS

CONTENTS

[7]

Contents

ACKNOWLEDGMENTS

No less than any other phenomenon, this book has been influenced and traversed by the texts and people that its author has chosen, but that have also chosen him. Such an interchange opens up the act of authorship to a process that is one of my subthemes here: the kind of collaboration and indebtedness that can never be fully acknowledged, because it was never fully controlled or present to consciousness. My indebtedness begins with what I owe the texts read in this book. I have also felt a steady influence from the exemplary acts of reading to be found in the work of Jacques Derrida and Paul de Man. Finally, for help and influence of a more personal sort I thank:

Richard Klein, for stimulating my interest in the question of chance long ago and being teacher, guide, and audience on so many occasions since. I hope this book has benefited from the kinetics of his reading praxis, where his grasp of a conceptual problem, the daring of his interpretive moves, and his pleasure in the surprising activate and renew one another.

Rodolphe Gasché, whose profound, nearly completed book on the relation between the philosophical problem of reflection and deconstruction has become a model of conceptual rigor for me. At three crucial points in the writing of this text, he generously helped construe richly packed passages of German. In the process, he helped lead me to some of the central ideas expressed here.

Dick Fly, whose passionate, lifelong meditation on Shakespeare has been consistently clarifying for me. By being willing to discuss anything about Shakespeare, on a moment's notice, for from three minutes to an afternoon, he helped to lead me through the labyrinths of

Acknowledgments

Hamlet criticism and know the pleasures of interpretation which could be shared even when our ideas diverged.

Biddy Martin, for generously sharing the thoughts and ideas emerging from a forthcoming book on Lou Salomé that will change our way of seeing her. In several long talks, she helped me gain a sense of how the Nietzsche-Salomé relationship might look from the woman's side, even while we confirmed our common differences from the conventional ways of understanding that relationship. In our talks I came to admire the way her thought blends an original theoretical project with an active sense of the human.

For valuable advice in revising, I am grateful to Cheryl Lester, Roy Roussel, William Graebner, Larysa Mykyta, and Carol Flynn. For helping with the preparation of this manuscript I also thank Rita Keller, Lisa Harmon, and Deborah Kloepfer. For staying with this project through an arduous process of revision my sincere gratitude goes to my editors Bernhard Kendler and Kay Scheuer.

WILLIAM B. WARNER

Buffalo, New York

Chance and the Text of Experience

INTRODUCTION

This book began with a speculative question: what is chance, and what bearing does it have upon the person who interprets the chance incident which befalls him or her? I carried this question through investigations of baseball, the *I Ching*, and Aristotle, until, for reasons this introduction will explore, I settled on a close reading of those texts which could most fruitfully support this intellectual venture: selected writings of Freud, Nietzsche, and Shakespeare. I soon realized that such an investigation cannot be limited to what has been written in these texts *about* chance; it must also seek to understand how chance has operated in the production and reception of that writing. But how can one pass from what is written of chance to the chances of its writing? These "chances"—never "spoken" by the text in their heterogenous plurality—appear as historical, biographical, experiential. The elusive ubiquity of chance vexes the effort to delimit a terrain for its study. How can one read the writings of Freud, Nietzsche, or Shakespeare in relation to what seems in important ways different from these texts—the incidents of their lives and their experience of these incidents (whether opaque or present to consciousness) as we might construe each from legend, letters, or the canonical text? To read text and experience in their exchanges, I need to go beyond a formal and conceptual analysis of the canonical text, so as to interpret what is adventitious about the experience of the person writing. I must risk doing some type of biographical reading. Such an effort opens this project to a debate recently joined in critical theory between two parties: those who would conceive literary studies as a subset of the deconstruction of texts, where "text" is the broadest possible term for a network productive of meaning, and those who would situate the study of literature and culture in the movement of their formation within a newly rejuvenated, global concept of history. Taking some of the coordinates of this debate will prepare us to embark upon our own study.

Text/Experience//Text/History

In the last few years deconstructive reading has been criticized for its purported inability or refusal to read the text in relationship to something outside the text—history, the social, politics, or culture. This criticism of deconstructive reading needs to be heard and modulated, so that, in revised form, it might serve our critical investigation of chance. With his accustomed vigor, Terry Eagleton includes deconstruction in a sweeping condemnation of literary theory as "extremist" in "its obstinate, perverse, endlessly resourceful refusal to countenance social and historical realities." Edward Said, in his introduction to *The World, the Text, and the Critic*, offers a more pointed description of the way American followers have appropriated the reading practices of Derrida and Foucault: "Textuality has therefore become the exact antithesis and displacement of what might be called history. Textuality is considered to take place, yes, but by the same token it does not take place anywhere or anytime in particular. It is produced, but by no one and at no time. . . . Literary theory has for the most part isolated textuality from the circumstances, the events, the physical senses that made it possible and render it intelligible as the result of human work." Seeking to overcome what he says has made "textuality" the "somewhat mystical and disinfected subject matter of literary theory," Said's account frames textuality within the empirical determinates of time, place, circumstances, and physical senses. More reluctant than either Eagleton or Said to define history as the proper and ascertainable ground for the interpretation of texts, Fredric Jameson nonetheless wishes to avoid seeing history as "simply one more text among others." He offers this formulation of the relation text/history: "that history is *not* a text, not a narrative, master or otherwise, but that, as an absent cause, it is inaccessible to us except in textual form, and that our approach to it and to the Real itself necessarily passes through its prior textualization, its narrativization in the political unconscious."[1] By the end of the long theoretical chapter of *The Political Unconscious*, Jameson is ready to confer the palm on "History": "History itself becomes the ultimate ground as well as the untranscendable limit of our understanding in general and our textual interpretations in particular."[2] Note the ambiguity of the relationship this statement posits between history and knowledge. On the one hand, history is the "ground" of understanding and interpretation. On the other hand, as a limit we can approach but never reach, as a horizon we can never go beyond, as a ground which is "ultimate" and final, and thus which may never really be plumbed, history is absent to us and can be approached only through textual interpretation.

Jameson's elevation of "History" over text does not take account of the practical consequences of history's intimate entanglement in language. A stark polarization of text and history allows each of these three commentators to insist on a proper—that is, a politically responsible—subordination of language to reality. It also mirrors in reverse the sweeping programatic claims made for language at the zenith of the structualist program of the 1960s.[3] But this assertion of the priority of "History" over text is vitiated by the way history fails to become the direct object of hermeneutic inquiry; rather, it is a liminal term that can be approached only indirectly, through the reading of texts.[4]

To read in the name of "history," to *choose* by fiat to privilege history over text, obscures a pivotal fact. Since each does not exclude the other, the opposition text/history is not a true binary opposition, any more than is its less encompassing affiliated opposition, text/experience. In fact, these oppositions put in question the oppositions

1. See Terry Eagleton, *Literary Theory: An Introduction* (Minneapolis: University of Minnesota Press, 1983), 196; Edward Said, *The World, the Text, and the Critic* (Cambridge: Harvard University Press, 1983), 3–4; Fredric Jameson, *The Political Unconscious: Narrative as a Socially Symbolic Act* (Ithaca: Cornell University Press, 1981), 35.

2. Jameson, *Political Unconscious*, 100.

3. In *Of Grammatology*, Derrida's readings of Lévi-Strauss and Saussure put in question the possibility of that systematic study of language which had been the mainstay of the structuralist project; but his oft-cited sentence "Il n'y a pas de hors-texte," "There is no outside of the text," echoes while revising the structuralist positioning of language at the center of the "human sciences." See *Of Grammatology*, trans. Gayatri Spivak (Baltimore: The Johns Hopkins University Press, 1974), 158.

4. I am indebted to Ellen Rooney for clarifying some of these issues. See "Going Farther: Literary Theory and the Passage to Cultural Criticism," *Works and Days* 5, 3, no. 1, (Spring 1985). Her article offers a critique of my earlier discussion of the relationship text/history in "Reading Rape: Marxist-Feminist Figurations of the Literal," *Diacritics*, 13 (1983), 12–32.

sign/referent and inside/outside that they seemed at first to repeat and confirm.[5] If as these "cultural critics" maintain, a particular text is produced in relation to time-bound, material conditions of history and experience, then history too is produced in language and the text, not just retrospectively but in its registering the first time. And by inverse argument, it is difficult to imagine a history or experience—whether as the "worldly events" or power relations Said focuses upon, or the almost mythically inaccessible "Necessity" Jameson invokes as the irreducible experience of History—as outside that textuality which would give them some form to the person or community. By the way they implicate each another, the orders of representation and history seem to function like partly miscible, partly immiscible fluids which enfold, penetrate, and repel one another. The attempt to fix or limit one in relation to the other is less a stable intellectual project than a symptom of interpretive desire.

By setting the historical or social beyond, apart, and above the textual, the three polemical statements briefly quoted end by construing and negotiating the opposition text/history in isolation from a reading practice. A reading practice might modify, in nuanced and unexpected ways, the relation between the text one reads and an outside—whether it be called "history" or "experience"—which textual production, as a social venture, both implies and necessitates. So in order to avoid the impasses that result from giving priority either to the text in its autonomy, or to "experience" as the text's absent origin and ultimate meaning, much of the practical conceptual work of this book is directed at finding middle terms which are neither *simply* text nor *simply* experience, but are always *both* text *and* experience. In my pursuit of a biographical reading of the writings of Freud and Nietzsche, and my narration of their life and thought in their reciprocal relation, chance emerges as a signal instance of such a middle term. For it is during the interpretation of chance that experience becomes so insistently entangled with a textual practice. By my interpretation, "chance" is neither an objective event in the world, nor merely reducible to its textual inscription in some personal narrative, but rather something which, befalling the person, and being construed by him or her, becomes a sign of a necessity that is opaque and resists the control of a presiding consciousness. This definition allows me to suggest, in a provisional fashion, the relationship between chance, text, and experience.

By entitling this book "Chance and the Text of Experience," I am

5. See Paul de Man's analysis of this whole issue in the first chapter of *Allegories of Reading* (New Haven: Yale University Press, 1979).

bringing several related ideas to my attempt to read the texts of Freud, Nietzsche, and Shakespeare in relation to "experience." Although we can know their experience only through the texts to which time has reduced their lives, we should not conclude that this experience has always been only text. It carries an excess and spills a surplus that is not entirely nameable or recuperable. But neither is a text, whether as the marks on the pages we now turn, or as obscure inscriptions at the origin, describable as experience. Thus, in the readings which follow, I have tried to allow a strange double perspective. Text and experience are not radically "other" to one another, but neither are they simply the same. In its elaboration experience is constantly involved with the conditions of writing and textual production. But the texts we read and write, whether by artists or thinkers or critics, are also "delivered of" experience—that is, they both come from and are cut off from experience.[6]

Reopening the Question of Chance

Chance is to be a key term in these readings, so we need to begin by grasping what "chance" might mean, and asking why the idea of chance, which has always had an urgent pertinence to the person has often been marginalized by the Western tradition. It is Nietzsche who suggests that our (largely illusory) sense of conceptual mastery and self-mastery is constructed upon a subordination of chance carried out early in our tradition. According to this argument, all of Western philosophy and science is based upon an idealist false premise: that chance and change and uncertainty are less real than

6. Derrida's writings have usually put the concept of "experience" under suspicion as too metaphysically determined a locus of the subject's self-presence to itself. See for example the aside and caution about the use of the concept of experience at one point in *Of Grammatology*: "As for the concept of experience, it is most unwieldy here. Like all the notions I am using here, . . . we can only use it under erasure. 'Experience' has always designated the relationship with a presence, whether that relationship had the form of consciousness or not" (60). An important critique of experience is implicit in Derrida's reading of Husserl. See *Speech and Phenomena*, trans. David B. Allison (Evanston: Northwestern University Press, 1973). It is, I think, true that a naive anti-textual version of experience will often seek to elide the gaps and aporias of life and turn the experience of the past, present, and future into what Heidegger calls a "pure sequence of Nows," present to a presiding conscious subject. See *Being and Time*, trans. S. Robinson (New York: Harper & Row, 1962), 377. This book has sought to avoid this tendency by textualizing the concept of experience, and reading it in relation to chance.

being and stasis and certitude. In turning away from those materialist philosophers who had made chance an integral part of their cos-
mology, the dominant current of Western philosophy, led by Plato
and Aristotle, systematically factored chance out of reality so as to
arrive at those identities and idealities with which we think reality:
time, space, being, the event, causality, history, gender, the cogito,
and character. These concepts allow us to replay and represent the
world to ourselves in a masterful mode. Then, an unruly material,
contingent reality will appear, in Yeats's words, as "but a spume that
plays / Upon a ghostly paradigm of things." Since philosophy promises access to the "ghostly paradigm" of truth, chance—the spume
upon the wave of reality—fades to insignificance.[7]

There are, however, other, more personal vantage points from
which chance appears central and decisive. If you are Oedipus con-
templating life-events that look more than coincidental; if you are
waiting for your horse to come in, or for the results of a biopsy, then
chance seems active, important, perhaps fateful. Few of us have
failed, at one time or another, to script ourselves as a latter-day Oedipus, who pauses to consider those times and places where chance
has subtly injected itself into our lives: one job, college, or city is chosen over another and then becomes the matrix of every subsequent
influential encounter; the seat found in the library brings you to the
table where you meet the person you marry; riding around that
curve at that speed on that night, a loved one meets another car
traveling head-on in the opposite direction. At these crossings in
time and space, where pasts intersect and futures fork in numberless
directions, chance seems decisive in the weaving of personal history.
We sometimes wish to forget, but cannot entirely elude, these commonplaces of critical coincidence.

Chance is habitually abridging the person's attempts at mastery;
but in doing so it brings intimations of pleasure as well as loss. In its
negative moments chance becomes a locus of anxiety for a life at
risk: cells have begun to grow too fast; a disease is indicated. But
chance also appears in a more neutral light, as if it had merged with
the genetic code and historical process which has delivered what is
most fixed and necessary about one's life: father, mother, gender,
wealth or poverty, all of one's past, the form of one's body—all of
what one takes as one's "lot" in life. Our thought about ourselves is

---

7. Yeats's lines on Plato are from "Among School Children." For one place among
many on this issue, see Nietzsche's discussion of Greek thought in *Ecce Homo* in *Basic
Writings of Nietzsche*, trans. Walter Kaufmann (New York, 1968), 729–30. Henceforth *BWN*.

[18]

so tied up with these things that we seldom dissociate ourselves from them enough to see them as arbitrary, bad or good, or even functions of the workings of chance. And finally, since the drabbest life of all would be a life immune to chance or change, chance can stamp its character upon that welcome event which inaugurates, begins, and brings new things. Like the good roll of the dice or a lucky lottery ticket, chance brings novel opportunities—as in the phrase "give the man a chance," or "the chance of a lifetime."

When chance challenges the person's accustomed sense of mastery and self-mastery, it becomes an urgent interpretive problem. Sometimes chance presents itself in the sublime metaphysical mode familiar from tragedy or times of national crisis: in war, storm, disease, when chance appears as an insistent fact, for things are in flux, and changes are coming suddenly and in excess of any imaginable cause-effect matrix, then the individual or the nation feels the possibility of loss, and the future yawns with uncertainty. Living thus in the brace of chance, we position ourselves opposite some "other"—the cosmos, fate, the gods, the Judeo-Christian God—and ascribe to this "other" sure knowledge of what has happened and what is to come. If we have before us a genuinely urgent question, then there opens what is perhaps the most uncertain and problematic of all scenes of reading: we scan the skies, the entrails of animals, the hexagrams of the *I Ching*, to find and read signs sent from the beyond. But we have a persistent suspicion that we are in the strange semiotic situation of being condemned to read signals that have not been sent. Perhaps the chance active in this moment is *merely* chance—it "means" nothing, is intended by no agency, is the function of no orderly process. Chance cannot even be the object of a focused question; it is an arbitrary mark that must be named, interpreted, and translated into a form with which a person can live. For someone venturing an interpretation of life that will make it seem intelligible, appropriate, and thus one's own, chance is scandalous: a scandal to the personal desire to construe one's own life as having a coherent incorporable meaning because it is determined by something more real and less alien, less arbitrary and more just than chance.

One recourse for the person is to strive for an objectivity that will suppress both chance and one's own position. Then chance will not only be a term to be pushed to the margins of one's life; it becomes an element to be strained out of the systematic body of knowledge. These two negations turn out to be related. For efforts at knowledge shaped on the conventional scientific model tame the indeterminacy of chance not only through the way they define their objects or through recourse to a science such as probability; they also begin by factoring out the position of the individual. This species of knowledge offers a description of things that will appear objective and hold true for everyone over time precisely because it is not tethered to the shifting moods, perspectives, and interests of an individual person.

An understanding of the way chance both peaks and frustrates a person's efforts at knowledge and self-knowledge allows me to hazard this definition. Chance is less an objective phenomenon than the way an observing subject characterizes some event in which it has a stake or interest, the interpretation of an event, in other words, which occasions loss or gain for the person. Chance intensifies the person's sense of the singularity of his or her position. Thus, although scientists have developed a systematic and objective definition of randomness, it is not at all clear that there is any "chance" event without some implied person to experience it as "chance."[8] An example will demonstrate this interrelationship. If you die in a fatal car accident, those friends and loved ones who think from your perspective will probably interpret this event as arbitrary, unnecessary, and chance. Your sudden death achieves this meaning through its antithetical relation to the horizon of your experience and the desires and interpretations which give that experience its distinct temper. This does not mean that the event cannot be understood in relationship to causal factors like speeding cars, changing lights, and absentmindedness—nor that this particular death cannot be melded into national accident statistics. And indeed, your death would probably seem no more chance or surprising to a visitor from outer space than the death of an insect. But from the perspective of the person, this event appears disturbing, significant, and chance.

That the person's position is somehow embedded in the very idea of chance is indicated by a pattern discernible in our language. Many of the words used in connection with chance have an etymological connection with the idea of falling. "Accident," "incident," "coincidence," and "chance" are derived, by different pathways, from the latin *cadere*, "to fall." In the most common word for "chance" in German—*Zufall*—and in the English verb "to befall,"

---

8. A random number may be formed from a series where the likelihood of the appearance of one digit will not be any greater than another. Thus if one counts the radioactive emissions per second from a given quantity of matter and records a "0" if the resulting number is even and a "1" if the omission count is an odd number, one can generate a number (00101101000 . . .) which is "random." There is no equally rigorous definition of chance.

this semantic linkage is particularly direct.[9] All these words refer to events that "just happen," in an apparently arbitrary way, like the way a die falls upon any one of its six sides. But "falling" is not a purely objective event; it includes within it, by implication, the position of the observing subject who defines which way is up or down. When considering events in astrophysics or particle physics, a science teacher will labor to divest students of this anthropomorphic, earthbound way of thinking. Why is there this habitual connection between chance and falling? Perhaps because gravitation, unlike light or fire, is a force manifest in its effects but invisible to the person; as such, it seems both mysterious and natural. When things begin to fall, the small part of the future concerned with this event suddenly appears open and indeterminate. And all our modern knowledge about gravitation and probability has not enabled us to foresee where or how, in a single instance, the cards will fall.

The ideas of the person, falling, and chance are closely linked in what Judeo-Christian scripture narrates as the first chance event and the first moment of history, because it is the first event that did not have to happen the way it did: the "fall of man" (and woman). Since orthodox Christian theology does not imagine God to be confined within human limits of time, space, or knowledge, there is a sense in which the Fall must be always already providentially known, and therefore not chance but necessary. Milton's narrative in *Paradise Lost*, however, gives prime emphasis to the human, time-bound perspective on the Fall. And there is a good doctrinal reason for doing so. The only way to link human freedom and moral responsibility in this event is by doing a narrative which makes it look fatefully contingent, the accidental cause of human history, the beginning and prototype of all subsequent human falls into chance-laden futures. At such a moment, a single person's "experience" is not private property, the possession or construction of the kind of essentialist subject phenomenology has postulated. "Experience" is woven of the language in which a person strives to construe an exterior event, or

9. Walter W. Skeat, *A Concise Etymological Dictionary of the English Language* (Oxford: Oxford University Press, 1881). In French this cluster of words comes from the Latin *cadere* through *choir*, the medieval word displaced by *tomber*, "to fall." See Jacqueline Picoche, *Dictionnaire etymologique du français* (Paris: Robert, 1979). For more on the etymology of the word "chance," and a valuable recent essay upon the subject, see Derrida's contribution to *Taking Chances: Derrida, Psychoanalysis, and Literature*, ed. Joseph H. Smith and William Kerrigan (Baltimore: The Johns Hopkins University Press, 1984). My own study of chance was completed before Derrida's essay was published, but I have tried to discuss some of the issues raised by the essay in my review of *Taking Chances*, in the special issue on comparative literature of *MLN*, 99, no. 5 (Winter 1984), 1195–1202.

sequence of events, as it impinges upon his or her life. Such experience, composed in bewilderment before what has befallen the person, may then become a pretext for revisions, speculations, narratives. But because it is determined, in its most decisive moments, by contingencies outside the person's apprehension or control, this experience continues to recede, appearing always somewhat beyond the grasp of the person who would know it.[10]

It is not easy to grasp or define this "experience" we all feel that we almost know. The conceptual narratives which compose this book illustrate this experience as an interpretive practice where the boundaries between inside and outside, matter and concept, object and subject, necessity and chance become crucially confused. My study of the way individuals interpret chance into experience gives special emphasis to what is strangely productive about this confusing movement. In articulating a relationship of chance and the person, narrative figures an experience for the subject which is obscure yet decisive because, in its single violent movement, chance helps constitute the very person it disrupts as a fixed identity. And narrative seems to be a privileged site for negotiating, and experiencing, this convergence of chance and the person. Thus something importantly similar is at work whether Hamlet is telling of the wonderful shipboard encounter with pirates which saves his life ("There's a divinity that shapes our ends . . ."), or Horatio promises a full explanation to Fortinbras and the ambassadors at the play's end ("So shall you hear / Of carnal, bloody, and unnatural acts . . ."); whether Freud makes an arbitrary choice of a line from Shakespeare's *Julius Caesar* to discover the logic of an important dream; or Nietzsche rejoices at the "dear chance" which has brought him Lou Salomé as an intellectual companion. Given the importance of chance to both the narratives of experience and the conceptual texts of Freud, Nietzsche, and Shakespeare, it becomes all the more noteworthy when chance and experience are excluded from these texts by the commentaries of

10. In the context of asserting the importance of the category "experience" to feminist discourse, Teresa de Lauretis defines "experience" as a process shaped coequally by the insistence of that which is "outside" and "inside" the person, in their ongoing exchange through time. By her account, experience has a mobile relation to the "reality" it encounters, the subjectivity it assumes, and the discursive practices within which it unfolds. Experience is not "a fixed point of departure or arrival from which one then interacts with the world," but an "achievement unending or daily renewed." Experience is that "process by which, for all social beings, subjectivity is constructed. Through that process one places oneself or is placed in social reality, and so perceives and comprehends as subjective . . . those relations—material, economic, and interpersonal—which are in fact social and, in a larger perspective, historical." *Alice Doesn't: Feminism, Semiotics, Cinema* (Bloomington: Indiana University Press, 1984), 159.

Freudians, Nietzscheans, and Shakespeareans. In fact the erasure of chance and experience becomes the condition of the possibility of the authority and "timelessness" claimed for these texts when they function as guides for the disciplines of psychoanalysis, philosophy, and literary studies. But how have the texts of thinkers and artists like Freud, Nietzsche, and Shakespeare acceded to a privileged and masterful position above historical contingencies? Once we have some understanding of how this position is constructed, we will be ready to attempt reading them in another way.

Interrogating Textual Mastery

When a major thinker becomes the focus of prolonged and attentive critical study, and when his thought is discovered to have so direct, provocative, and resonant a relation to truth that it becomes the ground for critical work, then this thinker's text becomes a privileged matrix for intellectual effort and exerts special influence upon the practice of reading.[11] But the special privilege accorded the theoretical text is a problem for the institution of literary studies. Since readings embarked on under the sponsorship of a privileged theoretical text often seem to return to the conceptual framework of that text, it can become the limit and enclosure of those readings. And because of the especially masterful relation to truth the theoretical text is presumed to possess, it is often fixed into an idealized truth system immune to the effects of chance, time, and history. Literary texts read under the aegis of such a theoretical text have usually, in their turn, been separated from those biographical, political, historical, and social texts and contexts to which they have a more than adventitious relation.

This idealization of the theoretical text should have an uncanny familiarity for any student of literature. For the special authority conferred upon Freud and Nietzsche by recent critical theory is sim-

11. Why have some texts had this kind of influence in this century? I can only offer this hypothesis. In the absence of generally accepted criterion of truth, and with the dispersion and specialization of the discourses so characteristic of modernity, the performative efficacy of a theoretical text seems to arise from the way it provides a semi-independent, "free-standing" system, with a coherent, mutually illuminating set of terms which, though not "natural" and "inevitable" in themselves, nonetheless allow it to become an effective matrix for thought and action. They function as a secular scripture.

ilar, in many essentials, to the special authority accorded Shakespeare by literary studies. How does a text acquire this position of mastery in relation to the discursive space it inhabits? It seems to depend on a strangely circular interaction between the text's intrinsic properties and its reception, between the text's formal and conceptual properties and the way it is repeated and countersigned by readers. Here, it seems to me, are the minimum necessary elements for the ascension of a text to a position of special discursive power: the work of a prolific writer and thinker becomes broad enough in scope, coherent enough in conception, and original enough in its expression that other thinkers, writers, critics turn in large numbers to that text and use its central concepts, forms of analysis, themes, and "method" as the basis or object of their own intellectual projects. With the continued increase of its authority and value, readers may undergo a transference to the text/thinker, imagining that it is the single most important repository of truth.[12]

The intellectual prestige accorded such a text by such readers engenders a double imperative for reading. On the one hand, there is an effort to translate the message of the theoretical or artistic text so that it will circulate widely; on the other, it must be protected against vulgar misuse and oversimplification. Consequently, efforts at summary description are often accompanied by the warning that what follows "does not begin to exhaust" the truth of the text, that it is but a partial beginning of the exegesis of a text that contains mysteries to which I have not yet penetrated (or you are not yet ready to penetrate). This interpretation situation leads to particular types of writing: producing editions both "authorized" and "standard"; doing a detailed, loving, and scrupulous exegesis of the text; carrying forward a lively defense of it against the misinterpretations of adversaries or false disciples. These kinds of writing are woven from at least four distinct moments of interpretation: "to understand what *X* means by this . . ." (the immanent reading informs us we are in a discursive space shaped by the master's subtle multiple intentions); ". . . it is essential to understand another concept or passage over here . . . " (the holistic reading mandates reading each part in relation to the whole); " . . . and even though he says this here, elsewhere he balances this half-assertion with its near opposite . . ." (so that each position is countered ironically in such a way that the

---

12. For an analysis of the transference to Freud as the "master" of psychoanalysis by his disciples, see François Roustang, *Dire Mastery: Discipleship from Freud to Lacan*, trans. Ned Lukacher (Baltimore: The Johns Hopkins University Press, 1982).

text can never be limited to a single assertion); ". . . and besides, this idea cannot be taken literally, it must be understood figuratively to mean . . ." (the movement into an allegorical reading; any simple relation to the signified has been overcome). These modes of reading, taken together, keep the text always slightly beyond the grasp of the reader.

The authority of the privileged theoretical or artistic text is often explained, and secured from explanation, by an insistence that the work is the creation of a "genius." The OED points out that the contemporary meaning of "genius," given definitive form in the Romantic period as "an exalted and mysterious power of mind," was explicitly distinguished by German theoreticians from an earlier sense of "genius"—an individual's distinct, remarkable, but finally intelligible "talent." "The former [was regarded] as the higher of the two, as 'creative' and 'original,' and as achieving its results by instinctive perception and spontaneous activity, rather than by processes which admit of being distinctly analyzed." The favored new sense of the creative power of "genius" harkens back to the earliest, most superstitious sense of "genius" (or "genii") as "a tutelary god or attendant spirit allotted to every person at his birth." The Romantic conception of "genius," when applied to the creator of a theoretical or artistic text, has the effect of transporting the conceptual and aesthetic achievement of the text outside history, whether history is understood as rationally causal or chaotically contingent.

An author who receives the accolade of "genius" becomes strangely difficult to know. The sense grows among an interpretive community that the architectonic greatness of his text cannot be explained by reading the traces of life in the writing, whether they are etched there by consciousness, the unconscious, ideology, the structure of institutions the person inhabits, the *zeitgeist*, or some overdetermined combination of these. The ideas and perspectives contained within the text seem to multiply and accelerate. It is no longer possible to think of this text as a subset of the writing of a historical person. Their human profile has gone through a "fade-out." And ironically, autobiography can facilitate the effacement of the traces of the life in the writing. Thus Freud, in writing of the origins of his science in *The History of the Psycho-Analytic Movement*, deletes Wilhelm Fliess from his story. In this case biography furthers the invisibility of its subject so as to increase the author's authority. With Shakespeare the reciprocal expansion of authority and invisibility reaches its logical limit. The nearly complete absence of information about his life, when combined with the extraordinary range of his rhetoric and his use of commonplaces and borrowed plots, allows Shakespeare to be, in Keats's words, "everything and no thing."

Under the force of these shaping presumptions about these texts, what has gradually been lost is the possibility of thinking of their authors as having biases of viewpoint, disabling obsessions, a limiting social position, and contingencies of personal and public history which helped to effect that viewpoint, those obsessions, and that position. The disappearance of the singular chance experience of the person who produces art and theory is part of the fascination, pleasure, and idealizing power of both art and theory. In the last movement of this book, I will try to demonstrate how such a disappearance enables the sublime idolatry extended to Shakespeare by most of the scholars of his text. It also operates in the kind of idolatry that the followers of Freud and Nietzsche have sometimes extended to their heroes.

By rereading Freud and Nietzsche, I am registering my sense of a situation of general indebtedness. I do not think we are yet ready to write off our debt to them, to pass "beyond" them. Instead, my rereading affirms the continued value of their texts, both for the way they have seeded so much recent intellectual work and for the critique of mastery they make possible. Like the debt of Western literature to Shakespeare, our debt to these texts is not easy to calculate. But neither is it immeasurable. Rather, this "debt," because it is also a legacy, will be valuable to investigate and assume, assume *by* investigating.[13] To do so, we will need to understand the initial allure of these texts and most particularly, the claims to mastery made in their names by those disciples who seek the most intimate and faithful repetition of them. This involves reading Freudians, Nietzscheans, and Shakespeareans. Rather than being competitors to outdo, in this book they become an integral part of the textual situation I am interpreting, and also inhabit. But if Freud, Nietzsche, and Shakespeare are to be jolted out of the masterful metaphysical role they are too often given, they must be read again, and read in another way. Thus my rereadings of Freud, Nietzsche, and Shakespeare seek to elude the metaphysically confining modes of reading they have often been used to serve. Then the authority they have fairly won can be seen as the effect of discrete interpretations which

13. See Sam Weber's useful and suggestive essay entitled "The Debts of Deconstruction and Other, Related Assumptions," in *Taking Chances*, ed. Smith and Kerrigan.

are time-bound, language-bound, and contingent. This book labors to trace the effects of these binding contingencies.

The distinct perspective of this reading venture arises from the way I will continue to depend upon those texts I subject to critique. Thus I will not proceed by returning to a naive pretheoretical reading, which would divest these texts of their conceptual or artistic power or their involuntary moments of reflexivity, so that they end framed within an impoverished causal explanation in biology, biography, history, psychohistory, and so on. Instead, my reading seeks to travel in reverse direction the path by which these theoretical and artistic texts have been stripped of their relation to chance and experience. Thus by doing a biographical reading of Freud and Nietzsche I will attempt to undo the invisibility of the life behind (and within) the writing. This involves enlarging the scope of our critical reading to include letters, journals, biographies, and legend. By reading the official, canonical text in relation to this larger body of life-writing of which it is a part, I hope to engage those events which appear both critical to a life-narrative and contingent—which, happening a certain way, did not have to happen the way they did. Finally, in opening these texts to the historicity of their production and reception, I want to rethink the way literary study has conceptualized (and resisted conceptualizing) the effects of mastery won by the texts of Freud, Nietzsche, and Shakespeare.

Reading Life-Writing;
Writing Conceptual Narratives

The intimate relationship I am suggesting between chance and experience has helped shape my strategy for reading Freud, Nietzsche, and Shakespeare: to read the "life" and "thought" of their writings, in relation to each other, and in view of the question of chance. Each of my narratives stages itself around a conceptual turning point of considerable consequence in the articulation of the text read. In these narratives, chance is not situated as an object, a hypostatized entity with the character of being and identity, as it is sometimes presumed to exist in an ideal time-space continuum. Instead, so that chance can be grasped in its Heraclitean activity, it is here examined in the more fugitive and aberrant locus of its action: as it appears to a person or character living in a shifting temporal manifold, in full exposure to its single decisive movements. In each of these texts "chance" is named and conceptualized in quite different terms. Shakespeare's engagement of this problematic is aligned with Christian (and not-so-Christian) ideas of providence, fortune, and chance. Although both Nietzsche and Freud assume a secular, nonprovidential concept of the world's workings, we shall see each giving "chance" a meaning peculiar to the trajectory of his own project. Thus, for example, Freud imagines the unconscious as a place where nothing chance can happen; Nietzsche figures chance as that disturbing fact which tests our power to affirm the value of life. In spite of these differences, with all three of these writers, chance is a term that challenges the conceptual stability of the life and thought these writings figure. By understanding it in a rather open and skeptical way, as an event's not having to happen the way it did, I make chance the operator of my readings, a thematic and problematic that will tease from each text read a disclosure of its productive involvement with a chance none controls.

Of course there is a long-recognized risk to the inclusion of biographical material in any critical reading. We do not read Nietzsche because he went mad or may have contracted syphilis, but for the language and ideas of his texts. Details about the life of a great person can take on the delicious currency of gossip, offering an illusory sense that *they* are more "telling" than anything else. Further, like any ad hominem argument, biography can lead us to forget the conceptual and artistic work of the text we read. Thus a double focus operates everywhere in my conceptual narratives of Freud and Nietzsche. On the one hand, I seek to enter the conceptual field of text and thought, so as to grasp its integrity of terms and goals as they effect certain conceptual work. But, at every turn I also risk reading biographically, for only in that way can I explore the way the contingencies of the personal life are not some incidental added term, but a pivotal factor in the production of the texts. Because I narrate the facts of the life only as they illuminate the unfolding of the thought, I call these readings "conceptual narratives." I hope this kind of reading contributes to the polemical effort to lift the ban on biographical reading that has been one of the implicit corollaries and practical effects of most critical theory since the New Criticism.[14]

14. In a recent issue of *October* devoted to discipleship in psychoanalysis, Joan Copjec's contribution, "Letters and the Unknown Woman," offers this warning about

In reading Freud and Nietzsche's texts in relation to their lives, I have tried to show how their intellectual work proceeds in a collaboration with significant other people which is only partly voluntary, partly controlled. To think of Freud, Nietzsche, or Shakespeare as collaborators challenges one of the main ideas with which criticism has protected the mastery of the artistic or theoretical text from uncontrollable contingencies—the idea of the genius who, working in profound isolation, discovers original truths through the operation of an obscure but necessary creative process. I have tried to show that, on the contrary, because in the "life" there is no innocent state of being apart for the person, and because for the "writing" there is no condition of standing apart in the mode of pure consciousness to express an idea, life and writing are always already inscribed in the traces of a complex historical formation I will call "life-writing." Life-writing often seems to be written to, for, with, and/or against another person. In these narratives these other persons bear the names "Fliess" and "Salomé." It is not just the "life" that functions as matrix and context for the "writing," but the "writing" that weaves the matrix and disseminates the repertoire of tropes, which then become the condition of the possibility of life's thought and thought's life as each unfolds within the life-writing of the person. This life-writing becomes the larger object of my effort to reread the texts of Freud and Nietzsche.

To describe the distinct kind of biographical reading attempted here, I offer this example. Conventional biographical reading has usually sought carefully to distinguish "canonical" texts, like Freud's *Interpretation of Dreams*, from "secondary" texts, like his letters to Fliess, which are then said to help us understand the personal and intellectual context "out of which" the canonical writings are supposed to rise. The fundamental idealism of this separation of the texts of the thought from the texts of the life is not compromised by giving great prominence of place to these "secondary" texts. Thus the editors of the 1954 edition of Freud's letters to Fliess have honored the volume with the title "The Origins of Psychoanalysis," and a less complete edition of the correspondence stands as Volume One of the Standard Edition. But by separating these letters from the works that follow, they have achieved a surgical walling-off of the ca-

the kinds of studies Roustang and others have done of Freud: "the concepts elaborated by Freud are not necessarily imprinted with, or molded by (their) 'origins.' . . . One will not evaporate the concept of the unconscious by simply revealing the history, no matter how prolix, of its discovery." *October*, 28 (Spring 1984), 70.

nonical theoretical texts from that larger network of life-writing of which these texts are a part. Such an editing operation is fully compatible with the kind of biography Ernest Jones has written of Freud. A narrative of selected connections between life and thought allows Jones to certify certain interpretations of pivotal psychoanalytic concepts—for example, the relationship between fantasy and memory. The partial erasure of other connections between canonical text and life-writing, the disinclination to read the canonical text *as* life-writing, enables biography to serve as the anecdotal footnote and frame to set off the body of theory and ensure its higher truth. Traditional biography can serve art in much the same way.[15]

I have pursued a different strategy. By giving new importance to a thinker's uncontrolled collaboration with another person, and in challenging the subordination of a writer's "life" to his "thought" and the separation of the two, the conceptual narratives that follow seek to practice a different species of biographical criticism. This requires a realignment of critical attention. Because they reveal how the thoughts of these "great" thinkers mediate and are mediated by their personal experiences and social exchanges, the letters that record Freud's intense relationship with Fliess and Nietzsche's love for Lou Salomé become as important to this study as *The Interpretation of Dreams* or *Zarathustra*. Here the incidents of the life no longer offer an empirical grounding to the thought, and the shapes of thought no longer appear to be controlled by the guiding intention. The "life" is finally no less and no more obscure, coherent, and fragmentary than the "thought" a life attempts to speak. Life and thought interpenetrate each other to become a "life-writing," or "bio-graphy" composed of letters, journals, published works and those acts which have left some written trace. Not an after-the-fact-reconstruction by a historically removed commentator, this original "bio-graphy" composes (and decomposes) the biographical subject.

By reading Nietzsche's life-writing in the year 1882, I can interpret the conceptual work of his philosophical writings without dispensing with an interpretation of a series of decisive experiences of 1882. Such a reading shows for example that those notorious words, spoken to Zarathustra by an old woman—"You are going to women? Do not forget the whip!"—need to be read in terms of a

15. Below we will take note of the particular excisions made in Freud's letters by the editors of *The Origins of Psychoanalysis*, so they will serve as a separable "Origin" of psychoanalysis. See pages 79–81. In the last two years, Jeffrey Masson's revisionary biography and editing have opened up the issue of Freud's theory of seduction and the relationship of fantasy and memory to heated debate. See page 53 for a discussion of issues raised by Masson.

series of contingent events: Nietzsche's writing of "Sanctus Januarius" as it prepares the new desire to "go down among men" and women, in high hopes of social rejuvenation; the intense, blissful, eight-month love relationship with Lou Salomé; the crisis which the angry breakdown of that relationship posed to Nietzsche's thought; and finally, Nietzsche's writing of *Zarathustra*. Then these words in *Zarathustra* can suggest an ironic and caustic revision of the photograph taken upon a happy day in May 1882, to commemorate the decision made by Salomé, Paul Rée, and Nietzsche to form a collective living arrangement the following winter. In the picture Nietzsche and Rée are standing in the traces of a small cart, while Lou Salomé, kneeling in the cart, holds her hand cocked back, and wields a small . . . whip. In such an analytical sequence, "life" is traversed, marked, and scarred by a contingency that becomes indelibly inscribed into the writer's life; and similarly, because of the way "writing" concatenates one series of words and has then avoided others, this "writing" opens and is opened by the arbitrary contingent path it takes, and finds itself taking. Then the written text does not evidence an architectural obedience to some anterior design, but displays that same strange mixture of "action" and "event" one so frequently finds in a "life." With intentionality subtly displaced, the life-writing the biographical subject has lived/written takes on the character of a pointed improvisation.

If one tries to read Shakespeare's life-writing as I do Freud's and Nietzsche's, one is brought up against an unsurmountable obstacle. There is no "writing" that we can attach with any confidence to the "life" behind the production of *Hamlet*. Further, because the language we have is woven from commonplaces, borrowed plots, and an astounding rhetorical range, it encourages us to believe that it subsists at a masterful distance above human limitation. But an analogy encourages us to probe this impression. Although the taste of bread won't allow us to identify the wheat's producer, we nonetheless know a person was once busy with its growing. We can safely assume that Shakespeare's text is marked with his "life," and that each of his texts is a fragment of life-writing. This life will not only reside at some mysterious and determining inside of the text; it will also leave its folds and traces everywhere on the surface. Shakespeare's life haunts the text like the ghost that legend has it he played in an early production of *Hamlet*. But we cannot read this writing *as* life-writing, or see the ghostly countenance of this author. This absence of a biographical subject has engendered strange ruses in Shakespeare criticism, including the effort to get some more visible author (such as Marlowe or Bacon) to assume the role of authentic author of the plays, and the attempt to do biography through supposition. So rather than try, as some psychoanalytic critics do, to speculate the image of Shakespeare as author into being, I would like to suggest the quite extraordinary effects of Shakespeare's invisibility.

Shakespeare's invisibility helps his writing pull off, more effectively than the work of any other artist of our tradition, one of the central ruses of art: everywhere his works give us the illusion that texts capable of representing the human encounter with chance are themselves immune from the effects of chance. Shakespearean tragedy is like tragedy in general in the way it can be read as an extended meditation upon chance. While religion reduces chance to the byproduct of the human failure to comprehend a divine controlling order, tragedy has provided the West with its most compelling way of enacting and meditating the intersection of chance with the life of the person. In tragedy, the fall of the protagonist and the events that lead to that fall appear opaque and mysterious. The fall seems both necessary and contingent; it is willed by some higher force or god, but is also somehow the responsibility of the protagonist it befalls. But this aesthetic representation of chance in tragedy is recorded with consummate design. It becomes nearly impossible to imagine the artistic text as exposed to the kinds of contingencies it represents. In fact, the artwork as a form, and the aesthetic as a mode of representation, seem to be organized by chance-ridden lives *against* chance, so as to occult the operations of chance. Shakespeare's invisibility is a concomitant of the powerful illusion that art has raised its producers and consumers above life's binding contingencies. In *Hamlet*, and the dominant criticism of *Hamlet*, chance has been displaced from being an obscure element of historical formations to being an object of scenic representation, from being a necessary condition of the play's production and reception to being the conscious thematic focus of its central characters. In my reading of the play, I will seek to question and reverse this aesthetic neutralization of chance.

My choice of Freud, Nietzsche, and Shakespeare for reading is strategic rather than inevitable. It is not just that these writers are especially influential. They are also particularly well suited for the development of a general analysis of the way chance constitutes and disrupts the text of experience. For it is Freud who offers our century's most persuasive and important theory of personal history and its interpretation; and Nietzsche writes a philosophy that is both compatible on many points with Freud and also begins the modern critique of the flight from chance. To pursue the interplay of chance and experience in a work of art, I have chosen a genre (tragedy) and a particular literary text (*Hamlet*) where chance is a salient aspect of plot and theme. But however useful these writers are for developing this inquiry, my selection of particular texts by each seems only partly justifiable. I could have chosen other dreams besides the "*non vixit*" dream for extended consideration, and emerged with much the same analysis of Freudian interpretation and a similar description of Freud's rivalrous relationship with his contemporaries. Nietzsche's relationship with Wagner and his wife would have offered as fruitful a matrix for charting the exchanges between life and thought in life-writing as the texts and experiences of the year 1882. *Macbeth, Othello*, and *Julius Caesar* seem as preoccupied with arbitrary contingency as *Hamlet*. My choices of particular texts for extended readings seem the most opaque and symptomatic aspect of my critical effort. I cannot explain or justify them because I cannot become fully conscious to them. They betray the fact that on these pages the general question of chance and the text of experience is engaged by a single person. Like every contingent event, once the die has been cast, what has happened comes to seem like a necessary fact. Thus, I have the illusion that it is not I who have chosen these texts but the texts that have chosen me. They have made themselves part of a life-writing which cannot be claimed as "mine." So in writing my readings, I will lean up against Freud, Nietzsche, and Shakespeare and thereby borrow from the conceptual work of their thought and art; but by tracing the conceptual threads of their writings, my conceptual narrative of their life-writing, when concatenated in this book, will compose another conceptual narrative of my own telling.

Here is a brief map of the narrative terrain you are invited to enter. So as to challenge the psychoanalytic annulment of chance as a factor of psychic life, the first movement of this book reads Freud's interpretation of the *non vixit* dream. Freud investigates an overlapping set of remembered scenes as they open around the primal scene he finds operating behind both the dream and the many scenes of rivalry the dream has "cited." Something has chanced to happen back there, which now seems decisive and primal: in a single early scene of rivalry with his nephew John, Freud has ambivalent feelings of hostility and affection that he is condemned to repeat in all his subsequent relations with contemporaries. By following three threads of Freud's work in the 1890s, my reading of Freud's reading of the *non vixit* dream complicates the determinism implied by this primal scene. Freud debates whether the primal scene (*urszene*) represents the memory of a single actual event or the projective repetition after-the-fact of the scene as fantasy (he finally concludes it must be both). In the text of the dream interpretation, a line from Brutus' speech of self-justification in Shakespeare's *Julius Caesar* becomes in its interability the condition for the possibility of the single (dream, self, interpretation). And finally, the personal and biographical context of the dream interpretation shows how Freud exercises an interpretive leeway in writing this text, in order to transform his relationship to his closest friend, Wilhelm Fliess, so that instead of being the "father" in a transference relationship, Fliess becomes a nephew Freud can defeat in battle. In this way the *non vixit* dream, in both its dreaming and its subsequent writing, wins Freud the self-mastery to "father" psychoanalysis.

In the second movement, in order to draw closer to the way contingent events traverse the life of a single person, I do a detailed biographical reading of Nietzsche's life and writings in 1882. Here chance appears to Nietzsche as what he calls the "dear chance" of Lou Salomé, and coincidence becomes the privileged figure for interpreting his life: the coincidental coinciding of two (Nietzsche, Salomé) in one (love). But Lou Salomé does not just "happen" to Nietzsche. In writing the fourth book of *The Gay Science* in the first weeks of 1882, Nietzsche has developed an ethos of aesthetic affirmation, and made the decision (wearing the mask of Zarathustra) to "go down among men." These compositional acts create the space within which Lou Salomé can be met, experienced, and loved (as a contingent happening, a "dear chance"). My narrative records what befalls Lou Salomé and Nietzsche: the plan for living together that Salomé, Paul Rée, and Nietzsche contrive; the love Nietzsche experiences; and the way his love and its failure lead him toward a new conception of the will (as conflictual, multiple, unconscious) which requires a fundamental revision of *The Gay Science* as *Zarathustra*.

To discern the traces of the relationship of Shakespeare's tragic art to the contingent, I proceed indirectly, first though a thematic reading, then through a reading of the critical responses to *Hamlet*, and finally through a textual reading. Because Hamlet is embarked upon an effort to regain a lost paternal mastery, and because he seeks an acutely conscious grasp of his situation, *Hamlet* is, among all tragedies, a particularly useful text for reading the relationship of mastery, chance, and the person. Through my reading I seek to take account of the elaborate means Hamlet uses to evade the radical contingency of his situation. These include his idealization of the father, his misogyny, his privileging of the inner self, his program for a truthful representation of things, and his plan for a restorative act of revenge. Hamlet also entertains, by turns, a skeptical-ironic neutralization of the will and a trust in an overarching Christian order. But finally, in the duel scene of Act V, for reasons which have everything to do with his acquisition of a more detached and playful relationship with language, he is able to project himself into an active and accepting relationship with a chance none controls.

Because critics of *Hamlet* have been just as discomforted by chance as Hamlet himself is, they have devised their own strategies of evasion, which have shaped their interpretations of the drama and are woven into the very mimetic categories that undergird their interpretation of interpretation. Their own distrust of chance has blocked critics from taking full account of the strange chiasmic form of Hamlet's encounter with chance in the play's final scene. The duel that wins Hamlet his revenge (and death) and brings young Fortinbras to the Danish throne is a singular repetition of the duel King Hamlet fought with old Fortinbras thirty years earlier, upon the day of Hamlet's birth. I hope to demonstrate the way this uncanny reversal of fortunes—by a son intent upon imitating a father he believes to be masterful—takes the reader to the textual limits of mastery: Hamlet's, Shakespeare's, and our own. Then we shall be in a position to see the way the mastery of this text is an effect of the same textual labyrinth which compromises that mastery.

MOVEMENT ONE

FREUD, CHANCE, AND THE PRIMAL SCENES OF READING

And a man's life is no more than to say 'one.'

—Hamlet

O heaven over me. . . . That is what your purity is to me now, that there is no eternal spider or spider web of reason; that you are to me a dance floor for divine accidents, that you are to me a divine table for divine dice and dice players.

—"Before Sunrise," *Thus Spake Zarathustra*

Freud's writings have a certain objective discursive authority: they have provided the dominant theory of the self in this century, one that has challenged the status of one of humankind's most prized possessions—consciousness, and the free will presumed to be concomitant with consciousness. By bringing the idea of the unconscious into view, Freud decentered the mastery of reality through thought that consciousness seemed to make possible; and by developing ways to read and work with unconscious thought, Freud's ideas seemed to his first followers to carry a "discovery" which challenged many of the settled and soothing assumptions of Western culture. But Freud's influence does not turn on a single idea such as repression or the unconscious, the pleasure principle or the death drive, or the first or second typologies of the mind. Instead, there are certain conceptual and formal properties of Freud's text which prepare its larger authority: it is rigorous, self-consistent, comprehensive, original, fecund. In its great range his thought interprets neurosis, dreams, childhood, forgetting, slips, sex, laughter, coincidence, character development, religion, art, and culture. The range and "greatness" of Freud's thought have given it the influence readable in the many types of cultural production opened in the wake of this text: the institution of psychoanalysis; the development of modern psychiatry; the writings of those moralists and philosophers who have read the culture, and its possibilities, in the light of Freud's ideas; and the manifold developments of Freudian concepts in art, theater, film, literature, and criticism. Thus commentators have celebrated Freud as a "genius" and insisted that his work is one of the most important nodal points of modern culture.[1]

For those, both inside and outside psychiatry, who become his disciples, Freud's text is the origin and medium of every legitimate development of psychoanalysis. Every intellectual effort must begin and end with a quote from the master, and the only proper task is to carry forward Freud's work. But this is also an impossible task. For the more energetically one works, thinks, and writes, the greater the danger, in spite of every intention, that one's ideas will become singular, independent and thus different from Freud's. Then Freud might declare (as he did about Jung, Adler, and others) that this work stands outside psychoanalysis.[2] A second double bind also operates: to win the sole laurel crown, to become the heir to the master, becomes the shared goal of the group, for only in that way can one's work gain the final imprimatur of legitimacy; but it is also an impossible goal—because there are so many able claimants, because it turns out the only one who can wear Freud's crown is . . . Freud himself. Criticism in this century has usually borrowed from Freud with a more independent spirit. But recent critical theory does not stand entirely outside networks of indebtedness to Freud. Since Freud's writings have helped to generate the methods and terms of much of critical theory I engage throughout this volume, I find I owe my own debt to Freud and Freud's text.[3]

François Roustang's critique of the "dire" consequences to psychoanalysis of mastery, whether it is conferred upon Freud or Lacan, allows me to clarify how I will read Freud. To read the mastery of Freud's text, I will need to expose my reading to the masterful force of Freud's thought. But how can one do this, without becoming sub-

1. I offer two examples. In *Freud and the Culture of Psychoanalysis: Studies in the Transition from Victorian Humanism to Modernity*, Steven Marcus ends one chapter by remarking how "rarely genius of revolutionary proportions occurs in both science and other theoretical disciplines. And . . . how when such a genius occurs the world changes" (Boston: George Allen & Unwin, 1984), 39. Paul Ricoeur, in his book on Freud, describes Freud's work "as a monument of our culture, as a text in which our culture is expressed and understood." See *Freud and Philosophy: An Essay on Interpretation*, trans. Denis Savage (New Haven: Yale University Press, 1970), xi.

2. I am indebted for this perspective upon discipleship to François Roustang's fascinating analysis in *Dire Mastery: Discipleship from Freud to Lacan*, trans. Ned Lukacher, (Baltimore: The Johns Hopkins University Press, 1982).

3. See "The Debts of Deconstruction and Other, Related Assumptions," by Sam Weber in *Taking Chances: Derrida, Psychoanalysis, and Literature*, ed. Joseph E. Smith and William Kerrigan (Baltimore: The Johns Hopkins University Press, 1984). I have written a short review essay on this book unified around the issue of each writer's "debts to deconstruction." See *MLN*, Comparative Literature Issue, 99 (Winter 1984), 1195–1202.

ject to that thought, without turning that text into a "master text" that is determined in advance as the metaphysical locus of truth? What I need is an itinerary of reading that will take me close enough to the architectonics of Freud's text so that I can hear the call of its mastery, but can still stand apart from that mastery, acknowledging debts to Freud's text without trying to define their exact limits. For what is most crucial here is not whether one chooses to exalt or reject Freud's thought; rather, one's relationship to Freud's mastery is determined by the *way* one reads and repeats his text. One way to justify my own strategy for reading is to mark my distance from a mode of reading Freud which is at once too slavish (in its repetition of Freud's concepts) and too voluntaristic (in its application of those concepts to new and better uses). So, in the reading of Freud that follows, I will not do what a wide spectrum of critics have done. I will not use Freud's thought as a marble quarry of useful concepts, which can be selected, cut away from their adjacent concepts, shorn of the particular language where they emerged as thought, freed of the negativity and necessity of their initial reading instance, so that, thus abstracted, they can be transported into another conceptual context where they can play a part in a scenario for cultural emancipation.[4]

For reasons broached in the introduction, I can best gauge, unsettle, and resituate the mastery of Freud's text by bringing this question to his thought: how is chance operative in Freud's thought and life, as both concept and event, during the time psychoanalysis is being invented? The story I tell in response to this question is not the only one possible. It proceeds by considering the several different levels—personal, conceptual, textual—upon which some notion of chance and the contingent operates during the formative years of psychoanalysis. I shall begin by describing what in the conceptual terrain of psychoanalysis has led most commentators to emphasize not the aleatory in psychoanalysis but that about it which seems deterministic.[5]

---

4. In spite of their enormous differences and rich variety, I find these common interpretive procedures operating in the well-known treatments of Freud by Paul Ricoeur, Norman O. Brown, Herbert Marcuse, Gilles Deleuze, and Félix Guattari. See Deleuze and Guattari, *Anti-Oedipus: Capitalism and Schizophrenia*, trans. Robert Hurley, Mark Seem, and Helen R. Lane (New York: Viking, 1977).

5. Freud discusses the tension between the determinism of psychic events and the *feeling* that we have free will in *The Psychopathology of Everyday Life*, ed. James Strachey, *Standard Edition of the Complete Psychological Works of Sigmund Freud*, hereafter *S.E.* (London: Hogarth, 1953–74), VII, 253–54.

The Psychoanalytic Neutralization of Chance

At first glance, Freud seems to give chance a marginal but significant place in his interpretation of psychic life. Thus, in the "primal" scenes of early childhood that later become traumatic, events happen which seem contingent and arbitrary; but they will later be both necessary and decisive in the constitution of the person. Or so it seems. But the more one takes account of the temporal movement beyond a primal scene, follows how the memory of it gets displaced, and accounts for the work of fantasy and the unconscious, in other words, the more one sees how it is always already riven and traversed by all that comes later, the more the very idea of the blank slate and first time where chance could leave its mark begins to seem only an abstract and problematic byproduct of our analytic work, instead of a time or place one could really locate.[6] Finally, within the psychoanalytic understanding of life there is quite literally no place for chance (to happen). Freud often says as much. And why should this be so? I shall sketch those motifs from the conceptual field of psychoanalysis which exclude or severely restrict the play of chance. They undergird the official determinism of psychoanalysis.

The compulsion to repeat. Freud gets us to see a vast portion of human behavior as the repetition, in safe and disguised form, of repressed memories, scenes, and affect. Repetition of something "back there" in the past and "down there" in the unconscious happens in the form of dreams, symptoms, personal rituals, slips, defense mechanisms, jokes. There are several things to note about this repetition: it is highly determined in its form; it is uncontrollable—there is no way to choose or not choose repetition; and, in *Beyond the Pleasure Principle*, Freud even elevates repetition to a tendency of the psychic mechanism independent of considerations of pleasure and unpleasure, safety and reality.

The traumatic memory. The memory of a traumatic scene imposes a certain tyrannical necessity upon the psyche. This memory-trace is presumed by Freud to be indelible; it will last "forever" in the timeless present of the unconscious. It is the object of complex maneuvers of escape, censorship, and repression. And like everything that has *happened*, it confronts us with an apparent finality: it cannot be undone.

6. In my treatment of Freud in what follows I am indebted to Derrida's important essay "Freud and the Scene of Writing," published in *Writing and Difference*, trans. Alan Bass (Chicago: University of Chicago Press, 1978), 196–231.

The drive to fantasy. In psychoanalysis, fantasy does not have the qualities often ascribed to the imagination and fancy: it does not emerge from the subject's "free" expression, and does not invent vacation realities and alternative worlds. Instead, fantasy obeys the logic of most of the forms of psychic life. It wells up from impulses to pleasure and the avoidance of unpleasure, and it works with and toward the signs of preexistent memory-traces and the affect with which they are imbued.[7] If fantasy produces the *effect* of innovation, it does so by giving expression to material in the self which only seems new because it has been unconscious.

Oedipus Rex. Freud accords special privilege to Western literature's most remarkable representation of fateful repetition. Thus Oedipus' life, in this myth, is traversed by three repetitions of the oracle whose text his life-story is condemned to repeat. That Oedipus' life seems shaped by terrible coincidences is just a snare prepared for Oedipus and the unwary spectator by the gods, Sophocles, and Freud. In his interpretation of the drama, Freud makes belief in these coincidences—that Oedipus "happens" to meet his father on the road, and "happens" to marry his mother—an illusory effect of repression. Repression of what?—of Oedipal desire. On stage, only one person can believe in these coincidences—Oedipus; he does not (yet) know the Oedipus story. And off stage, the only spectators who will continue to believe in these coincidences are those who refuse knowledge of Oedipal desire.[8]

The unconscious. If, as Freud asserts in *The Interpreation of Dreams*, "physical events are determined" and "there is nothing arbitrary about them," then this so because of the unconscious.[9] The special priority of the unconscious may be gauged from the remarkable

7. See Jean LaPlanche and Jean-Baptiste Pontalis, "Fantasy and the Origins of Sexuality," *International Journal of Psychoanalysis*, 49 (1968), 1–18. Also by the same authors, the entry under "Fantasy" in *The Language of Psychoanalysis*, trans. Donald Nicholson-Smith (New York: Norton, 1973), 314–19.

8. In *The Interpretation of Dreams* Freud writes, "It is the fate of all of us, perhaps, to direct our first sexual impulse towards our mother and our first hatred and our first murderous wish against our father" (*S.E.*, IV, 262–63). In the first mention of this idea, in a letter to Fliess (10/15/97), Freud is still less equivocal: "Everyone in the audience was once a budding Oedipus in fantasy, and each recoils in horror from the dream-fulfillment here transplanted into reality." For Freud's letters to Fliess, I have generally used *The Complete Letters of Sigmund Freud to Wilhelm Fliess (1887–1904)*, trans. and ed. Jeffrey Moussaieff Masson (Cambridge: Harvard University Press, 1985), hereafter *CL* plus date. At times I have needed to refer to the first edition of the letters to Fliess, *The Origins of Psychoanalysis*, ed. Marie Bonaparte, Anna Freud, Ernst Kris (New York: Basic Books, 1954), hereafter *Origins* plus date. *The Interpretation of Dreams*, vols. IV and V continuously paged in the *Standard Edition*, is hereafter cited *ID*.

9. *ID*, 514.

qualities Freud confers upon it in an article on the subject in 1915: it contains drives which exist side by side and are exempt from mutual contradiction; in it there is no negation, no dubiety, no varying degree of certainty; its forms and processes are timeless, not being ordered temporally or altered by the passage of time; and, having no indication of "reality," the unconscious is a substitution of pscyhic reality for external reality.[10] All of this is to say that there are no gradations of reality in the unconscious. Memory-traces in the unconscious may carry varying amounts of energy cathected to them, but most crucially something is either in the unconscious (and therefore has being) or it is not in the unconscious (and therefore it is not). By this analysis, unconscious thoughts possess some of the primordial reality Parmenides ascribes to Being. From the standpoint of the unconscious it is impossible to take account of those things in the world that trouble the ideas of truth and being by partaking of both the real and the unreal: for example a fiction, a memory, a dream, a promise, the words "I shall always love you," a fantasy, the past or the future, and, most important for this book, language or chance. And in conceptualizing the unconscious, Freud excludes chance from the object he takes to be most real.

Chance is illusory. Now we are in a position to understand Freud's most characteristic way of interpreting (away) chance. Something happens or is done: a verbal slip, a lapse of memory, a bungled action. It appears to consciousness as merely chance, but Freud's interpretative work shows that it is a highly determined effect of the unconscious. Freud is walking through the deserted streets of a provincial town in Italy, when he finds himself in the red-light district. He "hastened to leave" by the next street, but after wandering about for a while he "suddenly found" himself back on the same street "where my presence was now beginning to excite attention. I hurried away once more, only to arrive by another detour at the same place yet a third time."[11] In the popular mind repetition—especially threefold repetition—is the token of coincidence; for Freud it is the sign of unconscious desire, working in a covert but determined way.

Superstitious and paranoid interpretation. Freud finds two other kinds of readers who foreclose the province of chance: the superstitious, who understand every chance event as an act or sign from the hidden spirit world; and the paranoid, who assume a plenum of (hos-

10. "The Unconscious," *S.E.*, XIV, 186–89.
11. The anecdote comes from the discussion of involuntary repetition in "The Uncanny," *S.E.*, XVII, 237.

tile) intentions directed at them by others, evident in even the others' smallest actions. Freud extends a certain qualified approval to
these modes of overreading. For, strange to say, paranoids are often
right, and superstitious persons are in some way more correct in
their way of reading than rationalists. All these modes of interpretation make chance disappear by weaving a context for an event that
gives each observed effect a determining cause. Freud's expansion
of the scope and force of interpretation is predicated upon the rigorous parallelism he insists holds sway between his interpretations as
analyst and the interpretations shaped and acted out by the psychic
apparatus. But, one might ask, is there any limit to the efficacy of
these interpretations, and the annulment of chance they effect?
Freud distinguishes himself from the superstitious in the following
way. He tells us, "I believe in external (real) chance, it is true, but
not in internal (psychical) accidental events."[12] Thus one year, at
the beginning of the therapeutic season, Freud hires a cabman to
take him to the house of a very elderly patient. The cabman takes
Freud to a house of similar appearance and the same number on a
nearby street. The superstitious would see an "omen" in this incident, while for Freud it is "an accident without further meaning."
However, Freud tells us, if he had made this error while "absent-
mindedly" walking "deep in thought," it would have betrayed unconscious forebodings about his patient's death.[13]

Uncanny accident. Freud never tells us whether his elderly patient
did die that year. After all, the intimations of the superstitious will
have to be right sometimes. Freud separates himself from the superstitious through appeal to a hard-and-fast opposition between, on
the one hand, the inside and psychical, where nothing is chance,
and, on the other hand, the outside and physical, where chance is
"real." By aligning two sets of terms—outside/inside and chance/
necessity—Freud makes strategic use of the concept of chance to
isolate the psychical as the locus of interpretation. But we shall come
to see that this step makes for a problem rather than a solution, is
less an answer than a locus of questions. For doesn't the psychic apparatus take shape in part through its encounters with the outside?
Again, in *Beyond the Pleasure Principle* and his essay on "The Uncanny," Freud cannot stop returning to consider incidents that seem
to evade this neat rational opposition between inside and outside.
And he cannot stop noticing frequent repetitions of certain num-

12. *The Psychopathology of Everyday Life*, S.E., VI, 257.
13. Ibid., 256–57.

bers—like 51 or 62—which appear "uncanny" and "lure" him into the superstitious ascription of "a secret meaning to this obstinate recurrence of a number; he will take it, perhaps, as an indication of the span of life allotted to him."[14]

Given the vantage point of this broad overview of these motifs, Freud's neutralization of chance seems iron-clad and unequivocal. In part this is so because my initial grasping of the question of chance—through panoptic thematic summary—does what too many readers of Freud attempt: makes psychoanalysis into an autonomous interdependent system of reified atemporal, nonhistorical terms, where the space and time for contingent events has vanished. But there are at least three places upon this analytic terrain where chance (as that which, happening the way it does, did not have to happen the way it did) obtrudes in its otherness: it does so *conceptually*, in the very idea of those primal scenes postulated by Freud where the person receives his or her particular defining marks; and *historically*, through the chain of accidental encounters and decisive influences and nonnecessary language acts which have so much effect upon the emergence of psychoanalysis; and *pragmatically*, in the central therapeutic venture of psychoanalysis: to stage the collaboration of analyst and patient in the hope of shaping feelings and life directions away from painful ritual repetitions toward greater happiness. We can get Freud's text to "face" toward the question of chance and the person in a new way by stepping down from the high plain of his metapsychological pronouncements, so as to read the particular language of certain moments of his text and life closely, and in relation to each other. I will focus on the decade of the 1890s, when his work on hysterics and dreams led to the textual work that founded psychoanalysis, and I will recount and analyze three related "episodes": episode one—the debate about the competing roles of "memory" and "fantasy" in the aetiology of neurosis; episode two—Freud's readings of the "*non vixit*" dream in *The Interpretation of Dreams*, a text that pivots upon the way an early primal scene of rivalry repeats itself in subsequent scenes of psychic life; episode three—the way this interpretation of the *non vixit* dream performs Freud's self-analysis, his career ambitions, and his theoretical

14. Freud suggests this superstition about the number 62 in "The Uncanny," *S.E.*, XVII, 238. Early in the century he experienced a similar superstitious belief that he would die at 51, in 1907. Here he had been influenced by Fliess's theory of periodicity (23 + 28 = 51). See *ID*, 438–39. For further discussion of Freud's superstitions about this see *Psychopathology of Everyday Life, S.E.*, VI, 250. For other discussion of uncanny repetition in psychic life see section III of *Beyond the Pleasure Principle, S.E.*, XVIII.

leap beyond physiology as all three unfold within his relationship to Wilhelm Fliess. From the vantage point of this conceptual narrative, psychoanalytic interpretation, whether practiced in analysis or in everyday life, no longer seems only like an instrument of mastery. It also comes into view as the venturesome act and obscure event by which the person is propelled into contact (through language) with life's chances.

Memory versus Fantasy

The question of chance and the person enters psychoanalysis when Freud thinks about the contingent factors in the earliest and most decisive scenes of childhood. How, Freud asks, does an event in the past (perhaps a single chance event) affect the nature of a particular person? And a corollary question: how does something that happens outside the person become a fixed inner part of that person? Of course, Freud does not pose these questions in this form. His problem in the 1890s is the aetiology of neurosis—how it came to be, for example, that a person manifested severe symptoms of hysteria. He follows Joseph Breuer by tracing hysteria not to some anomaly of brain physiology, but "back to the scene in and through which it originated . . . the traumatic scene."[15] And, because the traumatic scene is said to contain "accidental aetiological factors," this scene—whether single or plural in its happening—functions as an accidental cause.[16] Thus it is fundamentally arbitrary in its shape, because it did not have to happen the way it did, but once it does, it has a decisive effect upon the person, his neurotic symptoms, his relationships with others, his style of thinking and feeling—in other words, it is a contributing factor in much of what we take an individual person to be.

Freud's analysis of the aetiology of neurosis follows two lines of thinking—the first developed around the idea of memory, the second around the concept of fantasy. Here is a schematic version of that analytical journey. Freud first encounters the traumatic scene in patients who develop symptoms as a defense against the memory of some disturbing scene. A patient named Emma will not enter a shop alone, for it stirs up an unconscious memory of a childhood scene of

15. From "The Aetiology of Hysteria" (1896), *S.E.*, III, 193.
16. From "Further Remarks on the Defence Neuro-Psychoses" (1896), *S.E.*, III, 163.

being molested by a grinning shopkeeper. But what is meant by "memory?" For "memory," Freud uses the German word *Erinnerung*, literally "a making inner," a bringing inside the psyche. But what outer element enters the psyche to become memory? Not any element in the empirical substratum of the traumatic scene, where there is no limit to the number of events that could be said to be happening in each second. Not any one of numberless impressions which might have been registered in the psyche, either clearly or faintly, in that time and place. A scene is not traumatic even when, in getting registered in the psyche, it causes feelings of unpleasure intense enough to be subjected to repression. Freud found that many of the most disturbing events of early life never become traumatic because they are successfully repressed. For a scene to be traumatic, it must *return* in later life. It must be followed by a second moment and a second scene, when, years later, often after the onset of puberty, something happens to stir the menacing memory of that early scene into new life. At age twelve Emma enters a shop where two shop-assistants, one of whom attracts her sexually, are laughing at her clothes. She rushes out in fright. Now, finally the first scene becomes traumatic and wounding; a symptom is formed that will block the return of that scene as memory: Emma will not enter a shop alone.[17]

This concept of trauma operates in the "seduction theory" Freud develops to explain the aetiology of neurosis. In an 1896 article entitled "The Aetiology of Hysteria" Freud expends a good deal of polemical energy to convince a reader, who he assumes will be skeptical, of a discovery he takes to be "a momentous revelation": the origin of various types of neurosis can invariably be traced back to some form of seduction of the child by an older person. In the light of this theory, the patient and the analyst focus their energies on the memory of a scene that has become traumatic; the neurotic develops symptoms to stop the memory from coming to consciousness; the analyst works to bring that memory into the light of consciousness so as to dissipate the negative affect associated with it. Freud's account of the seduction theory becomes more and more complex, but he never wavers in his commitment to an actual event behind the sexual memory: stimulation of the child so that he or she has, as he puts it, a "pre-sexual sexual shock."[18] But suddenly, in September 1897, Freud drops his adherence to this theory. He writes to Fliess: "And

17. The story of Emma is narrated as a case of hysteria in "Project for a Scientific Psychology" enclosed with the letter of 10/8/95 (see *Origins*).
18. This expression is used in *CL*, 10/15/95.

now I want to confide in you immediately the great secret that has been slowly dawning on me in the last few months. I no longer believe in my *neurotica*" (*CL*, 9/21/97).

A series of related factors discredit memory of an actual event as the nuclear cause of neurosis. First, Freud finds that he can never "get back" to this postulated primal ground of memory and event: "even in the most deep-going psychosis the unconscious memory does not break through, so that the secret of the childhood experience is not betrayed, even in the most confused delirium." Second, a series of factors put in question the veracity of these memories: their striking similarity among very different patients; their strange resemblance to early accounts of demonic possession; and finally, the difficulty of believing that so many fathers "had to be accused of being perverse." But perhaps, most decisively, Freud has the "certain insight that there are no indications of reality in the unconscious, so that one cannot distinguish between the truth and fiction that has been cathected with affect." But if Freud cannot account for neurosis by keying his analysis to the vicissitudes of the memory of an actual event, then how is he to account for it? A force and factor quite different from memory needs to be taken into account. By September 1897 it has already become an epicenter of his speculations. Its name is "fantasy."

When Freud questions the aetiological priority given memory—as the internalization of an actual event—he has embarked upon a fundamental shift in his understanding of the psyche. Little wonder he tells Fliess, "Now I have no idea of where I stand" (*CL*, 9/21/97). Later, in *The History of the Psycho-Analytic Movement* and in his *Autobiographical Study*, Freud reports of this pivotal moment that he felt "helpless bewilderment," "completely at a loss," because, as he puts it with considerable precision, "reality was lost from under one's feet."[19] Freud's disorientation comes from a loss of belief in a reality which could function as a ground for the traumatic childhood scene that lay behind later adult neurosis. But this loss of grounding opens a clearing for an understanding of fantasy, and the "psychical reality" that must be "taken into account along side actual reality."[20] Freud folds "reality" back on itself so that it becomes fissured, discontinuous, and double. How is this done? If "memory" begins outside the subject in some actual fortuitous event, and is then modified by its transcription into the psyche, then fantasy emerges from in-

19. "The History of the Psycho-Analytic Movement," *S.E.*, XIV, 17; and *An Autobiographical Study*, *S.E.*, XX, 34.
20. "The History of the Psycho-Analytic Movement," *S.E.*, XIV, 17–18.

side the psyche, where it obeys the law of the pleasure principle by winning pleasure through discharging unpleasure. The new importance accorded fantasy is cognate with Freud's increased interest in dreams and the discovery of everything defined as inward, prime, and primal in psychoanalysis: the unconscious, the drives, primary process, primal scenes and fantasies, and the compulsion to repeat. Within this matrix fantasy emerges in a particular form, described by Jean LaPlanche and Jean-Baptiste Pontalis as "an imaginary scene in which the subject is a protagonist, representing the fulfillment of a wish (in the last analysis, an unconscious wish) in a manner that is distorted to a greater or lesser extent by defensive processes." But this wish and desire exceed any simple physical need; a wish is caught up in the pathways of language and the signifier and may be fulfilled only through the restoration of "indestructible infantile signs" which are "bound in the unconscious to the earliest experience of satisfaction."[21]

The concept of fantasy brings desire and language into relation to one another at the forefront of Freud's understanding of the psychic processes. Now dreams—the purest language-texts of desire—receive concerted attention from Freud, and symptoms as well as dreams are interpreted as wish-fulfillments. The language-bound, fictive shaping power of fantasy allows Freud to understand a range of new phenomena: how family anecdotes could become interpolated into the psyche and function as powerfully as memory in organizing psychic life; how unconscious scenes—like seduction by the father—could have so much continuity among diverse members of the culture; and how symptoms could use puns in language in their formation.

Whatever its new importance, fantasy never becomes a simple *alternative* to Freud's analysis of the function of memory. Fantasy and memory sustain an obscure relationship to each other in the aetiology of neurosis, where they supplement each other in their operation. This relationship helps explain what one might call a systematic equivocation upon the origin of neurosis. If neurosis is the product of two discontinuous functions like memory and fantasy, organized along the axis fact/fiction and strung between the empirical event and the play of unconscious desire, how then can one locate the spot, the place, the time, the origin of hysteria? How can one really arrive at the wounding primal scene if memory and fantasy are the

21. See LaPlanche and Pontalis, *The Language of Psychoanalysis*. This is the primary definition offered under the heading "Phantasy (or Fantasy)"; then a clause from "Fantasy and the Origins of Sexuality."

only pathways back, and function sometimes as complementing pairs and sometimes as deflections and subversions of each other? Of the "architecture of hysteria" Freud writes in a draft to Fliess: "The aim seems to be to arrive [back] at the primal scenes. In a few cases this is achieved directly, but in others only by a detour *via* fantasies. For fantasies are psychic façades produced in order to bar access to these memories. Fantasies simultaneously serve the tendency towards refining the memories, towards sublimating them. They are manufactured by means of things that are *heard*, and utilized *subsequently*; . . ." (*CL,* 5/2/97, "Draft L").[22]

But to say the words "both . . . and . . ." of an unmatched pair like memory and fantasy involves us in seeing the way Freud's account of the psychic process will never allow us to say only "memory" or only "fantasy." Freud's strategic, nonsynthetic equivocation on memory and fantasy forces his reader to recognize two impossibilities. The first impossibility is that the mind ever contains something which is just memory—a pure repeatable fact in the mind that one could retrieve—even in the "deepest reaches" of the unconscious. For the psyche is always affecting, shaping, repressing, sublimating, and symbolizing a term which cannot be lifted away from the interested, desire-laden *work* of the unconscious. And even if you could go back to the very instant of the postulated event, you cannot keep the unconscious away from the term to be represented, traced, written into the unconscious, because in order to record this term the mind must offer itself and its language to that term. It must go out, halfway, to meet it, and this action forever compromises the event in its purity.

The direction of Freud's inquiry into the aetiology of hysteria takes him further and further toward an appreciation of the powers of fictive transformation at work in fantasy. Thus he eventually discards the theory of an actual seduction, in favor of seduction as a wish which is later subject to repression. Then *Oedipus Rex* can become a master text. But this expansion of the explanatory role of fantasy reaches its limit with a *second impossibility*. Freud never accepts the idea that fantasy carries forward so much fictive revision that all contact with an "actual event" disappears, so that the psyche is carrying on an improvisation according to exchanges of energy and affect which never makes contact with an outside, an event "out

---

22. I have retained the translation of *Urszenen* used in *Origins*, "primal scenes," rather than "the earliest [sexual] scenes." Masson uses the latter so as to distinguish Freud's broader use of this term in the 1890s to refer to any sexually charged repressed scene, from the technical meaning it acquired after 1904, of the child's real or imagined sight of parental coitus.

there" objectively considered. Fantasy is not a form of flight which provides a "lift-off" away from common reality. In "Screen Memories," an 1899 article written just after *The Interpretation of Dreams* was completed, the analyst (Freud) and "patient" (also Freud) investigate a memory from his early childhood: upon a rectangle of meadow, two boys gang up to steal the cluster of bright yellow dandelions picked by a girl playmate; then she runs off, with the two boys following, to receive slices of delicious bread from a peasant woman and a nursemaid. The analysis shows how this memory becomes a screen upon which the patient as adult has projected fantasies of sexuality, marriage, and abstinence. At the climax of the analysis the patient announces he has "lost all faith in the genuineness of the dandelion scene." To justify his suspicion that this scene is not the memory of an actual event, the patient shows how all the elements of the scene can be understood as fantasy projected back. But now the analyst disagrees:

> I see that I must take up the defence of its genuineness. You are going too far. You have accepted my assertion that every suppressed phantasy of this kind tends to slip away into a childhood scene. But suppose now that this cannot occur unless there is a memory-trace the content of which offers the phantasy a point of contact—comes, as it were, half way to meet it. Once a point of contact of this kind has been found—in the present instance it was the deflowering, the taking away of the flowers—the remaining content of the phantasy is remodelled with the help of every legitimate intermediate idea—take the bread as an example—till it can find further points of contact with the content of the childhood scene. ["Screen Memories," *S.E.*, III, 318]

In the intricate interplay of fantasy and memory as they "meet halfway," what certifies the reality of some sort of event behind this scene? It is the hallucinatory power of two details of memory: the yellow of the dandelions and the deliciousness of the bread offered the children. These two memory-traces are the indelible residue of the outside inside the psyche. Freud's tenacity in holding on to this concept of memory, when it would have been simpler and clearer to dissolve memory into the operations of fantasy, has several important consequences. First, the memory is the trace of events which were once arbitrary from the standpoint of the person, but become a necessary constitutive aspect of the person. The potentially traumatic memory becomes an instance of chance-become-necessity. The facticity of these memories makes them a token of materiality, necessity, and our eventual death. But the memory-trace also gives us access to a certain wealth: it insists with the specificity of its shape and tone so as to mark each person with memory; this chain of single marks of memory confers a sense of being onself—of being *this* one self, and no other.

If Freud's psychology locates the formation of the psyche upon what I have called a nonsynthetic equivocation between the claims of the memory of a real event and fantasy projection "après coup," this is less a dogmatic position than a pragmatic way to avoid two untenable alternatives. Nonetheless, it is in the midst of this strange analytic equivocation where Freud repeatedly situates the psyche as the interpretive "object" of psychoanalysis.[23] Given the complex trans-rational quality of this position on memory and fantasy, it is not surprising that some followers of Freud would seek to subordinate the claims of "memory" to the human power of "fantasy." This is one way to understand Jung's concept of the "collective unconscious," his downplaying of castration anxiety, and the generally thematic and religious tone of his cultural meditations, all criticized by Freud in his "history" of the psychoanalytic movement. Bruno Bettelheim's recent reinterpretation of psychoanalysis around the term "soul" and the myth of Psyche (rather than Oedipus) develops the idealizing potential of a concept such as "fantasy."[24] Other readers of Freud move in an opposite direction upon this conceptual terrain. By thinking rationally and empirically about the conditions of development, ego psychologists subordinate "fantasy," not so much to the "memory" as the fact of a real event. In a recent book, Jeffrey Masson has carried this position to one of its logical limits. In *The Assault on Truth: Freud's Suppression of the Seduction Theory*, Masson seeks to expose Freud's revision of the seduction theory, and Freud's development of the concept of the role of fantasy in the aetiology of hysteria, as nothing more than a complicated (and largely unconscious) "coverup" scheme to protect Fliess from receiving the blame for a botched operation on one of Freud's patients. Masson's appeal to the real (somewhat criminal) event behind the very concept of fantasy is part of his effort to save all of us from the invidious effect of psychoanalysis—the guilt-engendering idea that we are complicit with our neuroses and our own unhappiness.[25]

23. Thus in several case-histories, especially those of the Wolf-man and the Rat-man, we find this same equivocation upon the counterclaims of "memory" and "fantasy."

24. For Freud's discussion of Jung, see "The History," *S.E.*, XIV; Bettelheim's book is *Freud and Man's Soul* (New York: A.A. Knopf, 1983).

25. Masson, *The Assault on Truth* (New York: Farrar, Straus & Giroux, 1984). For a discussion of the issues raised by Masson's challenge to Freud, see Janet Malcolm's *In*

In our preliminary sketch of psychoanalytic determinism, we noted how Freud excludes chance from the arena of psychic events he takes to be rigidly determined. But this neutralization of chance is predicated upon drawing a firm boundary between the inside and psychic, which will not be open to accident, and the outside world, which will be traversed by "real" accident. Freud's meditation upon the role of "memory" and "fantasy" never reaches a simple answer to the question of how something external and accidental becomes psychic and internal. But the complex turns of his analytic journey lead him to challenge and traverse the boundary between the psychic and nonpsychic. The "memory" is the trace of the outside; in *Studies on Hysteria* it is described as wandering like a "foreign body" within the psyche, forcing the psyche to defend itself against the trauma-causing potential of an alien object.[26] Fantasy may *seem* to operate according to its own intrinsic processes to win pleasure for the psyche. But to do so, it must win an imagined restoration of those infantile scenes which are bound in the unconscious to the earliest experiences of satisfaction. Thus fantasy cannot leave memory behind. And in functioning in and around determining primal scenes, both "memory" and "fantasy" are taken up into the partly external, partly internal medium of language.

It is in the middle space of language where memory and fantasy meet, that a particular kind of chance—the psychic aleatory as textural aleatory—will have a part to play in the unfolding of psychic life. And this chance evades the traditional opposition between that which is determined and that which is open and "free." But to understand this kind of chance we will need to define with much more precision how an earlier unconscious scene superimposes itself upon and repeats itself within the subsequent scenes of life, and how this process is caught up in the network of language. By interpreting Freud's interpretation of a dream of his own that circles around his relationship to Fliess, the *non vixit* dream, we will have access to a striking instance of how this happens in Freud's own life in and through writing *The Interpretation of Dreams*. Only by doing this kind of close reading can we reach a nexus where contingency and life-

---

the Freud Archive (New York: Knopf, 1984). The position I am arguing here is fundamentally at odds with Masson's effort to collapse fantasy into an empirically determined "memory" of an actual event—the seduction of the early "seduction theory." In spite of my differences with Masson's project, I am very grateful for the energetic intervention which has led to the publication of the complete letters to Fliess.

26. *S.E.*, II, 6.

writing are reciprocally involved in that interpretation, both conscious and unconscious, which guides a masterful theoretical text.

The Primal Scene of Rivalry

At its most explicit level the *non vixit* dream circles around one of the
most disturbing and familiar kinds of psychic necessity: a feeling of
separateness and separation from those to whom one also feels very
close. In the dream this separation seems both bizarre and purely
situational.

> *I had gone to Brücke's laboratory at night, and, in response to a gentle knock on
> the door, I opened it to (the late) Professor Fleischl, who came in with a number
> of strangers and, after exchanging a few words, sat down at his table.* This was
> followed by a second dream. *My friend FL. [Fliess] had come to Vienna
> unobtrusively in July. I met him in the street in conversation with my* (deceased)
> *friend P., and went with them to some place where they sat opposite each other as
> though they were at a small table. I sat in front at its narrow end. Fl. spoke
> about his sister and said that in three quarters of an hour she was dead, and
> added some such words as "that was the threshold." As P. failed to understand
> him, Fl. turned to me and asked me how much I had told P. about his affairs.
> Whereupon, overcome by strange emotions, I tried to explain to Fl. that P. (could
> not understand anything at all, of course, because he) was not alive. But what I
> actually said—and I myself noticed the mistake—was, "*Non vixit.*" I then
> gave P. a piercing look. Under my gaze he turned pale; his form grew indistinct
> and his eyes a sickly blue—and finally he melted away. I was highly delighted at
> this and I now realized that Ernst Fleischl, too, had been no more than an appa-
> rition, a "revenant" ["ghost"—literally, "one who returns"]; and it seemed
> to me quite possible that people of that kind only existed as long as one liked and
> could be got rid of if someone else wished it.* [*ID*, 421]

The remarkable thematic consistency of these two related dreams,
which Freud treats as one, emerges in the way almost every element
of the dream dramatizes the distance between him and others. Thus
in each situation of the dream Freud is the outsider: alone in the lab
at night when Professor Fleischl and a group of strangers enter,
coming upon two friends on the street already talking, and at the
small end of the table. In these settings Freud is alternately silent,
asked a disturbing question by Fliess, makes an error in communication ("*non vixit*"), annihilates Joseph P. with his gaze, feels delight at

[55]

an inappropriate moment, and finally, in what gives the whole dream a strangely gothic turn, is aware he has been in the presence of two who are ghosts.

This dream and the analysis which follows it take Freud into one of the paradigmatic situations explicated by psychoanalysis. Joseph P. is the brilliant younger colleague who followed Freud as a demonstrator in Brücke's lab, and Freud is quite sure of his own fondness for P. Fliess is the most passionate attachment of Freud's adult life, one who Freud tells us in the course of this analysis "means more to me than ever the others could" (*ID*, 486). Freud has the sense of knowing, and being in full possession of his feelings for these two men. And yet, the dream and its analysis disclose strong hostile unconscious feelings for Joseph P., Fliess, and others. Something strange has happened. Something intercedes, some thing—an obscure force or factor Freud will later call *das Es*, the It—intercedes between Freud and his dear friends, something which dispossesses Freud of feelings he is sure he has.

Freud's dream and dream analysis show how the scenes and relationships of later life can fall prey to a compulsion to repeat one scene in a relationship from the earliest period of life. Thus this dream text conflates and condenses, in its references and transposition of persons and affect, the scenes and situations of three different epochs of Freud's life: his training in neurology in Brücke's laboratory (when Freud is in his early twenties); his intimate relationship with Wilhelm Fliess at the time he is writing *The Interpretation of Dreams* (Freud has recently turned 42); and last, Freud's decisive early relationship with his older nephew John (when Freud is between the ages of one and three). Connected with this last relationship, there is a scene of rivalry which repeats itself uncontrollably. To understand this repetition it is necessary to follow how these three periods of Freud's life converge in the dream text.

Rivalry and ambition in Brücke's laboratory. Freud works in the Vienna Physiological Institute. It is a place of instituted hierarchies and instituted authority. Ernst Brücke is the "great man" in charge, a man who has "terrible blue eyes" "which retained their striking beauty even in his old age" (*ID*, 422). A subordinate works under the watchful eyes of his superior hoping for approving glances and advancement. But sometimes things happen differently. Freud tells us about such an episode:

> [I] was due to start work early in the morning. It came to Brücke's ears that I sometimes reached the students' laboratory late. One morning he

turned up punctually at the hour of opening and awaited my arrival. His words were brief and to the point. But it was not they that mattered. What overwhelmed me were the terrible blue eyes with which he looked at me and by which I was reduced to nothing—[*ID*, 422]

The gaze and judgment of a "great man" like Brücke, and the discipline of science he embodies, open a scene of rivalry in the laboratory he oversees. There, some will succeed and make their mark in science, and after they are gone memorials will be unveiled to confirm their worth and perpetuate their visibility. Thus, Freud takes the words "*non vixit*" from the Kaiser Josef Memorial, and has this dream only a few days after the unveiling of the memorial to Fleischl, when he has also seen the Brücke memorial once again.

But where there are winners, there are usually losers. At the unveiling for Fleischl, Freud tells us he "must have reflected (unconsciously) with regret on the fact that the premature death of my brilliant friend P., whose whole life had been devoted to science, had robbed him of a well-merited claim to a memorial in these same precincts" (*ID*, 423). Freud's regret about P.'s early death overlaps with his concern about his own place in the future, a theme he often touches upon in the letters to Fliess. In one letter, Freud asks for just ten more years of work and wonders if a marble tablet will someday be erected before the house where "the secret of the dream revealed itself to Dr. Sigm. Freud" (*CL*, 6/12/1900).

In a space of intimate proximity and devotion to the same cause, is there any wonder that friendship and rivalry are entangled? In both rivalry and friendship the self sees the other as a version of the self—a good version (a friend) or bad version (rival), or a good and bad friend in rivalry. Thus Freud labels Joseph P. "good" but treats him in his dream as someone who is "bad." Freud tells us he once reproached Joseph P. for giving loud expression to his impatience for advancement, exactly at the time his superior, Professor Fleischl, was seriously ill. Freud's dream punishes P.'s ambition: "As he could not wait for the removal of another man, he was himself removed." But Freud confesses that "a few years earlier, I myself had nourished a still livelier wish to fill a vacancy." He also confesses to an "indiscretion" that caused trouble between two friends (Fleischl and Joseph Breuer) in the laboratory, by "quite unnecessarily telling one (friend) . . . what the other had said about him." Socially embarrassing disclosure will be a recurrent problem and worry for Freud.

Contemporary attachment to Fliess. At first glance, Freud's account of Fliess's part in the dream thoughts seems very remote from the psychodynamics of rivalry in Brücke's lab. Fliess, who lives in Berlin, undergoes an operation, and the first reports from his relatives "were not reassuring and made me feel anxious" (*ID*, 480). This is the "exciting cause" of the dream. Freud knows Fliess's sister had died in early youth after a very brief illness. Freud would have made the journey to Berlin himself, but he was then "the victim of a painful complaint" which made movement a "torture" to him (*ID*, 480–81). In the dream thoughts Freud supposes that "after getting some worse news of him, I should make the journey after all—and arrive *too late*, for which I might never cease to reproach myself." The guilt about not attending Fliess in his illness and anxiety about arriving too late get represented in the dream by Freud's late arrival in Brücke's laboratory. In addition, Fliess's relatives warned Freud not to discuss his operation with anyone. Freud tells us, "I had felt offended by this because it implied an unnecessary distrust of my discretion" (*ID*, 481). This warning and Freud's actual indiscretion in Brücke's laboratory are represented in the dream by Fliess's disturbing question to Freud of P.: "How much have you told him of my affairs?" But there are more complex connections between these two settings in the dream text. Freud's anxiety about Fliess's possible death is represented in the dream not just by two people who are dead (Fleischl and Joseph P.) but by two rivals Freud has outlived, one of whom Freud murders in the dream, and whose disappearance stirs a "delight" in Freud at the dream's end. How does it feel when a very close friend, someone who is like you, but not you, how does it feel when *they* (you) might die . . . but in such a way that you (but *not* they) will continue to live? Freud's dream analysis uncovers the anxiety and guilt he feels at this prospect. But, the cross-connections with the rivalry in Brücke's lab indicate that Fliess too must fall prey to the primitive delight that Freud had "once more survived someone, because it was *he* and not I who had died" (*ID*, 485).

The primal scene of rivalry. Freud's dream and dream analysis draw his contemporary relationship with Fliess into the scene of explicit rivalry in Brücke's laboratory. How does Freud explain this connection? He does so by making these two scenes part of a chain in a series that goes back to an original scene or rivalry. This movement back into the past and down into the unconscious is what makes Freud's analysis not just a sociology of rivalry, but a psychology— that is, an analysis that will account for Freud's engagement as a particular person in scenes of friendship and rivalry. Here is how he describes this decisive early relationship with his nephew John:

Until the end of my third year we had been inseparable. We had loved each other and fought with each other; and this childhood relationship, as I have already hinted above [pp. 198 and 231], had a determining influence on all my subsequent relations with contemporaries. Since that time my nephew John has had many reincarnations which revived now one side and now another of his personality, unalterably fixed as it was in my unconscious memory. There must have been times when he treated me very badly and I must have shown courage in the face of my tyrant; for in my later years I have often been told of a short speech made by me in my own defence when my father, who was at the same time John's grandfather, had said to me accusingly: "Why are you hitting John?" My reply—I was not yet two years old at the time—was "I hit him 'cos he hit me." [*ID*, 424–25]

Below we will have occasion to give this scene close analysis. But at first glance it can be seen to allow Freud to carry through the most deterministic possible account of psychic life. He makes this primal scene of rivalry the originary cause of a whole chain of subsequent effects. It also becomes the interpretive key to the dream. This scene allows us to see what all three scenes and the dream scene have in common: they are a space for rivalry between equals, where there is anxiety about failure, "delight" for the victor, and judgment for wrongdoing (lateness, indiscretion). Here it is easy to be overcome with sudden feelings of hostility to and estrangement from those of whom Freud insists he is actually quite fond. But these three scenes are not of equal importance. The primal scene seeds Freud's relationships with ambivalence. In each scene the characters may change, but the roles and action remain the same. To put it most starkly, Freud carries this scene around in his head, "inextinguishably fixed . . . in unconscious memory," and he is compelled to repeat it. This scene gives a particular form to Freud's life: Freud desires to be first (in science, at his friend's bedside, in winning the object all want); but in fact he is late and in the wrong (in his arrival at laboratory, in not going to Berlin, when might prevails over right in battle with his nephew). This "lateness" can engender guilt and anxiety because rivalry is conducted under the gaze of a judge (Brücke, Fliess's relatives, Freud's father), and a negative judgment could lead to annihilation rather than the memorial built to remember the worthy. And in this constellation of unconscious oppositions Freud's coming first and earning a memorial will bring "delight" from having "won" life (by forestalling death); in doing so he will have superseded and outlasted those friends who come later and suffer annihilation by having been overtaken by death. In this fantasmatic unconscious scene, Freud's assertion of selfhood will require replacing the avatars of John, who must be vanquished over and over again. And since they are from the first day he knows them only ghostly repetitions—*revenant*—"those who return," there is a wonderful precision in the error in the dream by which Freud says of Joseph P. *not* "*non vivit*," "he is not alive," as Freud "meant" to do, but "*non vixit*," "he did not live." That is, even when he was drawing breath and I knew him, he did not really live as himself for me, but as a "revenant," a ghostly repetition of my nephew John, and as such was condemned to act out a part already determined by the unconscious.

It is worth noting what allows Freud to give the primal scene of rivalry the explanatory power it has. First there must be some clear way to represent the primal scene, in spite of its remoteness in time, and all the obstacles of distorting memory. Then if the primal scene is to function as the kernel of psychic reality, in shaping the self and its relation to others, then it must remain unchanged in its essence as it is translated into the different epochs of life. For if it were too drastically distorted in its later "editions," would there really be repetition of a single primal scene? So, Freud must have available to himself a clear and compliant language to represent the primal scene and its repetitions. And finally, although Freud is analyzing himself, his analysis must not be distorted by this fact. All of which is to say that Freud can make his text an efficient conveyor of meaning of this primal scene only if his own text is not symptomatic.

This is a very strange demand to make of Freud, who in interpreting dreams, and most other texts, pays attention "to every shade of the form of words in which they were laid before us" (*ID*, 514). And lest we are willing to be left in the position of the *ingenu*—a Donatello among the *fauves*—his example impels us to do the same. If we look carefully at the form of words, we can note that evidence for the primacy of this primal scene comes from a sexually charged shift in the word used for "to hit" between early and late childhood—from *schlagen* to *wichsen*—which in turn shifts *non vivit* to *non vixit*. Freud's emphasis on this fact is suppressed by the English translation. A literal translation of the German would read:

> "Why are you hitting John?" My reply—I was not yet two years old at the time—was "I hit [ge(sch)lagt] him 'cos he hit me." It must have been this scene from my childhood which diverted "*Non vivit*" into "*Non vixit*," for in the language of later childhood the word for "to hit" [*schlagen*—"thrash"] is "*wichsen*" [pronounced like the English "vixen"].

The dream-work is not ashamed to make use of links such as this one. [*ID*, 425]

Why is this shift important? Though Freud remembers his passionate friendship with John, his memory of this early childhood scene has been completely repressed. It comes to him in the form of his father's anecdote. But the deflection of *"non vivit"* to *"non vixit"* shows that this scene is linked to experience in later childhood, where, perhaps during puberty, this scene was remembered, received a new charge of affect through *deferred effect (nachträglichkeit)*, and then was submitted to renewed repression. This possibility is not explored by Freud, but it seems likely when one notes that the word *wichsen* has, in some parts of the German-speaking world, including Austria, the sense of the English word "whack off" (to masturbate).[27] In addition, the screen memory of Freud and his friend ganging up on a girl playmate to "deflower" her (steal her flowers) involves the same period of very early childhood and the same nephew John. Their "victim" was John's sister Pauline. The primal scene of rivalry behind the *non vixit* dream could receive a sexual charge with the onset of puberty through making an unconscious connection with the screen memory it resembles.

All of this reminds us that the primal scene Freud repeatedly postulates in the 1890s is not what it sometimes seems to be—a fixed datum or memory-trace in the unconscious that operates continuously in one predictable fashion upon the psyche. Instead, in its effects on the person, it undergoes a complex interaction as memory and fantasy, and never stops being affected and displaced by what it displaces and affects. And if one considers how the primal scene behind the *non vixit* dream is discussed and represented in *The Interpretation of Dreams*, one finds the same processes of distortion and displacement at work in Freud's writing of the text. Freud recognizes this fact and justifies it as the need to *not repeat* once more, through an indiscreetly revelatory analysis, what he has done in the dream, the primal scene, and its later repetitions: "sacrificing to my ambition people whom I greatly value." But in evoking this moral censor—which will arrest repetition—Freud must frustrate an almost atavistic intellectual and aesthetic pleasure in showing everything behind "this fine specimen" to the reader. He tells us that this dream exhibits so many of the "puzzling characteristics of dreams"

27. This information comes to me from several native speakers of German, above all, my colleague Peter Heller of the SUNY Buffalo Modern Languages Department, who spent his early years in the same Viennese linguistic environment as Freud.

that "I would 'gladly give my life' to be able to give a full solution of its riddles" (*ID*, 422; my translation).

In fact the conflict announced at the beginning of Freud's interpretation of this dream partakes of the larger conflict at work in his taking himself as the exemplary object of analysis throughout *The Interpretation of Dreams*. On the one hand, Freud must desist from full analysis, replace names by initial letters, and hold back information at crucial junctures. He is aided in all of this by the theoretical superstructure of *The Interpretation of Dreams*, which justifies him in subordinating his analysis of a dream like the *non vixit* dream to concerns indicated in such subheadings as "Speech in Dreams" and "Affect in Dreams." But, on the other hand, in order to analyze the relation between dream and waking life he must do more than hide. He must risk indiscretion by making things visible; and in fact he usually tells much of the story in a covert manner. Thus, while seeing *The Interpretation of Dreams* through the press, Freud writes to Fliess: "My central accomplishment in interpretation comes in this installment, the absurd dreams. It is astonishing how often you appear in them! In the '*non vixit*' dream I am delighted to have outlived you; isn't it terrible to suggest something like this—that is, to have to make it explicit to everyone who understands?" (*CL*, 9/21/99). Thus in writing this text, Freud cannot prevent himself from encountering one of the central problems in the dream, the problem of indiscretion. Freud detects this theme in the dream text in this way: "The reproach of being unable to keep anything to myself was attested in the dream by the element 'unobtrusive' (*unauffällig*) and by Fl.'s [that is, Fliess's] question as to *how much I had told P. about his affairs*." And after describing how potential indiscretion about Fliess's operation undergoes displacement and condensation with actual indiscretion in Brücke's laboratory, Freud concludes that here these processes of the dream work "as well as the reasons for them, are strikingly visible (*augenfällig*)" (*ID*, 482). The linguistic echo of *unauffällig* and *augenfällig* dramatizes Freud's problem. How can he make his conclusions about the mechanisms of psychic life *augenfällig*—evident, manifest, and obvious—while still keeping the evidence upon which he bases those conclusions discreetly "unobtrusive" (*unauffällig*)?

If one reads Freud's text as a suspicious psychoanalytic reader, several features of the *non vixit* dream analysis stand out.

(1) Freud tells us his decision to share his dream analysis will lead him to "content" himself with selecting only a few of its elements for interpretation. But, in fact, he discusses many more than "a few" of

its details; this is one of the more complete examples of dream interpretation in the book.

(2) Next, although we can never be sure where Freud has exercised discretion and censorship, the division of the analysis into two
large parts offers a clue. In Part I of the analysis Freud almost entirely omits reference to Fliess, even though he is a principal figure
in the dream. Only in Part II do we discover that his operation is the
dream's "exciting cause." And everything we know about Freud's relationship to Fliess makes dream thoughts about him prime material
for Freud's conscious discretion and censorship.

(3) Finally, and perhaps most strangely, this two-part analysis involves Freud in an enactment of the very repetition he has placed at
the thematic center of the dream analysis. Thus Part I of the analysis
gives a one-paragraph description of the primal scene of rivalry with
Freud's nephew. Then Part II does not just summarize and extend
the first description, it *repeats* the earlier description, using many of
the same phrases, in an enlarged displaced two-paragraph analysis
of the primal scene.

What do these three features mean? First, Freud seems to write
more than he first intends. Now whether he does so because of his
strong, affective engagement with the material, or whether it is a result of his wanting a fuller understanding of the material he begins
to analyze—in either case, Freud seems to expose his analysis to
uncontrollable unconscious processes. We do not know how he drew
upon his notebooks of dream analyses in writing *The Interpretation of
Dreams*, but the two-part distribution of this analysis indicates that
he may have at first, in Part I, completely succeeded in suppressing
all discussion of Fliess, but that in writing Part II, under the sub-
heading "Affect in Dreams," though he could treat the subject ade-
quately in relation to Joseph P. and Fleischl, he could no longer re-
strain himself from a discussion of Fliess. At first Freud separates
Fliess from the impulses toward murderous rivalry focused upon
Joseph P., but he then concedes that even in the case of Fl., he must
have felt unconscious "delight" at having outlived yet another "edition" of his nephew John. There seems to be the same element of
compulsion at work in Freud's return to the primal scene in Part II,
where he repeats the words used to describe it in Part I. In Freud,
repetition is repeatedly the sign of compulsion. Thus, in writing
more than at first intended, in returning to discuss Fliess, and in returning to analyze more fully a primal scene he only imperfectly understands, Freud seems to be participating in an exploration of unconscious material which is at least in part involuntary. In describing

this process in the case of "Little Hans," Freud uses a metaphor most apt for our discussion of a dream with two ghosts: "a thing which has not been understood inevitably reappears; like an unlaid ghost, it cannot rest until the mystery has been solved and the spell broken."[28]

These three features of the text of the dream analysis lead me to ask the basic question: to what extent is Freud in control of his interpretation? Are these features of the dream analysis merely the checks of conscious censorship, as some might say, or are they compromise-formations that result from the conflict of unconscious desire and repression, as I have tried to indicate? In *The Interpretation of Dreams* Freud points to the way censorship and the "dream-distortion" caused by repression are aligned with one another: "the phenomena of censorship and of dream-distortion correspond down to their smallest details" (*ID*, 143). I suspect that distortion due to conscious censorship and distortion due to the conflicts of repression and unconscious desire are utterly entangled with each other in this dream analysis.

If we do a close reading of the language of Freud's analysis of this primal scene of rivalry, we will be able to understand the special power the scene exercises over his later life. This is not a simple task, because the two parts of Freud's dream analysis offer two very different accounts of what an early scene judged to be primal is and how it operates in psychic life: the first emphasizes "oneness" and primacy and atemporality, while the second sees this oneness as an effect of the scene's inscription in the textual and temporal displacements of psychic life. To trace these two ways of thinking the primal scene (*Urszene*), we need to look more closely at the two versions Freud offers.

Doubling the Primal Scene

Here is the last paragraph of Part I of the dream analysis. Freud has just discussed the way he has, in the dream text and in his relationship with Joseph P., played the part of Brutus—a friend who must murder out of a sense of justice. This theme allows Freud to

28. *S.E.*, X, 122.

introduce his early relationship with his nephew John, and make his first case for the primacy of that relationship.

> Strange to say, I really did once play the part of Brutus. I once acted in the scene between Brutus and Caesar from Schiller before an audience of children. I was fourteen years old at the time and was acting with a nephew who was a year my senior. He had come to us on a visit from England; and he, too, was a *revenant,* for it was the playmate of my earliest years who had returned in him. Until the end of my third year we had been inseparable. We had loved each other and fought with each other; and this childhood relationship, as I have already hinted above [pp. 198 and 231], had a determining influence on all my subsequent relations with contemporaries. Since that time my nephew John has had many reincarnations which revived now one side and now another of his personality, unalterably fixed as it was in my unconscious memory. There must have been times when he treated me very badly and I must have shown courage in the face of my tyrant; for in my later years I have often been told of a short speech made by me in my own defence when my father, who was at the same time John's grandfather, had said to me accusingly: "Why are you hitting John?" My reply—I was not yet two years old at the time—was "I hit him 'cos he hit me." It must have been this scene from my childhood which diverted "*Non vivit*" into "*Non vixit,*" for in the language of later childhood the word for to hit is "*wichsen*" [pronounced like the English 'vixen']. The dream-work is not ashamed to make use of links such as this one. There was little basis in reality for my hostility to my friend P., who was very greatly my superior and for that reason was well fitted to appear as a new edition of my early playmate. This hostility must therefore certainly have gone back to my complicated childhood relations to John.
>
> As I have said, I shall return to this dream later. [*ID*, 424–25]

How does this particular scene and relationship achieve its power over Freud's psychic life? Through its oneness. Freud and John, though two people, were one in being "inseparable." In this one relationship they reconciled antithetical activities like loving and fighting. It is the single intensity of this dyadic relation which forms one envelope of time and space—one scene. The oneness of this scene is given emphasis by the way Freud's text echoes with the word "one": Freud really did play Brutus "once"; his nephew was "one" year older; and Freud has hinted "once so far" as to the decisiveness of this relationship. But why is this "one" scene so important? It partakes of the more general character of the idea of the "one." Something that happens "just once" can be subordinated to recurrent natural processes because the single is incidental and accidental, and therefore gratuitous. But the single, by being small or momentary and so much itself, can have the oneness of an atom. Being nuclear, the "one," like the soul, cannot be broken into parts. In this way the "one" can quickly become the token of the particular, the specific, the unified, and the unique. But in Freud's consideration of a single decisive scene from early life, the "one" gets a more specific meaning. The oneness of the single scene is both cause and effect of its being "prime"—first in time and therefore first in importance. Freud never says that John's is the decisive friendship of his life, because coming first, it makes all subsequent friendships later editions of itself; this is implied by Freud's analysis, both here and elsewhere. This equation of temporal priority and causal priority is crucial for psychoanalysis. It is part of its most concerted flirtation with metaphysics and allows the primal scene to stand as the origin of the single person, the "one" self. And Freud confers astonishing power on this one scene. Because of the way its single doubleness is "inextinguishably" inscribed in unconscious memory, this scene of friendship can imprint its character on all the subsequent moments of life, which revive now this side and now that side of John's character. And, in the second part of the dream analysis, when Freud repeats these ideas in new words, he insists that the psyche shows an infallible efficiency in furnishing him with new incarnations of John: "My emotional life has *always* insisted that I should have an intimate friend and a hated enemy. I have *always* been able to provide myself with both" (*ID*, 483; my emphasis). The word "always" is an index of what has happened. Not only does the primal scene subsist in its remote oneness as a temporal island of continuous presence; it also seeds all subsequent psychic reality with its oneness. Through a repetition of its essential character, each subsequent scene and moment of life become perfectly reproduced "editions" of this one primal scene of life. Pure repetitions of this one scene annul the otherness and contingency of time and history. It seems that in staging involuntary repetitions of this primal scene, the unconscious accedes to Godlike power.

The anecdote Freud's father tells of the dissonant moment in his childhood friendship with John has an equivocal status in this text. As a fragment of this early relationship, it confers external authority on Freud's psychic involvement with this time of oneness. Because the lines of this early dialogue have the archetypal simplicity of every accusation—"Why did you do this?"—and the chiasmic simplicity of every justification of violence—"I did it to him because he

did it to me," because these are memorable as only the endlessly repeated seem to be, the anecdote becomes a model of pure repetition,
a repetition which escapes the displacements that befall most forms
of repetition. For these reasons this anecdote partakes of the permanence of the written trace to which Freud appeals in explaining the
timelessness of memory-traces in the unconscious. In all these ways
it enhances the oneness and timelessness of this primal scene of rivalry. But the content of the anecdote—a fight—also points to a
breakdown of oneness. And beyond this, it recalls an episode which
was forgotten, and thus repressed, by Freud. The repression invites
us to register the first suspicion of this scene of friendship: perhaps
its status as a timeless edenic time-before is an effect of forgetful-
ness. Perhaps there are several strata of scenes and times—and a
plethora of repressed incidents—before and after this scene, which
are operating covertly to give it its appearance of scenic oneness and
visibility and clarity. A multiplicity of psychic material operating behind the scene helps explain the linguistic displacement of one word
in the anecdote (from *schlagen* to *wichsen*), as it comes under the
pressure of the psychic experience of later childhood, perhaps, as I
speculated above, puberty. Such modification of the primal scene
through *deferred effect* shows the anecdote and the childhood relationship failing to function as pure repetition; instead the scene is
importantly displaced in its repetition. Time, history, and chance—
in their otherness—have all the time been contaminating the primal
scene in its apparent oneness. By following the turns of Freud's interpretation of the *non vixit* dream, we can find another more plural
way to think the primal scene in its operation in psychic life.

I noted above that Freud does not just talk about repetition of an
early primal scene in later life; he also *enacts* this repetition in his
text, by repeating his description of the scene in the second part of
his dream analysis. In its textual repetition the single primal scene is
befallen by a temporality that obliges us to see it in a different light.
Now the oneness and priority of that scene are a necessary illusion
engendered in a psychic middle space, what Freud calls the *Mittel-
stücke* of the dream thoughts—a textual space where past, present,
and future meet through the operation of "memory" and "fantasy,"
the work of unconscious desire, and an encounter with the outside.
We can watch this process by tracing the repetition and displacement of the primal scene in the second part of the dream analysis.

There are several general reasons Part II of the dream analysis
contests the atemporal conception of the primal scene developed in

Part I. The very fact of a return to previously discussed material creates an impression of temporal succession for the reader; and so does the unexpected length of the analysis. The five paragraphs of Part I move from Brücke's laboratory, to the connection between "*non vixit*" and Julius Caesar, to the first description of the primal scene. By contrast, the eleven paragraphs of Part II undertake a much more extended "genealogical" analysis of how the dream might have emerged in time: from its origin in the day residue (Fliess's operation), to the theme of indiscretion (with Fliess, and in Brücke's lab), through the long second description of the primal scene, to an accounting for the delight Freud expresses in the dream (an infantile glee for outliving everyone), and a comic coda (expressing "legitimate" delight at his current good fortune). But perhaps most important, by assuming a much more urgent personal tone in discussing his feelings about Wilhelm Fliess, Freud registers emotions which presuppose a sense of temporality. Thus Freud's anxiety about Fliess's operation and Freud's own ambitions for psychoanalysis tether him to an uncertain future. And in an analogous fashion, Freud's guilt about not going to Berlin and his shame about his "indiscretion" in Brücke's lab turn him toward a past which, because of gradations of memory and the work of repression, is mobile and plural in its aftereffects.

The second account of Freud's scene of rivalry with John deconstructs the primacy of the primal scene by carrying through three displacements: a displacement through representation, a displacement from the first to the middle, and displacement through a loss of primal oneness.

Displacement by representation. The second account of the primal scene shows that it is befallen by temporality in a particular way: by getting caught up in the displacements and deferrals of representation. Freud has described this primal scene, as it subsists in the unconscious, as a continuous presence. In its metaphysical absoluteness it is both timeless and before language. It apparently has no need of means of representation. But if the primal scene wants to repeat itself, if it wants to re-present its presentness, then it can do so only by using the reality outside itself as a language that can imitate it. The primal scene can *be* primal, and act as a cause and origin of the self's oneness, only by repeating itself in that which it is not: the nonprimal. To do this it must allow itself to be reduced and formalized into that which can be repeated. In the first version of the primal scene Freud said that later incarnations of John revived now this side and now that side of this fixed "character" (*Wesens*). The word *Wesens* also means "being, reality, or essence," and so it is charged with metaphysical plenitude. In the second version of the primal scene, later friends are said to be incarnations of this first form or figure (*ersten Gestalt*). Later versions will not be perfect copies of John, they will be ghostly figures of his form—*revenants*, those who return in a form less full than he. The loss entailed in these belated, less adequate versions justifies the tone of regret which is solicited by Freud's citation from Goethe's dedication to *Faust*. There the author summons shades that have "long since" appeared before his "cloudy or troubled gaze."

But later repetitions and imitations of the primal scene only partially compromise the authority and plenitude of the original. Things are more complex than this. The belated secondary quality of these repetitions also helps to guard and enhance the primacy of that early scene. Thus Freud tells us he has "always" been able to provide himself with "an intimate friend and a hated enemy," "and it has not infrequently happened that the ideal situation of childhood has been so completely reproduced that friend and enemy have come together in a single individual." Here Freud is dangerously close to making later reproductions *equivalent* to the original primal relationship. Thus he adds this important proviso: "though not, of course, both at once (*gleichzeitig*) or with constant oscillations, (*wiederholter Abwechslung*), as may have been the case in my early childhood" (*ID*, 483). The primacy of the original scene is protected by the inferiority of later versions, which are less able to hold the antinomies of love and hate in a primal oneness. This inferiority extends to John himself, who in returning when Freud is fourteen is no more than a "revenant," a ghost of his former self. Freud and John cannot relive their old shared intensities, so they act them, with John playing Caesar and Freud playing Brutus, before an auditorium of school children. Later Freud will find himself playing Brutus to others . . . among them Joseph P. and Fliess. The resort to stage drama merely makes explicit what life after the primal scene must be: an imitation of positions that once seemed to have oneness and plenitude, but have become roles to repeat.

A displacement from the first to the middle. Where does Freud place the primal scene? In Part I of the analysis the primal scene of conflict and rivalry came from a surmise based upon an anecdote: "There must have been times when he treated me very badly . . . for in my later years I have often been told . . ." And here we confront an irony. The very absence of information about this early relationship, which necessitates recourse to an anecdote, helps to invest this childhood scene with a firstness and beforeness that makes it primal. And Freud begins Part II of his description of the primal scene by using language traditionally linked to all that is primal, powerful, and psychic: he explains that in the dream work, anger at Fliess's relatives for worry about his possible indiscretion received "reinforcements from sources (*Quellen*) from the depth (*Tiefe*) of the mind and thus swelled (*schwillt*) into a torrent (*Strom*) of hostile feelings toward those of whom I was in reality fond." Where are these powerful sources that can replace a recent occasion for feeling with their own affect? "The source of these reinforcements flowed from my childhood." The hydrolic metaphors used here give emphasis to two qualities ascribed to the primal scenes of life: their mystery (who knows the origin of the spring?) and their necessity (none can hold back a torrent of water; it will find a way to flow and express its force).

However, as the paragraph proceeds, Freud does things which displace the primal scene away from the beginning and toward the middle. For one thing, he begins his description of the scene by equivocating in a strange way: "For the purposes of dream interpretation let us assume that a childhood memory arose, or was constructed in fantasy, with some such content as the following." Above, we followed Freud's investigation of the traumatic primal scenes that lie behind symptom-formation among neurotics, in which he failed to trace such scenes back to some prehistoric primal ground of "memory." He found instead that they were composed by an interaction between memory-traces deposited by actual events and fantasies as they were shaped by unconscious desire. This interplay can never be fully described because both memory and fantasy are deposited as indistinguishable traces in the psyche, and this process can be affected by factors as incommensurate and unpredictable as anecdotes told within the family, the delayed onset of full sexuality in humans, and the work of repression. Where does all this happen, where is the primal scene formed? In between and in the middle; temporally, between the remote (and repressed) past, and the present; typologically, between the work of conscious and that of unconscious psychic processes; and in the middle space of mediating language, between the language forms inside the psyche and those that come from outside. Little wonder that Freud calls this scene the "intermediate nodal point in the dream thoughts"—for it is the point of maximum density and complexity, where all the threads of psychic life converge, a knot or nodal point (*Knotenpunkt*) the analyst must unravel if he is to interpret the dream (*ID*, 513).

[70]

This middle placement is confirmed by the sentence which follows Freud's narrative of the primal scene in the *non vixit* dream:

> This memory, or more probably fantasy, which came into my mind while I was analyzing the dream—without further evidence I myself could not tell how—constituted a middle portion (*Mittelstücke*) in the dream thoughts which gathered up the emotions raging in them as a well (*Brunnenschale*) collects the water that flows into it. [*ID*, 484]

Where is the primal scene? It is at the nodal connecting points of psychic life; it is a middle portion or middle piece of the dream thoughts; or, more precisely still, it is like water collected in a *Brunnenschale*. A *Brunnenschale* is not just a "well"; it is a vessel placed at the head of a well where cattle might drink. It receives what comes from inside the well and holds it in its shell (*schale*) or vessel, so it will be open to the outside, before the water flows off on to the ground or into a stream. This middle space is not predetermined in its character by "torrents" of affect that "swell" from the "depths." It receives "emotional stirrings" from below, but its intermediate space can also be a place of comparative quiescence, variegated influences, and new directions. Finally these waters will be affected and modified by what they meet from outside in the middle space of the *Brunnenschale*.

A displacement out of primal oneness. In passing from Part I to Part II of the analysis the primal scene in the *non vixit* dream undergoes elaboration and grows in length and detail. Instead of saying that he and John "loved each other and fought with one another," Freud reports: "I early learned to defend myself against him, we were inseparable in living with one another and loving one another, and between, according to the testimony of our elders, we fought and— *accused* each other" (my translation; Freud's emphasis). And the scene Freud describes has many more elements than the anecdote his father recalled:

> The two children had a dispute about some object. (What the object was may be left an open question, though the memory or pseudo-memory had a quite specific one in view.) Each of them claimed to have *got there before the other* and therefore to have a better right to it. They came to blows and might prevailed over right. On the evidence of the dream, I may myself have been aware that I was wrong ("*I myself noticed the mistake*"). However, this time I was the stronger and remained in possession of the field. The vanquished party hurried to his grandfather—my father—and complained about me, and I defended myself in the words

which I know from my father's account: "I hit him 'cos he hit me." [*ID*, 483–84]

There are several ways in which this primal scene is displaced out of its putative oneness. Since Freud says he was the stronger "this time," it must not have been the first time they fought. With rivalry of any kind it never seems possible to locate a primal beginning or first time. Thus rivals can never agree in answering the question, "who started it?" And, in its second rendering this scene of rivalry is not described as a passionate union of two—a primal dyad bonded together with love and hate. Instead, these two are divided by the object that lies between them and each seeks to possess. Here is the paradigmatic situation of rivalry and desire: two do battle over a single object (a person, a treasure, a body of knowledge). And Freud chooses to leave the object indefinite. Why? First, because (as René Girard and Hegel show) desire for the object does not arise from the nature of the object; it is caused and mediated by the desire of others for that object. Then too, though desire and rivalry persist, the identity of the object will change as time goes on and life proceeds. But Freud insists that the memory/fantasy *did* have a single particular object in view, though it is not named. In this way he asserts the specificity of the scene—it happened once, in a single particular way; but since the object is not named, the scene has general significance. Finally, and most obvious, this object becomes the locus of Freud's censorship. He chooses to suppress its identity so he can represent this scene.

But it turns out Freud and John are separated by more than their common desire for a single object. When Freud defeats John, John goes outside their circle of friendship and rivalry, and appeals to Freud's father. John has divided the primal friendship with an "accusation." Such a use of language exposes a most profound division in this primal scene. For in order for Freud to be *accused*, there must be a symbolic order of language and shared signs, and the social system within which that language circulates, and the instituted hierarchies that are part of language and society, and are guaranteed by a father who could hear and judge the accusation.

Why does this scene become primal for Freud? Most obviously because "*this time*" he was the stronger and took possession of the object. This is a moment of triumph, mastery, and "delight" at having defeated his rivals. But possession of the object is only part of Freud's triumph; his real victory comes from his use of language before his father. We can get at this side of his victory by asking why

Freud's father would have remembered this little scene. Perhaps because of how little Freud must have appeared to his father, when, to his stern question, the son replied "I hit him, 'cos he hit me!" It is not difficult to imagine the father's response: "look at my son, he is not even two, and yet he stands up to my question most bravely, and offers this cute little speech of self-justification!" This may not have been Freud's first assertive use of language in a complex social setting, but his father's anecdote gets it to serve as such for the purposes of family history. Later, the anecdote, together with the scene formed around it, becomes a model for how Freud can cope with the rule of his father (or one like Brücke who, with a castrating gaze, could ask "why are you late?"); it also offers a strategy with which to overcome the power of his nephew, who, being older, is stronger and usually wins, and always seems to be in the right, having come to everything one year before Freud. How does Freud prevail? Through his use of the signifying process to designate meanings. Thus if one looks at the *content* of this scene of rivalry, it can be read as an allegory of the way possession of the object is won and protected through the arbitrary imposition of meaning, modeled on the use of language. Recall the situation: claim to the object does not arise from the nature or identity of the object, but "who got there first." Thus, anyone could get there first, Freud might have gotten there first, but he did not. Freud got there later, he was in the wrong, but he exercised force and won. In fact he exercised two kinds of force: physical force in taking the object from his nephew, and then, in defending his object before his father, the force of signification, of interpretation, and of a (very short) narrative. And this confronts us with an irony constitutive of the very idea of a primal scene. The scene which is to confer a quality, a natural identity, and a oneness upon the self is articulated by a series of relations of quantity: differences in the time of arrival at the object, differences in force in appropriating the object, and in defending it before the father. It is this series of arbitrary and contingent differential relations that produces the locus of a coherent identity for the self. Freud got there later, but because of his use of language and its power to impose meaning, "might" prevails over "right." It is this constellation of meanings that becomes formed into a scene which will appear primal and causative for the scenes of rivalry which open in Freud's later life.

The primal scene: it is not easy to grasp the strangeness of Freud's use of this idea. A one-sentence formulation by way of summary, would go something like this: although the primal scene is always already displaced from its originary oneness, and it is in large part a construct of the analytical process, in spite of this, it is an indispensable idea for thinking the person. What does this mean? We have traced the three ways the primal scene is always already displaced out of originary oneness: first, it is inmixed with forms of representation that, by repeating it both contrive and compromise its priority; second, the primal scene does not happen at the beginning, it is composed in an (impure) middle; and finally, the oneness of the primal scene is not an expression of identity or quality, but of arbitrary differential relations that happen on the model of signification. For all these reasons the primal scene invites its own impure repetition and displacement. There is a second dimension to the strangeness of this particular primal scene. Freud repeatedly equivocates as to whether it is a memory or fantasy and adds that it "came into my mind while I was analyzing the dream." Later in *The Interpretation of Dreams* Freud explains. When the analysis was "held up," he was led to the primal scene "by way" of lines from a Heine poem. The poem tells of a failure of mutual understanding until two friends find themselves together in the mud or shit (*Kot*) (*ID*, 513). Freud does not say why these lines led him to the fully elaborated second version of the primal scene. But his use of them shows how he "lets himself go" during interpretation, engaging in a process that approximates free association. This fills out a primal scene with detail, but ends by making it an undecidable synthetic amalgam of elements. This "primal scene" is a construct of the analytic process; it has no clear claim to existence.

This leads us to the final strangeness and irony that subtend this primal scene. What emerges from this process is an indispensable missing link and middle term for understanding both the dream and Freud's relationship with his contemporaries. The scene has both the specificity and generality to offer ways to interpret a whole complex of terms in their intricate and highly determined relation to one another: the ambition, rivalry, and affection which are active in Freud's friendships with others; his anxiety about arriving late; his desire to be first; and his fear of death. Freud's use of the idea of the primal scene avoids doing what many commentators have done and continue to do: push the decisive scenes of life further and further back, until every person is assimilated to a time and place (in front of the father, at the breast, in the womb) of mythic abstraction and undifferentiation. The primal scene Freud uncovers and composes behind the *non vixit* dream is the most rigorous and coherent way to interpret Freud. This primal scene is not a "cause" in the narrow sense of that term, where time and difference are annulled because a subsequent effect is somehow already contained in its prior cause. But it stands *in the place* of a cause, as a (fictive) site for an original articulation of a self. It still has reason to be called a primal scene because it is an idea that becomes important and necessary as soon as one tries to think how a particular person might have come to be so particular.

The Friendship of Freud and Fliess

In writing *The Interpretation of Dreams*, Freud takes a series of steps to separate his dreams and dream analyses from the personal history within which they unfold. He disguises the identity of the main characters in his dreams; he offers us only fragments of the fuller dream analyses done in his notebooks. Above all, he does not here use dream analysis as he does in his case histories and in the self-analysis carried out while he was writing *The Interpretation of Dreams*: as an integral part of the psychoanalysis of the dreamer. Instead, the reader of this text becomes party to a rather abstract game of interpretation. Each dream specimen is read in terms of the very limited information Freud provides in his interpretations. Both dream and dream analysis are supposed to be exhibits in a rambling but painstaking demonstration of topics like the subject matter, the characteristics, or the informing mechanisms of dream production. Thus the *non vixit* dream is discussed under the chapter subheadings of "Speeches in Dreams," "Affect in Dreams," and "The Forgetting of Dreams." This method allows Freud gradually to draw his reader toward the fundamental categories and processes of his new science: repression, the unconscious, and so on. Given the way the compositional placement of the dream circumscribes its reference outward, is it any wonder that the dream and dream analysis often appear as virtual constructs, immuned to chance, and predestined in their form by the operation of the unconscious?

In fact both dream and dream interpretation are everywhere affected by the accidental contingencies of Freud's life which they in turn labor to affect: his friends, his social class, his ambitions, the prejudices he encounters . . . but most especially and above all, in the 1890s, his friend Wilhelm Fliess. As almost every biographer affirms, Fliess plays a critical role in those episodes of Freud's personal history which enable him to write *The Interpretation of Dreams* as the inaugural text of the new discipline of psychoanalysis. And because it takes its author and his dreams as privileged objects of study, and because it is seeded with the elements of the self-analysis Freud begins in 1897, this book also functions as Freud's spiritual autobiography. Only by offering a description of Freud's intellectual and emotional history in the 1890s can we see how his interpretation of the *non vixit* dream acts within and upon that history.

By soliciting the biographical context of *The Interpretation of Dreams* we can pose a question that will deepen and amplify our understanding of the *non vixit* dream and its analysis: what is the meaning of this dream and its analysis when they are considered in relation to Freud's life-situation in the 1890s? We have noted that that life-situation is dominated by Freud's passionate friendship with an ear, nose, and throat specialist from Berlin named Wilhelm Fliess. A casual interpretation of this friendship, in relation to the *non vixit* dream, seems to make Fliess the last in a series of avatars of Freud's nephew John. At first, Freud resists this idea through excision of all but the slightest mention of Fliess from Part I of the dream analysis. But this resistance is overcome in Part II, where Freud announces that even his dear friend Fliess has fallen victim to ambivalent childhood feelings about John. Freud nonetheless avoids the logical conclusion of this analysis—a break with Fliess is imminent—by· giving the final paragraphs of the dream analysis a comic turn. Thus, he exempts Fliess from the fate of all previous friends: "How fortunate that I have found a substitute for them and that I have gained one who means more to me than ever the others could, and that, at a time of life when new friendships cannot easily be formed, I shall never lose his!" (*ID*, 486). Freud offers no reason for arresting the chain of substitutions with Fliess. He does so through wishful assertion. Then he calls attention to a recent event which accents the renovating aspect of loss, succession, and substitution. Fliess's beloved sister has died, but a daughter has been born to Fliess, and Freud is sure Fliess will "transfer the love" felt for the sister to this new baby girl. There is even a coincidental detail in the birth which allows Freud to experience the event as a wonderfully recuperative loop back into the very scenes of early childhood invoked by this dream analysis:

And now the associative links between the contradictory components of the dream-thoughts were drawn closer by the chance fact that my friend's baby daughter had the same name as the little girl I used to play with as a child, who was of my age and the sister of my earliest friend and opponent. It gave me great *satisfaction* when I heard that the baby was to be called "Pauline." [*ID*, 486]

Events contest this hopeful close of the dream analysis. In the last year of the decade a new distance comes into the Freud/Fliess friendship, and six months after the publication of *The Interpretation of Dreams* there is a decisive break. One can only conclude that in writing the *non vixit* dream analysis, Freud had given his readers all the clues necessary to see what he himself could not then admit: that Fliess must succumb to Freud's compulsion to repeat the very same scene of childhood affection and rivalry that had shaped all his other relationships with contemporaries. By this interpretation, the *non vixit* dream analysis is a signal instance of the way a scene which is past and unconscious determines current experiential reality.

But there is a very different way of seeing all this. If one looks more closely at Freud's life situation in the 1890s, and sets that situation opposite the *non vixit* dream and analysis, the writing of this analysis may be seen to act upon the Freud/Fliess relationship so as to make it circulate within an economy of heterogeneous terms whose exact relation is difficult to calculate. The Freud/Fliess relationship is drawn into an interpretation which is both an effect and a subsequent cause within Freud's shifting life-situation and intellectual adventure in the 1890s. This interpretation forges the beginning, the advent, of psychoanalysis. Fliess becomes the catalyst that allows a series of transformations: in Freud's theories about the relationship between memory and fantasy, in Freud's way of articulating his own self, and in the force and direction of his career ambitions. How does it happen that Freud's relationship with Fliess becomes the condition for the possibility of psychoanalysis as it is formulated in the 1890s? From a reading of Freud's letters to Fliess and the biographical studies of Ernest Jones and Octave Mannoni, certain salient features of this remarkable "friendship" emerge. I offer them in a narrative that reflects how they seemed to happen—with terms from Freud's personal life entangled with fundamental shifts in his intellectual position.[29]

When Fliess meets Freud in Vienna, in the fall of 1887, there is

29. Ernest Jones, *The Life and Work of Sigmund Freud*, vol. I (New York, 1953), and the one-volume abridgment, ed. Lionel Trilling and Steven Marcus (New York, 1961). Octave Mannoni, *Freud*, trans. Renaud Bruce (New York, 1971). Masson's new book, cited above, does not alter the basic picture of this strange friendship as presented by Jones, Mannoni, and the letters.

much the two men share. Both come from middle-class Jewish families in trade, both are concerned with establishing a medical practice and maintaining growing families, and both have been trained in the teachings of the Helmholtz school of physics and physiology. Freud's first letters to Fliess demonstrate the strong and immediate mutual attraction the two felt for each other. In the letters and meetings that follow, Freud and Fliess share the zeal of their ambition: to make an important contribution to knowledge, one that would merit a permanent place in the annals of science, and a marble monument in the catacombs of the university. As the decade of the 1890s proceeds, new ties are woven between the two friends. Freud and Fliess periodically escape from their respective cities and families to meet for a "congress" of two, for one to three days of incessant intellectual exchange. The further Freud takes his theories on the sexual aetiology of neurosis the more estranged he becomes from Joseph Breuer and other Viennese colleagues. The congresses become more and more important, as Fliess is now Freud's only real companion and confidant. The two think of collaborating on a book. And to the distress of later historians of psychoanalysis, Freud entertains a lofty estimation of Fliess and confers enormous authority upon Fliess's work and ideas. He also trusts Fliess's judgment on a series of medical problems, including spells of arrhythmia that afflict Freud in the early 1890s. He even suspects Fliess of concealing knowledge that he, Freud, has some dire illness; Fliess performs two operations on Freud's nose during this period. Finally, and somehow cognate with the trust he extends to Fliess as a physician, Freud makes Fliess the judge, arbiter, and censor of his own work and speculations. Many of Freud's early formulations are sent in drafts to Fliess along with his letters. Thus, for example, the only fair copy of many early draft sections of *The Interpretation of Dreams* was sent to Fliess for "corrections" and a speedy return. Freud often accepted Fliess's judgments. Freud initially had one specimen of a complete dream analysis in the book, but it was removed when Fliess counseled against this.[30] In a very real sense, most of Freud's work in the 1890s, and especially *The Interpretation of Dreams*, unfolds in the margins of the correspondence with Fliess.

How does Fliess become so important to Freud? Because of the two decisive, intricately related roles Fliess plays in Freud's life-story in that decade: first, as an intellectual partner and collaborator in

---

30. Letters from Freud to Fliess concerning the manuscript and Fliess's deletions are from the summer of 1899. See *CL*, 8/20/99.

discovering the premises of human psychology; and second, by oc-
cupying the position of the "analyst" and father-figure in the transference triggered by the self-analysis Freud undertakes after his real
father dies in 1896. In both these roles Fliess is a stabilizing authority whom Freud begins by esteeming and overvaluing; this attitude
allows Freud a time of adventurous exploration; finally, a disillusionment sets in which makes Fliess a false "father" and authority
Freud must overcome. To make clear how Freud and Fliess saw
their projects as shared, I will briefly sketch the intellectual itinerary
they followed. Both are interested in the problem of the aetiology of
neurosis, and both are looking for alternatives to the narrowest explanation of pathology offered by the neurophysiology of that day
(and this one): a mental patient is abnormal because certain brain
cells are damaged or are failing to function correctly. This research
leads Freud and Fliess to studies on the boundary of physiology and
psychology, between the mind's "body," the brain, and the more abstract structure of interrelated signs which allow the brain to function as a mind by storing, rearranging, and emitting new representations. To account for crucial human behavior between birth and
death, Fliess develops two hypotheses: the life rhythms of both men
and women run in periods of days, in the male 23 and in the female
28, during which secretions are regularly emitted that affect the
nervous system; next, disturbances in sexual functioning are due to
problems in the mucous membrane of the nose, which is connected
to the genitals. These ideas seemed scarcely less outlandish or implausible in 1895 than they do today. What did they offer Freud?
Like Freud, Fliess makes sexuality the fundament of human behavior; the period theory assumes the kinds of discontinuity in development Freud found so striking in humans; for Fliess every human being is bisexual; and the period theory, like psychoanalysis, allowed
one to think about the "normal" and "abnormal" patient with the
same conceptual terms. Throughout the 1890s Freud often writes
Fliess that they are investigating the same phenomena from two
complementary vantage points—Freud from the position of psychology, Fliess from the firmer ground of physiology. Thus Freud
might ascribe a woman patient's ability to have five orgasms in one
night to her realization of an unconscious childhood fantasy; Fliess
might attribute this to the biochemical secretions that trigger sexual
response; but these two explanations could operate in tandem.
   Freud's followers and biographers often seem chagrined that
Freud had the bad taste to work so closely with someone so much his
inferior. Yet in writing his biography, Ernest Jones read the com-

plete record of Freud's correspondence to Fliess, and he assures us
that the evidence for Freud's acceptance of many of Fliess's ideas is
indisputable. Thus Freud began writing his ambitious early attempt
to synthesize psychology with neurophysiology on the train back
from a "congress" with Fliess. Freud includes a draft of this incom-
plete "Scientific Project" in a letter dating from the autumn of 1895.
In a letter written on New Year's Day, 1896, Freud announces that
Fliess recently has told him things that modify all the terms of the
Scientific Project: "Your remarks on migraine have led me to an
idea which would result in a complete revision of all my own theories" (*CL*, 1/1/96). The editors of the first edition of Freud's letters to
Fliess acknowledge the importance of this correspondence to psychoanalytic thought by giving the book the title *The Origins of Psychoanalysis*. The "s" at the end of "Origins" is an index of plurality;
but the editors are intent that these origins be altogether Freudian.
The correspondence shows something different: the creation is impure, a hybrid, a bastard—of variegated and uncertain origins.
Freud collaborates with Fliess in founding psychoanalysis. But the
editors protect Freud's priority from any contaminating indebtedness by dismissing those passages where Freud parrots Fliess's ideas
so as to integrate them with his own. Thus in the last lengthy paragraph of letter 39 of the first edition, Freud links his speculations
with Fliess's theories about secretions triggered by the "nasal organ."
After the first sentence of this paragraph, the editors forewarn the
reader with a footnote: "Freud obviously wrote the following passage in the hope of building a bridge between Fliess's field and his
own. The ideas it contains played no part in the further development of Freud's theories" (*Origins*, 1/1/96). At other times, instead of
shaping the reader's response to Freud's text, the editors simply ex-
cise those parts of letters where he shows himself compromised by
contact with his interlocutor. Thus letter 53 begins with an ellipsis
and a footnote: "The beginning of this letter, not reproduced here,
contains a further attempt to connect Fliess's period theory with
Freud's own theories of the neuroses" (*Origins*, 12/17/96). I have no
intention of squabbling with Freud's progeny about what Freud
might have "borrowed" from Fliess. For me, rather, it is a matter of
defining another form of indebtedness and collaboration than the
one they seem to contemplate.

In spite of the cunning and solicitude the editors show in shaping
Freud's correspondence with Fliess, Freud himself never doubts
the fundamental compatibility of his project and Fliess's. At times
this must have been both an emotional and intellectual comfort to

Freud. His words in a letter written before one congress indicate some of the ways his overestimation of Fliess is connected with Fliess's secure affiliations with the "legitimate" science of the day:

> I feel a pall has been cast over me, and all I can say is that I am looking forward to our congress as to the slaking of hunger and thirst. I bring nothing but two open ears and one temporal lobe lubricated for reception. I foresee important things—I am that self-seeking—also for my purposes. With regard to the repression theory I have run into doubts that could be dispelled by a few words from you, in particular about male and female menstruation in the same individual. Anxiety, chemical factors, and so forth—perhaps with your help I shall find the solid ground on which I can cease to give psychological explanations and begin to find a physiological foundation! [*CL*, 6/30/96]

The editors of the first edition of the letters do not seem to consider the possibility that Fliess might offer Freud ideas which would later entirely "drop out" of the picture—but would be crucial for the design of what remained. But the passage just quoted may indicate how this happened. When Freud runs into doubts about an explanation of neurosis based on a new psychological concept like "repression," he finds it invaluable to fall back onto something Fliess might "supply": a "factor" located on the more "solid ground" and "firm basis" of "physiology." And this gives Fliess's work a double status in Freud's eyes. On the one hand it is a last (one is tempted to say "crackpot") vestige of the nineteenth-century physiology both Freud and Fliess had been trained to honor—in its bottom line appeal to physiology, a species of the science practiced by father-figures such as Brücke. But, on the other hand, Fliess's work is only a scaffolding and temporary support for the new conceptual structure Freud was all this time developing. And for this purpose, it is better to have a version of nineteenth-century physiology that has its own madcap speculative tendencies, something decidedly outside the main current of nineteenth-century science, so that, once it has served its purpose, it may quite easily be allowed to drop away.

Freud probably always remains unconscious of this particular usefulness of Fliess's work to the development of his own. Little wonder that it is so important for Freud to keep up the illusion of the compatibility of their investigations long after a third party would have dismissed the idea. But eventually conceptual incompatibility becomes evident. If so much of human behavior is determined by complex multiples of 23 and 28, and the physiology of the nose and "the nasal reflex," then what room is there for the kinds of dynamic psychological factors Freud's work is uncovering? While Fliess's "discoveries" constrain human behavior within predetermined rhythms that are mathematical, biochemical, and even cosmological, Freud's meditations take him away from any simple physical determinism. Thus, in treating a hysteric, Freud begins with a symptom like paralysis that seems physical in character. But he finds this symptom operating as a sign calculated to defend against the recognition of another sign—some early traumatic memory. This discovery locates the "cause" of the present illness in the mind or psyche and makes its physical manifestation secondary to its representational or ideational content. Lacan's work shows how this shift of concern toward questions of representation was to be crucial to psychoanalysis. But Freud takes another step away from the narrow historical determinism implied by this schema. His initial "seduction theory" emphasizes the event behind memory—the actual physical seduction of the child which later becomes traumatic. But above we have followed the steps by which Freud discovers that this "memory" is often half-constructed after the fact by fantasy directed by unconscious desire. Concepts such as "memory" and "fantasy," in the equivocal way Freud uses them, cannot be assimilated to the traditional protocols of scientific thought—the ground rules it assumes for thinking time, space, and causality. Gradually Freud develops a new language for interpreting the person: the typologies of the unconscious, consciousness, and the preconscious, and a later nonsymmetric tripart typology of the id, the ego, and the super-ego. These are explicitly psychological terms, because the relationship they have with the physiology of the brain is a question this terminology is explicitly designed to allow Freud to suspend. By cutting off his account of the person from any determining physiological or historical matrix, Freud can allow the new science of psychoanalysis to develop its own modes of interpreting the person—Freud's case histories and dream interpretations. Thus, when Freud seeks to account for his ambivalent relationships with contemporaries, we find him interpreting the play of memory and fantasy around a primal childhood scene of rivalry with his nephew John. And we have seen that the person does not emerge in a fixed original lucid scenic space, but in a displaced middle space of arbitrarily imposed meanings. Given the complexity and obscurity of this placement of the person, it is little wonder that Freud is finally no longer able to accept the mathematical determinism of Fliess's periodic laws. Some reticence on this subject is evident in his letters to Fliess as early as January 1899, but when he criticizes

Fliess in the final "congress" of the summer of 1900, Fliess responds by saying Freud is only a thought-reader—"and more—that he reads his own thoughts into his patients."[31] The collaboration is over.

If Fliess is a partner and companion of an equivocal sort in elaborating the conceptual terrain of psychoanalysis, he is no less indispensable for the other event in the 1890s crucial to the institution of psychoanalysis: the self-analysis that Freud undertakes in July 1897, and that becomes the prototype of every analysis which follows it. The self-analysis arises out of a matrix of disparate events and life-activities in the 1890s: the theoretical meditation on the aetiology of neurosis which begins to focus upon the way early childhood scenes impinge upon the development of the person; the death of Freud's father Jacob on October 23, 1896, which Freud calls later "the most important event, the most poignant loss of a man's life"; Freud's experience of entirely new intensities of neurotic turmoil, released by his father's death, feelings focused first on his father and then on Fliess. At the same time Freud has found a new instrument of inquiry: both personal and theoretical questions are pursued with the new forms of dream analysis he began to practice in 1895. Freud responds to these new parameters of his life in three ways. He brings new intimacy into his relationship to Fliess in the second half of the decade. He begins to shape his ideas and material on dreams into *The Interpretation of Dreams.* And in the spring of 1897 he begins his own self-analysis, which becomes his chief activity in the following summer and autumn.[32]

When Freud returns from a late summer holiday, he writes Fliess three letters in twenty-four days, making the conceptual leaps necessary to the institution of psychoanalysis. Freud's self-analysis has shown him the central place of fantasy and unconscious desire in symptom formation, dream analysis, and his own psychic history. Thus in the first of these letters he announces "the great secret" that he no longer believes in the seduction theory, by which the memory of an actual sexual seduction leads to repression and the later formation of neurotic symptoms. In May of that year, Freud had even had a dream which seemed to confirm the seduction theory by expressing an unconscious incestuous desire for his daughter Mathilde. He sees the wish behind his own dream: "The dream of course shows the fulfillment of my wish to catch a *Pater* [father] as the originator of neurosis, and thus [the dream] puts an end to my

31. Jones, I, 314.
32. Mannoni is particularly effective in illuminating the interrelationships between the different strands of Freud's work and life. See especially *Freud*, 36–58.

ever-recurring doubts" (*CL*, 5/31/97). Both dream and the seduction theory are functioning as resistance to the more fundamental insight that sexual desire has its origin in the child-become-adult who carries the memory/fantasy of childhood seduction. Freud's self-analysis exposes a quite different pattern, one described in the two letters that follow Freud's disillusionment with the seduction theory. By interpreting his own dreams and memories and consulting his mother about facts of his childhood, Freud finds this series of elements: an unconscious hostility directed at his father, an early erotic attachment to his mother (dating from seeing her nude at age two-and-a-half on a night train between Leipzig and Vienna), a problematic bond with a nurse who taught him to steal, and who was later taken from him at an early age when she was sent to jail, and finally of course his nephew John: "I have also long known the companion of my misdeeds between the ages of one and two years; it is my nephew, a year older than myself, who is now living in Manchester and who visited us in Vienna when I was fourteen years old. The two of us seem occasionally to have behaved cruelly to my niece, who was a year younger" (*CL*, 10/3/97). What takes form under Freud's analytical work is a network of original or primal scenes which articulate his desire in a particular way. Below we shall return to the question of how this network of scenes impinges upon the primal scene of childhood rivalry with John. In letters of October 3 and October 15, 1897, Freud makes two basic points about the material he has discovered. First, in spite of his new understanding of the power of fantasy to work with anecdotes and shape memory into entirely new forms, he insists upon "real points of references" being latent in these reconstructed scenes. Thus the dreams indicate the nurse was his "teacher in sexual matters" and used to wash him "in reddish water in which she had previously washed herself." The "horrible perverse detail" of the water's color is a token of some kind of reality behind this fantasy (*CL*, 10/3/97). Then Freud's mother confirms something indicated by one of Freud's dreams: that his nurse was connected with stealing coins. Freud's second point about these scenes offers a hint at a way of unifying responses as disparate as hostility to the father, rivalry with boy siblings, behavior with little girls, attraction to the mother, naughty scenes with a nurse: "A single idea of general value dawned on me. I have found, in my own case too, [the phenomenon of] being in love with my mother and jealous of my father, and I now consider it a universal event in early childhood" (*CL*, 10/15/97). Freud proceeds to attribute the "riveting power of *Oedipus Rex*" and the hesitation of a divided will in *Hamlet*

[84]

to an unconscious Oedipal desire. The importance of this step does not hinge upon the validity of the Oedipus complex as a hypothesis about human behavior. It emerges from the way this mode of interpretation opens a pathway toward the kind of psychoanalytic interpretation of the symptom, the dream, and the person which Freud could now carry through by writing *The Interpretation of Dreams, The Psychopathology of Everyday Life*, and the case histories.

In both Freud's self-analysis and the intellectual speculation that advances with it, Fliess plays the same role in a similar scenario. Freud is confronted with an initial loss: his emphasis on sexual factors in the aetiology of neurosis costs him Joseph Breuer's support and the interest of his Viennese colleagues; the self-analysis can begin when Jacob Freud dies. During the course of Freud's speculative adventures—in self-analysis, in finding the aetiology of neurosis— Fliess is companion, judge, and steady support. Fliess is imbued with those qualities of strength and omniscience the child attributes to the father. Later, when analysis is better understood, it will be seen to depend upon a transference by which the analyst and interlocutor becomes a figure of the father, and the "one who knows," so the patient feels strong enough to risk bringing repressed thoughts and feelings into the artificial play space shaped and guarded by the analyst. The discovery of each analytical trajectory is really the same: the central place of fantasy and unconscious desire in the life of the person. This insight changes, in the most radical way, the means by which the "memory-traces" of the past act to shape the person in the present.

That Freud goes through what later analysis will call a transference to Fliess breeds a certain irony. The very analytical work Fliess helps make possible also renders him unnecessary. Thus, the murderous feeling for the father-figure analysis uncovers is in this instance focused upon the authority of traditional physiology and the interlocutor in analysis. The "father"/Fliess must be overcome; the intimacy and collaboration with Fliess must end. And the end comes after Freud writes the book which consolidates the gains, both personal and intellectual, of this relationship. *The Interpretation of Dreams* is published in the fall of 1899, and the separation with Fliess begins in the summer of 1900, and widens into a split by the summer and fall of 1901. (See *CL*, 8/7/1901 and 9/19/1901.)

The three episodes which I have recounted around Freud's interpretation of the *non vixit* dream do not suggest that the trajectory of Freud's "thought" is simply determined by the circumstances of his biography or psychology. Instead, in the intricate interplay of "life"

[85]

and "thought" in these episodes, we watch Freud shaping a life and thought he cannot fully control. Thus these three episodes have within them an axis of terms and forces one of whose poles is something highly fixed and determined—in the debate between memory and fantasy the "memory" of a real event; in the analysis of the *non vixit* dream, the primal scene conceived as the causal origin of the person; and in Freud's relationship to Fliess, the whole compulsive cast to Fliess's indispensability to Freud. What is the opposite term on this axis? What stands opposite the determinism in Freud's text? *Not*, I hasten to say, the classical oppositions offered throughout Western thought: not that separate spiritual faculty called "free will" which Christian theological and ethical philosophers make the touchstone of the truly human; nor the corollary belief in the free randomness of the material substratum which, through its oblivion to human concerns, offers its own perverse comforts to those, like Stoics or Taoists, who would enjoy the freedom of matter at an ecstatic remove from the fatality they accept for the person's life in the world. Freud's text points somewhere else. Opposite the "determined" there is a compositional leeway and textual play at work in unconscious fantasy, in the elaboration of a primal scene in the middle space of language, or in Freud's wild expansion of his relationship with Fliess beyond the "normal" limits of friendship. If I were to give a name to this phenomenon or activity, I would call it "interpretation," or "self-interpretation." By using "interpretation" I am engaging two sets of meanings: the hermeneutical effort to make sense of any text or life situation; as well as the more Nietzschean sense of interpretation as the willful imposition of meaning by the subject so as to advance the interests of life. Freud's interpretation of the *non vixit* dream is an instance of both these kinds of interpretation coming together as a kind of "life-writing," which engages contexts that are indissolubly social and personal, intellectual and psychological.

We need to see with greater precision what this interpretation, by both what it presents and what it obscures, allows Freud to do. Freud's dream analysis concludes by aligning Fliess with the primal figure of rivalry, his nephew John. This interpretation ignores the equally strong links both dream and dream analysis suggest between Fliess, Freud's father, and a chain of father-figures. Thus in the dream proper Fliess occupies a dominant position of authority. He recounts the story of his sister and interrogates Freud so as to produce "strange" emotions in him. This aligns Fliess with two other judges and fathers: that "great man" Brücke, who reduces Freud to "nothing" with his "terrible blue eyes," Freud's own father, who "accusingly" asks Freud as a child: "Why are you hitting John?" A second factor links Fliess with Freud's father. Part II of the dream analysis indicates that the exciting cause of the dream is Freud's anxiety for Fliess's life, upon the occasion of Fliess's operation. We have seen that both the writing of *The Interpretation of Dreams* and Freud's intimate relationship with Fliess are in part responses to Freud's father's death. And Fliess's worrisome operation and the dream it occasions come "only a few days after" the unveiling of the Fleischl memorial (October 16, 1898). That puts the dream within a few days of another time Freud would be likely to be thinking about the loss of the father: the second anniversary of Jacob Freud's death (October 23, 1898). This temporal contiguity allows us to offer another perspective on the *non vixit* dream. It registers Freud's wish and fear that Fliess will occupy the position of the father who has died. Fliess could replace the father who is gone, but also become the father who will, like the previous father, pass away.

Freud's analysis of the *non vixit* dream is expert and probing. Yet, having established the links between Fliess, and other contemporaries, and his "decisive" early relationship with his nephew John, why would Freud ignore that about Fliess which links him with his father? The dream-text is equivocal on this question. It seems to link Fliess with both the father and the nephew, on a ghostly margin, threshold, or transition place between these two very different intrapsychic positions. But Freud's analysis refuses to take account of this ambiguity. It resolves the ambiguity through the force of its interpretation, by determining Fliess as the last—and Freud hopes final—substitute for his nephew John: "How fortunate that I have found *a* substitute for them and that I have gained *one* who means more to me than ever the others could" (my emphasis; *ID*, 486). Freud is no doubt quite sincere in writing this sentence. He is constantly writing versions of the same to Fliess in his correspondence. But the interpretive work achieved in the analysis of the *non vixit* dream actually takes him in a diametrically opposed direction. Freud's experience in the late 1890s—both the intellectual partnership and the self-analysis—has made Fliess a figure of the father. Fliess is strong, masterful, the "one who knows"—and utterly irreplaceable. As long as Fliess occupies this position in Freud's psychic life, Freud's feelings for him will be compelled to repeat those feelings of admiration, submission, and occasional hostile rebellion that Freud as child felt for his father. But Freud can move Fliess and himself out of this determining and predetermined matrix, by displacing Fliess into a different role and position in an intrapsychic network of roles and scenes. This displacement happens in Freud's writing of this dream analysis. The analysis carries out a reinterpretation of Wilhelm Fliess, so that he undergoes a shift from Fliess-as-father to Fliess-as-John, from being an indisputable external authority whom it would be most dangerous to challenge, to a friend and rival whom it is both necessary and desirable to challenge and defeat. This transformation allows Freud to carry through his central task of the late 1890s: to go beyond Fliess by completing his self-analysis and overcoming nineteenth-century neurophysiology.

What are the salient qualities of this particular form of interpretation? Though it is neither determined by something that has gone before, nor simply produced in the present as the "free" effusion of the self, dream analysis does seem to be the way Freud can act on his own life. The limited leeway in this interpretation comes from the writer-composer's ability to arrange, design, and redesign a space of preexistent intrapsychic positions. This interpretation is economical and conservative, constructed like a collage made from found objects. And this kind of interpretation is neither lucidly conscious nor simply unconscious; it seems to unfold so the interpreting subject is both conscious and unconscious of what he is up to. All of which could be said this way: there is no separate, conscious subject directing and controlling this sort of interpretation above the weave of texts being read and written.

Let us focus all this more precisely. The analysis of the *non vixit* dream does certain interpretive work by shifting Fliess from "father" to "nephew." But for this move to succeed, Freud must not really see what is happening. The reasons for this requirement are complex, and open on to another thing that is happening with this interpretation. The shifting of Fliess-as-father to the position of Fliess-as-nephew does not mean that the position of the father is left behind in its pristine earlier condition. The position of the paternal authority is displaced, modified, and internalized. Fliess in his role in Freud's self-analysis and Fliess as the authoritative figure for nineteenth-century science become subject to a more active intimate kind of relationship, with Fliess as nephew John. In this shift from father to nephew, Fliess carries some of the power of the father's position with him. Which is another way of saying that the shift of Fliess from "father" to "nephew" is never really complete. If the interpreter were fully and calculatingly aware of the way his dream analysis shifts Fliess from father to nephew, then it would not work as a modification of the self's earlier relationship to the father, because the father-figure would remain as external and all-powerful as before. And, in corollary fashion, if this shift from "father" to "nephew" were completely successful, the whole interpretation would be quite unuseful because the father-figure would have lost all its power and authority, instead, for example, of being very much in play and at stake in a covert way, in the scene of rivalry with nephew John.

The Fundamental Trajectory of Freudian Interpretation

The limited interpretive leeway Freud exercises here depends upon the operation of an interpretive "engine" that he invents and then uses to write *The Interpretation of Dreams*, to modify his own life, and to institute psychoanalysis. To understand the operation of this invention, we need to probe further into the workings of the *non vixit* interpretation, so as to sketch the fundamental trajectory of Freudian interpretation. What allows this interpretation to be produced the way it does? To begin, it emerges from a particular way of engaging language—of reading (other texts) and writing (a text not entirely one's "own"). To trace how this Freudian interpretation unfolds in language and as language, it will be useful if we return to a decisive juncture of Freud's analysis of the *non vixit* dream. Remember the progression followed in his analysis of that dream: first he takes up the annihilating gaze directed by Freud at P. as the "central feature" of the dream scene, and links this to the gaze Brücke directs toward Freud on the occasion of his lateness; next Freud traces the "*non vixit*" in the dream to the Kaiser Josef Memorial, and the other memorials, real and imagined, that signify ambition and great achievement in the dream thoughts; Part I of the dream analysis reaches its climax and conclusion when Freud describes his "determining" early relationship with his nephew John, and the single scene of rivalry documented by the anecdote Freud has heard from his family. The explanatory power of this part of the dream analysis arises from the way Freud interprets the dream scene in terms of the experiences and feelings in Brücke's laboratory, and then links both these scenes to the early relationship to his nephew. This act of connecting allows Freud to account for the surprising hostility

[89]

shown toward Joseph P. in the dream—hostility, Freud tells us, he never felt for P. during their friendship. There are obvious links between the dream scene and the time in Brücke's laboratory (the laboratory itself, Fleischl, P.); Part II of the analysis will elucidate equally manifest links between the dream scene and the current relationship with Fliess (Fliess's coming from Vienna, his speaking of his sister). But what justifies linking the dream scene, or the epoch in Brücke's lab, or his relationship with Fliess, with the early relationship with Freud's nephew? My whole discussion of Freud in this part of the book indicates why there is a lot at stake in this question. Much of the analytical power of psychoanalysis derives from the way it explains a dream, a current life-situation, or a proximate memory through a probing and sometimes surprising reference to an early primal scene that is said to be determining for the constitution of the person.

The answer to this question about Freud's method of reading is not obvious. It is quite correct to say that halfway through Part I of the analysis Freud develops a middle term—Brutus' speech of self-justification after killing Julius Caesar—which becomes a link that allows him to take the dream scene, the scene in Brücke's lab, the whole discussion of memorials for the dead, and connect them with the short speech of self-justification Freud gives his father when accused of hitting John. This connecting link has the power to make all the elements of the interpretation converge. It leads both backward to scenes of rivalry with John, where "strange to say I really did once play the part of Brutus" and forward into a present and future relationship with Fliess, where by writing this book, *The Interpretation of Dreams*, Freud will play Brutus to Fliess's Caesar. But what authorizes Freud's rather bizarre detour into the story of Brutus and Julius Caesar and the literary language of Shakespeare and Schiller? And what further purposes are served or effected? An answer to this question will allow us to grasp the mode of reading fundamental to psychoanalytic interpretation. Here is the relevant passage from the dream analysis. It will reward the closest attention.

By the rules of dream-interpretation I was even now not entitled to pass from the *Non vixit* derived from my recollection of the Kaiser Josef Memorial to the *Non vivit* required by the sense of the dream-thoughts. There must have been some other element in the dream-thoughts which would help to make the transition possible. It then struck me as noticeable that in the scene in the dream there was a convergence of a hostile and an affectionate current of feeling towards my friend P., the former being on the surface and the latter concealed, but both of them being represented in the single phrase *Non vixit.* As he had deserved well of science I built him a memorial; but as he was guilty of an evil wish (which was expressed at the end of the dream) I annihilated him. I noticed that this last sentence had a quite special cadence, and I must have had some model in my mind. Where was an antithesis of this sort to be found, a juxtaposition like this of two opposite reactions towards a single person, both of them claiming to be completely justified and yet not incompatible? Only in one passage in literature—but a passage which makes a profound impression on the reader: in Brutus's speech of self-justification in Shakespeare's *Julius Caesar* (iii, 2), "As Caesar loved me, I weep for him; as he was fortunate, I rejoice at it; as he was valiant, I honour him; but, as he was ambitious, I slew him." Were not the formal structure of these sentences and their antithetical meaning precisely the same as in the dream-thought I had uncovered? Thus I had been playing the part of Brutus in the dream. If only I could find one other piece of evidence in the content of the dream to confirm this surprising collateral connecting link! A possible one occurred to me. "My friend Fl. came to Vienna in July." There was no basis in reality for this detail of the dream. So far as I knew, my friend Fl. had never been in Vienna in July. But the month of July was named after Julius Caesar and might therefore very well represent the allusion I wanted to the intermediate thought of my playing the part of Brutus.

Strange to say, I really did once play the part of Brutus. I once acted in the scene between Brutus and Caesar from Schiller before an audience of children. I was fourteen years old at the time and was acting with a nephew who was a year my senior. He had come to us on a visit from England; and he, too, was a *revenant*, for it was the playmate of my earliest years who had returned in him. Until the end of my third year we had been inseparable. . . . [*ID*, 423–24]

The general point of view established in this passage must be familiar to any reader of Freud's work: it opens a scene and drama of interpretation with Freud as the protagonist, detective, and master interpreter. Freud does not pretend to give us a historical account of the steps taken or leaps made in his deciphering of the dream. Instead he writes something much more artificial: the unfolding of an argument which is gradual enough to disguise its leaps and weave an interpretation that serves two distinct purposes. It explicates the meaning of the dream, but does so in such a way that it constructs a compelling, purposive habitation for the dreamer/interpreter as a single person—a self. And Freud seeks to invest this interpretation with the mantle of necessity. How is this done? This passage will show us, as it takes a loop through the fundamental trajectory of Freudian interpretation.

Something's missing/There's something here. Freud begins by insisting there is an important gap in his account of how the "*non vixit*" has passed from his memory of the Kaiser Josef memorial to the words in the dream with which Freud consigns Joseph P. to oblivion. This is so, because the dream world could have found innumerable other ways for expressing hostility for P. Thus Freud is sure that the unconscious must have had other reasons, and be representing other things, in choosing precisely *this* way (the words "*Non vixit*") for eliminating P. This fact gets translated into "the rules of dream-interpretation" which lavish the language of dreams with an attention "to every shade of the form of words in which they were laid before us" (*ID*, 514). Freud treats a sign like "*non vixit*" as overdetermined in its meaning, and the meaning reached so far is less important than those not yet grasped. By locating a lacuna in his own interpretation, Freud's narrative insists upon a missing object— "some other element"—that will unravel the dream's deeper truth.

Elaboration/analysis/reworking. Freud next returns to the scene in the dream (Freud, Fliess, and P. at the café) to make a general observation. He finds a hostile and an affectionate current of feeling toward P. are both represented in the single phrase "*non vixit.*" Freud refers to the apparent reasons for these two currents of feeling: P. devoted his whole life to science, but, Freud later explained, he also was inappropriately impatient for advancement (*ID*, 484). The *way* Freud presents these reasons is of the utmost importance. He elaborates and reworks his own dream thoughts with these words: "As he had deserved well of science I built him a memorial; but as he was guilty of an evil wish . . . I annihilated him (*Weil . . . . aber weil . . . . vernichte ich ihn*)." Here Freud demonstrates a certain interpretive daring. With this sentence he reworks and acts out the mixed feelings in the dream he still does not understand. The sentence is a crux in Freud's interpretation. It constructs a linguistic bridge toward that "other element" still missing from the interpretation.

Freud asserts the "special" character of the sentence he has just written. It is easy to miss the strangeness and importance of this interpretive gesture. Freud writes, "I noticed that this last sentence had a quite special cadence (*besonderem Klang*), and I must have had some model (*Vorbild*) in my mind." As part of his ongoing search for the "other element" behind the dream's use of "*non vixit*," Freud draws this sentence of his analysis into the same frame he puts around the dream text. Here the very distinction between dream text and analytical text is shown to be impure. Each kind of text begins to bleed into the other. This sentence from the analysis offers another path to the truth behind the dream. It is a way of probing the psychic processes operating behind the dream because those processes are still active in the very language Freud is "now" writing and we are "now" reading. Freud is here carrying on something of an interpretive high-wire act, a blind hunt for treasure. Unsure of his goal, he projects himself forward, with the intuitive half-sense that the "special cadence," sound, or tone of this sentence is *familiar* to the mind; it is like the experience of the uncanny which baffles consciousness, but carries resonances that communicate to the unconscious, as if by an underground passage, messages that, strictly speaking, are not intelligible to it. Now Freud proceeds with his analysis. He is sure the special cadence he has heard is a repetition and echo of some earlier sentence functioning as a model for this one. In this way the singular distinct quality of this sentence will be the effect of its repetition of some quality of another sentence. This distinct linguistic echo allows Freud to focus his search. He is looking for the particular sentence to which the dream alludes.

Focusing the search with a question. Freud now characterizes the language he seeks. It will be language where a particular trope—antithesis—coincides with a certain psychic state—ambivalence: "a juxtaposition like this of two opposite reactions towards a single person, both of them claiming to be completely justified and yet not incompatible." And Freud gives urgency to his search, and implies the singularity of the object he seeks, by casting this conceptual and linguistic profile in the form of a question. "Where was . . . to be found . . . ?" This question implies its own answer; it implies . . .

Finding the single place. Now Freud is ready to answer this question and unveil his discovery. In only one single place (*An einer einzigen Stelle*) are both these conditions fulfilled—in Brutus' speech of self-justification (*Rechtfertigungsrede*) in Shakespeare's *Julius Caesar.* Then Freud stages his "find" by quoting the passage which, sure enough, has the same syntactical pattern and connectives as the sentence that started the search. "*As* Caesar loved me, I weep for him; *as* he was fortunate . . . ; *but, as* he was ambitious, I slew him (*Weil . . . ; weil . . . ; aber weil . . . erschlug ich ihn*)."

What has Freud succeeded in doing by moving through this intricate trajectory? Lurking behind and within the phrase "*non vixit*" he has found that single "missing element" which is the interpretive key to the dream text. It is this passage from Shakespeare's *Julius Caesar* which most specifically designates Freud's role in the dream text. He tells us, "Thus I had been playing the part of Brutus in the dream." This summarizes his behavior to P. in the dream and prepares for the climactic interpretive move of the analysis, when Freud points to his "determining" relationship with his nephew John, with whom he twice played the part of Brutus: once quite literally when John returned at age fourteen and they played a version of this scene from Schiller before school children, and much earlier, in a figurative way in that primal scene of childhood rivalry, where Freud gave what must have been his first "speech of self-justification" (*Rechtfertigungs-rede*): "I hit him, 'cos he hit me." The cogency of this interpretation of the dream comes from what Freud explicitly asserts: that he has found the "single" term which organizes all the elements of his psychic life activated by the dream. But conversely, it is the "special cadence" of this single sentence from Shakespeare, allowing it to function as a "model," seminal sentence in his own interpretation and articulate the ambivalence in all his relationships with contemporaries, it is this singleness that makes Freud's representation of himself as a person seem necessary, inevitable, and natural rather than arbitrary, adventitious, and accidental. That is the powerful illusion this interpretation effects. It does so through its subtle and gentle progression from a lacuna in the dream interpretation to the sentence Freud composes to the crucial lines from Shakespeare to the discovery of the primal scene behind the dream. In this way Freud's interpretation creates the sense of having articulated the single objective truth of at least one aspect of the person—Freud's ambivalent relationship with his contemporaries.

This is why Freud is so intent upon asserting the idea of the single and the one in this passage. He introduced his discovery of the sentence from Shakespeare by insisting that antithesis and ambivalence coincide in only this "one single place" in literature—even though antithesis must be one of the most common tropes in language, and ambivalence the most pervasive constellation of affect in the psychoanalytic understanding of human nature. For instance, both run through nearly every speech Hamlet gives about his mother in the bedroom scene. We have already noted how the rest of the passage is punctuated with the word "one": Freud looks for "one" other trace or track (*Spur*) of evidence to confirm the allusion to Julius Caesar: "strange to say," he really did "once play Brutus"; Freud's nephew John is "one" year older; and the two are one in being "inseparable." From a conceptual perspective, this cluster of "ones" is merely coincidental. But through a logic that resembles the production of overdetermined meanings Freud describes operating in the dream work, this pattern of repetition indicates the deeper tendency of this interpretation. By uncovering the single primal scene Freud seeks to establish the person in his or her uniqueness.

It is with the idea of the "one" and the single that this text engages the most powerful and familiar idea about the person. In Christianity the uniqueness of each person is certified by the idea of a soul which is both immortal and radically particular. This theological doctrine comes into secular contemporary life as the idea that each person, however ordinary, blends qualities, feelings, and styles into a configuration that is unique and irreplaceable. In psychoanalysis the primal scene offers a way to think of the single original site for self-articulation; the oneness of that site comes from its unity as scene present implicitly to the eye which sees all in that space. When the unity and visibility of the primal scene come into question, Freud's text falls back upon a more ambiguous way to articulate the person —with the writing that has traditionally been used to tell a single particular life-story in autobiography. Freud tells such a story about himself in *The Interpretation of Dreams.*

Here we must confront two contradictory senses of the single and the one. The single has long been connected with the oneness of the unified, the unique, and the self-identical. Thus Greek materialist philosophers gave pride of place in their systems to a single atomic particle, which, being nothing but itself, could be the elemental term for everything else. But the single is also a token of the incidental, the accidental, that which just "happens" by chance, on a single deviant occasion. Thus something as arbitrary as lightning is supposed to strike but once in the same place. So, at least, a familiar commonplace assures us. And in Freud's interpretation the assertion of singularity is closely connected with the arbitrary imposition of will. We have noted how Freud implausibly insists that antithesis and "two opposite reactions towards a single person" coincide "only in one passage in literature"—Brutus' speech in Shakespeare's *Julius Caesar.* But this is less decisive to this interpretation than the moment that does really point to that one speech in literature—when Freud frames his hostile and affectionate feeling for P. into one particular sentence: "As he had deserved well of science I built him a memorial; but . . . " Here is the place of arbitrarily imposed meanings. Does any reader believe that Freud could not have found a multitude of other sentence patterns to express the same idea? Yet it is the special cadence of the single sentence he does find which leads to Julius Caesar and nephew John and the whole coherent design of this interpretation. Freud acknowledges that he has here done more

[95]

than the usual cutting and fitting associated with interpretation. Thus he looks for some trace of evidence to confirm what he calls this "surprising collateral connecting link" between "*non vixit*" and lines from Shakespeare, and finds it in this detail of the dream text: "My friend Fl. came to Vienna in July." Because this statement is not true, July must be an "allusion" to Julius Caesar, the person for whom the month is named. But this connection points to a final irony. Freud offers it as a marginal addendum to confirm the validity of his interpretation. However, the appearance of Fliess in the analysis, carefully avoided so far, points to another locus of arbitrarily imposed meaning. For here we feel the pull and fore-effects of the future in view of which Freud writes: an (as yet unconscious) will to accede to a position of dominance by completing his self-analysis, overcoming neurophysiology, and ending the friendship with Fliess.

The separateness and authority of the single is compromised by something else besides the design of arbitrary imposition that works through this interpretation. Just as we found the primal scene displaced out of an original beginning into a middle space of language and representation; in similar fashion, the instances of the single in this interpretation are always already traversed by a repetition which makes the appearance of the single possible. This is most clear in the trajectory of this interpretation. Groping toward a further understanding of the phrase "*non vixit*," Freud *notices* hostile and affectionate feelings and then *composes* them into a sentence. The appearance of the sentence seems like the decisive single act/event of the interpretation, a new beginning, and an accidental cause of all that follows. But in order for Freud to notice a pattern of ambivalence and compose this sentence, he must be already hearing a pre-echo of the "special cadence" of the sentence he then composes and finds to be a copy and repetition of some model that he then locates in lines of Shakespeare. A network of repetitions resonates through this neat sequence of (non-)singular events. And since it has become difficult to judge what comes first, and what next, the logical temporal sequence of events Freud's narrative has labored to construct is upset. Once the single is traversed by repetition, it does not seem to come to rest. Thus Freud's interpretation finds its model in lines from Shakespeare which are indebted to words of Plutarch which are presumed to come from history. But Freud apparently met the story of Caesar and Brutus in a version from Schiller, which is indebted to Shakespeare but took on real importance to the psyche only because it repeated a primal scene from childhood. This textual network of overlapping repetitions is more than a curiosity of literary intertextuality; it coincides quite exactly with the interaction of roles he finds himself playing with contemporaries on each stage of life: Freud plays Brutus to the Julius Caesar of Joseph P. (in the dream), of his nephew John (in the primal scene), and finally of Fliess (in the scene opened by the writing of this interpretation, and subsequently acted out). Freud may wish for something quite different. He ends his interpretation expressing his good fortune for having found "one" friend in Wilhelm Fliess who is a gratifying substitute for all the others. But this desire to bring friendship to rest in oneness is itself inscribed in a larger uncontrollable regress of purposes and repetitions which soon overtake that friendship.

A Labyrinth of Primal Scenes

We are ready to take account of the complex and equivocal status of Freud's interpretation of the *non vixit* dream. Freud's project seems most straightforward when he follows the traditional protocols of science and interpretation by making his analysis an "act of explanation." Thus Freud directs his reading of the dream to uncover its meaning and to investigate the person who dreams the dream. The language he uses is presumed to be a transparent medium and neutral tool in this effort. His task will be to show what the symptomatic text is symptomatic of. Thus, the *non vixit* dream allows Freud to analyze the ambition, the affection, the ambivalence that lie behind his relation to contemporaries. In Part I of the analysis he follows a tortuous trail of language to the heart of the matter—the single primal scene of rivalry that accounts for his compulsion to repeat the role of Brutus. This scene also explains the meaning of the dream. After we read this act of explanation it will be entirely correct to ask if Freud has given the right or wrong interpretation of the dream or his relation to contemporaries.

But Freud's interpretation also operates on a more vexed and obscure register: as an act of composition, of arranging, and of bringing together, where his efforts at knowing are mixed in with the will and desire to shape a text that will engender new effects in the world. Whether in the uncontrollable interplay of memory and fantasy, or where affect and idea meet in the middle space of language, or when Freud's past (with John and Joseph P.) intersects with his present relationship with Fliess—in all these instances Freud's interpretation renders a complex "explanation" of the forms and forces operating within and behind the person and the dream. In Part II of the interpretation, the more amplified and detailed version Freud offers of the primal scene greatly enhances the scene's power to explain. It also does more, however. Now this explanation is itself a fictional construct or performance that shapes the life Freud lives. Here he is not separate from the texts he explicates. It no longer seems possible to say that Freud has offered the single possible account of the dream. The singularity of the primal scene is still there; but now it is part of a necessary but illusory unity ascribed to the person. Instead of whether this interpretation is "right" or "wrong," it seems more precise to ask if this arrangement of language is—like the criterion applied to the "performative" by J. L. Austin—one that is "happy" and felicitous or unfelicitous and "unhappy." Does it work for Freud? Does it work in the text he has written?

And one can go one step further in this direction. This interpretation of a symptomatic text is also symptomatic. From such a vantage this dream interpretation is not an "act," undertaken by and for the subject and under the conscious control of the subject considered as an agent, but an "event" that overtakes and traverses the person, and to which the person cannot be present in the mode of consciousness. Not as an "act" of any kind, but as a symptom. One arrives at this perspective through an eminently psychoanalytic tendency of thought—by saying: an interpretation may perform an act of explanation or composition within the restricted economy of the attempt to understand or arrange meaning . . . but these "acts" must themselves circulate within a broader, general economy of needs, purposes, and desires. What impels and compels these acts? Above, I offered one response to this question: Freud's project in the 1890s rearticulates his relationship to the father, to traditional neurophysiology, and to Fliess. But what lies behind this effort? That is, what is the cause behind these causes? This is the radical and self-reflexive moment of psychoanalysis, the moment when psychoanalysis is overtaken by its own conceptual projections. It is the kind of question (a strong) psychoanalytic thinking can never allow itself to desist from asking—the interpretative move it is compelled to repeat.

If one exposes this dream interpretation as both explanation and composition to the force of this question, strange things happen. There are two places in the trajectory of Freud's interpretation that are decisive to the design that results, but are also apparently arbitrary and accidental in their happening. We have noted how crucial it becomes for this interpretation that Freud mimes the syntax of Shakespeare in defining the dream's ambivalent feeling toward P. A second decisive point in the generation of this interpretation does not take place in its narrative unfolding, but in the "real time" of the analysis. There Freud tells us that while analyzing the dream, "the interpretation was held up (*stockte*)." By the rules of psychoanalysis this delay indicates resistance to what he is uncovering. Then Freud takes note of the "inconspicuous" phrase in the dream text "*As P. failed to understand him, Fl. turned . . .*" This phrase leads Freud back to the childhood fantasy scene of rivalry with his nephew John. How? After Freud reads a stanza from Heine that has the same word "understand" at its focal point:

> Rarely have you *understood* me,
> And rarely too have I understood you.
> Not until we both found ourselves in *the mud*
> Did we promptly understand each other.
>
> [*ID*, 513]

However, this explanatory account only raises new questions. Does Freud "just happen" on this stanza from Heine? Why does it help him explicate the question of mutual understanding between friends? What memory (or fantasy) whether conscious or unconscious is stirred by the poem's idea of two friends playing in the mud or shit (*Kot*)? Freud does not say. He *does* tell us that this stanza allowed him to proceed with the interpretation and fill out the primal scene as he reports it in the second longer version. Is Freud withholding something? If so, why? Or, does this function in the interpretation as what he elsewhere calls the "navel" of the dream, this interpretation's "point of contact with the unknown," which, like the belly-button, is an enigmatic trace or antistructure of an original but irretrievable connection with the place of origin (the womb) (*ID*, 111). Both this moment of interpretation, and Freud's unconscious echo of Brutus' speech, are obscure, decisive, and involve Freud in splicing his dream analysis with preexistent texts (Heine's, Shakespeare's). This splicing then helps to structure Freud's text as unified, explanatory—but also symptomatic. But symptomatic of what? What lies behind Freud's recourse to these texts in weaving his own?

Freud does not give us enough information to say. But we may probe the broader question of the origins of this interpretation by noting that the lines spliced in from Shakespeare and Heine both push the dream analysis in a particular direction: toward emphasizing the intimate and intense rivalry between two males of the same age in the dream scene, in Brücke's laboratory, in the primal scene, and in the current life-situation. And this emphasis is compatible with two other qualities of both the dream and the interpretation: here where boys or men compete, there is little overt sexuality; both dream and analysis are comic and upbeat, in bizarre ways, in spite of the fact that they incorporate loss and death. Thus in the dream scene Freud murders P. with his gaze, but feels delight that he can dispense people in this way; in the primal scene Freud presents himself as intrepid in his self-command, though he is called before the father to be judged; and the dream is apparently triggered by worrisome news about a best friend's operation, but it ends with cheery thoughts about the powers of renewal in life. In this whole cluster of scenes and situations, Freud somehow manages to end a happy, complacent winner.

How does one account for the selective tendencies of Freud's interpretation? Does it reflect what Freud was? what he wished to be? what he was seeking to hide? what he could not help but wish, be, or hide? These questions lead into a labyrinth of possibilities we cannot here explore. I will confine myself to suggesting a direction where this kind of psychoanalytic interrogation of the person encounters its limits.

We have seen how Freud's interpretation of the *non vixit* dream and of his relations with contemporaries is focused upon the primal scene of rivalry with his nephew, reconstructed in its full detail during this dream analysis. And clearly Freud felt that this early scene/relationship was one of the decisive factors in giving his self its particular conformation. But something interesting happens if the scene is put beside other crucial scenes from Freud's early life described in the letters and *The Interpretation of Dreams*. For it seems to be in subterranean communication with them by the way it resembles, inverts, and transposes them.

Here are three scenes that may be arranged around the primal scene of the *non vixit* dream. I will describe the primal scene and these three scenes so as to emphasize and explore the relation between these nodal points of Freud's self-analysis.

Freud and John. Two cousins fight for control of an object. Claim is based upon "who got there first." Though Freud is in the wrong, "might prevails over right," and he wins. When John appeals to Freud's father, Freud is called to judgment, and defends himself stoutly.

Transition. In his article "Screen Memories" Freud tells of a memory closely related to the primal scene behind the *non vixit* dream. The memory comes from the same epoch of life, involves aggression and rivalry in play with the same nephew John, as well as John's sister Pauline. But unlike the earlier scene, the overtones here are everywhere sexual, and the parental figure—a nurse—is nurturing and maternal.

Freud, John, and Pauline. While the three children are picking flowers on a sloping rectangle of lush green meadow, Freud and John gang up on Pauline to steal her bouquet of yellow dandelions—to "de-flower" her. (Freud calls attention to the pun in German.) She runs up the hill in tears and is given, "as if by consolation," black bread by a nurse and a peasant woman by the cottage. The two boys throw down the flowers, follow, and are also given bread, which "tastes quite delicious." In his discussion of this scene, Freud is concerned with the way the original memory becomes the screen for later feelings—a first infatuation at age seventeen, and a later decision to defer the sexual gratifications of marriage (the flower) so as to pursue his career (the bread).

Transition. Both these scenes involve rivalry among children, but in the second the potential rivalry between Freud and John for sexual possession of Pauline is suppressed to permit a collective attack on her. In both scenes conflict between children is superseded and annulled by a move into the more powerful arena of adults—where fathers judge and mothers nurture. This is in keeping with Freud's explanation of rivalry among children in *The Interpretation of Dreams.* It arises from the desire of each child to win and control *all* the parents' love. (See especially *ID*, chap. V, section D, part B.) In the first scene "love" means a favorable judgment; in the second scene sexual desire for mother and/or "sister" turns out to be both an alternative and further incitement to rivalry.

These two scenes are cheerful in tone and comic in structure; Freud's position never seems threatened by events. But affiliated with these two scenes in his writings are two scenes of genuine anxiety. In letter 70 from the correspondence, Freud seems to be referring to an x-rated version of the screen memory when he writes Fliess that his nephew John was the "companion of my misdeeds," and they occasionally treated Pauline "cruelly" (*CL*, 10/3/97). In the same letter Freud tells of an early memory of seeing his mother nude on a train. A dream indicates that his old nurse was "my instructress in sexual matters" and stole coins from Freud, for which Freud finds, after consulting his mother, she was sent to prison ("boxed up.") In the next letter to Fliess, Freud uses all these details to reconstruct a scene that has been recurring to him "for the last twenty-nine years."

Mother "boxed up"/mother lost. "My mother was nowhere to be found; I was crying in despair. My brother Philipp (twenty years older than I) unlocked a wardrobe (*Kasten*) for me, and when I did not find my mother inside it either, I cried even more until, slender and beautiful, she came in through the door" (*CL*, 10/15/97). Freud pieces together clues behind this memory. Philipp had gone to "fetch the policeman" who locked up Freud's nurse for theft. When Freud couldn't find his mother in the cupboard "I was afraid she had vanished from me just as the old woman had a short time before." The fact that Freud turned to Philipp "proves that I was well aware of his share in the disappearance of the nurse" (*CL*, 10/15/97).

This scene makes explicit something not evident in the primal scene of rivalry and the screen memory: the rivalry for parental love can be a high-stakes game of stark polarities. Here the anxiety at the terrible absence of a mother gone forever—even the wardrobe, the place where they put nanna, is empty—is balanced by the intense pleasure and desire triggered by her sudden reappearance: "slender and beautiful, she came in through the door" (*CL*, 10/15/97). And in this scene there can be no question of vanquishing or joining in alliance with the figures of male power—a brother twenty years older; a policeman who takes nanna away; or the law that locks her up. Freud's victory must come against a different and more equal rival —his nephew John.

Transition. The scene around the cupboard offers an anxious counterpart to the more carefree presentation of maternal love and female sexuality in the screen memory. Another scene—one of the most influential memories Freud narrates in *The Interpretation of Dreams*—stages Freud's ambition in view of paternal judgment so that ambition appears fraught with peril and anxiety. It complements the benign paternal judge in the primal scene of rivalry.

Judgment and humiliation before the father. "When I was seven or eight years old there was another domestic scene, which I can remember very clearly. One evening before going to sleep I disregarded the rules which modesty lays down and obeyed the calls of nature in my parents' bedroom while they were present. In the course of his reprimand, my father let fall the words: 'The boy will come to nothing.' This must have been a frightful blow to my ambition, for references to this scene are still constantly recurring in my dreams" (*ID*, 216).

Now the rival for the mother is the father. In his parents' room, little Freud brings out his penis. (In an aside Freud tells us "micturation" and "the character trait of ambition" are intimately connected.) But Freud's penis is small; he has been indiscreet. And, most cruelly, at this exuberant moment when he experiments with expressing his feelings of sexual potency and personal ambition, his father responds by delivering a judgment that brings humiliation and (castration) anxiety. Now ambition is connected with a scene which has all the elements of Oedipal rivalry for the mother.

I have narrated these scenes to indicate something about Freud's interpretation of the *non vixit* dream. His interpretation takes on its authority and aura of comprehensiveness precisely because it aligns a single (dream) text, through a complex regress of associations, with a single primal scene. If this one-to-one cause and effect relationship did exist, psychoanalysis *would* be the system of iron-clad determining mechanisms it sometimes seems to be. But to raise the question of the analysis as symptom is to push our analysis on a regress of causation that has no clear end-point (short of the womb); and to encounter other primal scenes of early life is to multiply the causes behind the primal scene of rivalry. Freud's interpretation of this scene begins to waver. Now a whole network of scenes seems to operate behind this primal scene, helping to motivate the ambition it bespeaks. Thus, this scene and its interpretation seem contrived to suppress and exclude a variety of strong bonds to another: the mutuality of a camaraderie with John, the pleasure of sexuality active in the pastoral scene with Pauline; the passion and attachment expressed in Freud's tears for a mother who is lost, and his inventive desire to stay in his parents' room. The primal scene of rivalry also removes any all-powerful figure of authority—whether the Philipp who manipulates Freud's feelings around the empty wardrobe, or the father who delivers a withering judgment on Freud's prospects. Instead Freud weaves a scene that makes the "father" benign and appreciative—one who might retell anecdotes. In this space of co-equal competition, mutual identification, and rivalry, each gain for oneself necessarily entails a loss for the other. The only pleasure seems to come from the joy of prevailing over the other.

This network of scenes shifts our view of the primal scene of rivalry. Now the primal scene is not a separate elemental term in the psyche. It acts out the desire for a mastery, untroubled by the need for maternal love, desire for pleasure, or anxiety before an all-powerful father. All these feelings are banished and excluded from the primal scene, but by the very fact of this exclusion they are operating in the scene that excludes them. In this way they become indirect causes of the primal scene of rivalry which acts as a cause of the *non vixit* dream and of Freud's compulsively repeated way of relating to his contemporaries (for example, as Brutus).

One way to organize this causal matrix so that it still has the coherence to be a causal system is to insist on the priority and centrality of the Oedipus complex. It would be easy to plot these four scenes into an Oedipal configuration. Then Freud's rivalry with his nephew John becomes a byproduct of a more primary rivalry with a powerful father and older half-brother (Philipp) for the love of the mother, and the later female figures of the mother. And in fact there is evidence Freud moves in this direction. Thus in the second of the two important letters where he reports the findings of his self-analysis to Fliess, he concludes a listing of an inchoate series of scenes, memories, and hypotheses with what is perhaps the most famous passage in the letters: "A single idea of general value dawned on me. I have found, in my own case too, [the phenomenon of] being in love with my mother and jealous of my father, and I now consider it a universal event in early childhood" (*CL*, 10/15/97). The subsequent course of psychoanalysis will make the Oedipus complex the seminal developmental matrix for the origin of the person, and thus a master-cause of the effect of the person. The hierarchical arrangement of early life under the concept of the Oedipus complex makes psychoanalysis a much more rigidly determined, comprehensive system for accounting for psychic development. Terminological changes also help consolidate the centrality of the Oedipal. A "primal scene" (*das Urszene*) is no longer any decisive early scene of life. After the 1890s it becomes the technical term for the child's traumatic sight, actual or imagined, of parental coitus.[33]

There are several things wrong with this way of organizing these four scenes. The Oedipal synthesis reduces their difference and particularity. It imposes an order and sequential logic upon experiences of desire, anxiety, pleasure, and the will to mastery which seem far from self-evident and universal. Above all it draws these four scenes into one "scene"—the Oedipal scene represented as the child aware of himself watching the mother with feelings of desire and the father with feelings of anger, anxiety, and rivalry. I will try to clarify the assumption operating behind Freud's interpretive *praxis*. He ex-

33. LaPlanche and Pontalis take note of this shift of terminology from early essays in the 1890s, where *das Urszene* has the broader meaning I have used in discussing the "primal scene" of rivalry behind the *non vixit* dream, to the more narrow and explicitly defined meaning (of seeing parental intercourse) it assumes in psychoanalytic literature after the case of the Wolf-man (1914).

plicates one dream text (for instance, the *non vixit* dream), and one quality of the person (rivalry with contemporaries), by aligning each with a scene from early life (whether memory or fantasy), whose singular coherence comes from what is implied by the very idea of the scene: that all can be present and visible to the participant who lives the scene or the analyst who reconstructs it, unobscured by that in it which may have been (temporarily) hidden by repression. But our analysis of the primal scene of rivalry indicates something quite different. This scene becomes complex and obscure in both character and origin the moment it is seen in relation to other scenes—I chose three, but there could have been more. Then each scene loses its virtual separateness and integrity. No scene can be comprehended in a single glance; each solicits other scenes that resemble it. Scene blends into scene, offering new ways to "read" one another, as each becomes a transposed and disguised version of other scenes. Eventually we have moved out of any intelligible visible scenic space. In reading the person as a catalogue of memories, dream texts, and free associations, we do not move before a life that looks like Rubens' cycle of "The Life of Marie de Medici." Instead, the life of the person appears as a loose and baggy monster: something as untidy in form as, for example, *The Interpretation of Dreams*, with its implausible accumulations of dreams, anecdotes, analyses, and hypotheses. And in the textual labyrinth Freud uses to represent, interpret, and explore himself, the person's sense of coherence cannot be established through a unified visible space, or even a series of discrete scenes. Instead an intuition of singleness happens through the echoes and repetitions of words and their cadences heard in a catacomb of linked chambers. Now singleness and repetition are not alternatives, but affect one another as effects. Here every place seems to be linked and crosshatched with obscure connecting passages. Now the attempt to hear or see any fixed interpretation of the person will be most problematic. But it is this very disability that wins the person something between "freedom" and the rigidly determined—the limited interpretive and compositional "leeway" Freud exploits in his analysis of the *non vixit* dream.

Instituting Psychoanalysis

And what does Freud do with this "leeway"? He solicits and displaces compelling preexistent scenes and the cadences of Shake-

speare's language, and much more, so as to draw them into an interpretation that allows him to institute psychoanalysis. This is the
specific task—a task he cannot yet fully comprehend—for which
this interpretation opens a clearing. For to institute psychoanalysis
Freud will have to act like the young hero of the primal scene of rivalry behind the *non vixit* dream. He will seize the object to which
others have some claim (the object is psychoanalysis) and he will do
so on the basis of priority ("each claims to have gotten there before
the other"). But Freud also admits he was/is/will be in the wrong. It
does not matter, though. Sheer might will make things right. (The
disciples write most of the histories.) So in spite of the collaboration
with Breuer and the complex dependency on Fliess I have described, and the plural case of paternity these relationships indicate,
Freud ends by claiming to be the (one and only) father of psychoanalysis.

Though Freud's analysis of the *non vixit* dream lays the groundwork for interpreting Freud as the founder of psychoanalysis, that
interpretation does not come to full articulation until he publishes
"The History of the Psycho-Analytic Movement" in 1914. That text
serves two related functions. Freud brings the movement's past under his control by writing a history of its origins; and he exercises
control over its immediate future by excluding from it two potential
rivals—Jung and Adler—on the basis of heresy. In this text, and
others concerned with priority, Freud repeats the basic gestures of
the primal scene of rivalry with John. The text opens with Freud
laying claim to his personal propriety over psychoanalysis in words
that are concise, direct, and sweeping:

> No one need be surprised at the subjective character of the contribution
> I propose to make here to the history of the psycho-analytic movement,
> nor need anyone wonder at the part I play in it. For psycho-analysis is
> my creation; for ten years I was the only person who concerned himself
> with it, and all the dissatisfaction which the new phenomenon aroused
> in my contemporaries has been poured out in the form of criticisms on
> my head. [*S.E.*, XIV, 7]

The "History" engages a rivalry with the contemporaries it addresses, describes, or displaces by insisting on Freud's having been
there first at the creation. But not only does Freud insist he created
psychoanalysis; he insists he did it alone. Expressing a certain nostalgia for the early days of the movement, he compares himself with
Robinson Crusoe on a "desert island," living out a "heroic age" in

"splendid isolation." Then he makes this sweeping claim: "I was not subject to influence from any quarter" (*S.E.*, XIV, 22).

This account of Freud's intellectual itinerary in the 1890s is bizarre reading for anyone who comes to it from a reading of the letters to Fliess, *The Interpretation of Dreams*, or other texts of the period. It is not just that the whole way psychoanalysis imagines the person makes the absence of "influence from any quarter" something most difficult to think. Specifically, how does Freud dispense with an influence nurtured so forcefully and continuously as that of Wilhelm Fliess? Freud could still read the elaborate compliments to this intimacy scattered through the texts of the early period. These passages are not suppressed in later editions, though Fliess is completely absent from "The History of the Psycho-Analytic Movement." Had Freud, by 1914, actually forgotten his intense intellectual and emotional relationship with Wilhelm Fliess? Of course, memory can be faulty. Freud offers a vivid example of motivated forgetting in a passage of *The Psychopathology of Everyday Life* that circles around the question of his relationship with Fliess and priority in the discovery of bisexuality:

> One day in the summer of 1901 I remarked to a friend with whom I used at that time to have a lively exchange of scientific ideas: "These problems of the neuroses are only to be solved if we base ourselves wholly and completely on the assumption of the original bisexuality of the individual." To which he replied: "That's what I told you two and a half years ago at Br. [Breslau] when we went for that evening walk. But you wouldn't hear of it then." It is painful to be requested in this way to surrender one's originality. I could not recall any such conversation or this pronouncement of my friend's. One of us must have been mistaken and on the "*cui prodest?*" principle it must have been myself. Indeed, in the course of the next week I remembered the whole incident, which was just as my friend had tried to recall it to me; I even recollected the answer I had given him at the time: "I've not accepted that yet; I'm not inclined to go into the question." But since then I have grown a little more tolerant when, in reading medical literature, I come across one of the few ideas with which my name can be associated, and find that my name has not been mentioned. [*S.E.*, VI, 143–44]

Freud puts this anecdote about relinquished originality to original use in his analysis of unconsciously motivated forgetting ("metalepsis") in *The Psychopathology of Everyday Life*. It also becomes a memorial to his very last meeting with Fliess. The permanent formal break came a few years later when Fliess directed public accusations against Freud for trying to steal priority in the discovery of bisexuality.[34]

"The History of the Psycho-Analytic Movement" asserts Freud's claim to possession of psychoanalysis. But Freud's anecdote about "forgetting" Fliess on bisexuality indicates a fundamental dubiety inherent in this assertion: the very discovery he claims priority in making (psychoanalysis) puts in question the grounds for making such a claim. So though Freud makes his bold assertion—"each of them claimed to have got there before the other"—he also undercuts this assertion—"I was in the wrong"—through his analysis of how he came to the idea of the centrality of sexuality as "the source of the propelling forces of neurosis." Here in the "History" the analysis follows a similar course to that taken in the subversion of Freud's claim to originality on bisexuality. Freud tells three anecdotes, all of which involve the same pattern: he becomes party to a consultation in which a senior physician—Breuer, Charcot, Chrobak—attributes the neurotic symptoms of a woman to sexual abstinence occasioned by the husband's impotence. (Later, in writing *The Autobiographical Study* [1925], Freud reports that he remembered these three incidents while he was writing "The History of the Psycho-Analytic Movement."[35] In writing the "History," he had been forced to forfeit claims to having discovered the sexual aetiology of neurosis. Freud had consoled himself for the idea's "bad reception" with "the thought that I was taking up the fight for a new and original idea." But memories of these three incidents "disturbed this pleasing notion" by showing this idea "had by no means originated with me." "These three men had all communicated to me a piece of knowledge which, strictly speaking they did not possess." Freud calls their engagement with this idea "a fleeting inspiration" and compares it to "a casual flirtation." But their insight can rest as latent memory-traces in the mind, and suddenly return to Freud where the idea can be taken as "literally" and seriously as "solemn matrimony." This return creates the effect of an original discovery. Freud reports: "these three identical opinions, which I had heard without understanding, had lain dormant in my mind for years, until one day they awoke in the form of an apparently original discovery" (*S.E.*, XIV, 13). Thus through a temporal delay traces with a fragmentary meaning may operate in the unconscious to emerge through *deferred effect* as a rep-

34. For a detailed discussion of this final episode of the Freud-Fliess relationship, see part IV of Ernst Kris's long introduction to *Origins*, 35–47.
35. *S.E.*, XX, 24.

etition that appears single, unique, and transparent (the discovery of the sexual basis of neurosis). This is the same structure Freud found operating in the emergence of an early childhood scene as traumatic for the person. And it is also at work in the primal scene of rivalry between Freud and John, and in Freud's institution of psychoanalysis.

Only if one takes hold of the double register of all these psychic social events can one understand what Freud's interpretation of the *non vixit* dream does. *First register*: To the extent that Freud asserts the originality of his discovery, and must (quite understandably) experience his own life as the origin of psychoanalysis, to that extent this interpretation is an act of will. Freud is the little boy one year younger who wins the object he desires from his nephew because he got there first. Freud successfully upholds his claim before his father; he can possess three objects—the self, *The Interpretation of Dreams*, and psychoanalysis—for these three objects are, we can now see, one object in the analysis of the dream text. Thus, in the primal scene of rivalry, Freud can seem to accede to the father's power, and inseminating himself into full selfhood, he writes his own life by doing autobiography. Bypassing others (Fliess, John) Freud can now father psychoanalysis. But—and this is the *second register*—to the extent that this singular (seminal) act is embedded in a network of repetitions echoing forward and back, this interpretation is also symptomatic (and disseminating). In the middle space of language, between the operation of memory and fantasy, a scene is remembered and composed where Freud prevails "this time" over his older and stronger nephew. This is more an uncontrollable event than an act. And this seminal victory—over John and Fliess and Jung and others—is not won because of the rightful priority of having got there first. No, this victory comes through a more powerful use of language as interpretation—language smartly mustered before the father, language woven into the text named *The Interpretation of Dreams*, language used to assert Freud's authority to start the movement of psychoanalysis. Within this use of language, Freud's assertion of priority, and the more general weight everywhere given the uniqueness of a single person's experience, will be the fiction necessary to summon the force to turn one man's works of life and writing and indebtedness and repetition into the pragmatic beginnings of something he and others will later be able to call "the" psychoanalytic movement. Freud's way of doing this communicates a knowledge of the fictionality of this priority and uniqueness which

[109]

strictly speaking he refuses to acknowledge; Freud's text thereby allows its reader to understand more than he or she is permitted to
hear said.

In the years that follow the turn of the century, Freud does things
so that the discoveries of the 1890s, as they are formulated in *The Interpretation of Dreams* and other texts, can be turned to use: he founds
the psychoanalytic association, his theoretical writings attempt to
give a systematic coherence to the new science, he writes about therapeutic technique, he even writes "introductory lectures" to guide
the layman to some understanding of his thought. Sam Weber has
shown how Freud's theoretical work develops psychoanalysis in an
inventive and fictive fashion.[36] Freud is also, however, at the same
time, working to increase his effectiveness and effect—upon patients, upon followers, upon the science and medicine of his day.
But my reading of his work also indicates the way any claims to mastery made in the name of his theory and practice, by both him and
his followers, are powerfully qualified by a close reading of the text
which invents that theory. Thus, by reading Freud's text against the
grain of intention, and exploring the interstices and cross-currents
of his argument, we have found that Freud's text gives the person a
most equivocal status: the person is both broached and constituted
by chance as singular repetition. This is not simply the paradoxical
terminus of our analysis. This (non-)placement of the person is indispensable if we are to account for the interpretive leeway Freud
demonstrates in displacing Fliess, and all he represents, from the position of preeminent authority to one of a rival open to substitution.
By setting three episodes in motion around one act of reading (the
analysis of the *non vixit* dream), we loosened the literality and fixity
of Freud's assertion. Then we could see how the appearance of the
primal scene of rivalry as something determining and natural is inscribed as memory-trace, as fantasy, as practical experience, and as
theoretical projection within an interpretation which Freud manages
but cannot fully control or apprehend. But finally, in order to turn
this interpretation to use, and in order to make it accomplice in
instituting psychoanalysis, Freud simplifies and reduces the problematic concept of the person implicit in this interpretation.

Why does Freud do this? In part he must guard the coherence of
the person in order to have an object of study. Thus Freud cannot
disseminate the primal scene of rivalry, as our analysis suggested

36. See Weber's subtle reading of Freud in *The Legend of Freud* (Minneapolis: University of Minnesota Press, 1982). For discussions of psychoanalysis as an institution
see Roustang's *Dire Mastery*, and *October*, 28, special issue upon "Discipleship."

one could, into other potentially innumerable scenes, until any ground for the being of the person drops away. But Freud does not just suppress this radically skeptical critique of the person. He goes further. In order to institute psychoanalysis and make it a teachable, repeatable form of treatment with methods of diagnosis, disease categories, and protocols for treatment, he had to convert a subtle, arduous, and personal interpretive paraxis into a system of interpretation that followers can operate. Freud proceeds to obscure that in interpretation which is arbitrary, inventive, and aleatory so that it can seem natural, inevitable, and simply a way of seeing, so that it can appear impersonal rather than shot through with the eccentricity of a single person's position, so that what had been willed, both in his self-analysis and in instituting psychoanalysis, should disappear and be all the more powerful for having disappeared.

So Freud makes something of a devil's bargain, trading knowledge for power, obscuring the radical insights of his interpretive praxis in order to institute a system that others could use, until psychoanalysis can grow into a far-flung church and empire with schools, canonical texts, heretical outcasts—and Freud as the acknowledged father and founder. But one must immediately issue a couple of provisos. Even while psychoanalysis is becoming an institution, Freud never stops taking risks, and pushing his thought into unimagined places, by writing such texts as *Totem and Taboo*, "The Uncanny," *Beyond the Pleasure Principle*, and "Analysis Terminable and Interminable." And beyond this, who is to say that Freud was not correct to take those steps necessary to turn psychoanalysis into an institution? Perhaps this was the most powerful conceptual form for the projection of his work? And by instituting the scene of analysis as the locus for therapeutic work, Freud also opened a valuable matrix for ongoing intellectual inquiry. It is an inventive textual matrix to which this reading of Freud is indebted, and which, I shall now repeat, displace, and "countersign," in my own way, so that it may aid me in reading Nietzsche's life and writing in 1882.

NIETZSCHE AND LOU SALOMÉ: A BIOGRAPHICAL READING OF THE COINCIDENCES OF LIFE AND WRITING IN 1882

Grief joys, joy grieves, on slender accident.

—*Hamlet*

One must have chaos in one's heart
To give birth to a dancing star.

—Nietzsche, *Thus Spake Zarathustra*

Standing apart is the guiding intention and the most ingrained impulse of Nietzsche's life and writing. It becomes the springboard for his effective mastery, as well as the source of specious claims to a masterful autonomy. Thus, in his writing, Nietzsche glories by turns in the disciplined superiority of the noble, the solitude of the sage, the daring of the explorer, and the iconoclasm of the revolutionary. Each becomes an (only partly) ironic self-complement. But Nietzschean apartness is not just thought, and then written; *so* that it may be written, Nietzsche lives out many registers of this independence. By not marrying, and by not continuing his university career after his illness, Nietzsche stands apart from the expectations of his family; he breaks with Wagner and other friends when he fears they might circumscribe his thought; he condemns his country's "herd responses"—its religion, nationalism, and anti-Semitism; his deconstructive reading of Western metaphysics allows him to expose and stand apart from its founding suppositions. By his experimentation in the aphorism and the fragment, he refuses the inherited language forms of philosophy, philology, and the moral essay. Nietzsche's position apart reaches its extreme, and even supercilious expression, in the not-so-playful headings of *Ecce Homo* ("Why I Am So Wise," "Why I Write Such Good Books," "Why I Am a Destiny"); its final experiential form is Nietzsche's terminal madness. Whether this standing apart is interpreted as a central trope of Romanticism or as one of the most familiar reflexes of the modernist avant-garde, it always seems to carry this implicit assumption: he who stands apart can see the larger curvature of the enclosing paradigm, which is hidden from those who instinctively endorse their society's collective

[115]

values and constraints of vision. In thus positioning himself, Nietzsche assumes that he who stands apart stands above; he may suffer isolation, but he will see more. This range of vision is the reward Nietzsche claims for "we daredevils of the spirit who have climbed the highest and most dangerous peak of present thought and looked around from up there—we who have looked *down* from there" (*GS, Preface*, 1886).[1]

For Nietzsche, his position apart is more than a rhetorical pose. It helps achieve an inventive conceptual independence the reader may share. Generations of readers have come to Nietzsche for his peculiar blend of opening skepticism, ruthless unmasking, and renovating affirmation. The masterful scope of Nietzsche's critique and reconception of the Western tradition has made his text seem to be, in spite of its recurrent critique of system, a system apart. But problems haunt this intellectual isolation: it can also become an exaggeration and (through the seduction of inflated self-estimations) an alibi. Just as Freud in his "History of the Psycho-Analytic Movement" grossly exaggerates his "splendid isolation" in the 1890s, so Nietzsche, like every great thinker, is less isolated, more indebted, and more in need of response than he often admits. Nietzsche may attribute his failure to find readers to "the disproportion between the greatness of my task and the *smallness* of my contemporaries" but his solicitation of an engaged and intelligent response from others is a constitutive dimension of his whole project (*BWN:EH, Preface*, 673). Nietzsche's own critique of the ascetic priest can be applied to himself: even the saint who fasts on the pillar in the desert has internalized the audience in whose name, and before whose imagined gaze, he makes his sacrifice. What is the value of Nietzsche's hard-won ori-

1. Throughout I have used the Walter Kaufmann translations of Nietzsche's work, except where I note the use of another translation. When the translation has been modified, usually only by a word or two, I have noted this. Also, there are times when I have suppressed the paragraph divisions so as to reflect the standard German edition I have consulted: *Nietzsche Werke*, ed. Giorgio Colli and Mazzino Montinari (Berlin & New York: Walter de Gruyter, 1977). I have abbreviated Kaufmann's texts as follows: *The Gay Science*, GS, section number; *The Will to Power*, WP, section number; *Zarathustra*, Z, part, section; and works in *The Basic Writings of Nietzsche: The Birth of Tragedy*, BWN:BT, section, page; *Beyond Good and Evil*, BWN:BG&E, part, section; *On the Genealogy of Morals*, BWN:GM, essay, section, and page; *Ecce Homo*, BWN:EH, chapter title, section, page. *The Will to Power* and *On the Genealogy of Morals* were translated with R. J. Hollingdale. All the Kaufmann texts with the exception of *Thus Spake Zarathustra* are published by Random House, Inc., and are quoted with the permission of that publisher. Quotations from *Thus Spake Zarathustra* are taken from *The Portable Nietzsche*, edited and translated by Walter Kaufmann, copyright © 1954 by The Viking Press, Inc., copyright renewed © 1982 by Viking Penguin, Inc., and are reprinted by permission of Viking Penguin, Inc.

ginality and independence if the very critique they produce keeps him both ignored and unread by the culture it is intended to serve and persuade, the very people whose reformation it is conceived to effect?

This problematic side of Nietzsche's isolation points to one of the biographical themes of his correspondence in 1882. The summer of 1881 has brought his first grasp of the idea of "eternal recurrence," and *The Gay Science* has offered the first formulations of that idea. But Nietzsche is disappointed with the sale of his books, and his retirement from the University of Basel has left him more intellectually isolated than ever. Perhaps writing his ideas in poetic form, and as the teachings of the god Zarathustra, will carry his message to a wider audience. In 1882, as preparation for writing *Zarathustra*, Nietzsche conceives the idea of a winter stay in a northern city, where lectures, companionship, and libraries are available. He also toys with the idea of finding a disciple—a person who may become heir to his project. For, as I indicate in the Introduction, the effective currency of someone's work is not validated until others (or at least *one* other) take up that work, and "countersign" it as their own. To express this new turn in his work and disposition Nietzsche assumes the mask of the god Zarathustra and imagines greeting the sun as it touches the peak of his mountain home upon the very morning he decides to "go down among men."

Nietzsche announces this arduous new phase of his philosophic project and life plans in "insipit tragoedia," the famous last section of *The Gay Science*, which he uses nearly unchanged a year later as the Prologue of *Zarathustra*. There Zarathustra, finding his "heart had changed," addresses the sun and announces his new intention: being "sick of my wisdom" Zarathustra will go find "hands outstretched to receive it." To do this he will "go under" like the sun, and for this risky venture of self-expenditure, he asks a solar blessing: "Bless the cup that wants to overflow in order that the water may flow from it golden and carrying the reflection of your rapture everywhere. Behold, this cup wants to become empty again, and Zarathustra wants to become man again." Examined in the light of this point in Nietzsche's career, this gesture is equivocal. Nietzsche, wearing the mask of Zarathustra, assumes the stance of the one who knows, but who, in order to impart his knowledge, must go down among men and translate his wisdom into their ways of knowing. In order to teach he also has to learn; and learning requires a fundamental displacement of his own ways of living and writing. Thus to "go under" is also to "break down" and "under go" metamorphosis.

He announces his readiness for the self-expenditure expressed in the final gesture and image of this passage: to inseminate men with divine solar wisdom, the god Zarathustra wants to become man; the overflowing cup is ready to spill itself.

In his letters Nietzsche quite explicitly calls on his friends to help realize the "second life" he feels stirring in him. He writes the composer Peter Gast: "Can't you find me some absorbing distraction? I should like to spend a few years in adventures, so as to give my ideas time, rest and manure."[2] In making this request, in taking a sea voyage to Messina, and in going to Rome to meet the new young woman Paul Rée had discovered, Nietzsche is following his own formula for learning: "one must be able to lose oneself occasionally if one wants to learn something from things different from oneself" (*GS*, 305). Adventure, travel, and something different from himself: all this was waiting impatiently for him in Rome in the person of Lou Salomé. She was the woman who would provide that useful supplement of lived experience which Nietzsche was groping to find in the spring of 1882 as he finished *The Gay Science* and meditated Zarathustra.

Excising Lou Salomé from 1882

Nietzsche's predisposition toward finding some "absorbing distraction" in the spring of 1882 has encouraged me to do a biographical reading of the interplay of his life and writing in that year—a more detailed and concerted act of biographical reading than I attempted with Freud and Fliess. In beginning this biographical narrative, however, two immediately complicating factors present themselves. Almost from the moment Nietzsche knows Lou Salomé, he loves her. She therefore appears to him as "something else" and something other—the advent and the omen of an adventure that cannot be controlled by any initial designs or accounted for by his own language. And this complication is affiliated with another that is inherent in my method: in following the way Salomé is woven into and

2. Elisabeth Nietzsche, *The Life of Nietzsche*, 2 vols. (New York: Sturgis & Walton, 1912–15), 2, 116. Note the way Nietzsche has subordinated "adventures" to his "ideas" by likening them to "manure"; Nietzsche refers to his "second life" in the letter to M. Meyerbug, *Life*, vol. 2,113. "Sanctus Januarius" alludes to the miraculous liquefication of a saint's blood. In more ways than one, Nietzsche's juices are flowing.

out of Nietzsche's life and writing, we will necessarily begin to confuse the boundaries between life and writing. The life lived begins to assume the qualities of a carefully contrived compositional effort; and the text written has those qualities—of will and pleasure, of arbitrary taste and perverse desire—that one associates with a particular life.

Because Nietzsche's biography became a polemical battlefield from the moment he went mad, knowing what Lou Salomé meant to Nietzsche is difficult. But strange to say, all his biographers, however heatedly they argue, agree on one matter: that Lou Salomé, though an important figure in Nietzsche's personal life, had no significant effect on his thought. Therefore, they seem to say, she may be safely excised from a serious narrative of the philosophical events of that year. Elisabeth Nietzsche contrives an ingenious account that represents Salomé as a failed disciple, who for a while distracted Nietzsche from the one important woman in his life (Elisabeth). R. J. Hollingdale begins his chapter on "the 'affair' of Lou Salomé" with a caution that puts it in "proper perspective": "At the time, Nietzsche thought it very important and his disappointment at its failure threw him off balance for a while: but there is no ground for thinking it changed him in any way or that his work from 1883 onwards would have been any different in its essentials if he had never met Lou Salomé." Walter Kaufmann treats Salomé as a valued but essentially passive (that is, womanly) intellectual companion, "to whom [Nietzsche] could speak of his innermost ideas, receiving not only intellectual understanding but a response based on Lou's own experience." Salomé is thus a kind of example and verification of Nietzsche's own thought. Kaufmann focuses his narrative on the misunderstandings which arise out of this relationship as they help explain (and explain away) the bitter recriminations Nietzsche makes in the summer of 1883. Above all, Kaufmann is delighted to report, in the fourth edition of his book, that Rudolph Binion has found evidence that Nietzsche never proposed to Salomé as Salomé had claimed. She, no less than Elisabeth Nietzsche, had engaged in "falsification of the record" and "tampering with the evidence." "Now we know that *both* women are unreliable witnesses." Rudolph Binion, in his monumental biography of Lou Salomé, and Ronald Hayman, in his recent biography of Nietzsche, both give Salomé a larger place in Nietzsche's emotional life. But Binion everywhere emphasizes that the influence flows from Nietzsche to Salomé; that finally Nietzsche rejects her rather than the other way around; and that in all this she is what the subtitle of Binion's book makes her—Nietzsche's wayward disciple.

Hayman's interpretation of the Salomé episode is compatible with Binion's. He makes it a difficult experience which Nietzsche struggles to put behind him. It may offer the occasion for many of the formulations of *Zarathustra*, but it does not effect its philosophical understructure.[3]

All these biographers display particular motives for writing narratives that place Lou at the margins of Nietzsche's philosophic project. But each is also subscribing to a series of metaphysically charged hierarchies which help us read what might be called the ideology of philosophy. Nietzsche is a man who lives a life of the mind, engaged in an impersonal quest for truth; by contrast Lou is a beautiful woman, necessarily more closely engaged with the body, whose proper sphere will be the personal life, where her hold on the truth will perforce be more tenuous. This ideological template is not the same as, but is deeply coimplicated with, the cultural subordination of woman. It elucidates key features of each biographer's response to Lou Salomé: Elisabeth's indignation that Lou Salomé could presume to treat herself as Nietzsche's peer; the dry assurance with which Hollingdale can define the identity of Nietzsche's life "in its essentials" without Salomé; the pleasure Kaufmann demonstrates in clearing Nietzsche (as ascetic priest) of the charge of having proposed to Salomé; and the zest he shows in detecting Lou Salomé's falsity, her tamperings, her "unreliability." At best "Frau Lou" could have only hoped to be the loyal disciple Binion finally labels "wayward." This way of marginalizing Salomé gains force from the assumption that Nietzsche must have been a "master" to this would-be disciple by the fact of his philosophic genius. Salomé and the Salomé episode may provide the fortuitous terms, the fugitive metaphors, the occasions of experience for Nietzsche's writing. But everywhere it is assumed that the genetic force of Nietzsche's genius is expressing itself at a profound conceptual level immune to contingent encounters with any "other" such as Lou Salomé. This is the assumption this section of my book will investigate and challenge.

Nietzsche himself, before meeting Lou, wants "adventures" that will serve as a manageable supplement to his work—time, rest, and manure as a useful supplement for his ideas. After meeting her, Nietzsche playfully postulates her as the "mother" for his "son"

3. Elisabeth Nietzsche, *Life*, 2, 119–25; R. J. Hollingdale, *Nietzsche: The Man and His Philosophy* (London: Routledge & Kegan Paul, 1965), 179; Walter Kaufmann, *Nietzsche: Philosopher, Psychologist, Antichrist*, 4th ed. (Princeton: Princeton University Press, 1974), 49; Rudolph Binion, *Frau Lou: Nietzsche's Wayward Disciple* (Princeton: Princeton University Press, 1968), hereafter B; Ronald Hayman, *Nietzsche: A Critical Life* (New York: Penguin, 1980), 256, 258, 259.

Zarathustra. But the metaphor of Salomé as mother (and wife) already suggests the experience of passion that will move him beyond any facile subordination of Salomé. Although Nietzsche himself attempts to limit the scope of this relationship, there is something perverse in the way his biographers separate Nietzsche's life and thought. One of the central aims of his philosophy is to do a psychology of philosophy: to show that what men and women think only seems, and can never be, divorced from what they live. This goal is implicit in Nietzsche's project when he interprets a chain of philosophical systems in terms of the all-too-human desires of their creators (*Beyond Good and Evil*), when he shows how the Western idea of man and the psyche comes from our historical conditioning, religions, passions (*The Genealogy of Morals*), when he insists on the importance to the personal life of suppressed nonideal terms like climate, diet, and so on (*Ecce Homo*). In all these analyses Nietzsche adheres implicitly to the ideal of a Protestant sense of vocation, which demands an arduously achieved consistency between beliefs and values on the one hand and the practice of life on the other. The letters of 1882 are full of moments where he applies to his life the very same formulations he has written in his books. Thus in one letter to Elisabeth, he says many kind things in his attempt to smooth over the distress Lou Salomé caused on her August visit to Tautenburg. But in the letter's close he is quite firm in denying Elisabeth her own self-righteous anger and the apology she is demanding from him: "My creed absolutely forbids me two things: 1) repentance 2) moral indignation. Let's be quite good friends again, my dear Lama!"[4] Nietzsche makes his life—especially in 1882—a laboratory where he tests what he thinks and seeks to learn what he thinks by what he lives (*GS*, 319). For this reason 1882 becomes a vexing and even bewildering year for him. To "have reached a point at which I live as I think," as he proudly informs Jakob Burckhardt he has, will also mean that his life has the power to expose what is wishful or deluded about his thought (L, 277;8/2/82). It is his own sense of the potentially ironic tension between what one thinks and what one lives that tempers one of the clearest statements he gives of

---

4. Throughout I will refer to the new standard edition of Nietzsche's letters edited by Giorgio Colli and Mazzino Montinari, *Nietzsche Briefwechsel* (Berlin: Walter de Gruyter, 1981) as L, giving first the number of the letter in volume III, 1, devoted to the period January 1880–December 1884, then the exact or approximate date of the letters as established by the editors: here 300; 9/9/82. This edition is most important, because the Middleton edition of selected letters in English, which I have made use of when possible, and the letters published by Elisabeth Nietzsche in the *Life* often contain serious errors and distortions as to text, dating, and translation.

this ethos: "Finally, I speak only of what I have lived through, not merely of what I have thought through: the opposition of thinking and life is lacking in my case. My 'theory' grows from my 'practice'—oh, from a practice that is not by any means harmless or unproblematic!"[5]

If one takes seriously this injunction to see life and thought together and looks carefully at the eighteen months of Nietzsche's life that begin on New Years Day 1882, then one cannot help but be as struck with those dissonances which sound between life and thought as with the harmonies Nietzsche sought. Thus "Sanctus Januarius" defines a "theory," an ethos of aesthetic affirmation, which creates a potential for practice that he seeks to put into effect in the Salomé episode. Things seem even more fortuitous than this. Salomé appears as wonderfully coincident with what Nietzsche has already thought. Her poem "To Pain" contains the same unconditional affirmation of life which Nietzsche took to be one of his central beliefs. Thus, Salomé can be read (and Nietzsche almost does read her) as a realization or creation of his philosophic project. But there are problems with this ideal image of their mutual imaging. First, Salomé is independent, resisting, and self-assertive. She refuses to let herself "be used"; in fact she has her own designs for use in this relationship. Second, the platonic living arrangement Lou, Paul Rée, and Nietzsche plan to advance their intellectual lives is swamped by the commonplace but powerful facts of Nietzsche's falling in love, Rée's falling in love, and a rivalry for Salomé's affection opening between them. As the locus of unexpected passion and conflict, she becomes a figure in Nietzsche's life for the resistant "other," the contingent which traverses life, displacing it out of its intended directions. By this argument the Salomé episode can be neither something uncalled for, completely exterior, and radically chance in its appearance, nor something choreographed by Nietzsche, a simple repetition of his desire; it is not even an "aporia" implied by Nietzsche's text. Rather this episode is both something that unfolds in a space invented for Salomé by the text of *The Gay Science*, and, in this happening, something that exceeds or violates that space. And this doubleness helps explain why the Lou episode must be thought not as a measured application of philosophical "theory" to living "practice," but as what comes between *The Gay Science* and *Zarathustra*; not as a

5. This is a quote from a discarded 1888 fragment of *Ecce Homo*, as cited by Walter Kaufmann in *BWN*, 796.

bridge, but as a fissure, a violent displacing, a challenge, a mockery, and a joke. After all Nietzsche's gratitude for Lou comes attendant resentment; after intensities of bliss, a backlash of wrenching loss. The episode is an acute challenge to Nietzsche's brightly affirmed ethos for saying "yes" to life. As a biographical supplement to Nietzsche's philosophic texts, this story will enable us to see the way "theory" and "practice," life and philosophy, become elucidating allegories, bizarre distortions, and impish disguises for one another.

From January 1882 through July 1883, Nietzsche's life and writing pass through three broad phases. In the first three months of 1882 Nietzsche writes the climactic fourth (and final) book of *The Gay Science*; in the next nine months, he meets and falls in love with Lou Salomé, makes her the central person in his life, and then, in losing Lou to Rée, has a falling out with nearly everyone important to him—Lou Salomé, Paul Rée, Elisabeth Nietzsche, and his mother; in the first six months of 1883 Nietzsche writes Books I and II of *Zarathustra*. By narrating these events, and reading the words and acts and philosophic texts of this period of Nietzsche's life in relation to one another, we will be able to do a critical articulation of the relationships of several pairs of terms which are not parallel in themselves, but which the contingent events of Nietzsche's life in 1882 make parallel: philosophy and love; writing and life; mind and body; man and woman; Nietzsche and Frau Lou. A sequential narrative of this epoch of Nietzsche's life will give us access to what is contingent, uncontrollable, and decisive in the encounter between the first and second of each pair. *The Gay Science* stages this encounter with a strong prejudice toward happy anticipation, aesthetic symmetry, and a philosophic commitment to affirm whatever comes of this encounter; the experiences of the year, as they unfold around the axis of the passion for Lou Salomé, test, confound, and displace the philosophic postulates of *The Gay Science*; and *Zarathustra* fulfills, short-circuits and sometimes even reverses the themes and positions of *The Gay Science*, as they are refracted and realigned around a quite new and much more conflictual concept of the will operating within interpretation. In telling this story I shall be less concerned with Nietzsche's avowed purposes—to cure Western cluture of its hatred of life, by offering an affirming counter-ideal to its nihilism —than with testing his writing on chance and the person against what we find chancing to happen in that life. This approach will disturb the pose of masterful assertion which the Nietzsche persona so often assumes.

How I Plan to Read Nietzsche

To define the ethos of aesthetic affirmation Nietzsche invented by writing "Sanctus Januarius," I will pursue a two-pronged strategy for reading. First, I will create a thematic unity for "Sanctus Januarius" by assembling its images, gestures, and ideas into a coherent statement. Then I will refine, test, and challenge this synthesis by doing a close, "deconstructive" reading of several passages of it. By coordinating these two ways of reading, I hope to avoid the most glaring liabilities of each of the two main currents of Nietzsche criticism. Readers like Walter Kaufmann, Gilles Deleuze, and a host of lesser commentators set out to describe the conceptual unity of a text composed of aphoristic passages, which are arranged as separate, but which, because of their multiple echoes and implied cross-references, can be composed into a more coherent system of meaning than Nietzsche ever described. This kind of commentary finds its justification in a presumption about the priority of the whole: because, although the links are covert, each of Nietzsche's major positions is conceptually dependent upon every other, his critique of Western thought can be fully appreciated only as a totality. Each reader dreams of being the person who will assemble the puzzle of fragments into a whole where every piece will have its place. This kind of reading quickly turns Nietzsche's text into a system of belief, and Nietzsche into what he sometimes feigned to be: an oracle of truth. Reading Nietzsche in this way allows a commentator to explicate one of Nietzsche's ideas—such as his affirmation of a world and life that is chance-laden—in such a way that Nietzsche himself, as both thinker and person, is by that analysis exempt from the force of chance's operation.[6] Crucial to the practice of this holistic commentary is the imposition of hierarchies among concepts and between texts—an imposition that will seem natural and conceptually inevitable to each individual practitioner of this method, though arbitrary and partial to others. The central poverty of holistic thematic commentary emerges from the way it levels the text into an undifferentiated surface of tonally equivalent positions; erased are the performative turns, the language play, and the strife of positions that give Nietzsche's writing its distinctive force. Thematic commen-

---

6. This, I think, is what Deleuze does in *Nietzsche et la philosophie* (Paris: Presses Universitaires de France, 1962). See especially chap. 1.

tary cannot take account of the way the conceptual excess and linguistic pyrotechnics of Nietzsche's writings have turned literature and philosophy into pre-texts for each other.

As a corrective to the weakness of the thematic collation that explicates the ur-system it finds resident in the text, a second, more recent body of Nietzsche criticism emphasizes the radicality of Nietzsche's language—its tropological displacement of concepts, its plurality and heterogeneity of styles, its way of throwing into question traditional assumptions about communication, the subject, being, truth, and the like. This linguistically centered reading of Nietzsche, practiced most persuasively by Paul de Man and Jacques Derrida, has proved a valuable antidote to interpretation by holistic commentary. It has also demonstrated the enormous deconstructive potential of the Nietzschean text.[7] But while it challenges most of the assumptions of holistic commentary, it provides another kind of radical innocence for Nietzsche, which might be called the innocence of the avant-garde. By being "beyond" the usual metaphysical complacency and blindness, Nietzsche's work becomes a scriptural "master text," a decisive guide for reading other texts, and an (impossible) example for writing. In giving predominant attention to the deconstructive work of Nietzsche's text, this reading practice also fails to find a way to talk about some themes of the Nietzschean corpus—such as the will to affirm—which, as central preoccupations and avowed goals of his writing, are something any full reading of his work must seek to construe. Finally, the language-centered reading of Nietzsche is too ready to make a virtue of its own deference. It defers any general interpretation of Nietzsche's work, making the hermeneutical desire for truth part of the metaphysics it would displace. But by the way it lingers around the Nietzschean text, it betrays its own strange blend of iconoclastic humility and hermeneutical desire. This patient willingness to defer is fully compatible with what the asserted radicality of Nietzsche's writing implicitly assumes: that Nietzsche's text, if not Nietzsche as a bio-

---

7. The most important deconstructive readings are those of Paul de Man in *Allegories of Reading: Figural Language in Rousseau, Nietzsche, Rilke, and Proust* (New Haven: Yale University Press, 1979) and Jacques Derrida, *Spurs: Nietzsche's Styles*, trans. Barbara Harlow (Chicago: University of Chicago Press, 1978). See also Sarah Kofman, *Nietzsche et la métaphore* (Paris: Payot, 1972), and Bernard Pautrat, *Versions du soleil* (Paris: Seuil, 1971). Other examples of this way of reading Nietzsche may be found in the Nietzsche special issue of *boundary 2*, 9, no. 3, and 10, no. 1 (Spring/Fall 1981): Rudolph E. Kuenzli, "Nietzsche's Zerography: *Thus Spoke Zarathustra*," 99–119; Gary Shapiro, "Nietzsche's Graffito: A Reading of *The Antichrist*," 119–41; Rodolphe Gasché, "Autobiography as *Gestalt*: Nietzsche's *Ecce Homo*," 271–95.

graphical-historical phenomenon, is exempt from the necessities and banalities of experiences like the wishful idealization of art or woman, the errancy of passion, and the revenge against woman that we will find overtaking his text, no less than his life, in 1882.

The radicality and innocence that a "deconstructive reading" wins for Nietzsche's text may have less to do with the systematic possibilities opened for reading by deconstruction than with the itinerary of purposes it has happened to pursue and the texts it has chosen to read and left unread. Thus in *Spurs: Nietzsche's Styles*, Derrida reads Nietzsche so that philosophy, art, and woman become problems and questions for one another. In this analysis, Derrida shows how Nietzsche's radical concept and practice of style disrupts the conventional parallel oppositions and hierarchies of our tradition: philosophy and art, man and woman, truth and error, the phallus and the absence of a phallus. Derrida suggests what is symptomatic about Heidegger's exclusion of the term "woman" from his reading of a passage of Nietzsche's text where she figures in an important way: the exclusion evidences philosophy's failure to comprehend its own desire and limit. Derrida's reading elaborates the series of contradictory relationships to woman suggested by Nietzsche's text, where each will have a strategic function in one moment of his philosophic project. As the locus of a mendacity and bad faith, woman is censured and debased; as the veiled one who triggers the desire which acts upon us at a distance, "woman" becomes the very figure of "truth," the locus of Christian virtue and pity, and the one who disreputably plays with truth; but finally, beyond these two negations of woman, woman is "recognized and affirmed as an affirmative power, an artist, a dionysiac." Thus for the Nietzsche who wields the spur, the pen, the phallus of a subversive new (anti-)philosophic style: "He was, he dreaded this castrated woman [as falsehood]. He was, he dreaded this castrating woman [as truth]. He was, he loved this affirming woman [as dionysiac]. At once, simultaneously or successively, depending on the position of his body and the situation of his story, Nietzsche was all of these. Within himself, outside himself, Nietzsche dealt with so many woman. Like in Basel where he held council."[8]

Derrida's reading of Nietzsche is an invaluable corrective to the tendency to read Nietzsche's pronouncements upon woman and feminism outside any broader reading of his thought. It also offers a powerful refutation of those feminist efforts, contested by Nietzsche

8. Derrida, *Spurs*, 96–97, 100–101; the words in brackets are my own addition.

as well as by Derrida, to reify gender oppositions by designating the nature of "woman." But the final lines of Derrida's suggestive typology of "woman" in Nietzsche's text suggest the locus for my reading of this terrain. Nietzsche did not just have women within a psychic "inside"; he also dealt with them in a social "outside." He did not just encounter them in Schopenhauer and the philosophical tradition; he also knew them in Basel and Rome and Trischben and Tautenburg. And the women within and without were constantly confused with one another. In my narrative Elisabeth Nietzsche and Lou Salomé function in many of the same ways Derrida interprets "woman" in Nietzsche—as art, as false belief and idealism, as embodying a "truth" to be deconstructed, and as the locus of a wisdom beyond the metaphysical concept of truth. But "woman" does not do so simply because Nietzsche has located woman and style and art as the suppressed terms of Western philosophy. "Woman" is also, *and at the same time*, something contingent, social, experiential, and personal: "Lou Salomé" and "Elisabeth" as specific positions in the love affair which engulfs Nietzsche's life and thought in 1882. My narrative analysis of his writing unfolds in relationship to a biographical space and text which is both before and after Nietzsche's general ideas about woman as art, as style, and as that which can unsettle our idea of "Truth." For this reason, Lou and Elisabeth cannot be collapsed into an abstract amalgam called "woman." In fact some of the efforts to generalize about "woman" in the years after 1882 are Nietzsche's revenge on Lou and Elisabeth. By reading Nietzsche's personal relationships as they can be known (and cannot be known) through the texts which have survived, I am seeking to explore what becomes an explicit problem and crisis within Nietzsche's philosophy: the exchange between "life" and "philosophy" Nietzsche seeks (in love), but which cannot be managed within the ethos for living formulated in "Sanctus Januarius." After the personal failures of his love affair with Lou Salomé, Nietzsche is impelled to think and write the relationship between life, art, and philosophy in a new way.

In the analysis of "Sanctus Januarius" which follows, I will attempt a syncopated act of reading that assumes that the synthetic reading and the deconstructive reading both have pertinence, necessity, and value in a common interpretive effort. Thus, if one takes seriously the claims of Nietzsche's project to offer a guide for (re)thinking and (re)living our tradition, there is no way *not* to do a kind of inventive thematic assembling and a gymnastic global interpretation of the text, even if this is done (as most do it) in the byways of the reading act, intuitively, informally, and impressionistically. Only if one

[127]

presses this text into larger coherence can it become the pragmatically useful guide for living Nietzsche hoped it would be. But like all language, Nietzsche's texts mean more than they say, betray more than they intend. Nietzsche's writing expresses a particularly vivid grasp of what might be called the double bind of every effort to assert meaning. A deconstructive reading will allow me to see how Nietzsche's use of the aphorism, irony, parody, and the fragment makes texts (no longer exactly "his") a fundamental challenge to a traditional authorial desire to make language a site for the control of meaning. But I hope to do more than balance a synthetic and deconstructive reading of Nietzsche. If one focuses almost exclusively upon Nietzsche's philosophical texts, both the thematic and deconstructive readings have the effect of asserting the self-sufficiency and the necessary design, and thus the masterful separateness and inevitability, of Nietzsche's texts. The biographical supplement to this reading is a calculated effort to unbalance the antipathetic symmetry of these thematic and deconstructive readings of Nietzsche.

The critic of Nietzsche who in some ways comes closest to the conceptual point of departure of my reading is Stanley Corngold. His article "The Question of the Self in Nietzsche during the Axial Period (1882–1888)," is compatible with my biographical reading of Nietzsche in a series of ways. We are both seeking to carry discussion of Nietzsche elsewhere than the "deconstruction of the subject" which is so central a theme for the readers of the "new" Nietzsche; we both want to take into account the way Nietzsche's philosophic project, including its moments of affirmation, presupposes some pragmatic operational conception of the self; finally, we both wish to do these two things by taking into account, rather than simply ignoring, the deconstructive reading of Nietzsche. Although a detailed critique of Corngold's argument is not possible here, such a critique would need to touch on the following issues.[9] It may be accurate

9. See the special Nietzsche double issue, *boundary 2* (Spring/Fall 1981), 55–98. I cannot here do justice to the full complexity of Corngold's argument, but a brief description of some of the main themes of his essay will offer a guide to the very important divergences in our reading of Nietzsche on the person. (Corngold would say "self," and there is the beginning of our differences.) In order to contest the "deconstruction of the subject" in Nietzsche, Corngold's article does several related things. It seeks to take account of the broad and varied range of Nietzsche's statements on the self. Corngold demonstrates how indispensable some concept of the self becomes for comprehending much of Nietzsche's philosophy: for example, the injunction to "become the being that you are," or the distinction between surface and depth, or the psychological kinetics of "self-overcoming," or the articulated distinctions of the social field. Finally, Corngold seeks to distinguish between "the subject" which Nietzsche

to make a terminological distinction between Nietzsche's use of the terms "self" and "subject," but that does not protect the "self" against the conceptual force of the deconstruction of the "subject" Paul de Man has argued so persuasively. Corngold does not reconcile the semiotic closure of the moment of "inspiration," celebrated by Nietzsche in *Ecce Homo* with the critique of representation he argues in "Truth and Lie in an Extra-Moral Sense." Finally Corngold does not show us where in a text of Nietzsche's the "strong self" speaks in such a way as to be immune to the "contaminating" effect of the irony the text engages. The greatest weakness of Corngold's essay is that he fails to do a close reading of any text of Nietzsche. Throughout the analysis, Corngold uses a thematic mode which does not seek to explore any possible tension between what is said and how it is said. Instead his argument marshals the elements of his thematic summary of Nietzsche on the self, so as to construct an all-inclusive self that would seek to incorporate its own deconstruction into its own being, making a deconstruction of the self a dialectical moment in the production of a "strong self." In this way Corngold puts out of play the deconstructive reading of Paul de Man—his real adversary in the essay—and works a favorable fate for the self by rescuing it from a disseminating deconstruction. The somewhat idealistic tone of his finale suggests a return (with significant displacements) to what I take to be the overly humanistic reading of Nietzsche developed by the person to whom Corngold's article is dedicated—Walter Kaufmann.

By writing an analytical narrative of the Salomé/Nietzsche relationship in view of the question of chance and the person, I hope to show how it is necessary and useful to engage some of the questions about selfhood Corngold puts forward, without dispensing with de Man's deconstruction of the subject in Nietzsche's text. While much of my initial analysis is deeply indebted to de Man's and Derrida's readings of Nietzsche, my problematic of chance and the person is

---

deconstructs and the "self" to which Nietzsche gives "special protection" (65). Thus, in contrast to the diacritical distance between the sign and referent that afflicts the subject, signs really converge to become "vehicles of the things they name" for this "self," in moments of "great health," where the self knows the special "inspiration" Nietzsche describes in *Ecce Homo* (72–73). While the "weak self" is open to the irony Corngold acknowledges to be part of Nietzsche's text, the "strong self" "neither perceives nor furthers its dissolution in irony" (79). For Corngold the "strong self" finally garners to itself certain qualities to which he clearly wishes to give general descriptive force: the self has a "unity" that can assert its fundamental self-certainty; the self exceeds its masks and doubles and in being hidden and powerful can take "responsibility" for its action; finally the self must live its "passion"—"the terrible necessity of its task" (86–87).

integrally tied up with an investigation of the person's pragmatic encounters in the world, the sort of singular chance-laden encounters
which may not be conceptually incompatible with, but have certainly
been pragmatically difficult to think about form the vantage point of
a steadfastly deconstructive reading. But chance also fails to be visible from the horizon of Corngold's polemical expansion of the self. I
can more precisely demonstrate the necessity of thinking both the
self and its deconstruction—so neither is collapsed into the other
—in the following way. In the narrative which follows, a certain coherence for the self is necessary in order for Nietzsche to narrate
and register his experience of chance. Nietzsche's ethos of aesthetic
affirmation, and the experience of falling in love with Salomé it prepares, involve Nietzsche in an enormous intuitive affirmation of the
metaphysics of the self. (It will be a self united with Salomé's self.)
But when the relationship breaks down, Nietzsche's text reinterprets
both the love and its demise in terms of a concept of the unconscious
will which renders his life as a kind of "life-writing" (that is, biography). In this way a deconstruction of the metaphysical self becomes an indispensable precondition for thinking the way selves live
in the world; and a more textual diacritical conception of self comes
to be necessary for understanding that writing of *Zarathustra* by
which Nietzsche seeks to "overcome" (and rewrite) the experience of
Lou Salomé.

"Sanctus Januarius" as a Philosophy of Life and a Matrix for Living

In the range of Nietzsche's writing, "Sanctus Januarius," the
fourth and final book of *The Gay Science*, has a special place. It is
written quickly and on impulse in January 1882, in spite of the fact
that he has just announced his intention to wait several years before
he attempts more writing, telling Peter Gast that he wants to wait
until he is "mature enough," and well enough informed, to deal with
ideas like eternal recurrence, which need "thousands of years to develop properly." Thus a first draft of "Sanctus Januarius" is produced in ten days, in an anomalous space between past and future
projects: as the supplement to the first three books of *The Gay Science*, which was itself first imagined as a supplement to his previous

book *The Dawn*.[10] Yet it also broaches the great themes of the late
work, by announcing the idea of the external recurrence of the same
and introducing Zarathustra in the passage where he announces his
decision to go down among men, the very passage later used to begin *Thus Spake Zarathustra*. In pivoting toward an as yet undefined
future in this text, Nietzsche's writing takes on a special warmth and
brightness of tone; it is gentle in its assessments and generous in its
judgments. "Sanctus Januarius" becomes a cycle of prose poems, acting toward the future as a catalyst, a manifesto, and a promise. Perhaps this is why Nietzsche urged his closest and most valued friends,
those to whom he sent copies of his new book in August and September 1882, to be sure to read "Sanctus Januarius." Here they
could find the risky writing project he was attempting to live.

But this text can also be coordinated with those more general horizons of Nietzsche's philosophic project, which can be traced in
every line he wrote. Thus in his psychology of Western culture,
Nietzsche finds that a resistance to chance had been bred like a reflex into our thoughts, our feelings, and even our desires. This reflex can be traced in the idea of Heaven, of Nirvana, of a final rest
and redemption; also in our lifelong desire for continuity, unending
youth, loyalty, love, and a reward tomorrow for today's virtues and
disappointments. To contest these predominant valuations of the
culture, Nietzsche launches a systematic critique of the timid eco-
nomics of the Christian condemnation of those aspects of life that
bring suffering—chance, change, sex, and the will to rule—and re-
cuperation of all the losses in this world in an unseen world after
life.[11] But this is not enough. Thus he begins "Sanctus Januarius"
with the statement of his wish for the new year, *amor fati*, "to love
fate," and his announced desire to become someday "only a yes-
sayer" (*GS*, 276). In the aphorisms which follow, more than in any
other text before *Zarathustra*, Nietzsche seems to be defining a textual space where he can invent values—an "ethos" that is more a
permanent set of values than a transient feeling of "pathos" (*GS*,
317). Such an ethos makes possible a new kind of experience: the
moods, sensations, and interpretations which could be an antidote
and counterthrust to Christian nihilism.[12] Each section demon-

10. See Hayman, *Nietzsche*, 240.
11. See *GS*, 109–10. On the spiritual negation of life see *Twilight of the Idols* (New
York: Viking Portable, 1954). "What I Owe to the Ancients" appeals to Dionysus and
Zarathustra. Also see the chapter of *Ecce Homo*, entitled "Thus Spake Zarathustra: A
Book for All and for None."
12. See *GS*, 58, where Nietzsche insists "we can destroy only as creators."

strates the way an artful interpretive shaping operates to weave and enhance the texture of a person's experience. It is this inmixing of art and the personal life which gives the person "the good will to appearance" and enables him or her to say a fundamental "yes" to life (*GS*, 107). "Sanctus Januarius" becomes a manual, training its reader to internalize what might be called an ethos of aesthetic affirmation.

But what is this ethos? If one composes the diverse fragments of "Sanctus Januarius" into an essay as organized as, say, "Schopenhauer as Educator," or "Truth and Lie in an Extra-Moral Sense," then what systematic statement does one find there?

First, something warned against and subjected to critique: all the subtle and various ways a society reins persons in and bolsters them against what is new in themselves and their future. These include the idea of a "reputation," which trains all persons to regulate themselves according to collective values that will make them into useful, predictable instruments of society (296); religion, which by promising the perfection of life and self in some place elsewhere and hereafter, allows the person's strength to "flow out into a god" (285); and that irritable "self-control" which does not enable a person to "entrust himself to any instinct or free wing beat," or feel the most beautiful fortuities of the soul, or lose himself in something besides himself (305). The narrator saves his praise for the people of Genoa, who, having ventured to the Orient, come to see the law and their "neighbors as a kind of boredom," and build mansions and gardens which "lay between themselves and their neighbors their personal infinity" (291).

The central value of this ethos: the new, the single, the salient, and accidental. Over half the aphorisms provide an example: the strange new figure of music one must learn to love (334); the new year's wish with which Nietzsche begins "Sanctus Januarius" (276); the series of apparently chance events in life, each of which soon "must not be missing" (277); the error at the concert which is turned into a beautiful necessity by the cunning art of the player (314); the moment of embarking on the emigrant's ship (278); that ultimate beauty of a work "that comes but once" (339). In each case this singular event or motive is declared to be beautiful, to be what gives "style to one's character" (290). While men who judge each other take actions as like equivalents for one another, in fact "every action that has ever been done was done in an altogether unique and irretrievable way" (335). Each carries "galaxies" in himself, and if he looks, he "knows how irregular all galaxies are" (322). Marked by "dear chance," "the luckiest dice throws of existence," and "the rarest of lucky accidents," the salient event that etches the life of a person carries a double valence—it is incalculable and uncontrollable, but also precipitates beauty and value into life (277, 288, 339).

How does one get to this valued moment or place of the singular? Perhaps several things are necessary: first, one must be willing to act impulsively and take risks by "embarking upon uncharted seas" and living dangerously (283, 289). Here there is a valuing of expenditure not in view of gain, but in itself and without reserve. Then one must *not* do what Socrates does in dying: turn suffering into a reproach against life. Instead one must see pain and joy as equally essential to a life well lived, especially if one wants to do what Homer and Prometheus did, and what Nietzsche hopes to do—create a god (341, 300, 302). What life brings to the risk-taker who accepts suffering will often have the character of an obstinate necessity. So one must learn the art of negating by simply stepping aside, or looking away (321, 276). Then one will perforce be emulating the cunning, the patience, and the agility of those gardeners and performers who know how to shape accident, error, and vagueness into a single ruling taste and aesthetic pattern (303, 290, 299). Even the "ugly" may be "reinterpreted and made sublime" (290). Are there limits to the powers of art to transmute the negative into something that provokes a "yes"? In "Sanctus Januarius" Nietzsche's narrator does not try to pose those limits.

That in view of which this ethos is practiced and its central mythos: the self is promised or asked "to become the being that you are." In that way people can become "human beings who are new, unique, incomparable, who give themselves laws, who create themselves"(335). This ethos justifies suffering and makes Zarathustra a hero and teacher (338, 342). In places in "Sanctus Januarius," and in the letters to friends in 1882, Nietzsche seems to assert the weak sense of this idea, whereby a process of personal development allows one to uncover or grow toward the "being" which one already, at some deeper level, is. But as Rodolphe Gasché's reading of *Ecce Homo* demonstrates, "becoming the being that you are" cannot mean a development toward either a fixed being or a perpetual being of becoming.[13] Instead Nietzsche develops a particular mythos for expressing the person's life in chance, in expenditure, in the singular as that which is both painful and beautiful, but which can also be affirmed: the idea and image of the eternal return of the same (341).

By comparison with the transience usually associated with feelings,

13. See Gasché, "Autobiography as *Gestalt*."

Nietzsche's ethos of aesthetic affirmation is supposed to be something stabilizing. But Nietzsche's privileging of the single, unique, and accidental creates a kind of instability at the heart of this ethos which will express itself when he tries to put it to practical use in 1882. Perhaps this tension between cohesion and dispersion explains why Nietzsche himself resists arranging this ethos into a coherent essay, and instead merely suggests what can be constructed (as I have) by the interpreting reader in the interstices of the text. This is also why the most recent tendency of Nietzsche criticism, a detailed and scrupulous reading of his texts in terms of the plurality of their styles and voices, is a valuable corrective to the longstanding tendency to make Nietzsche's writings into some sort of system.

To show how this ethos for aesthetic affirmation emerges in "Sanctus Januarius," how it is woven into and spun out of particular moments of "experience" we find staged, "lived," and reflected there—so that we can go on to take account of what in its very enunciation will make the attempt to live this ethos most problematic—let us look at the somewhat self-contained triptych of texts at the book's opening. The first, "For the New Year," expresses the wish to learn to love fate as that which is beautiful; the second, "Personal Providence," describes the ways and the reasons that single, apparently random events become that which "cannot be missing" from our lives; and the third, "The Thought of Death," affirms the value of life against the all-too-certain claims of death. These texts are typical of many others in *The Gay Science* in several obvious ways. In the foreground there is a rhetorically adept, but very engaging narrator, who opens a meditation which advances in several different registers. First, he asserts the "thisness" and immediacy of a contemplative space that makes the reader a participant in the experiential matrix which supports and delivers the meditation; second, he carries forward a meditation upon some general conceptual question by writing in relation (sometimes in the mode of parodic inversion, sometimes in the mode of affirmation and emulation) to some explicitly invoked, or subtly implied text of the Western tradition; finally, through the act of enunciation, the narrator seeks to define an ethos for living which will make Nietzsche's aphorism exemplary. A critical reading of these aphorisms will allow us to investigate the grounding assumptions of the ethos of aesthetic affirmation. These include the newness and singularity of what is being valued; the coherence of the self implicitly affirmed so that this ethos can be expressed; the hierarchical valuation that chooses affirmation over negation; and the dubieties of the conscious will presumed to be operating within the self who constructs the wish to affirm the new as beautiful.

"For the New Year" is about one of the happiest, but most problematic, moments of life: the act of beginning, wishing, and intending—of making pledges and promises to ourselves for the future. Nietzsche presents this moment in the margins of the text of Descartes, the philosopher who argued most cogently for the presence and authority of an autonomous faculty of consciousness in humans. Nietzsche's revision of Descartes's text, in the first sentence of "For the New Year," shifts the grounds for this act in a most fundamental way. Here is the whole text of "For the New Year:"

276

For the New Year.—I still live, I still think: I still have to live, I still have to think. *Sum, ergo cogito: cogito, ergo sum.* Today everybody permits himself the expression of his wish and his dearest thought; hence I, too, shall say what it is that I wish from myself today, and what was the first thought to run across my heart this year—what thought shall be for me the ground, security, and sweetness of my life henceforth. I want to learn more and more to see as beautiful what is necessary in things; then I shall be one of those who make things beautiful. *Amor fati*: let that be my love henceforth! I do not want to wage war against what is ugly. I do not want to accuse; I do not even want to accuse those who accuse. *Looking away* shall be my only negation. And all in all on the whole: some day I wish to be only a Yes-sayer. [Translation modified]

How does Nietzsche rewrite Descartes? In the Second Meditation, Descartes attempts to define the essential being of man. As he sits before the fire in his room, Descartes names all the ways he knows a particular piece of wax—through its color, shape, fragrance, and so on. But in a moment he must reject the idea that the being of the wax inheres in any or all of these things—for the wax melts and changes all its qualities, which now appear only accidental and inessential. On further reflection Descartes rejects the concept of body or extension as the ground for the being of the wax. He does so because the mind cannot grasp the infinity of possible forms the wax might take. Having cast the senses under suspicion and rejected any concept of being independent of the cogito, Descartes proceeds, in analogous fashion, to strip away all the accidental, external, physical qualities of a particular human life: name, family, history, body, temperament, and so forth. The only certain ground of a man's being is his ability to think. This single certitude justifies Descartes's celebrated formula in the fourth part of *The Discourse on Method:*

cogito ergo sum, "I think, therefore I am." For Descartes this is the kernel of the truly human—thought, consciousness, and most especially self-consciousness (that is, being conscious of being conscious). This discovery in philosophy is an early episode in the continuing saga of what Nietzsche calls in *The Will to Power*, the human tendency toward the "absurd overestimation of consciousness" (*WP*, 529).

In "For the New Year" Nietzsche rewrites Descartes in a very precise way. He begins the text, "I still live, I still think." These words do not point to an origin of living or thinking. Both have been going on for some time, and are continuing now. Notice the order: Life comes before thought, because, as Nietzsche argues in "Truth and Lie in an Extra-Moral Sense," consciousness is "not concerned with any further mission transcending the sphere of human life. No, it is purely human and none but its owner and procreator regards it so pathetically as to suppose the whole world revolves around it."[14] But notice that here, in "For the New Year," Nietzsche does not separate thought from life: thought comes right along with life. So for Nietzsche there is no preverbal ultra-real self some psychologists suppose exists. Then Nietzsche writes, "I still have to live, I still have to think." Life and thought are not chosen or willed—each is part of necessity, that which human life necessarily is. Now Nietzsche is ready to offer us the Cartesian formula, but he does it backward and then forward so as to put being before thought, and then creates a circle that leaves the two hopelessly intertwined. *Sum, ergo cogito: cogito, ergo sum.* Thought has grown out of life instead of having a pure autonomous epistemological or ontological value. And now we can notice that the setting Nietzsche creates for his citation of Descartes has shifted the terms of Descartes's meditation—not "being" but "living" (*Leben*) has been played off against thinking. This small but important shift reflects the way Nietzsche situates being in *The Will to Power* and elsewhere. The idea of "being" is an attempt to hypostatize and eternalize a life which is mobile, energetic, and transient. In this abstract way, man affirms his own feelings of power and self-certainty. He does so with a certain metaphor, uncovered by Nietzsche when he points to the etymological grounding of the Latin *esse*, "to be," in "to breathe." This origin shows that the notion of a universal idea of being is merely a metaphoric and anthropomorphic projection of human beings' way of living—by breathing—onto everything else.[15]

14. See *The Philosophy of Nietzsche*, ed. Geoffrey Clive (New York: New American Library, 1965) 503–15.

15. See Nietzsche, *Philosophy in the Tragic Age of the Greeks*, trans. Marianne Cowan (Chicago: Regnery, 1962), 84.

Descartes and Nietzsche move in opposite directions to locate the person. Descartes's meditation strips away every accidental exterior quality from the person. This allows Descartes to focus down and in toward that pure faculty of conscious will whose vectoral act of self-reflection founds the cogito. By contrast, Nietzsche's meditation begins with a most proximate and immediate thought ("I still live"), embeds that thought in the obscure fortuities of a certain time and place (Genoa, January 1882), and moves up and out of the space of self-reflection toward an ethos of engagement with all that is other and outside the self: the necessary, the beautiful, and that which one must avoid negating. In analogous fashion it is the singularity of Descartes's thought—*cogito ergo sum*—which allows it to be the philosophic act that secures a ground of being for the person. But for Nietzsche, because his single wish is not a thought of the self focused on the self thinking, this wish implies a multitude of past and future conditions and desires. I will try to demonstrate why this is so.

Having situated the speaking subject, Nietzsche risks his wish, a wish that is unusual because it brings together two things not usually conjoined: desire and necessity. Usually we desire the unusual, the fugitive, the perfect. Instead Nietzsche wishes to love the fateful and necessary. Of course this has always been the position of the wise man who welcomes the necessary negative moments of life—for instance, death. But we shall see that Nietzsche blocks this gesture as a negation of life, as an escape into a metaphysical antiworldly world. How do we "love fate"? This conjunction of love and necessity is presented as an arduous achievement. Like every New Year's wish, it stirs powerful resistances in the heart. But Nietzsche makes "yes-saying" seem possible by the way he stages his wish. First he describes this thought as "the first thought to run across my heart this year." The wish appears like a crystal entering a supersaturated solution—capable of reorganizing a life susceptible to this first (*zuerst*) thought. It is the firstness and newness of this thought which allows it to appear as the "thought [which] shall be for me the ground, security, and sweetness of my life henceforth."

How could a "first thought" have the initiatory power Nietzsche seems to confer on it? After all, even coming on the first day of the new year, doesn't this thought cross a mind with a mix of conscious and unconscious drives and a host of memories from every earlier year of life? A partial answer to this question comes at the beginning of the second essay of *The Genealogy of Morals*, where Nietzsche describes the difficult beginnings of memory in man, and the astonishing development of the "right to make promises." Memory and

[137]

promises have to fight against what is more primary in man, "forget-fulness . . . an active and in the strictest sense positive faculty of repression . . . [it gives us] a little quietness, a little *tabula rasa* of the consciousness, to make room for new things . . . active forgetful-ness . . . is like a doorkeeper, a preserver of psychic order, repose and etiquette . . . there could be no happiness, no cheerfulness, no hope, no pride, no *present*, without forgetfulness" (*BWN:GM*,II,1, 493–94).

Read in light of this passage, the new beginning Nietzsche repre-sents in "For the New Year" should not be construed as an originary moment of self-creation. Instead this moment *appears* to us as a be-ginning precisely because it does not come about simply through an act of conscious will. For how could we will to forget, without re-membering what we are trying to forget? Instead we are aided in be-ginning anew through the operation of an involuntary and largely unconscious faculty of forgetfulness. This forgetting (or repression) creates the condition for the possibility of the new thought, wish, and beginning, the new and renewing thought for the new year. This unconscious process supports and undergirds, in ways which cannot be calibrated or controlled, the more conscious artistic shap-ing the narrator advocates here: "looking away" as one's only nega-tion and learning to "make things beautiful." All are necessary for Nietzsche's coming meeting with Lou Salomé, and the newness of both his love and her beauty.

"For the New Year" makes its readers conscious of how he or she confronts the future. But every new venture implies a reflection on what the self has been. The next section of *The Gay Science* turns us toward the past so that an explicit meditation upon chance becomes an urgent matter. Here Nietzsche reports a surprising experience common to most of us: many of the things which happen in our lives—even the most trivial or painful—take on an appearance or pattern which creates a strong intuitive sense that they mean some-thing and have value. Much of the coherence of personal experience and the self as the locus of that experience emerges from this sense of meaning and value. Nietzsche's use of the word "providence" in the title invokes the Christian idea of providence; and his whole text imitates the meditation form used for centuries by Catholics and Protestants to bring their lives into alignment with God's providen-tial design. The Christian meditation begins with an earnest and of-ten troubled reflection upon the events and feelings of the personal life. In the course of the meditation, the chaotic facts of individual experience yield to an intuition of God's presence. By opening up to this powerful "other" beyond the self, the speaker of the meditation finds himself/herself transformed from a refractory spirit of rebellion into one in peaceful reconciliation with God's providential design. Nietzsche's text blocks any belief in divine providence; but he parodies religious meditation so as to report an analogous experience in a much more secular key. Here is the whole passage, preserving the absence of paragraph division and the sentence breaks of the German original:

277

Personal providence.—There is a certain high point in life: once we have reached that, we are, for all our freedom, once more in the greatest danger of spiritual unfreedom, and no matter how much we have faced up to the beautiful chaos of existence and *denied it all providential reason and goodness, we still have to pass our hardest test.* For it is only now that the idea of a personal providence confronts us with the most penetrating force, and the best advocate, the evidence of our eyes, speaks for it—now that we can see how palpably always everything that happens to us turns out for the best. Every day and every hour, life seems to have no other wish than to prove this proposition again and again. Whatever it is, bad weather or good, the loss of a friend, sickness, slander, the failure of some letter to arrive, the spraining of an ankle, a glance into a shop, a counterargument, the opening of a book, a dream, a fraud—either immediately or very soon after it proves to be something that "must not be missing"; it has a profound significance and use precisely for *us.* Is there any more dangerous seduction that might tempt one to renounce one's faith in the gods of Epicurus who have no care and are unknown, and to believe instead in some petty deity who is full of care and personally knows every little hair on our head and finds nothing nauseous in the most miserable small service? Well, I think that in spite of all this we should leave the gods in peace as well as the genii who are ready to serve us, and rest content with the supposition that our own practical and theoretical skill in interpreting and arranging events has now reached its high point. Nor should we conceive too high an opinion of this dexterity of our wisdom when at times we are excessively surprised by the wonderful harmony created by the playing of our instrument—a harmony that sounds too good for us to dare to give the credit to ourselves. Indeed, now and then someone plays with us—dear chance; now and then chance guides our hand, and the wisest providence could not think up a more beautiful music than that which our foolish hand produces then. [My emphasis; translation modified]

In both Nietzsche's text and a Christian meditation, a certain experience is described in a testimonial style: apparently arbitrary or random events in life are incorporated into a pattern that makes them seem necessary. This is a moment of danger and vulnerability—a "high point in life"—appropriate to a meditation where the Christian will seek to assimilate his position to God's design; it is also appropriate to any effort—the philosophic or scientific one, for example—to look down on things and know them as they are. This moment is "high" in the sense of lofty and important; but Nietzsche's text indicates that it is also capable of making one "high" in the sense of giddy, dizzy, and susceptible to a fall. Thus Nietzsche narrates the scene as a temptation or seduction—as when Satan appears to Christ, takes him to a great height, and offers him domination of the kingdoms of the world if he will be of Satan's party. What is the temptation here, the "test" we all have to pass? It is that sense we have that once something happens, it "must not be missing"; "it has a profound significance and use precisely for *us*." This feeling could tempt us into belief in the Christian God. But Nietzsche dismisses that possibility by deflating the high seriousness of his own meditation with some mockery of the anxious and "petty" deity that would not be nauseated in personally concerning himself with every hair on our head (a slight to the praise of the scope of God's concern in the Gospel according to Matthew). Instead of recourse to some higher deity for explanation, Nietzsche suggests that his experience is the effect of something else at a high point—"our own practical and theoretical skill in interpreting and arranging events." But there is more. For when the harmony of events just sounds too good, Nietzsche suggests that someone plays with us, "dear chance" (*liebe Zufall*). What does this mean?

We can approach an answer by focusing attention on the series of personal experiences which provides the point of departure for Nietzsche's meditation. The narrator presents this series so that it has special immediacy: it comes "now," articulating a dramatic present for the text; the idea "confronts us" with a "penetrating force" (or "urgent authority," *eindringlichsten Gewalt*); and last this idea has its "best advocate" in our eyes and our hands. What is it that makes this idea come across so directly and forcefully, in such a way that one believes in personal providence, and the reality of the "person" and his/her "personal" life? Just a simple series one could find in any life, consisting of a glance, the opening of a book, a dream, and so on. This series has a triple character: (1) It appears to be random in nature. It is not ordered according to any apparent logic. In fact it seems to be ordered against logic. Thus these events exist in every possible register: they are great and small, good and bad, social and private and physical. (2) The series has density. This is so not because it includes objects (like bad weather or the opening of a book). Rather all the elements in the series *appear* as objects to the reader because they are arranged in the form of a series. The result is that each thing that happens looks solitary, immobile, mute, resistant to interpretation and turned in on itself. (3) Last, this series has a pronounced aesthetic quality. The scattering of detailed random events creates a texture to daily life. Its elements become part of a provisional aesthetic unity—one's life—so they "must not be missing." Their muteness and eccentricity are poised opposite the individual person and have meaning precisely for him. And like all art, this series casts a mantle of value and celebration over what it adorns. Daily life acquires a poetic quality. For this reason, chance events are converted into events that seem necessary and have "significance and use precisely for *us*." Now these events seem inevitable. What finally emerges from the series is an unexpected harmony—a condition in which many different elements sound well together. The chance series has become music.

The first five sentences of "Personal Providence" make use of a skeptical critique of Christian providence so as to create a symmetrical argument. It is not anything *outside* the individual—like God—which brings a sense of personal providence; it is the individual's own internal "skill in interpreting" that does so. Personal providence is an effect of interpretation. But the last two sentences of the text throw this argument into an important asymmetry. Nietzsche introduces a metaphor for the individual's activity—this interpretation is like the dexterity (*Fingerfertigkeit*) used in playing music on an instrument. Then he insists that we sometimes produce a surprisingly wonderful harmony, a music which is just too good to allow us to take all the credit. This excess or remainder which cannot be accounted for leads to a new formulation. It is neither something outside, "God," nor simply inside, our own interpretation, which produces personal providence; it is both our own skill in interpreting and something outside—chance—and the mysterious interplay and collaboration between them which produces an aesthetic moment of surprising harmony. Personal Providence, like music, has harmonized diverse elements into a provisional unity that allows us to step back and, looking at our personal life, say yes, it's good, we've got it right, how provident!

It is important to see what Nietzsche's text does here. "Personal Providence" seems to tell us how the events of life become proper and provident for the person, a personal life, a self. But the text does this by opening a performative space which exceeds the self and person in important ways. There the self comes up against a chanciness, material otherness, and aesthetic praxis that displace the self away from the conditions of control, knowledge, and self-consciousness which have been the hallmarks of the self in traditional philosophy, and were the focus of critique in "For the New Year." Instead, the "person" emerges through an uncontrollable interplay between what is inside the mind (interpretation) and outside the mind (chance), the ideational (one's mind works) and the material (but so do one's hands), the voluntary and conscious (one wants and schemes to make it right) and the involuntary and unconscious (but it only becomes "right" when an enigmatic partner, Chance, plays with us, and guides our "foolish hand"). What results is paradoxically more beautiful than the wisest providence could produce; and the "person" performing who knows personal providence, who performs this providence, is now no one, no single self but a performer that is a function of the fore-effects and aftereffects of a performance that can no longer be said to be his/hers. This performance is without actor, script, director, or audience—more a happening than a performance; it wins the person an ironic moment of knowledge. In "performance" the person knows the personal life as real and provident, at the very moment that life touches, participates in, something "other"—impersonal patterns which are beyond (his/her) control or understanding: the movement of hands and eyes, the play of chance and interpretation.

There is another way of saying this. Nietzsche's text seems to demonstrate the special effect of personal providence: how it may be possible that a random series is shaped into a personal life, a person, a self. But because this text describes personal life as made out of a chance series of elements, it opens up a more aberrant and opposing possibility. Since the series is not ordered by a relation to some end or goal or by the logic of cause and effect and since, like every series, it moves through time, both the future and the past, in a chance and indefinite way, one can project this hypothetical possibility: If the series which Nietzsche postulates were extrapolated backward indefinitely, then the "person" of the personal life would spin apart, and there would be no subject—the narrator's, Nietzsche's, or the reader's (all of which Nietzsche assumes so as to write this text)—no subject to incorporate random elements into a personal providence. This is the final irony of Nietzsche's text, an irony upon which it would be easy to construct a Borgesian parable about the radically fictive quality of selfhood. For here the dispersal of the subject is latent in the randomness of the very series Nietzsche uses to present the experience of personal life as cohesive and provident.

Personal providence makes chance appear as enhancing to life. It is the kind of overarching interpretation of the events of 1882 which will seem most appropriate when Nietzsche meets and falls in love with Lou Salomé, and then calls this meeting a "dear chance" (*liebe Zufall*). But chance, by the singleness and suddenness of its operation, and the obscurity of its happening, can also be violent and negating. If "Personal Providence" makes the person a byproduct of a chancy life performance, then death is the thought of the performance's punctual termination. When the performance is gone, there is no person. This idea of the person-as-nothing in death is implicit in "Personal Providence." It becomes the problem Nietzsche takes up in the next section of *The Gay Science*, "The Thought of Death."

In "The Thought of Death" Nietzsche announces the impossibility of thinking death the way traditional wisdom literature does—as the standpoint for an indictment of human desire. Here is the whole text:

278

The thought of death.—Living in the midst of this jumble of little lanes, needs, and voices gives me a melancholy happiness: how much enjoyment, impatience, and desire, how much thirsty life and drunkenness of life comes to light every moment! And yet silence will soon descend on all these noisy, living, life-thirsty people. How his shadow stands even now behind everyone, as his dark fellow traveler! It is always like the last moment before the departure of an emigrants' ship: people have more to say to each other than ever, the hour is late, and the ocean and its desolate silence are waiting impatiently behind all of this noise—so covetous and certain of their prey. And all and everyone of them suppose that the heretofore was little or nothing while the near future is everything; and that is the reason for all of this haste, this clamor, this outshouting and overreaching each other. Everyone wants to be the first in this future—and yet death and deathly silence alone are certain and common to all in this future. How strange it is that this sole certainty and common element makes almost no impression on people, and that nothing is further from their minds than the feeling that they form a brotherhood of death. It makes me happy that men do not want at all to think the thought of death! I should like very much to do something that would make the thought of life even a hundred times more appealing to them.

This text reverses the rhetorical stance of wisdom literature; according to which the sage, warning of death, speaks the truth of

spirit and eternity against the illusory claims of the transient pleasures of life. Like that sage, Nietzsche writes his text at the intersection of desire and death, and his emigrants' ship recalls the passage
of the dead to Hades across the River Styx and the ways this image
enters Christian iconography, as in Michelangelo's depiction of the
Last Judgment. But Nietzsche does not invite us to realize our peril-
ous proximity to death and repent our ways. Instead this text leaves
the reader strangely suspended with his/her desire. The traditional
image of a ship of transitional passage has been displaced. There is
no "other shore" to which this emigrants' ship will surely pass. It
seeks passage to the new world, but its actual destination is indefinite. Also, Nietzsche does not identify with death as the end of
life—either as valuable goal or necessary terminus. Instead death
appears as one of the three Fates: Death is the one who cuts the
threads of life. Her name is Atropos, because death is what cannot
be "troped": death cannot be figured (that is, represented); death
cannot be finessed (that is, gotten round). And yet, though we cannot know death direct, we still know of its coming, we can (and
must) experience the *thought* of death. Nietzsche's text unfolds
within the ambiguities of the person's relationship and nonrelation-
ship with death.

This text places us in an ironic position, watching the person and
his desire confront death through this series of antitheses: life's
noise and death's silence; "everyone" and his "dark fellow traveler"
(death); the emigrants and the ocean; the desire for future and its
grim certainty; and the speaker's initial response to this spectacle:
"melancholy happiness." This stark opposition between the claims of
life and the fact of death generates the central irony enunciated by
this text: "Everyone wants to be the first in this future—and yet
death and deathly silence alone are certain and common to all in this
future." Nietzsche's text presents this irony as inescapable. It is not
something wisdom would allow one to overcome; rather life as
desire is founded upon it. Since a person cannot know or master
death, one is for the most part blind to death. It may be "strange"
but it is entirely appropriate that death "makes almost no impression
on people." Death is the (impossible) limit of personal life. Since the
person ceases to exist at death, it is impossible for the person as person to be present to death.

If "The Thought of Death" opposes life, noise, emigrants, and ignorance to death, silence, the ocean, and knowledge, where does
Nietzsche's speaker place himself vis-à-vis this scene? At first it may
seem as if, as the silent observer of the scene he describes and as one

who carries the truth of certain death, Nietzsche, like the wise men of all the ages, must be aligned with death and knowledge. But he carries no wisdom or truth with which to speak about death. And he is not silent. Instead he repeats the position of naive desire and joins his text to the crescendo of noisy, life-thirsty people who offer this vulgar human spectacle and performance. Here the performance means carrying life on in a happy, blind role entailing naive desire, participation in the physical, with the body exposed to chance death. Here "death" should be written with a capital D; it is figured as the murderous crouching element and monster that awaits us: "the ocean and its desolate silence are waiting impatiently behind all of this noise—so covetous and certain of their prey." To counterbalance this grim Death, Nietzsche's speaker celebrates an energetic vitalistic will to Life. The whole text seems to counsel an eager participation in Life and a willing blindness to Death; for otherwise the thought of Death could become a silencing silence within humans. The speaker ends by choosing between these two symmetrical alternatives—Life and Death—and stating his intention to make Life more appealing.

But there is something wrong with all this. Can one really choose between Life and Death? And if doing so entails a blindness to Death, how is Neitzsche's speaker to efface the awareness of death his words so clearly evince? The text goes through several positions on life and death. First there is a covert rejection of the tendency of wisdom literature to denigrate life by speaking from the position of death. Then Nietzsche's speaker engages in a naive affirmation of Life over Death. But the language of this text takes us much further, dissolving the metaphysical categories of Life and Death as pure symmetrical opposites figuring Presence and Absence. Instead, life (with a small l) and death (with a small d) come into a subtle and essential relationship to each other. Death is not some hostile devouring "other," and life is not a vitalistic energy flowing from a self-identical subject, who is living life on a splendid, if temporary, dispensation from death. Now life subsists in death, death in life, so the thought of death is drawn into an economy of life. This is most explicit in the double quality of the last moment (*letzten Augenblicke*) before the departure of the emigrants' ship: on the one hand, this is a moment when desire and expectation reach a crescendo; those embarking are actually beginning a journey; the moment also figures something more uncertain—the beginning of the desired life in a new world. On the other hand, it is an ending for an old life, a time for partings and departure, which prefigures the final parting

[145]

brought by death. The moment of embarkation is paradigmatic, because it brings to the fore something which subtends every moment of human experience: one simply cannot choose between life and death, for they are copresent in each instant and constitutive of each other. Life stands in our foreground, but death stands just behind.

This text offers two striking ways of figuring the relationship between life and death. Death stands behind us like our shadow (*Schatten*), and this simile is most suggestive because the shadow is a "likeness" of the self, but it is also nothing; it is dark (as death), but only happens in the light (of life). In an analogous fashion the silence this text repeatedly links with death is not the antipodal opposite of the noisy, shouting, life-thirsty people Nietzsche's narrator celebrates. Just as all sound must be framed by some silence so as to be heard at all, so the silent thought of death is a necessary supplement to life and its noisy voices. But neither death nor its thought can be recuperated by life: death is not negated, abstracted, and rendered a mute partner of life. In this scheme, death as a thought is never really absent or forgotten—it lurks in a contrapuntal way in the silences and shadows. Death is half-there, half-heard, half-acknowledged. It shadows us just as our own shadow does, just as silence shadows our voice.

We are not in a position to generalize about the compositional process working in this triptych of texts. While some definitions of art will emphasize its impersonal objectivity as an end in itself, here Nietzsche turns life into art, by taking banal and ordinary fragments of personal experience—a new year's wish, a random sequence of incidents, the departure of an emigrants' ship—and turning them into moments with a strongly aesthetic character. Over the course of his reflection upon each fragment of experience, Nietzsche's narrator encounters a horizon of resistance, with something beckoning and dangerous, which he can finally judge to be both valuable and beautiful. The construction of an aesthetic moment begins with an encounter of two terms that become a potential challenge and refutation of each other: In "For the New Year," necessity and the beautiful, in "Personal Providence," the person and "dear chance," in "The Thought of Death," life and death. The interaction of these terms weaves the fabric of personal experience as discrete moments with a strongly aesthetic character. But we might ask: what brings these disparate terms into a new relation? What grounds and generates this experience? It would be tempting to say, "Nietzsche does." Even if we leave aside the question of what Nietzsche-as-author might be, his texts always seem to have a witty, lively, and ironic narrator who enjoys exercising rhetorical and conceptual control. In fact this is the chief seduction and duplicity of the Nietzschean text. But the language of each passage complicates the position of the narrator. Each text engages a trope that has contradictory and not completely predictable effects: it offers support to the position of the narrator, but it also puts the authority of that position into question. Thus in "For the New Year" Nietzsche uses synecdoche to rebegin his life: he takes the "first thought to run across [his] heart" to stand for all the thoughts, conscious and unconscious, which may have traversed his mind at that moment. Synecdoche allows him to posit a new origin for his life. In "Personal Providence" the narrator uses the series to project the unexpected purposefulness and beauty of the events of life. The series enables Nietzsche to adumbrate an intuitive teleology and end-directedness (as an aesthetic effect) at the very moment that a divine teleology is discounted. Finally, in "The Thought of Death" the trope of antithesis is used to reverse the wise man's condemnation of Life from the standpoint of Death. Nietzsche's narrator asserts a new hierarchy and valuation of Life over Death. The three metaphysical categories engaged by the representation of Nietzsche's narrator—the origin, teleology, and the instituted hierarchy—help to suppress chance and randomness. To put it simply, if life could proceed from a pure origin to a fore-seeable (that is, "pro-vident") end, under the guidance of a hierarchy of forces and values, then man would be exempt from the vagaries and violence of chance. This freedom from chance would vindicate the will of the artistic subject which seems to speak, in the mode of aesthetic affirmation, behind each of these texts.

But our readings have shown the equivocal and multiple effects of a troping process in each text of this triptych. Thus in "For the New Year," what appears as an origin—with the newness and glow of all beginnings—is made possible by the synecdoche which posits the "part" as its beginning, but cannot entirely forget or leave behind the "whole" of past life. Nor can this new year's thought fail to carry the negative as a resistant nondialectical moment of its positive yes-saying movement. Remember, it is only "some day" that the narrator can hope to be only a Yes-sayer. And, in a similar way, what appears in "Personal Providence" as a teleological progression—events leading properly to some meaningful if undefined end—is put in question by the arbitrariness and potential randomness of the series. Finally, we have seen how the antithesis which organizes "The Thought of Death" into an ironic opposition of life and death triggers a valuable figural interplay between voice and silence, light and shadow, and life and death. In this way antithesis undoes the naive hierarchical valuation of Life over Death proclaimed by the narrator.

The Climax of the Aesthetic Moment
in "Vita Femina"

When the Lou Salomé episode is kept in the background of one's reading of "Sanctus Januarius," its texts still read as systematic statements on a range of philosophic issues, but they also double as a matrix for living. But in both the letters to friends in 1882 and "Sanctus Januarius," ideas which are quite commonplace in themselves can be organized into a moment of mastery, epiphany, and a freedom above life, by the fact of the reader's or writer's participation in an aesthetic moment. This dependency of conceptual assertion upon the aesthetic helps explain Nietzsche's glowing tributes to art throughout *The Gay Science* and his other texts (*GS*, 60, 107). Art is Nietzsche's engine of ascent; but it is precisely this glorification of art which becomes most treacherous for Nietzsche in 1882. Almost every section of "Sanctus Januarius" is organized around a redeeming aesthetic moment, which is enthralling because it enhances life, but also seductive because it invites us to suspend our inclination to criticism. One of the last sections of "Sanctus Januarius" is entitled "Vita Femina," Latin for "life is a woman." No section of the text more completely prefigures the abandon—at once ecstatic and aesthetic—with which Nietzsche will throw himself into his love for Lou Salomé. But this text also makes possible a self-reflection upon the linguistic resources used to produce the aesthetic moment. A close reading of "Vita Femina" will allow me to probe the conceptual underpinnings of the ethos for aesthetic affirmation devised in "Sanctus Januarius" and applied in the experiences of 1882.

In "Vita Femina" Nietzsche proposes to name the way we can fulfill our desire to see the "ultimate beauties of a work." But beyond this, "Vita Femina" offers a glimpse of the special conditions under which this kind of affirmative moment happens. Here is the whole text:

339

Vita femina.—For seeing the ultimate beauties of a work, no knowledge or good will is sufficient; this requires the rarest of lucky accidents: The clouds that veil these peaks have to lift for once so that we see them glowing in the sun. Not only do we have to stand in precisely the right spot in order to see this, but the unveiling must have been accomplished by our own soul because it needed some external expression and likeness, as if it were a matter of having something to hold on to and retain control of itself. But it is so rare for all of this to coincide that I am inclined to believe that the highest peaks of everything good, whether it be a work, a deed, humanity, or nature, have so far remained concealed and veiled from the great majority and even from the best human beings. But what does unveil itself for us, *unveils itself for us once only.* The Greeks, to be sure, prayed: "Everything beautiful twice and even three times!" They implored the gods with good reason, for ungodly reality gives us the beautiful either not at all or once only. I mean to say that the world is overfull of beautiful things but nevertheless poor, very poor when it comes to beautiful moments and unveilings of these things. But perhaps this is the most powerful magic of life: it is covered by a veil interwoven with gold, a veil of beautiful possibilities, sparkling with promise, resistance, bashfulness, mockery, pity, and seduction. Yes, life is a woman. [Translation modified]

This text is organized by three discrete movements, each provoking a certain question. First Nietzsche stages the moment of beauty. How and why does this beautiful moment come? Then a series of qualifications seem to withdraw the possibility of this moment: it is "rare for all of this to coincide": it comes once only; the Greeks prayed for more, but though the world is full of beautiful things, it is poor in beautiful moments. Why is this moment withdrawn as an actual likelihood just after its enactment? Why should it come just once? Finally the beautiful moment of unveiling is inscribed as a remote possibility behind the image of life as a woman, where the veil that ensures desire now seems necessary and inevitable. Why is the beautiful moment withdrawn behind the veil of a woman? A lot is at stake in these questions, because whatever this beautiful moment is, its process seems to undergird the valuable chance-laden moments of personal experience represented throughout *The Gay Science.*

The moment of seeing the ultimate beauties of a work cannot be brought on by a controlling ego, even if it uses all its will and knowledge. Nor is it simply a property of the object we see. This text challenges the idea that we, dwelling in our consciousness, look out "there" for the beautiful so as to accede to the beautiful moment. This assumption of everyday experience is cast under suspicion by "Vita Femina." Coming from neither the ego, nor the "other" we see, this moment must be the "rarest of lucky accidents" (*glücklichen*

Zufälle). The metaphor for such an accident presents the moment of beauty so that it *appears* a random coincidence. The movement in time and space of the observer, the cloud-veils, and the sun in relation to the mountains must so coincide that we receive a singular and momentary glimpse of the mountains unveiled. Not while we are elsewhere, nor while we are looking elsewhere, but while we are exactly here, with our eyes and mind fixed on these mountain peaks, does the cloud-veil lift so we may see them glowing in the sun.

By looking at the language used to stage the moment of beauty, we may decipher this moment's deeper meaning. Here a metaphoric chain is used to represent the ultimate moment of beauty. First there is the "external" event: cloud-veils lift to expose peaks glowing in the sun. This image is spare, so it seems like an unmediated fact: it simply seems to be there. The second clause begins to describe the proper conditions for "us" to experience this sight—"we" must stand in just the right spot. This clause moves us closer to the person and his vision, and therefore is the first marking of an inside (person)/outside (mountain) boundary. But this second clause is introduced with the words "not only"; standing in the right spot turns out to be an initial proviso. For this external unveiling must have been already doubled by the soul's having pulled the veil from itself. This act of our soul is said to coincide with a need to find some outer expression and likeness (*Ausdruckes und Gleichnisses*) which would be external to itself because it would be in language. Let us retrace these steps. The first clause appears as fundamentally external, and the second inside (and personal) in relation to the first, but external as a positioning of the person before the mountains in time and space in relation to the third clause, where the soul's unveiling is inside in a most emphatic psychological way. Then the fourth clause attributes a logic or motivation to this psychic unveiling—the need to find an outer expression or likeness for itself. (The German word for "expression"—*Ausdruckes*—implies a verbal or linguistic expression.) This need may lead to an inner unveiling, but it also leads to seeing the outer unveiling as an expression of the psyche. At this point in the progression of clauses there is a profound confusion of inside and outside, person and "other," language and event, as the scene of the cloud-veil lifting in the first clause is inscribed in the soul by the soul's doubling of that act, and the person is caught up in the use of expression and likeness which represents that (double) event with the outerness of language. All this activity is given further explanation in the last two clauses: it happens as a way to find an external stay or hold so the self can keep a separate independence for itself. Some clauses of this sentence could be interpreted differently as to whether they focus on the inside and psychic or the outside and natural. The "likeness" (*Gleichnisses*), as a troping event and relation, defies this distinction by being both inside and outside to different terms of this scene: inside in terms of the sun on the mountain, outside in terms of the cogito. The language of this sentence performs the moment of beauty as a moment of likeness between nature and person; and this moment is a kind of double unveiling, precipitated by a double troping which appears radically coincidental.

In his article "Sign and Symbol in Hegel's *Aesthetics*," Paul de Man suggests what conceptual presuppositions structure the aesthetic in general and this kind of moment in particular. First, behind this event there is a subject using language, deploying what Hegel calls "the greatness of the sign." Unlike the symbol, which is proximate and enslaved to the object it represents, the sign, by forging an arbitrary relationship between form and meaning, uses the world with independence, freedom, and violence. This use of language allows the subject to subordinate the "other" it represents (here "the ultimate beauties of a work") through a process of interiorization which it effects and then disowns, by an appeal to a quality said to inhere in the aesthetic object ("beauty"). De Man writes: "The commanding metaphor that organizes this entire system is that of interiorization, the understanding of aesthetic beauty as the external manifestation of an ideal content which is itself an interiorized experience, the recollected emotion of a bygone perception. The sensory manifestation (*sinnliches Scheinen*) of art and literature is the outside of an inner content which is itself an outer event or entity that has been internalized." It is this inner-ing—*Erinnerung*—which in the aesthetic brings history and beauty together.[16]

This analysis suggests the way one stratum of this text engages the metaphysics of the aesthetic. When the aesthetic moment becomes the model for a relationship between the person and another, when in other words Salomé becomes for Nietzsche the one who figures "Life" as a woman, this aesthetic moment creates a sense of an effortless internalization of the "other," which puts the "other," as genuinely other, out of play. Stanley Corngold writes vividly about this illusion: Nietzsche "is aiming to create an aesthetic mode in which the world may appear as already interpreted, already mas-

---

16. See "Sign and Symbol in Hegel's *Aesthetics*," *Critical Inquiry*, 8 (Summer 1982), 771.

tered."[17] Of course, this effortless coinciding of self and other is one of the central illusions of love. From the vantage point of our analysis of "Vita Femina," Nietzsche's repeated use of the word "likeness" in the correspondence to describe his fundamental similarity with Lou becomes problematic. In both the letters and "Vita Femina," Nietzsche's own will to interpret, master, and subordinate the other is occulted by an appeal to the quality of the moment lived and the object seen: its "beauty." Later, when Nietzsche becomes suspicious of this kind of moment, he describes it as one of the high points in the exercise of the will to power, where, under the sign of beauty, "opposites are tamed"; moreover, this is done "easily" and "pleasantly," and "without tension" (*WP*, 803).

Because the aesthetic moment has been forged from a tropological movement of language which as written language permits exact repetition, it is a moment which is a spot of time that seems to stand outside all time. This is an implicit metaphysical pretension of the aesthetic moment. It appears to us, in Yeats's terms, really to be part of "the artifice of eternity." As such, it is heir to identity, immutability, and perfection. But to be protected, it must be withdrawn from time and our probing eyes. It is for this reason that Nietzsche ends "Vita Femina" not in full possession of the moment of unveiling and beauty, but by drawing this moment back behind a veil. Since the word for "truth" in Greek is "aletheia," literally "to unveil," this text seems to have described a rare and lucky glimpse of that woman "Sophia" who is the object of philo-sophy's love. The veil she wears coyly covers a body that would keep secrets; but it also ensures philosophic desire by the implicit promise of an ultimate moment of unveiling. What is this veil? Since throughout *The Gay Science* veils and clothes are privileged metaphors for language and text, this is a veil of language and tropes behind which the impossible moment of beauty (and truth) has appeared and then withdrawn. The veil of language determines the peculiar bind of the philosopher. The philosopher, as an enlightened and impious seer, would tear away the veils that obscure his vision of the truth. But the very language he uses to do so reifies and reveils the body he would unveil. Little wonder that the veil becomes hopelessly and interminably interwoven with what it veils. But Nietzsche ends on this note of consolation: it is this veil's very refusal of a final vision of truth which gives it the power to rearticulate desire, so that the beautiful moment, the fugi-

17. Corngold, "The Question of Self in Nietzsche," 71.

tive moment of fulfilled desire, can be reinscribed as text in the text as an object of desire.[18]

"Vita Femina" rehearses a moment of maximum aesthetic pleasure that prefigures Nietzsche's falling in love with Salomé. She will be the particular "woman" who becomes the figure of "life." When the ethos of aesthetic affirmation is transported into personal life, love becomes the aesthetic moment, the beloved the aesthetic object. But this text does something more strange. By also challenging what is unitary and affirmative about such a moment, and putting in question the mastery and coherence of the subject which seems to preside over the moment and benefit from it, it also anticipates the failure of the Salomé-Nietzsche relationship. We can develop this idea by posing a question of the text. If the moment of ultimate beauty is the result of the finding of an expression or likeness between inside and outside, then *who* produces this figure or trope? Is Nietzsche's narrator writing this experience for himself? The question is important. For if the cogito's resources—whether conscious or unconscious—structured this moment through an original need to express externally something that has some prior form, however indefinite, then this moment would not be "rare," "lucky," or accidental because it would not be new; no, this moment would be merely an externalization, a raising to the surface, of a beauty that lies hidden (most of the time) within the psyche, and that has continuous being there. This account of things accedes to the whole metaphysics of writing as an expression or efficacious transcription of a prior self-identical self. "Vita Femina" suggests all this but also opens another contradictory possibility. It suggests a transaction between self and a genuine "other" that is *not* presided over by a cogito operating in a continuous state of self-reflection, but one that is traversed by a troping process that is chance and aberrant because nobody can be said to be in possession or control of it. How is this so?

First because the "oneness," plenitude, and identity of this moment are illusory. The figure for the moment of seeing the ultimate beauty of a work looks like a pure identity: the sun (the source of planitude) glowing on the mountains (traditionally an image of the spiritually lofty, and the home of the gods). Both art and love engender such an illusion of the purity of being. But this moment does not come from a physical object, or from an experiencing subject, or from the interchange between these two. Instead the moment is, as

18. See Derrida, *Spurs*, 82–95.

we have seen above, modeled upon a turn of and in language: it is generated by a troping relation by which two terms suddenly appear alike. These terms are not two physical objects; nor does the moment achieve a correspondence between a physical peak and an internal psychic height. No, it is the likeness between two fugitive moments of unveiling that produce the "same" beautiful moment of unveiling. This text shows this unveiling is double: the singular moment of beauty emerges from a structure of repetition where inner and outer unveilings appear as a-like, repeat each other, and so are experienced as the same.

Why just "once"? "Vita Femina" twice repeats the words "one time" or "once": "But what does unveil itself for us unveils itself for us once (*Ein Mal*) only." And one sentence later "for ungodly reality gives us the beautiful either not at all or once (*Ein Mal*) only." The usual way one writes "once" in German is "*einmal.*" By separating one word into two words, and capitalizing the E in *Ein* and the M in *Mal*, this text does several things. We are given another reminder that one emerges from two, that behind the unity of this moment is a complex double relationship. But the capital E also emphasizes the one-ness, facticity, and irreducibility of this moment. This moment's appearing, like all chance accidents, is a violent intervention in the ordinary flow of things. And this is compatible with the second cluster of meanings the word *Mal* has in German: "sign, mark; landmark, monument; stigma, stain, spot, birthmark, mole . . ." The moment, coming one time, marks experience with an isolated single meaning; its meaning is its enigmatic separateness as coming and being apart from everything else. Coming once and by coincidence, this moment becomes a figure for the singular unincorporable quality of chance. Why can't this moment be known in a continuous mode of self-reflection, as having the continuous quality of being? Because the singular, pointed, chancy event happens when a troping relationship suddenly opens between the self and "other." This relationship is a fugitive moment of repetition constituted by the likeness between terms in motion, which disappear as quickly as they appear.

The "other" can come to the self, as "other" with genuine "otherness," only once—in a singular accidental moment. This singleness not only suggests the opaqueness of this moment to consciousness; it also opens upon the negative side of the aesthetic moment. The oneness of the moment marks it as a moment of loss, not just because we want but cannot have this moment more than once, but because the reformation and idealization of self and other needed to make them a-like is predicated upon betraying and deforming both so their difference disappears. Then too, this making a-like is risky, fragile, unstable. The oneness, the punctuality, the ellision of distances and boundaries that this moment precipitates—all make it an instance and instant of erasure and obliteration. The aesthetic moment is a spasm of affect and knowledge; bringing bliss and oblivion, it is like lightning striking. It comes like lightning in a way that can be repeated only as another accidental coincidence, that cannot be assimilated to a form of knowledge or consciousness. The clouds reveil the mountain, obscuring the sun as the moment of beauty is gone.

Nietzsche between Lou and Sophia: A Biographical Supplement

Above I noted a general condition that justifies a biographical supplement to this study: Nietzsche risks using his life as a testing ground for his thought. Moreover, the important changes in Nietzsche's thought between *The Gay Science* and *Zarathustra* are not part of a natural and inevitable development but are entangled with, and cannot be understood without reference to, the contingent, violent events of 1882. The life-episode becomes a supplement to Nietzsche's text which expresses the contradictions and inhibitions hidden by the compositional desire of "Sanctus Januarius" to affirm; in this way, the Salomé episode decenters, unravels, and reopens the philosophical assertions of "Sanctus Januarius." Before proceeding, however, I need to offer a few cautions upon the uses and abuses of biographical writing.

The writing of biography is motivated by a particular desire: to make the person of the past come to life in writing; to write the story of a life, so that the person comes into presence in his or her thoughts, feelings, and experiences across the hiatuses of time and in the "silent" medium of life-writing. Biography is perhaps always written as a reparation for the loss of the person it represents. In taking the attendant risks (of nostalgia, of mystification, of engendering impossible illusions) here as part of an effort to interpret Nietzsche's thought in 1882, I hope to steer between two sets of paired antithetical assertions which have too often dominated discussions of the efficacy (or impossibility) of biography. The first pair of assertions: On the one hand there is *the biographical reduction* by which the meanings of the text are referred to and limited by what is offered as the true "context," the privileged origin, and "real" signified of the text. In reaction to the limitations and banalities of the biographical reduction, many new and newer critics effect an *excision of the biographical* from the reading of the "primary text." But by separating the text from the contextual matrix of its emergence, a matrix the author and text are often in conscious and unconscious dialogue with, this reading procedure has a secondary effect. It focuses the reader's attention upon the "text proper" in such a way that a whole series of taboos and proprieties for reading are put into force. This process reifies and idealizes the text and makes it a comforting aesthetic enclosure for the critic's hermeneutic attentions. My alternative effort: to see both "text" and "context," work and life, as texts equally open in their meaning, and pertinent to each other as allegories, translations, and transpositions of one another.[19]

An epistemological problem of whether and how one may know another person organizes the second set of paired antithetical assertions. On the one hand, there are the "happy biographers" who, assuming that there is a universal substratum of the human, project themselves empathically into the life of the person they study, know his thoughts and feelings, and (by implication) mark the difference between themselves and the subject their biography represents. In opposition stands the critic who insists that there is a fundamental epistemological bar to knowing another person. Since each man and woman is an island entire to him- or herself, we must desist from biography as a delusive act of appropriation. My alternative effort: although the difference and similarity between the interpreting self and the subject of biography cannot finally be calibrated, and although the life written cannot help but become a screen, pretext, and allegory for the life of the person writing, within the adventurous biographical criticism I will attempt, there can be an illuminating exchange between the two.

Nietzsche's life is known to us through biographies—most espe-

---

19. Nietzsche insists, against some romantic aestheticians, that art cannot be a transcription, it must be a displacement of the life of the artist. Thus in section 5 of *The Birth of Tragedy*, he seems to be saying, "If Homer were Achilles he would not have had to invent him" (*BWN*, 48–52). For an example of the "biographical reduction" by a usually intelligent commentator, see the way Hayman glosses Nietzsche's advocacy of winter's ardors in Book III of *Zarathustra*: "It is the unhappy Nietzsche, freezing in his underheated room, who is recommending unhappiness and discomfort, while anathematizing overheating as one of the detrimental characteristics of city life" (270–71). This way of reading cannot be shown to be "wrong," but it certainly tends to explain away more than it explains about the meaning of the text.

cially those of Elisabeth Nietzsche and Walter Kaufmann—which do more than describe and interpret his life and give sequential narrative summaries of his writings. They are also a species of what Nietzsche called "monumental history": the effort to change humankind in the present and future, through an active appropriation and strong interpretation of the past.[20] Monumental biography will find and build examples so as to exhibit within its own narrative an exemplary spiritual encounter with life. This process usually monumentalizes the subject of biography in another sense: as a "great man" he must tower over almost all of his contemporaries. Thus Elisabeth Nietzsche, in attempting to justify her brother's loneliness in later life writes: "At heart every man of genius is and remains lonely."[21] Such a point of view is distorting when one tries to understand what happens in Nietzsche's life in 1882. Although Nietzsche's special gifts were apparent to most of his friends, he was far from famous, he had not written his greatest work, and his published work seemed eccentric, marginal, and often obscure. For Salomé, and Rée, Nietzsche was talented and special but still one of their company, another completely human person with whom there could be a mutuality of feeling and a reciprocity of action. In setting Nietzsche radically above every contemporary except Wagner, monumental biography loses this perspective and slights the vantage points and claims of the other parties to the action.

Beside these general issues of balance and point of view in biographical narrative, there are special reasons why the Lou Salomé episode is an embarrassment to monumental biography. First there is an awkwardness to Nietzsche's falling in love. Nietzsche wrote about the absurdity of the married philosopher; these biographers are interested in protecting against the image of an infatuated one. So they seldom quote from letters which give expression to the extravagant hopes Nietzsche entertained for his relationship with Salomé. What was naive and unwise about the projected living scheme also gets cursory treatment. And when Nietzsche descends to outrageously unfair invective, the biographers are embarrassed. Nietzsche was the first to point out that his violent recriminations against Rée and Salomé in the summer of 1883 were wildly out of keeping with the values of his own ethos ("looking away," being strong enough

---

20. See the second of the *Thoughts out of Season*, usually known under the title "The Use and Abuse of History," but better translated as "The Advantage and Disadvantage of History to Human Life." See *Untimely Meditations*, trans. R. J. Hollingdale (Cambridge: Cambridge University Press, 1983), 57–124.
21. See the *Life*, 2, p. v, subtitled by Elisabeth, "The Lonely Nietzsche."

not to "forgive" injuries but to simply "forget" them). Throughout their accounts, the major effort of the biographers is to protect Nieztsche's character and his priority vis-à-vis Salomé. This goal helps explain the considerable effort they expend to discount her claim that Nietzsche proposed to her in the spring of 1882; to insist that nothing sexual happened between Lou Salomé and Nietzsche; and to blame Elisabeth Nietzsche's rancorous machinations for the recriminations Nietzsche directs at Salomé and Rée. To me these interpretive efforts seem very strange. The technical question of whether (or when) Nietzsche uttered a proposal to Salomé does not loom so very large when one takes note of the completeness of his love for her and his intense if unrealistic desire, by the fall of 1882, to live his life with her. From what we do know, it does not seem likely that Lou and Nietzsche had a full sexual relationship. But, because neither had a friend in whom to confide such matters, there is simply no way to gauge the extent of their amorous contact. Finally, given Nietzsche's adeptness at handling Elisabeth throughout the Salomé episode, and his clear understanding of her jealousy, Elisabeth cannot be given more than a modicum of the blame for Nietzsche's attacks on Salomé and Rée. In the biographers' handling of these matters, what seems at issue is power and subordination: the effort of the monumental biographers is to make sure that Nietzsche as a major figure of Western thought is not contaminated by the sexuality, femininity, and passion this episode evidences; that no matter how intricately Nietzsche is entangled with Lou Salomé and his sister, the two women do not rise out of their properly subordinate position to "the great man."[22]

I suspect that few biographies—this biographical supplement included—can escape entirely the desire to exalt their subject. It would be interesting to relate this tendency of biography to one that lurks at its periphery: the wish to "set up" that subject, by showing

22. A valuable corrective to the tendency to subordinate Lou Salomé to the famous men in her life—Nietzsche, Rilke, and Freud—will be available when Biddy Martin's book on Salomé, written from a feminist perspective, is published. Her article "Feminism, Criticism, and Foucault," *New German Critique*, 27 (Fall 1982), 3–30, offers reasons why Lou Salomé has become an object of erotic fascination and scandal to Binion and others: "the importance of establishing her sexual identity [becomes part of her critics'] attempt to normalize and control" (25); Martin takes note of Salomé's strong attachments to women which the biographers have regularly ignored; finally, Salomé's concept of narcissism enables her to distinguish herself both from the male representation of Woman as men's "Other," and from nineteenth-century feminist suppressions of their difference from men in the name of full and equal treatment within a patriarchal culture. Martin's book will do a reading of Salomé's writings as they develop a feminist critique of thinkers such as Nietzsche and Freud, and then go on to develop independent feminist theory and practice.

that this man or woman was all too human after all. Finally the biographer seems to wish to win out over rival biographers by "taking sole possession" of the subject. Such an imbroglio of intentions are operating with Nietzsche. Elisabeth Nietzsche is ridiculed by Kaufmann and others for her archival distortions and her strange mixture of self-effacement before and cooptation of Nietzsche; Kaufmann has been an invaluable interpreter and translator of Nietzsche for the English-speaking world, but when one is urged manifold times while reading his standard translation to go to his writings on Nietzsche, his embrace seems hardly less claustrophobic than Elisabeth's. In a similar way, Binion's biography of Lou Salomé has performed an invaluable service through its publication of inaccessible material, and the accuity of its scholarship and detective work. But the heavy-handedness of Binion's Freudian analysis of Salomé, whom he always calls "Lou" or "Frau Lou," and the often condescending tone of his discussion of her leaves one with the impression that he did not really like his subject very much. See, for example, the way Binion describes Salomé's desire for an independent relationship with Nietzsche: "only well out of Nietzsche's gigantic presence was she ever able to take exception to his proud design on her" (B, 54). This, though Salomé abandons the plan for living with Nietzsche while seeing him regularly in Leipzig. Although this book does not escape a hermeneutic and narrative subordination of Lou Salomé (and others) to the central issues in Nietzsche's life, I have tried to acknowledge that problem and take note at certain points of how differently things might look from others' vantage points.

The relationship between Nietzsche and Lou Salomé comes to us not as "hard facts" or a chain of pristine events, but lodged in the texts of letters, journals, letter-journals, biography, and autobiography. Were this writing to disappear, this "episode" would be no more visible than (the likely) analogous events of Shakespeare's life. The relationship's subsistence as writing means that every event in this love affair comes to us shaped, censored, and interpreted by some interested party. For this reason, my first step will be to make some initial estimates about the factors motivating the writing done around and within this episode in 1882, and the writing it has triggered since. My narrative will begin by describing the two rather opaque actions/events that give the episode its peculiar trajectory and character: first the plan for a living arrangement between Lou Salomé, Paul Rée, and Nietzsche which provides its initial matrix; and second, Lou Salomé's quarrels with Elisabeth Nietzsche, and then with Nietzsche, which arise out of indiscreet comments

Salomé made about Nietzsche at the Bayreuth Festival. The offense caused by this incident is overcome at the time, but it becomes the focus of negativity and anger with the collapse of the plan for a trinity. What unfolds between and within these two actions/events is in many ways a perfectly typical instance of romantic love. So I will narrate the episode in its most salient, visible, and transparent moments as they participate in a love story which is entirely typical. But I will also take account of what makes this affair nontypical and noteworthy—the way it becomes a test for Nietzsche's thought. The love for Lou Salomé is shaped in its very happening by the ethos of aesthetic affirmation devised in *The Gay Science*, exceeds and offers resistance to that ethos, and, after the failure of the relationship, triggers a fundamental rethinking of some of the central terms of Nietzsche's thought. In the process, the life and writing of the eighteen months shaped by this episode become a case history for the interplay of experience and thought, life and philosophy.

The Arrangement

In Lucerne, on May 13, 1882, after a good many weeks of debates and negotiations, Lou Salomé, Paul Rée, and Friedrich Nietzsche agree to form a "holy trinity," to live and study together the following winter in Vienna. To commemorate the moment, Salomé prevails upon Nietzsche and Rée to be photographed pulling a small cart, with her in the driver's seat wielding a small whip. At the moment they assume this playful pose, do the parties to the plan and the picture have an intuition of the pleasure and suffering their act will entail? The forging of the arrangement is an act which is opaque and symptomatic in the way it exceeds conscious intentions and projects these three people into unforeseen relations. A collaborative act, it nonetheless expresses divergent purposes and interpretations. Thus, the arrangement is at once a parody of the marriage convention and a substitute for it. By blocking the need to think of marriage, it seems to foreclose the very intimacy it also promotes. This arrangement serves to illustrate, perhaps more than Nietzsche would have liked, the assertion about actions in "Sanctus Januarius": "Every action that has ever been done was done in an altogether unique and irretrievable way" (*GS*, 335).

The parties to the "trinity" felt they were doing something quite daring and original with this arrangement. Nietzsche calls it "our Pythagorean friendship" and, apparently unmindful of the dangerous properties of triangles, insists in a letter to Rée that "it raises me in my own esteem to be really *capable* of it. Yet it does remain laughable?" (B, 61). Malwida von Meysenbug, who had introduced Lou Salome to Rée, is displeased by this living scheme from the start. In a letter to Salomé she remonstrates in the name of simple good sense: "the experience of a long lifetime tell[s] me that it will not work without a heart's cruelly suffering in the noblest case, otherwise a friendship's being destroyed. . . . Nature will not be mocked, and before you know it the fetters are there. . . . I wish only to protect you from nearly unavoidable sorrow" (B, 62). Undeterred by the advice and skepticism of others, the trio organizes their summer and fall to lay the groundwork for their heterodox living plan. It is a summer Salomé spends traveling between Rée and Nietzsche. She visits the Nietzsches' dear friends the Overbecks just after Nietzsche does; after travel with her mother, she visits Rée's family estate in Stibbe to get to know him and his family better; then she joins Elisabeth Nietzsche in Bayreuth for the world premier of *Parsifal*. She spends most of August with Nietzsche and his sister in Tautenburg, and returns to Stibbe for most of September. By the time Salomé and Rée join Nietzsche in Leipzig, to audit some classes and make final plans for living together in the winter, the rivalry between Nietzsche and Rée for Salomé's affection is in full swing.

Why did two men in their thirties and a young woman of twenty-one embark on this arrangement? Each seems to have very different reasons. For Lou Salomé the projected living arrangement expresses the tension between two currents of her life and character. On the one hand, it allows her to pursue a new, more equal relationship with men by sharing a coequal intellectual quest. On the other, it forges this independent relationship by articulating a sexually and romantically charged scene of rivalry, where two men will vie for her attentions. One can see these conflicting currents of Salomé's motivation in the way she defends the living plan in a letter written to Gillot. Gillot, a married Lutheran minister, had fallen in love with Salomé while serving as her confirmation teacher. She first demonstrated her remarkable independence of spirit when she developed a strong passion for Gillot. Taking Salomé on a protracted tour of the continent was her mother's way of removing her from this awkward situation. When Salomé begins to urge the idea of the "trinity" upon Rée, even before Nietzsche arrives in Rome to meet her, her mother has Gillot write Salomé to discourage the idea. Gillot writes that he had conceived her travel and education as part of a "transition" to some more permanent condition (marriage? marriage to him?).

Salomé's response is a kind of manifesto of her intention to win her own freedom by challenging Victorian convention: "Just what do you mean by 'transition'? If some new ends for which one must surrender that which is most glorious on earth and hardest won, namely freedom, then may I stay stuck in transition forever, for *that* I will not give up. Surely no one could be happier than I am now, for the gay fresh holy war likely about to break out does not frighten me: quite the contrary, let it break. We shall see whether the so-called 'inviolable bounds' drawn by the world do not just about all prove to be innocuous chalk-lines" (B, 50). In terms quite compatible with "Sanctus Januarius," Salomé here endorses an idea of life as a condition of ongoing transition and adventure and risk-taking. There is a youthful zest and exuberance in the way she joins the "gay fresh holy war" against convention. To the Germans with whom she is now waging this war, convention weighs much more heavily. Thus in the same letter to Gillot, there is a note of condescension in the way she describes her efforts to persuade Rée to embrace the idea of a trinity. Salomé describes her assault on the inviolable bounds of convention as a scene of seduction: "[Rée] too is not completely won over yet, he is still somewhat perplexed, but in our walks by night between 12 and 2 in the Roman moonlight, when we emerge from gatherings at Malwida von Meysenbug's, I put it to him with increasing success" (B, 50). These walks shocked Malwida, and she cautioned against them. But Salomé is intent on finding a risky new way of living in a European world she believes to be too much defined by strict convention.

Salomé seeks to ensure her independence of any one man, not by removing to a distance from all men, but by stationing herself between two who love her equally. Thus this very description of moonlit walks must cause Gillot some difficult moments, at the same time that it challenges him to be clear about the proposal he may have hinted at. When Salomé visits Rée at his Prussian family estate in Stibbe, she brings a portrait of Gillot in "an ivory picture frame." When she visits Nietzsche at Tautenburg in August, the ivory picture frame is placed on her dressing table, but the photograph found within is of Rée.[23] By making each male attachment one term

23. There are many examples of this pattern. Salomé meets Rée's friend Heinrich von Stein at the Bayreuth festival, first mocks him in letters to Rée, but then makes plans to visit him in Halle. Much later in her life, Salomé begins her study of

in an open series, Salomé sustains an ambiguous relationship to the conventions of courtship her contemporaries assumed her to be operating within. This ambiguity allows her to chart these male relationships so as to advance her intellectual itinerary. To effect an ingenious negotiation of Victorian constraints, Salomé makes use of all the persuasive skills at her command. When it is time to leave Rome, she finds a way to bend her mother's travel plans to coincide with Nietzsche's and Rée's, delays things until Nietzsche is well enough to travel, and charges Rée with the task of gaining Nietzsche's cooperation. One line of the letter to Rée on the subject asserts her authority by pleading her lack of power: "It is unpleasant to be able to do nothing but plead in a matter so close to one's heart." She ends the note, "most commanding Miss Lou" (B, 53). In order to be free to visit Rée and Nietzsche later that summer, Salomé orchestrates for her mother an impression that she will be chaperoned by Rée's mother. Thus Salomé's efforts to gain considerable independence in 1882 meet with remarkable success; but the victory is merely a prelude to difficulties.

Since the two met in 1878, Rée has become Nietzsche's best friend, the one with whom he shares the closest intellectual interests and the most social pleasure. Rée is the author of two books, and in 1882 he is preoccupied with a subject which also interests Nietzsche—the origin of morality and guilt. When Nietzsche took Rée by Bayreuth as his guest, in spite of Rée's being Jewish, this was taken as an insult by Wagner, and helped to formalize Nietzsche's break with Wagner. Rée and Nietzsche have long talked of forming a small group for enlightened intellectual companionship, and the trinity seems the realization of that idea. Like Nietzsche, Rée has been reluctant to marry; the trinity offers an intimate living situation with a woman short of marriage. Rée counts on Nietzsche's providing the intellectual excitement his own sense of inferiority has led him to feel was deficient in himself; Nietzsche is quite sure he could rely on Rée's flexibility, generosity, and social genius.

Nietzsche looks for several benefits from the living arrangement. It means a return to human community after the severe isolation of the previous four or five winters; Lou Salomé might be a receptive student and "heir" for his ideas; and because Nietzsche's eyesight has deteriorated, there has been the need to find people to help with manuscript copying. In explaining the trinity scheme, Elisabeth

---

psychoanalysis in Vienna by participating simultaneously in two hostile circles of study—Adler's and Freud's (B, 335–37).

Nietzsche puts great emphasis upon these factors, which also make it possible for her to discount a much more compelling factor. For Nietzsche's reservations about the idea are not overcome, and the plan does not really strike fire, until Nietzsche takes a long hike with Lou Salomé up a mountain in the Alps, shares his most cherished writing plans with her, and discovers a special spiritual kinship with her. Until, in short, he falls in love. Then he works to blend, meld, harmonize, and reconcile Lou Salomé with his great new project, Zarathustra. In thanking Malwida von Meysenbug for introducing him to Salomé, Nietzsche can be seen doing this:

> My life belongs now to a higher aim, and I no longer do anything that does not suit that aim. No one can guess it, and I myself must not yet betray it: but I will confess to you—and to you more gladly than anyone—that it needs a heroical way of thinking (and by no means one of pious resignation). If you find any persons of this way of thinking, let me know, as you did in the case of the young Russian lady. This girl is now united to me by a bond of firm friendship (so far as anything of the sort can be firm on this earth); it is a long time since I made so great an acquisition. Really, I am extremely grateful to you and Rée for your agency in the matter. This year, which in many respects marks a crisis in my life ('epoch' is the right word—an intermediate stage between two crises, one behind me and one before me), has been made much happier through the charm and brilliance of this youthful and truly heroic soul. In her I look for a disciple, and, if I am destined not to live much longer, an heir who will carry on my work. [L, 264; 7/13/82][24]

This letter belongs to the first phase of his relationship with Lou Salomé, the time between their first acquaintanceship in Rome and the Alps and her extended August visit. What is most remarkable about the letter is the many ways he finds to figure Salomé's subordination to his work, a cooptation and incorporation into his project that is all the more complete because he is sure she has become indispensable to it. Salomé is an "acquisition," who is to become a "disciple," and possibly an "heir." Nietzsche does not just thank Malwida; he urges her to send along any others she turns up who might be as usefully "heroic" as Salomé. In subordinating Salomé to the single "higher aim" of his life (his work), Nietzsche echoes the hierarchical valuations of the monumental biographies of genius. But he is not being disingenuous. Nietzsche clearly *does* believe that the

24. The Greek root of the word "epoch" means "to pause."

pathway toward his next work lies through a relationship with Lou Salomé. Rather than the pious and resigned style Nietzsche associates with his sister, Salomé has the heroic soul which will be compatible with *Zarathustra* as he now imagines it. Thus, he tells Overbeck's young wife to warn Salomé that he is "always pursuing only his own mental aims and thinking only of himself" (B, 56). In linking Salomé to the "higher aims" of his work, Nietzsche no doubt feels he pays her the richest compliment he can give.

I wonder what Lou Salomé would have thought if she could have read Nietzsche's "thank you note" to Malwida? Although Nietzsche is much more circumspect in describing what he expects from Salomé in the letters he sends her in this period, much the same message can be read between the lines of the exultant letter he writes her after she accepts his proposal that she spend August with him and his sister in Tautenburg. This letter of July 3 tells us a lot about how Nietzsche was seeking to weave Salomé into his future (L, 256). Salomé received it, but quite uncharacteristically, she never answers it. Perhaps she did read something between the lines she did not care to see.

To Lou Salomé (Tautenburg, July 3, 1882)
My dear friend:
Now the sky above me is bright! Yesterday at noon I felt as if it was my birthday. *You* sent your acceptance, the most lovely present that anyone could give me now; my sister sent cherries; Teubner sent the first three page proofs of *The Gay Science*; and on top of it all, I had just finished the very last part of the manuscript and therewith the work of six years (1876–82), my entire *Freigeisterei*. O what years! What tortures of every kind, what solitudes and weariness with life! And against all that, as it were against death *and* life, I have brewed this medicine of mine, these thoughts with their small strip of *unclouded* sky overhead. O dear friend, whenever I think of it, I am thrilled and touched and do not know how I could have *succeeded* in doing it—I am filled with self-compassion and the sense of victory. For it is a victory, and a complete one—for even my physical health has reappeared, I do not know where from, and everyone tells me that I am looking younger than ever. Heaven preserve me from doing foolish things—but from now on!—whenever you advise me, I shall be *well* advised and do not need to be afraid.

As regards the winter, I have been thinking seriously and exclusively of Vienna; my sister's plans for the winter are quite independent of mine, and we can leave them out of consideration. The south of Europe is now far from my thoughts. I want to be lonely no longer, but to learn again to be a human being. Ah, here I have practically everything to learn!

Accept my thanks, dear friend. Everything will be well, as you have said.

Very best wishes to our Rée!

Entirely *yours*, F. N. [L, 256]

This letter is organized around a series of explicit messages: joy and gratitude at the way an excess of gifts have coincided in their arrival; a sense of personal triumph that a whole phase of his writing has been completed against the worst odds; and surprise that even his health and youth have returned. Over all there glows the joy of expectation at a new beginnings in his relationship with Salomé and Rée and in his work. But behind these explicit messages is a fictive design of more covert ones which express the scope of Nietzsche's demands on Salomé. In sending her "acceptance" of the proposal that she stay with Nietzsche in Tautenburg, she has given him "the most lovely present anyone could give me now." It is this gift (of herself) which has brought back his health, youth, and vigor. In the long heroical self-description of his "complete triumph" in finishing his writings of the free spirit, Nietzsche transforms himself into the intrepid hero of romance: he has overcome tortures, solitudes, weariness, and finally even death. Salomé's gift is no longer freely given; it is a reward for Nietzsche's bravery. She is put in the position of the maiden who has offered herself as reward to the conquering knight who has returned in triumph with the holy grail. Quite ironically, the letter's grandest compliment to her knowledge and independence covertly subordinates her to Nietzsche's work: Salomé is not to be Nietzsche's student but his teacher. For though it had been implicit in their relationship that Nietzsche was to function as a teacher, by giving her the role of the teacher, he not only implies that he can be as receptive and compliant as a pupil; he invites Salomé to subordinate her itinerary and interests to his needs for companionship and socialization. In this role, she is not to show the narcissism of the student, but the selfless generosity of a teacher (and woman).

Nietzsche's heroical representation of his "complete victory," and his way of making Salomé both his reward and his teacher, help to elucidate the way he implicates her in the curious periodization of his life alluded to in the letter to Malwida. "This year . . ." Nietzsche tells Malwida "marks a crisis in my life ('epoch' is the right word—an intermediate stage between two crises, one behind me and one before me)." What does this mean? By making the time he is setting aside for Lou "an epoch," I suspect he makes it a bridge between two more crucial and "critical" phases of creative work and transformation: the hardships and effort of the previous six years of work, and the new "heroic" trials that await him in writing *Zarathustra*. In this way, what can happen now between him and Salomé may be important personally, but it also is somehow fundamentally secondary. It is research, background work, a time out for pleasure, eating cherries, and learning to be "human"—all on the way to the more important work that lies ahead. But by the very emphasis in his assertion, Nietzsche's text implies what it excludes: that this intermediate stage, a "*mittelzustand*," could be like the middle space where the primal scene gets elucidated. This living space *could* become the place of the kind of assertion and artistic composition associated with writing. Here too events could "befall" Nietzsche which are punctual, singular, and violent. This is what his anticipatory quarantine of the Salomé experience, in an "epoch" space of transition between, seems designed to forestall.

In both these letters Nietzsche expresses enormous confidence in the new turn to his life which pivots around Lou Salomé. But in separating himself from the accustomed primacy of his sister, who was always unstinting in extending to Nietzsche the self-sacrificing support he accepted, and in forsaking the winter refuge provided by real blue skies of the south (as opposed to the metaphorical ones provided by Salomé, or his own writing), Nietzsche shows some sense that he is doing something risky and impulsive. Thus he qualifies his assertion that Salomé is "united to me by a bond of firm friendship," with the words "so far as anything of the sort can be firm on this earth"; and he surmounts his own self-caution—"heaven preserve me from doing foolish things"—with an enunciation of his faith that when Lou advises him, he will be well advised. This expression of trust in Salomé implies what he does not quite acknowledge: that by embarking upon uncharted seas, he is, in the words of "Sanctus Januarius," "living dangerously" (*GS*, 283).

The Quarrel

As the summer continues, Nietzsche, Salomé, and Rée begin to live the relationship they have so far only imagined in prospect. Inevitable strains appear. Nonetheless, whenever a threat to the living arrangement emerges, each shows agility in keeping the triangular relationship in balance and the project on course. When Nietzsche presses Salomé for a solitary rendezvous near Berlin, she deflects his request, but coyly adds that she is taking his book *The Dawn* to bed. Rée warns Lou Salomé that Nietzsche may try to use her as a secretary or turn her into a disciple. When Salomé passes these accusations on to Nietzsche, he is easygoing and good-humored in deflecting them. After Salome's visit with Nietzsche, Rée senses how much Nietzsche has come to engross her imagination, so he offers to withdraw from the arrangement. She reassures him of her continued attachment to him and forbids his withdrawal (B, 67, 88).

The only serious threat to Nietzsche's relationship with Lou and their projected living plan comes with the action/event that can be grouped under the title of "the quarrel." While at the Bayreuth Festival, Lou Salomé is quite open in describing the plan, even to Wagnerites most hostile to Nietzsche. After receiving his sister's report of these incidents, Nietzsche calls off her visit to Tautenburg and the whole living arrangement. But when Salomé's hurt and dismay are evident, Nietzsche relents and forgives her. He writes, "Do come, I am suffering too much for having made you suffer: we shall bear it better together. F. N." (L, 279; 8/4/82). Then, in new arguments about the living arrangement with Elisabeth during their journey to Tautenburg, Salomé's insistence upon Nietzsche's baser motives scandalizes his sister. Again Elisabeth Nietzsche reports Salome's transgressions, again the visit is canceled, but again Nietzsche forgives her. There are several reasons why this episode calls for careful analysis. The quarrel shows how a relationship aglow with convergent intentions becomes complex. First, we have seen the ways the arrangement's symmetries of purpose were only apparent. Lou's indiscreet comments and the subsequent quarrel are an index of her refusal to be coopted, in a passive and compliant manner, into Nietzsche's writing plans. Then, the obstacles to this plan are more than personal. To develop a daring antitraditional relationship like the trinity, one must put out of play the prior claims of the society one inhabits, with its interests, laws, and morality. But, how does one exclude (one never can exclude) this social law from intruding into a privately contrived society imagined as a place where a select few can live freely, apart from convention's constraints? In this instance the social law comes to Nietzsche and Salomé in the form of a jealous sister. In August 1882, it is Elisabeth who reports Salomé's indiscreet comments to Nietzsche; and years later, in her biography of her brother, she replays this quarrel for posterity, as the chief exhibit in her moral indictment of Lou Salomé. The quarrel, as produced and directed by Elisabeth's carefully modulated disclosures, indicates the perilously complex geometry of Nietzsche's new relationship with Salomé: it is not just one side of a triangular relationship with his best friend, Rée; at the very same moment, it is one side of another, adjacent triangular relationship with his sister.[25]

Almost the moment the plan for the trinity is settled upon, Nietzsche is confronted with the problem of who should know of it. He speaks buoyantly of the plan with his most trusted friends, the Overbecks. But there are practical dangers. Such a living scheme is quite startling for a German university professor to plan. It could lose him both his small readership and the stipend he is receiving from the the University at Basel since illness forced his retirement. Then he knows quite well that the strict morality of his mother and sister—which he has begun to call "Naumburg virtue"—will be dead against the project. Finally, there is something Nietzsche is perhaps less willing to acknowledge to himself: the emotional intimacy of living with Lou Salomé will displace his sister from the position of primacy she has occupied since the earliest days of their childhood. Little wonder that Nietzsche's first letters to Salomé are organized around the theme of silence and discretion. Since, as he writes, "[I] heartily wish that you and I should not become subjects of European gossip," he suggests that "we should firmly decide to *initiate* only the necessary persons." In the same letter he marks the differences of temperament which may lead them to act divergently upon the matter of silence: "Nature gave each being various defensive weapons—to you a glorious openness of will." As for himself, he wrote, "I love the hiddenness of life" (L, 239; 6/10/82). Secrecy is fine for Nietzsche, but for Salomé, just starting her studies and having published no books, her chief source of importance and pride is this newly conceived relationship with Nietzsche and Rée. Nietzsche keeps the plan secret from his mother, but he finally has to tell Elisabeth, as she is in correspondence with Paul Rée's mother, and it becomes convenient to use his sister to accompany Lou Salomé from Bayreuth to Tautenburg.[26]

25. Binion assumes that Lou Salomé's refusal to answer Elisabeth's public accusations about her behavior at Bayreuth imply an acquiescence in the truthfulness of these charges. They also may indicate Salomé's refusal to be drawn into a display of invidious public self-justification.

26. That Salomé challenged Nietzsche's request for profound silence on the arrangement may be inferred from Nietzsche's responses to her letters from Stibbe. Rée has warned Lou that a summer visit with Nietzsche's sister might be a problem, but Nietzsche denies this and even makes light of "my whole hush-hush" (*Stillschweigerei*): "I analyzed it today and found as its basic cause: mistrust toward myself. I was down-

Since Elisabeth Nietzsche is the only witness to record an account of Lou Salomé's indiscreet comments at Bayreuth and the subsequent quarrels, Binion relies upon her account in reconstructing the episode. Although we will never be sure of the accuracy of Elisabeth's account, it has this pertinence: it is the version which influenced the Salomé-Nietzsche relationship. Here, as in so many of those human affairs mediated by gossip, the interpretation of the event is more influential for subsequent events than some hypothetically postulated real event at the origin. As Binion reconstructs the episode, the "quarrel" has two parts. At Bayreuth, "by Elisabeth's account, Lou declared against Nietzsche to his Wagnerite enemies and, flaunting the Lucerne photo, 'told whoever would or wouldn't listen that Nietzsche and Rée wanted to study with her and would go with her anywhere *she* wanted'" (B, 74). After the Tautenburg visit is canceled and uncanceled, Lou delivers her memorable speech to Elisabeth, expressing her anger at Nietzsche's vacillations and designed to disabuse his sister of her ideal notions of Nietzsche's purity. Elisabeth's narrative is written about a month after the incident, in a letter to the friend with whom both women were staying (in Jena) on their way to Tautenburg:

Lou burst forth with a flood of invective against my brother: "he's a madman who doesn't know what he wants, he's a common egoist who wanted only to exploit her mental gifts, she doesn't care a hoot for him but if now they didn't go to a city together it would mean she weren't "great," that's why Fritz doesn't want to study with her—so as to shame her. What's more, Fritz would be crazy to think she should sacrifice herself to his aims or that they had the same aims at all, she knew nothing of his aims. Besides, were they to pursue any aims together, two weeks wouldn't go by before they were sleeping together, men all wanted only that, pooh to mental friendship! . . ." As I, now naturally beside myself, said that might well be the case with her Russians only she didn't know my pure-minded brother, she retorted full of scorn (word for word): "Who first soiled our study plan with his low designs, who started up with mental friendship when he couldn't get me for something else, who first thought of concubinage—your brother!" And just as she was repeating in the most malicious tone of voice, "Yes indeed your noble pure-minded brother first had the dirty design of a concubinage!" in you came. . . . [I was] utterly out of my element: never in my life had I heard such indecent talk (here I have reproduced it all with propriety at

right bowled over by the fact of having acquired a 'new person' after overly strict seclusion and renunciation of all love and friendship. I had to keep silent. . . . Now, I tell you this for laughs" (L, 251; 6/27–28/82).

that). . . . In the evening . . . she broke out again in a fury against Fritz
and became downright grossly indecent, as when she said full of deri-
sion: "just don't go thinking that I care beans for your brother or am in
love with him, I could sleep in the same room with him without getting
worked up." Would you believe it possible? I too was altogether beside
myself and shouted at her repeatedly: "Stop this indecent talk!" "Pooh,"
she said, "with Rée I talk a lot more indecently." She had also told me
Rée had told her that Fritz was thinking of a concubinage. So now I told
her: All right, I would ask his mother, whereupon she was furious and
threatened to get back at me, and she did. I was utterly miserable and
didn't sleep a wink. . . . Oh what a martyrdom for my sensibility the
whole story was! . . . The moment she believed she could draw no further advantage from his fame she fell upon him like a wild animal and
tore his good name and reputation to bits [B, 76–77].

This text stages a struggle of interpretations around Nietzsche, for
Nietzsche. But Nietzsche also simply offers the occasion for each
woman to assert the kind of person she intends to be. In the battle
Lou Salomé makes use of the shock value of direct disclosure, so as
to unmask the social properties Elisabeth Nietzsche so values. Without the counterpressure of Elisabeth's sense of virtue, much of what
Salomé says here might have gone unsaid. Elisabeth counters with
all the force of outraged modesty; her censored and delayed disclosures will help make this scene of Salomé's anger into a scandal.
Since the quarrel and its tirade cannot be ascribed to one person, it
needs to be interpreted from both Salomé's and Elisabeth Nietzsche's position.

So, from Salomé's vantage point, what does this quarrel evidence?
First, and most blatantly, her desire for a sense of control. Thus the
Lucerne photograph is now given a new meaning. Taken as a jest
and a lark two months before, it becomes a warrant of Lou's mastery
when shown at Bayreuth, coupled with a disclosure of the projected
living scheme. By insisting, quite accurately, that the men would follow her choice as to the site of their winter residence, Salomé has
found a way to make her mastery seem quite complete. But her casual disrespect for Nietzsche also indicates something else. Like the
graduate student who seems ready to say almost any scathing thing
about a professor, at Bayreuth and Jena Lou Salomé is protecting
herself against an intellectual engulfment by Nietzsche at the very
moment when she is opening herself up to his influence as part of
her own intellectual project. When Nietzsche simply cancels their
plans, she must feel her actual powerlessness and unimportance
most acutely. How pleasant it must be to have found in these vitu-

perative scenes a way to express her anger with Nietzsche by making his devoted sister squirm.

Salomé's tirade brings to the fore what is contradictory and symptomatic about the whole living scheme, and subsists as a problem in her relationship with Nietzsche. When the plan for a trinity is formed, sex is quite explicitly left to one side.[27] To conceive the "holy trinity" is for Salomé and Nietzsche and Rée a critique of the way marriage turns relations between men and women into a crude material and sexual transaction. It is also an assertion of faith in a particular ideal: that men and women can know each other in and through a shared intellectual quest. This idealism is implicit in Salomé's judgment of Nietzsche for "soiling" the study play with "low designs." But the trinity is also flirting with becoming a *menage à trois* —and a rather kinky one at that. Thus, even before Nietzsche meets Lou, his letter to Rée about the living plan assumes the arch and cavalier style of men talking of women they intend to share: "Greet the Russian girl for me, if that makes any sense: I am greedy for souls of that species. In fact, in view of what I mean to do these next ten years, I need them! Matrimony is quite another story. I could consent at most to a two-year marriage, and then only in veiw of what I mean to do these next ten years" (B, 49). Here superiority to marriage is not ideal, but an effect of masculine license and licentiousness. Of course, Nietzsche's words strike a pose much more consciously ironic than the ardent passion he ends experiencing with Lou Salomé. Nonetheless, when Nietzsche's and Rée's feelings for Salomé intensify, the term whose exclusion made the trinity thinkable—sex—returns. At Stibbe, Rée describes to Salomé the letter in which Nietzsche limits interest in her to a "two-year marriage," and this reference becomes the "concubinage" with which Salomé shocks Elisabeth. From the beginning the trinity was fascinating—to both the eager principles and the skeptical observers—for the way it triggered curiosity and suppositions. But when the officially excluded term returns, misunderstandings quickly engulf the parties to the plan. Now "mental friendship" seems a sham screen for "something else," and sex becomes the ulterior motive which threatens to make the plans for study, and the whole intellectual life, a pretext and charade. Salomé may take pleasure in "talking indecently" with Elisabeth or Rée; but she is also wrestling to find a way to protect the integrity of the plan for living and study she hopes to put into effect.

Elisabeth's response to Salomé is shaped by one overriding goal:

27. See, for example, Nietzsche's letter to Peter Gast explicitly precluding a "love affair": "We are *friends*, . ." (L. 263; 7/13/82).

to protect her passionately sustained central position in Nitezsche's life from the incursions of this gifted but unprincipled interloper. From early childhood she has saved every scrap of his writing; in old age she will labor tirelessly to establish the Nietzsche archive at Weimar. Because she also has stayed unmarried, Elisabeth can always be available to do small services to make Nietzsche's life easier and his health less harried—from mailing things south and arranging summer residences to dealing with publishers. Her solicitude for Nietzsche's reputation extends to urging him to do those things which will increase his influence and celebrity: write books in a nonaphoristic style, resume his teaching at the university, patch up his differences with Wagner. Little wonder that Elisabeth believes she is the only proper custodian of Nietzsche's work and reputation. All her service to him is paired with the intense personal affection one can read in her description of the happy days she spent helping him copy the manuscript of *The Gay Science*, in June 1882. "Once more, as in his student days, our little green verandah rang from morning till evening with merry laughter. The laughter, indeed, had sometimes to be suppressed, so that our mother should not enquire as to the real meaning of our allusions" (*Life*, 2, 123). Elisabeth little suspects that Nietzsche's new passion for another woman is the single most important reason for his joy and health that June. Nietzsche is well aware of the jealousy his sister will feel, so his letters of that spring carefully screen her from any romantic interpretation of Salomé.[28] But this solicitude does not prevent Nietzsche from asking the ever useful Elisabeth to serve as chaperone to facilitate his reunion with Salomé in Tautenburg (L, 268; 7/16/82).

Elisabeth has received justifiably harsh treatment from Nietzsche scholars for her self-interested tamperings with Nietzsche's letters and writings, but the difficulty of her position when Salomé became the focus of Nietzsche's attentions should win more understanding than it has. Upon meeting Salomé, Elisabeth must have quickly seen that her intelligence and charm made her a dangerous rival, one who might be able to share Nietzsche's mental life in a way she never could. Elisabeth assembles evidence against Salomé at Bayreuth without Salomé's having any inkling of her feelings.[29] Her (cen-

28. Nietzsche's descriptions of Lou Salomé to Elisabeth are completely different from those sent to others. Thus, in one letter, Lou Salomé is "plain," Nietzsche is suspicious of Rée's enthusiasm, he even wishes she were a man.

29. Salomé shows a youthful egotism in assuming that Elisabeth would relinquish her position of centrality in Nietzsche's life without a fight; she shows her youthful naïveté in failing to understand that the most important rivalry between people is hidden. Thus at the very moment Elisabeth is describing Salomé's behavior at Bayreuth, Salomé writes Nietzsche of "your sister, who is now almost mine too" (B, 76).

sored) description of Salomé's indecent accusations in Jena give her material for a second brief. Both are part of her effort to end a relationship with Nietzsche before it really begins. There is little doubt that Elisabeth is largely unfair in her criticisms of Salomé. Nietzsche soon finds her scathing judgment of his new friend to constitute unacceptable meddling in his life. But nonetheless Elisabeth probably conceives her battle with Salomé—and it lasted until long after Nietzsche's death—as a battle for his soul and reputation. In a letter, written about this period Elisabeth Nietzsche describes her brother's life and thought as compounded of the morally corrupt and the spiritually redeeming. Thus when, under her very eyes at Tautenburg, Nietzsche and Lou Salomé begin to explore the many grounds of their shared response to life, Elisabeth writes to a friend of Salomé's: "I cannot deny that she really personifies my brother's philosophy: that rabid egotism which tramples on anything in its way, and that complete indifference to morality."[30] But she is still indignant when Salomé accuses Nietzsche of being an egotist who would sacrifice her to "his aims." Elisabeth loses the battle for influence over Nietzsche in the summer of 1882. But that small part of Lou Salomé's tirade which Elisabeth withholds from Nietzsche, Rée's betrayal of "the design of concubinage" he attributes to Nietzsche, makes it possible for her to imagine Salomé as the true enemy of Nietzsche, operating in tandem with Rée to undermine her unsuspecting brother.

The arrangement for living together and the quarrel that informs Nietzsche's life in 1882 are both strangely insubstantial. The arrangement is no more than an idea, a hope, and a plan that never comes off. But it orients a great deal of his language and desire in 1882. The quarrel is no less textual: it is made of words and signs—a picture shown indiscreetly, a youthful woman bragging about her importance, a sister's countervailing self-righteousness, skepticism about sexual motives, and a torrent of "indecent" language. Since Salomé's supposed indecency inheres in the words Elisabeth's propriety forbids her to repeat, the quarrel cannot be fully contained in Elisabeth's exhaustive narrative. Depending upon the interpretive pressure applied to it, the indiscretion and the quarrel fade in and out of focus, acquiring different force and meaning. Therefore when Nietzsche's urgent desire to be close to Salomé prevails, it becomes quite easy to erase the quarrel. Under the sign of youthful indiscretion, and a "first quarrel," Nietzsche forgives Salomé, and sim-

30. Hayman, *Nietzsche*, 251.

ply will not hear the stern judgments that Elisabeth continues to express (L, 301; 9/9/82). Elisabeth's description of the scene of Salomé's reconciliation with Nietzsche shows how easy it is to dissolve the quarrel into laughter. Elisabeth paraphrases Salomé: "'Heavens, she had never imagined I still had such retarded views, so what if he had intended concubinage? That would be nothing degrading surely, they were above conventionality so it couldn't degrade Fritz and she hadn't meant it to.' Then she made Fritz believe Rée had told her that about him only so as to benefit from it *himself* should she consent and so it went and Fritz swallowed it all and with her made fun of his family and me" (B, 78).

But indiscretion and quarrel have not really vanished. As long as all goes well with Nietzsche and Salomé, they are successfully suppressed. They subsist, however, in faint outline under the trinity, as a gathering point of potential conflict. When Lou Salomé leaves Leipzig in November with Paul Rée, and fails to make plans to rendezvous with Nietzsche in Paris in the ensuing weeks, the themes of the quarrel return. Thus in a letter to Rée of December 1882, Nietzsche describes his sense of injury at Salomé's behavior the previous summer at Bayreuth, and hints at the information he has about her indiscretions which he has never discussed with her (L, 339; 12/82). In his correspondence with Salomé that December the whole issue of sex and Nietzsche's ulterior motives returns in a new and much more rancorous tone. By the following summer, a copy of a letter of Elisabeth's written to Rée's mother ("a female masterpiece," Nietzsche calls it) represents the quarrel so as to give him "new lights and new tortures" (B, 105). Now Nietzsche interprets the whole episode under the sign of betrayal. "Of a sudden Dr. Rée steps into the foreground: to have to *relearn* about someone with whom I shared love and trust for years is frightful" (B, 105). In a bizarre letter written to Rée but never sent, what he had partially heard last summer but successfully suppressed now returns as dirt: "So the defamation of my character stems from *you*, and Miss Salomé was only the mouthpiece, the very unclean mouthpiece for *your* thoughts about me? You it was who, behind my back of course, spoke of me as a common low egoist always out to use others? You it was who maintained that I pursued the dirtiest of designs in regard to Miss Salomé beneath the mask of ideality?" (B, 106). The indiscretion can return as a scandalous betrayal only because Nietzsche had forgotten the methods of his own forgetting: selective attention, conscious goodwill, and unconscious idealization . . . all aided in their operation by the inventive compositional pressure of love.

[175]

A Story of Love

In doing a biographical supplement to this study, I have assumed a perspective where the accidental particularities of person, place, and time make a difference in the life lived and the text written. But in improvising their relationship, Nietzsche and Lou Salomé draw upon something which is available to everyone in our culture as a template for living: love. The power of love is that of a collective, partly conscious, partly unconscious cultural text, where everyone always already knows the whole script: the roles and plots, the stations and scenes of the self's merger (in love) with another. Here one does not just "feel love"; the lover "falls in love," so love is felt as an overwhelming metaphysical system, whose force reorganizes life. Then the lover does not just contemplate from afar, but feels him/herself and the beloved *to be* that perfect circle whose center is everywhere and whose circumference is nowhere.

From outside this circle of illusion, the lover looks like a puppet danced upon the strings of the puppeteer Love. The spectator says, "Ah, yes" with a bemused smile, for from the glimpse of the smallest fragment, the whole seems immediately readable. Why is this so? Perhaps because here a single historical love story resonates with the types of the one story of love. To read what is typical in Nietzsche and Salomé's story, we must intentionally, if only for one cycle of interpretation, bracket everything personal about them as lovers: their past, their interiority, a lot of their words, and even their ideas of the future. For in moving through love's trajectory, they are the mute members of a mime troop, whose silence and removal to the middle distance imposes those very limits upon knowledge which allow the spectator to apprehend their reenactment of love's pantomime.

Love is not the *whole* story of what happens between Lou and Nietzsche in 1882. It does not account for the ethos of aesthetic affirmation Nietzsche brings to this relationship, nor for the eccentric qualities of the central figures in the drama, nor for the particular conflicts of will and circumstantial incidents that give the episode its determined shape. But love is *part* of what happens between these four people in 1882, a part which tosses them pell-mell into those ordinary human feelings and that loss of mastery and self-mastery characteristic of the most ecstatic states. So in what follows I will try to narrate the events of the year as moments in a typical love story.

Only after doing this will I be in a position to describe the ways Nietzsche interprets this love while he lives it; and how, when its failure makes it appear an arbitrary event which is violent and wounding, it pushes Nietzsche toward a more comprehensive interpretation of the will, so as to become part of the new writing project of *Zarathustra*. Throughout the trajectory of this episode, Lou Salomé seems as deeply involved but not as deeply in love as Nietzsche.

In 1882 the trajectory of Nietzsche's love for Salomé coincides with the progress of the seasons. Their meeting in the spring engenders in Nietzsche a sense of keen anticipation and hidden hopes, where everything seems possible between them. The summer brings the happy idyll in Tautenburg, with its mutual celebrations and its difficulties surmounted. Here the lyric apogee of love gives Nietzsche a serene sense of possession. With the autumn comes the end-stage of this love, with a permanent parting, concomitant self-doubts and reproaches, and Nietzsche's angry mourning for the loss of the wonderful companion he hoped he might have for a lifetime. Within this broad movement, things are said and done and attitudes are struck which mark the stations of love's progress. I shall describe them briefly.

First meeting: By prearrangement Rée escorts Salomé on April 21 to St. Peter's Basilica, where she and Nietzsche meet. She reports that Nietzsche's first words are, "What stars have sent us orbiting towards each other?"[31] These words make their love seem destined by an obscure fate.

Alone together in nature: On May 6, Rée is left behind with Lou's mother, and Nietzsche and Salomé climb Monte Sacro, a mountain near a Franciscan monastery. Both represent their personal prospect of the future to the other: Nietzsche tells of Zarathustra and "eternal recurrence," and Salomé of her ambitions. By the time they have returned tardy, each has discovered in the other a kindred spirit. Nietzsche imagines fashioning her according to his philosophical ideal; she writes Malwida von Meysenbug that his is "a religious nature." This future of two together is made all the more alluring by the particularity of the other person (B, 54).

Submission to the beloved: At Salomé's request, Nietzsche and Rée pose for a photo in Lucerne drawing a small cart, with Salomé in the driver's seat. Nietzsche's ego acquires the elasticity to assume unaccustomed roles. No matter how distinguished his mien, as a lover he has become the slave of the beloved, accepting a reversal of the

---

31. Ibid., 245.

usual hierarchies with humor and good grace. The photo suggests that this submission may entail pain: the beloved holds a whip.

A sentimental visit: On May 14, the day after the Lucerne photo, Nietzsche takes Salomé on an excursion to Tribschen, the former home of Wagner. It is the site of Nietzsche's other great passion: his idyllic days with the "master" and his wife, Cosima, and his painful but necessary renunciations of that intimacy. By bringing Salomé here, he can make his new love the climax and summation of the best of past life.

Reciprocal gifts: Salomé gives Nietzsche a copy of her poem "To Pain," which, he feels, offers an uncanny coincidental repetition of his own affirmation of life. In return Nietzsche gives Salomé a copy of his essay "Schopenhauer as Educator." This selection points in two directions: he hopes to be Schopenhauer to her Nietzsche, overcoming the opposition between self and other in discipleship, so that his teaching will only aid her in becoming the being that she is. Thus there is to be no coercion, no conflict of wills. Within the magic circle of this relationship, everything done by these two seems reciprocal, symmetrical, effortless (B, 56). In the chiasmic exchange of gifts the lovers give themselves to the beloved, but these selves will turn out to be a version of what the beloved already is.

Rash desires, sudden impulses: After several weeks of being apart from Lou, Nietzsche is made agitated and restless by the pain of separation. Salomé has pleaded practical obstacles to every proposal for an immediate meeting. Nietzsche writes to her on June 15, describing his "melancholy" at her refusals, and announces with grandiloquence: "Now see what manner of man I am! Tomorrow morning at 11:40 I *will* be in Berlin, Anhalter Station." On this impulse he takes the trip; Salomé does not meet him, or leave him a message. The trip is a (comic) disaster (B, 65). As a lover, Nietzsche must sometimes wear the fool's cap.

The coincidence of two in one on a forest walk: On August 14, after differences about Salomé's indiscretion have dissipated, and Salomé has recovered her health, she and Nietzsche take a long walk in the forest near Tautenburg. Salomé's diary letter to Rée describes this high point of their coming together. It must have seemed to betray rather more feelings for Nietzsche than she was willing to entertain, for it is followed immediately by her explicit disavowal (to Rée) of any feeling of love (for Nietzsche).

> In the quiet, dark pine forest alone with the sunshine and squirrels. . . .
> Conversing with Nietzsche is uncommonly lovely . . . but there is quite

special charm in the meeting of like thoughts and like emotions; we can almost communicate with half words. . . . Only because we are so kindred could he take the difference between us, or what seemed to him such, so violently and painfully. . . . The content of a conversation of ours really consists in what is not quite spoken but emerges of its own from our each approaching the other half way. He gave me his hand and said earnestly and with feeling: "Never forget that it would be a calamity if you did not carve a memorial to your full innermost mind in the time left to you." . . . But is it good for him to spend the whole day from morning to night in conversation with me, hence away from his work? When I asked him this today, he nodded and replied: "But I do it so seldom and am enjoying it like a child." The same evening, though, he said: "I ought not to live long in your vicinity." We often recollect our time together in Italy . . . and he said softly: "*monte sacro*—I have you to thank for the most bewitching dream of my life." [B, 79–80]

Here in the forest, the place where passion proverbially reaches beyond accustomed limits, Lou's narrative description defines the chief figure of love: the coincidence of two in one. Between these two people, kindred thoughts and emotions touch in a place "half way" between, where meaning comes in "half words" that are "not quite spoken." Each knows what the other intends immediately, automatically, without effort, even before it is fully enunciated. In this strange conversation everything said by one about the other applies with equal force to the self: as when Nietzsche enjoins Lou/himself to "carve a memorial" to his/her "innermost mind." Since these two are already one, the experience of distance, however illusory, is painful and violent. The coincidence of lovers overrules the order of the day, stretching conversation from morning to night and making work impossible. But since it brings the innocent pleasures of a child, it cannot be denied. In a few hours, however, a reflexive moment of caution arrives: this kind of proximity "ought" not to continue long. But caution is forgotten with the memory of the still more astonishing occasion when they walked up *Monte Sacro*. So even this August day, lived out as singular and unique, is only a repetition of a more original moment of coming together, when upon a sacred mountain Nietzsche dreamed the most intoxicating vision of his life,—perhaps of a life like this, lived in complete coincidence with Salomé, as he has this day, in the forest near Tautenburg.

A collaboration: When Salomé leaves Tautenburg, she leaves Nietzsche a copy of her poem, "Prayer to Life," and Nietzsche comforts himself on her departure by setting it to music. His music frames and adorns her words; two collaborate in making one thing, as music and words coincide in time and space. As with the Dionysian revels, music is the place where an excess of energy may blur the boundaries between persons. Nietzsche's letter announcing the musical setting ends with these words, "In fond devotion to your destiny—for in you I love also my hopes" (L, 293; end 8/82).

Imitation: In Tautenburg, Salomé is writing an essay on woman. Nietzsche annotates her essay with questions and ideas. On going to Stibbe, she decides to write a book about Nietzsche. In Leipzig she shows him aphorisms written in his style, which he annotates with suggestions for revision (B, 82, 90–92).

Invitation to abandon: The trinity is about to put its living plan into effect. But in Leipzig, Salomé's feelings have become complex. Nietzsche is apparently happy but inwardly uneasy. Salomé is too entangled with Rée for there to be any question of a proposal, so he inscribes her copy of *Human, All Too Human* with an eight-line poem. These verses are a coy and oblique invitation to abandon herself to a southern journey with him. The poem warns a lover against those Genoese who feel, like Columbus (and Nietzsche, whose winter residence has been in Genoa) the sirenlike allure of the sea, and ends with these words: "If he loves, he lures afar / In space and time too eagerly: / Above us star shines unto star, / Around us roars eternity" (L, 321; 11/82). This dream of a passionate leap into the elemental is perhaps also the first intimation of this love's extinction.

Yearning and loss: Upon leaving Leipzig with Rée, Salomé has said there was something she wanted to tell Nietzsche. Nietzsche writes, "I was full of hope" (B, 94). But to speak his desire directly has become impossible. Where is the locus of her demand? Everything has become uncertain. Perhaps Salomé wants nothing from him? The wait for the only word that really matters from the beloved—a definitive "yes" or "no"—has become agonizing. So Nietzsche's letters to Salomé now lack the tide of communication which once gave them such buoyant cheer. They become short, telegraphic, and indirect. "You had something further to say to me?—I like your voice best when you are requesting. But this is not heard often enough.—I shall be studious.—Ah, this melancholy! I am writing nonsense. How *shallow* people are to me today! Where is there a sea left in which one can still really *drown*? I mean a person. My dear Lou, I am your faithful F. N." (L, 325; 11/7/82). When love is balked, it stutters, or begins to speak in lyric fragments. There is so much surplus energy of feeling, but no large responsive body (like Salomé, or the sea) into which one might leap. So Nietzsche dreams of peace in death; but it is a death that is aesthetic, metaphoric, and (somehow) communal. He would drown in Salomé.

Multiple voices: As the failure of the plan to form a trinity becomes evident, Nietzsche refinds the power of direct communication. But now there are multiple voices, constantly fading into new tones, which express the ambivalence of the passions speaking through him. Thus in the letters of November and December, there are a series of incompatible communications: reasoned requests for explanation, veiled reproaches about Lou's indiscretions, appeals to Rée for help in patching up disagreements, the hope of a clear understanding of differences on good terms, an act of renunciation ("Rée, Lou is yours"), the marshaling of a stern judgment against her, scathing accusations (she has the "predatory pleasure lust of the cat . . . Monstrosity! A brain with only a rudiment of soul"), and repeating to Salomé Hamlet's question to Ophelia: "Are you honest?" At last, in the deepest December's despair, there is a veiled (but also somewhat trite) threat of suicide.[32]

"*Lou*" *as a* "*Dear Coincidence*"

To live within the purity of one's love, especially in its ideal moments, is dependent upon a repression and suppression of complexity, common sense, everyday demands, old self-concepts, and perhaps, above all, the distance and difference between lover and beloved. But Nietzsche does not arrive at this state through "believing" in love, or some simple intoxicating oblivion, but through ingenious frenetic interpretation. Ingeniously reflective people like Nietzsche can "fall in love"—not by slowing but by accelerating the interpretation which will then make possible the forgetting indispensable to love. In the spring and summer of 1882 forgetting is greatly facilitated by Nietzsche's having at hand a fully articulated

---

32. There is little explanation of why Salomé's feelings for Nietzsche changed. One diary entry from the Leipzig period suggests that her accusation of sensuality was in part a self-accusation: "so can the most ideal love become sensual again in its ideality just because of the great tensing of feeling. An unlikable point, this revenge of the human element . . . the point of *false pathos*, at which truth and integrity of feeling are lost. Is this what is estranging me from Nietzsche?" An aphorism of the period implicates women as well as men in this moment: "The sensual moment is for women the last word in love, for men the first" (B, 93).

interpretive matrix—"Sanctus Januarius"—which will enable him to turn Lou Salomé, and his love for her, into a practicing ground for the ethos of aesthetic affirmation.

One strand of Nietzsche's correspondence this summer offers a rational interpretation of his relationship to Salomé. In the letters to Franz Overbeck, the sturdy church historian he had known from his days in Basel, Lou Salomé is explained as part of an effort to live in a new way: "in the way I *here* mean to act and shall act, I am for once altogether the man of my thoughts, or my innermost thinking." In this letter from early June, "this *concordance*" of thought and action means living the ethos of "Sanctus Januarius"—taking risks, living dangerously, affirming the future—or, as he explains here, being "fatalistic in my 'submission to God' (I call it *amor fati*)." This love of fate is necessary to the new way of writing projected for composing *Zarathustra*. "There are lots of life secrets of mine bound up with this *new* future, and tasks remain that can be carried out only through deeds" (L, 236; 6/4–7/82). In September, Nietzsche reports back to Overbeck with an account cast in the same terms: The "long, rich summer was for me a testing time; I took leave of it in the best of spirits and proud, for I felt that during this time at least the ugly rift between willing and accomplishment had been bridged." There have been difficulties, "hard demands made on my humanity," but "[I have] crossed a tropic," and in this "whole interim state between what was and what will be" turned from an old writing (the philosophy of the "free spirit"), and old way of living (alone), toward the "trinity" and "the *terrifying* face of my more distant life task"—Zarathustra (L, 301; 9/9/82). This same letter announces that there has been "a real break" with his sister and mother.

What has made possible this new way of living? What are the "deeds" promised in June which have been enacted by September? Above all what is involved is Nietzsche's new relationship to Lou Salomé. She is the catalyst and midwife for the heroic deed that enables Nietzsche to transform himself. She can function in these roles because her nature is so proximate to Nietzsche's: "we" have such a "likeness in our views and mental equipment," "such a deep affinity between our intellect and taste," where even our differences make us "the most instructive objects and subjects of observation for each other," that Nietzsche concludes "it is not possible for two people to be more akin than we are" (L, 300, 301; 9/9/82; L, 327; 11/10/82). Because she already concides with what Nietzsche is, Salomé can become the agent that will enable Nietzsche's thought and life to coincide. I have already noted how this attitude subordinates Salomé to his itinerary. Feminism has richly demonstrated how men repeatedly take women as the intercessors between themselves and their own subjectivity. But by insisting on the objective character of his "likeness" with Lou Salomé, Nietzsche can also circumvent a most banal psychological observation. There are always similarities and differences between two people, but the *feeling* that there is a profound likeness between oneself and another, and a *recurrent representation* of that likeness is one of the chief signs of love.

Perhaps because he is writing to an artist, in Nietzsche's letters to the composer Peter Gast, he finds a way to describe his "likeness" to Lou Salomé which takes account of the uncanny aesthetic quality of their coming together and their rightness for each other. Nietzsche has sent Gast copies of recent poems written in Messina, as well as a copy of Salomé's poem "To Pain." The timing has led to a possible confusion about the identity of the latter's author, which Nietzsche's letter seeks to clarify. But the way he does this and the way he introduces the "discovery" of Salomé only tend to confuse the boundary between Lou's identity and Nietzsche's:

> The poem "An den Schmerz" [To Pain] was *not* by me. It is among the things which quite overpower me: I have never been able to read it without tears coming to my eyes; it sounds like a voice for which I have been waiting and waiting since childhood. This poem is by my friend Lou, of whom you will not yet have heard. Lou is the daughter of a Russian general, and she is twenty years old; she is as shrewd as an eagle and brave as a lion, and yet still a very girlish child, who perhaps will not live long. I am indebted to Frl. von Meysenbug and Rée for her. At present she is visiting Rée; after Bayreuth she is coming here to Tautenburg, and in the autumn we are going together to Vienna. She is most amazingly well prepared for *my* way of thinking and my ideas. [L, 263; 7/13/82]

This letter is marked with obvious clues to Nietzsche's emerging love for Salomé: the depth of his feeling for her poem; the mutual plans for the future; the way she unites and overcomes contrary qualities in herself—shrewdness, bravery, girlishness, and short life. But most decisively, to describe their relation to each other Nietzsche uses two figures of coincidence: the coincidence of the "voice" in Lou's poem, and that which Nietzsche has been awaiting since childhood; the coincidence of Nietzsche's ways of thinking and that for which Lou is "prepared" (*vorbereitet*).

The covert rhetoric of the discovery of this coincidence is all too obvious (and also fully compatible with Salomé's narrative of their

[183]

day in the Tautenburg forest)—either the beloved is another version of the self, or obscure but powerful forces are bringing them together; in either case, Lou Salomé and Nietzsche are "meant" for each other. So after assembling that message, Nietzsche quite explicitly suppresses it. The letter continues: "Dear friend, you will surely do us both the honor of keeping far from our relationship the idea of a love affair. We are *friends*, and shall keep this girl and this confidence in me sacrosanct; what is more, she has an incredibly definite and clear character (*sicheren und lauteren Charakter*), and knows herself exactly what *she* wants without asking all the world or troubling about the world" (L, 263). What makes Lou appear to have the "definite and clear character" so valued in "Sanctus Januarius"? What makes her appearance singular, punctual, and decisive? And what allows this particular coincidence to engage the whole mythos of the beloved as the other self, destined for the beloved? To answer these questions we must note the way this passage does not make Nietzsche and Salomé into discrete individuals and preexistent identities who "happen" to come into coincidence. Both, before they even meet, are already versions or models of each other. If Nietzsche has been waiting for this voice since childhood, it is something he has "pre-known," something he has known before it appeared to him. Conversely, if Salome is "prepared" for Nietzsche's thought, this foreshadowing is an anticipatory repetition of his unique thought. The miraculous singularity of each, both in their individuality and in their coming together in a single love, is both broached by and dependent upon the way they repeat each other. Their anticipatory repetition of each other expresses the "fatality" of the past which mobilizes itself behind the singular appearance of their "chance" coming together in one single time and place. The love of two in one (love), as both chance and fated, is an instance of singular repetition.

This way of figuring Nietzsche and Salomé is capable of disrupting, in an uncanny fashion, the concept of temporal linearity which undergirds the normative concept of causation. Gast, in his response to the July 13 letter, evidently calls attention to the way Nietzsche's poems written in Sicily before he met Lou seem to anticipate her. Nietzsche underlines this fact in the penultimate paragraph of his reply of July 25, and adds: "But perhaps you also feel that, as 'thinker' and 'poet' as well, I must have had a certain presentiment [*Vorahnung*] of Lou? Or is it 'coincidence'? Yes! *Dear* coincidence! (*Ja! Der liebe Zufall!*)" (L, 272). The phrase "dear coincidence," or "dear chance," is the same used in the rousingly affirmative close to "Personal Providence." This second letter to Gast adopts a similarly celebratory tone as it itemizes a whole list of felicitous coincidences: the arrival of Gast's score joins the other gifts of the summer (finishing *The Gay Science*, the bowl of cherries sent by his sister, but above all Salomé; the musical score is difficult, "but at just the right moment, as if heaven-sent, . . . a serious and reliable musician" turns up; "by a coincidence, I met him for half an hour, and by another coincidence, when he arrives home from this meeting, he finds a letter from a friend beginning, 'I have just discovered a splendid philosopher, Nietzsche . . . '" (L, 272). What does this proliferation of coincidences mean, and why does Nietzsche mark them? Here the "likeness" of terms is multiplied and condensed so as to exceed rational composition by an interpreting subject. Not God, nor our interpretive dexterity, but "dear chance" plays with us, making what happens seem both destined (as the orbits controlled by the stars) and necessary (—that which "can not now be missing"). In this letter, these coincidences are dense with meaning and weighted with (a wonderful) future.

What that meaning and future are begins to become evident in another coincidence marked in this letter to Gast. Nietzsche's mind is very much on Bayreuth in these closing days of July, because there the world premier of Wagner's *Parsifal* is about to take place. Nietzsche's estrangement from Wagner makes his attendance awkward, but Elisabeth goes. She even shares a room with Salomé, who is most enthusiastic about meeting the many intellectual luminaries sure to be in attendance at this great cultural event. Nietzsche tells Gast that he recently went to Naumburg, "to prepare my sister a little for *Parsifal*." He describes an interesting little scene.

> [The music] felt strange enough. Finally I said, "My dear sister, precisely this kind of music is what I was writing when I was a boy, at the time when I wrote my oratorio"; and then I took out the old manuscript and, after all these years, played it—the *identity* of *mood* and *expression* was fabulous! Yes, a few parts, for example, "The Death of Kings," seemed to us more moving than anything we had played from *Parsifal*, and yet they were wholly Parsifalesque! I confess that it gave me a real fright to realize *how* closely I am *akin* to Wagner. [L, 272; 7/25/82]

We have time only to pause before the irony of the way this passage wins a victory over Nietzsche's former "father-figure," Wagner, not just by giving the "son" priority in creating, but also by giving him the palm in a contest with the greatest msuician of the age. What most counts for our discussion is the way the "identity" of mood and expression between *Parsifal* and Nietzsche's childhood oratorio has the force of an uncanny coincidence. It evidences the remarkable kinship of their two creators—a resemblance which resembles the resemblance of Salomé and Nietzsche. And this double resemblance—between Nietzsche and Wagner, between Nietzsche and Salomé—becomes a problem.

How can Nietzsche know once again such passionate intimacy with another person, without repeating the end of that passion? He addresses that problem, in a covert way, in a letter written on July 16 to prepare Salomé for (and against) Bayreuth. In this letter Nietzsche explains his break with Wagner so as to clear a space for a new and unique relationship with Lou Salomé. But by the *way* he does so, he describes the same pattern of passion, renunciation, and the rediscovery of himself that the relationship with Salomé will end by repeating.

> As for Bayreuth, I am satisfied not to *have* to be there, and yet, if I could be near you in a ghostly way, murmuring this and that in your ear, then I would find even the music of *Parsifal* endurable (otherwise it is not endurable). I would like you to read, beforehand, my little work *Richard Wagner in Bayreuth*; I expect friend Rée has it. I have had such experiences with this man and his work, and it was a passion which lasted a long time—passion is the only word for it. The renunciation that it required, the rediscovering of myself that eventually became necessary, was among the hardest and most melancholy things that have befallen me. The last words that Wagner wrote to me are in a fine presentation copy of *Parsifal*: "To my dear friend, Friedrich Nietzsche. Richard Wagner, Member of the High Consistory." At precisely the same time he received from me my book *Human, All-Too-Human*—and therewith everything was perfectly clear, but also at an end.
>
> How often have I experienced in all possible ways just this—everything perfectly clear, but also at an end!
>
> And how happy I am, my beloved friend Lou, that I can now think of the two of us—"Everything is beginning, and yet everything is perfectly clear!" Trust me! Let us trust one another! With the very best wishes for your journey.
>
> Your friend Nietzsche [L, 269]

Nietzsche characterizes the coincidental similarity and difference of his relationship with Wagner and Salomé by using the figure of chiasmus, the crossing of a first term by a second moving in the opposite direction. With Wagner "everything was perfectly clear, but also at an end"; with her "everything is beginning, and yet everything is perfectly clear!" The movement of Wagner's and Nietzsche's works in the mail traces a similar crossing pattern. The letter describes the predominant recurrent pattern of Nietzsche's life as a permanent loss which accompanies clarity about the difference between two people. In this letter, and in his relationship with Salomé, Nietzsche is using the figure of chiasmus to take account of this pattern of repetition while he guards against it. For chiasmus registers a movement of repetition *and* reversal. Lou Salomé is to be the singular exception in his life, which, like the ultimate beauty of a work described in "Vita Femina," if it comes at all comes just "once" (*Ein Mal*), and then only by the "rarest of lucky accidents" (*der seltensten glücklichen Zufälle*). This singular moment is possible only because so many similar things—like the movement of clouds, the sun, and the sensible observer before the mountain—happen to "coincide" (*gleichzeitig*). That Nietzsche is trying to compose just such a moment in this letter is indicated by the way it begins. Because Lou Salomé has not answered his last letter, Nietzsche asks if it is possible she had not received the letter that described the happy arrival of the proofs of *The Gay Science*, cherries from his sister, and Salomé's own acceptance of a visit. Nietzsche writes of the (possible) nonarrival of his letter: "That would be a pity; in it I described for you a very lucky moment (*glücklichen Moment*)—several good things came my way all at once (*auf Einmal zur mir*)." And, as we have seen, Nietzsche does not fail to find a plethora of coincidences to signify the singular turn (he hopes) his life is taking. All these coincidences seem to certify that, if "life," as "Vita Femina" begins and ends in saying, "is a woman," then Lou Salomé is just *the* woman for Nietzsche's life.

The text of this letter shows us what militates against Nietzsche's hope for a singular happy coincidence of Lou Salomé and Nietzsche (in love). For Wagner as he is described here is not meant just as Nietzsche's contemporary. "Wagner" also stands for the chief instance of a pattern which Nietzsche's life seems compelled to repeat. It might have a predictive power. If only Lou could be inoculated from coming under the sway of this force—perhaps by reading Nietzsche's essay "Richard Wagner at Bayreuth." Then she might not become someone like Wagner whom it would become necessary to renounce, so that Nietzsche could find himself again. That such a dispensation is neither likely nor easy helps explain why Nietzsche ends the letter: "Trust me! Let us trust one another!" Such a trust would not be necessary if Salomé's and Nietzsche's coincidence were the result of their likeness as identities, or the work of obscure but irresistible forces. In fact this letter betrays a final evidence of the alterity and otherness undergirding both the Nietzsche-Salomé relationship and their correspondence: Nietzsche's previous letter was not lost, it just went unanswered. We cannot be sure why. Lou Salomé was usually a regular correspondent, and she wanted the trinity to work. But during this July period at Stibbe, she was becoming closer to Rée; also Rée was sowing suspicions of Nietzsche's motives. Or, perhaps, as I suggested above, she found something in the very intensity of Nietzsche's pleasure at her acceptance of his invitation to Tautenburg to which she could not respond. Then too, what appears as an extraordinary coincidence of events to Nietzsche might have seemed not so remarkable to Salomé.

The Breakdown of the Ethos of Aesthetic Affirmation

We can follow the appearance of difference between Nietzsche and Salomé by tracing the variations his letters work on the reiterated injunction to authenticity he gives to her. In an early letter, Nietzsche closes a compliment to Lou's "glorious openness of will" with the words, "Pindar says somewhere, 'Become the being you are'!" (L, 239; 6/10/82). Here the words help express a wonder and pleasure at the uniqueness of Lou Salomé's character—a definiteness and clarity and density of being which will make its more complete coming-into-being an adventure he plans to share. After Salomé has spent three weeks with Nietzsche and has returned to Rée at Stibbe, Nietzsche's first letter ends, "Lastly, my dear Lou, the old, deep, heartfelt plea: *become the being you are!* First, one has the difficulty of emancipating oneself from one's chains; and, ultimately, one has to emancipate oneself from this emancipation too!" (L, 293; end 8/82). Here Nietzsche has coupled the "old . . . plea" with a warning about the way an agent of emancipation can become a new kind of enslavement. This points in two directions: while he urges Salomé to be independent of the influence of the last three weeks (Nietzsche), he warns her against the influence of the next four (Rée). But Nietzsche may also be expressing his own ambivalence about the chains that now tie him to this new love.

One of the attractions Nietzsche finds in enjoining Lou Salomé to be true to herself is that it appears disinterested on his part. Of course, as we have seen, his identification with her becomes so complete that her self-becoming will be his, his hers. Lou Salomé's life has become the object of Nietzsche's *autobiographical* solicitude. This identification helps explain the form of the reproaches and regrets that emerge in the weeks after Salomé and Rée leave Leipzig for Berlin without Nietzsche. He writes to her that his own suffering "is all nothing to me as against the question of whether you find yourself again" (B, 98). Such a reclamation of herself is an implied requirement for his continued love. Nietzsche writes Rée that he would like to erase the "painful" memory of this year, "not because it offends me, but because it offends Lou in me" (L, 339; beginning 12/82). He is still struggling to hold on to the coincidence of their selves which their love has made seem indisputable. But he shows signs of relinquishing this idea. In a sentence crossed out in his notebooks, he announces that Lou has become "the caricature of my ideal" (B, 98). Finally he accuses her of a duplicity that makes her poetry a lie: "in your mouth, such a poem as 'To Pain' is a deep untruth" (B, 101). By marking a difference within Salomé, Nietzsche will be able to begin thinking a difference between her and himself.

In diagnosing the failure of their relationship, Nietzsche makes accusations against Salomé in the last weeks of 1882 that charge her with not having read, or properly read, or read and duly adhered to the program for self-becoming outlined in his early essay "Schopenhauer as Educator." This text was Nietzsche's first gift to her in the spring, and a short description of some of its main themes shows why Nietzsche felt that it offered a road map to the direction their relationship should follow. The essay begins with an emphatic assertion of the essential uniqueness of every person, which no "extraordinary chance" will allow to come a second time. The problem of life is to live and develop in an authentic relationship to the singular being that you are. This necessitates eschewing all the false bridges to other selves and systems by which every young person is tempted. Education begins by taking risks, and guiding oneself in the direction of what has truly stirred one's passion. But because the self is mysterious and obscure, help in becoming yourself is essential. A crucial passage of the essay describes the way this help can be won:

> . . . for your true being lies not deeply hidden in you, but an infinite height above you, or at least above that which you commonly take to be yourself. The true educators and molders reveal to you the real

groundwork and import of your being, something that in itself cannot be molded or educated: your educators can be nothing but your deliverers.[33]

The bulk of the remainder of the essay describes how for Nietzsche, Schopenhauer became the philosopher who enabled Nietzsche to educate himself. By this argument, true education finds a way to overcome the potential tension between self-becoming and some significant relationship with another. As we have seen, in the spring of 1882, Nietzsche imagines a reciprocal teaching relationship with Lou Salomé, so that each could become the other's catalyst in a process of education, "delivery," and self-becoming. Little wonder that Nietzsche is appalled when Salomé suggests, in their autumn arguments by mail, that what Nietzsche was really expecting in return for his knowledge was what she suspects all men finally want from women—sex.

How could Nietzsche have been so mistaken about the essential "likeness" of himself and Salomé? He later comes to see himself as having engaged in image-making. In a letter to Olga Overbeck in the summer of 1883, he is still making this practice sound disinterested: "I had the best intentions of remaking her into the image I had formed of her" (B, 69). The precision of Nietzsche's word choice, however, indicates the violence ("of remaking") and egotism endemic to image-making, whether it be part of the romance of philosophy or of love. Salomé shatters Nietzsche's image of her with two acts of will: a refusal to go through with the living arrangement, and a refusal to retract the accusations she has made about his ulterior motives. After heading south for the winter, Nietzsche appeals to Salomé to renounce those "suspicions" which endanger his higher feelings for her: "I feel every stirring of the *higher* soul in you—and love nothing about you but such stirring. I am glad to renounce all intimacy and nearness if only I may be sure that where we feel *at one* is just where common souls do not attain" (B, 96).

Nietzsche's demand that Salomé apologize for her cruder accusations is a way of punishing her; but it is also a last effort to rescue the memory of their ideal summer love. Her refusal to retract releases the full tide of Nietzsche's anger. In a few weeks, he has given up the effort to believe in their underlying spiritual coincidence. He mocks Salomé and himself for the delusive quality of his idealizations: "Formerly I was inclined to take you for a vision, for the

---

33. "Schopenhauer as Educator," in Clive, 330; translation modified.

earthly apparition of my ideal. Observe: *I have poor eyes."* This is more than a rhetorical flourish. If the aesthetic intensities of "Vita Femina" lead its reader to the enthralling, veiled image of the woman who is life (and truth), then Salomé's refusal to assume this ideal position puts Nietzsche's vision in question. Nietzsche's caustic irony is testimony to his continued involvement in this failed ideal. His delusive love for Salomé and this ideal seems the effect of the "intoxication" induced by another dangerous woman, the witch Circe. A later analysis in *The Will to Power* describes this process: "love" has done with reality to such a degree that in the consciousness of the lover the cause of it is extinguished and something else seems to have taken its place—a vibration and glittering of all the magic mirrors of Circe—" (*WP*, 808).

By December 1882, Nietzsche has invested an enormous aesthetic and emotional energy, and a large part of his life's project, in a grounding idea of what he and Salomé share, and this idea has collapsed. We need to grasp the scope of Nietzsche's dilemma. A few passages from a Christmas Day letter to Franz Overbeck state the problems vividly:

> This last *morsel of life* was the hardest I have yet had to chew, and it is still possible that I shall *choke* on it. I have suffered from the humiliating and tormenting memories of this summer as from a bout of madness ——. . . the most essential thing . . . involves a tension between opposing passions with which I cannot cope. . . . Unless I discover the alchemical trick of turning this—muck into gold, I am lost. Here I have the most splendid chance to prove that for me "all experiences are useful, all days holy and all people divine"!!! All people divine. My lack of confidence is now immense. . . . My relation to Lou is in the last agonizing throes—at least that is what I think today. [L, 365; 12/25/82]

Nietzsche intended that the life he led in 1882 would confirm the ethos of aesthetic affirmation defined in "Sanctus Januarius"; instead, the failure of the "trinity" and the passions that attend the loss of Lou Salomé seem to refute much of his philosophy. Nietzsche repeats the glowing epigraph from Emerson that appeared on the title page of the 1882 edition of *The Gay Science* so as to mock himself. How could the experiences of this year be "useful," these days of mad misery be "holy," and Salomé, Rée, or Elisabeth be "divine"? How can Nietzsche love fate if it is his fate to love Salomé, and Salomé has left? How can "looking away be his only negation," when the objects of his angry judgment do not lie at some aesthetic dis-

tance from himself, but swirl like demons within. Nietzsche had lost
that unity of feeling and tranquillity of will which the ethos of "Sanctus Januarius" had so carefully nurtured. In its place are "opposing
passions": rankling memories of last summer's bliss and quarrels, his
continued love for Salomé alongside a new hatred for her, and finally, his continued commitment to his thought beside an immense
new lack of confidence in it. For Nietzsche the alchemical trick of
turning muck [*Kothe*] to gold does not just seem necessary for writing *Zarathustra*, it seems necessary for continued survival.

To pull off this compositional "trick," Nietzsche needs to work a
significant shift in his categories. What that shift will be can be di-
vined from the last paragraphs of a letter written to Salomé after he
has gone south, still with hopes for a reconciliation. This passage
sounds like a rejoinder to a high-minded defense by Salomé of the
properly ideal, spiritual quality of their relationship. It also implies
a fundamental revision of the categories with which Nietzsche had
been living and interpreting his love for Salomé.

> Spirit? [*Geist?*] What is spirit to me! What is knowledge to me! I esteem
> nothing but impulses [*Antriebe*]—and I would swear we have something
> in common here [*Gemeinsames*]. Do look through this phase in which I
> have lived a few years—look behind it! Don't you be fooled about me:
> you surely don't believe that "the free spirit" is my ideal? I am—
> Excuse me! Dear Lou, be what you must be. [*Liebste Lou, seien Sie, was
> Sie sein müssen.*]   F.N. [L, 335; 11/24/82]

By the way it asserts their psychic commonality and urges an esteem of impulse, this text has a kinship with the love poem about
Columbus quoted above. It urges self-abandon that they might then
share. By both its message and tone, however, the letter's staccato
series of unsubordinated clauses are also expressive of the angry
haste of Nietzsche's iconoclasm. He would topple Salomé ideals. But
since Nietzsche had called the books from *Human, All-Too-Human*
through *The Gay Science* his "philosophy of the free spirit," his vehement renunciation of *Geist* is also a self-renunciation. *Geist*, usually
translated as "spirit" or "mind," implies a refined and reflected consciousness, a higher faculty of the person, which makes possible
meditation, self-control, and civilization. In its place Nietzsche
speaks up for *Antrieb*, the "impulse" which is an expression and con-
ducting medium of force, energy, and power. To embrace impulse
is to accept the necessity of a certain uncontrol, an abandon to the
self's unconscious wills and drives.

Nietzsche's advocacy of impulse leads the content of this letter to shortcircuit its informing desire. Nietzsche had always admired Salomé's "glorious frankness of will," and he imitated her risk-taking impulsiveness and independence by joining her in the scheme for a trinity. So now when Salomé has put an end to the scheme and taken her future away from Nietzsche, she *may* be wrong in her polemical appeals to the lost ideal of a *Geist*-filled intellectual arrangement. But perhaps she is also being quite true to her own inward necessary impulse to end their relationship. It is this possibility which seems to force Nietzsche to shift his letter away from reproach. Breaking in mid-sentence, he apologizes, and then offers a revision of his old moral injunction: not "become the being that you are," but "be what you must be."

In "Sanctus Januarius," Nietzsche's narrator overcomes obstacles by practicing a kind of aesthetic finesse of the negative. But the breakup of his relationship with Lou shoves Nietzsche, quite rudely, toward a confrontation with the problem of the will. He wills to have Lou, but Salomé will not have him. He wants the self-composure which accompanies an affirming and unified will; instead, he must try to swallow conflicting passions, many of which are entirely negative. In the three major texts written in the years that follow this crisis—*Zarathustra, Beyond Good and Evil*, and *The Genealogy of Morals*—Nietzsche moves toward a new concept of the will. The will is (1) unconscious as well as conscious, (2) multiple in number and discontinuous in type, (3) conflictual in origin and expression, and (4) expressive of the necessity of the *fatum* (fate) which is the self. Although this concept of the will seems remotely descended from the primacy accorded the much more abstract "Will" operating in the Dionysian chorus of Greek tragedy, the new idea is much less abstract and less indebted to Schopenhauer. We can grasp the nuanced and analytical precision of this idea of the will by pausing before several passages in the later works which result from and allow a reinterpretation of the Lou Salomé episode.[34] In the first of three contiguous sections of *Beyond Good and Evil*, Nietzsche describes how the "spirit's" desire to be master in its own house (the self) leads it not to truth but to the pleasures of a creative aesthetic flexibility that

34. In these three major texts Nietzsche seems to be using a concept of the will as a way to interpret the process of interpretation. Thus the various philosophical systems considered at the beginning of *Beyond Good and Evil* are instances of very different wills operating covertly beneath the announced collective desire of philosophy "to know truth." The circuitous, multiple, playful qualities of the will as a subduing power are implicit in the famous description of interpretation given in the second essay of *The Genealogy of Morals* (*BWN:GM*, II, 12, 513-14).

comes with a series of mendacious activities. His description of this process becomes a list of some of the subtle unconscious ways his will worked, in his love affair with Lou Salomé, to hide the manifest differences between him and her from himself. They include: appropriating the new and foreign to old values and ideas, so as to win a "feeling" of growth and increased power; saying "no," shutting one's windows, "in a state of defense against much that is knowable"; an occasional will of the spirit to let itself be deceived, by merely accepting such and such to be so, although one knows it is not, perhaps out of a "capricious" delight in all uncertainty and ambiguity, and a jubilant enjoyment of "the secrecy of some nook"; and finally a will to deceive others, and dissimulate in front of them, so as to enjoy the "multiplicity and craftiness of [one's own] masks" (*BWN: BG&E*, VII, 230).

One reason for this elaborate self-deception is suggested in the next section, where Nietzsche touches upon the necessity that works like a law in and through our will. "But at the bottom of us, really 'deep down,' there is . . . something unteachable, some granite of spiritual *fatum*, of predetermined decision and answer to predetermined selected questions. Whenever a cardinal problem is at stake, there speaks an unchangeable 'this is I'; about man and woman, for example, a thinker cannot relearn but only finish learning—only discover ultimately how this is 'settled in him'" (*BWN:BG&E*, VII, 231).

Here Nietzsche assumes that much of the self is fixed and necessary. The issue is neither to learn about external truths, nor to acquire the agility and goodwill to love fate. Instead, learning happens by coming to terms with our "granite of spiritual *fatum*" (fate). Little wonder that our lives do not readily yield to the pressure of the will of a spirit postulated to be free. Especially when it comes to a vexing "cardinal problem" like "man and woman." Nor can Nietzsche's opinions about "woman as such" be expected to be anything but his "truths."

Having given fair warning, he launches into one of his most sweeping assaults on the woman's movement of his day and its pretension to win "emancipation" by gaining equality with men. In many ways this text is simply a witty recirculation of traditional dicta about woman's true nature and proper sphere. But it also reads as a more pointed herangue against the modern woman for refusing to occupy an aesthetic role and position vis-à-vis men: one "of grace, of play, of chasing away worries, . . . of a subtle aptitude for agreeable desires . . . [of practicing an art that makes them] beings under

[194]

whose hands, eyes, and tender follies our seriousness, our gravity and profundity almost appear to us like folly" (*BWN:BG&E*, VII, 232). In this text Nietzsche reaffirms the connection of art and woman that he had developed in Book II of *The Gay Science*, and that had operated in ways unbeknown to him in his idealization of Lou Salomé. What made that love so intoxicating was the feeling that it "just happened." Like the power of beauty to be completely itself, their love, as a precious "coincidence," seemed to come about without the operation of anything like a will driving experience and interpretation, and the interpretation of experience, like a hidden motor. Only with their sudden differences did the will enter their relationship. Now Nietzsche's sweeping complaint against modern woman, for failing her aesthetic calling, arises from woman's daring to will.

It is not until the notebook entries to *The Will to Power* that Nietzsche offers a fundamental revision of his alignment of beauty, woman, will, and art. There, in sections 800 through 809, he interprets the experience of beauty and falling in love as instances of a will to power that seeks to idealize and perfect woman as an aesthetic object, which then seems to possess everything of value. Just as Nietzsche's adoration of art in *The Gay Science* prepared him to fall in love, so falling out of love enabled him to write a skeptical critique of art. In arguments which anticipate contemporary ideas about "the feminine mystique," Nietzsche tries to demonstrate the way women, through the orchestration of feminine beauty and sensibilities, enter into an unconscious complicity with male desire. By this interpretation, the naturalization of both beauty and the whole phenomenon of one person falling in love with another is just the final ruse of interpretive efforts which enhance the authority of their interpretations by occulting their own operation. From this analytic vantage point, not only Nietzsche's experience of Salomé's beauty, not only his feelings of love for her, but also the sense that their relationship was dictated by their fundamental likeness and coincidence are all interpretations that deny the fact of interpretation, acts of will that conceal the impulsive will by making it seem unreal beside a rapturous aesthetic moment of coincidence.

Lightning Strikes

. . . in the end, one experiences only oneself. The time is gone when mere accidents could still happen to me; and what could still come to

> me now that was not mine already? What returns, what finally comes
> home to me, is my own self and what of myself has long been in strange
> lands and scattered among all things and accidents [*Zufälle*].
>
> [*Zarathustra*, III, 1]

Given the violence of the accidents and experiences which helped
shape his life in 1882, it is not difficult to see why Nietzsche would
seek to earn the position, described by Zarathustra, where no "mere
accidents" could happen to him. It's comforting to know that everything that could possibly count for the self is already right here in
its "home." For one weary of uncontrollable encounters with the
strange lands of other people and passions, the grandiose claim that
after all there is nothing outside the self will be a kind of warranty
against further disturbances. For readers of Nietzsche's thought and
life there are two very different ways to confer upon Nietzsche the
invulnerability to accident the fictive god Zarathustra here imagines
for himself. First, one can conceive of Nietzsche's writings as a self-
enclosed arboretum where a limited number of germinal ideas of
the early and middle periods gradually grow, by cross-pollination
and ingenious grafting, to achieve the strength and mutual consistency of his mature work. Or, one can imagine Nietzsche as the most
acrobatic of artist-thinkers, whose genius allows him to take daring
leaps of speculative knowledge. These two versions of Nietzsche are
not incompatible, but the first emphasizes his thought's continuous
development, while the second insists upon its sudden shifts. Both
makes every part of Nietzsche's writing seem inevitable: the first by
the entelechial purposiveness of vegetative growth, the second by
the artistic and conceptual necessity presumed to attend the cre-
ations of genius.

Walter Kaufmann, in his account of Nietzsche's "discovery of the
will to power," shows his ingenuity by employing both these arguments at different points. Kaufmann's account of the "discovery" begins by insisting that the idea of the will to power "did not spring
from Nietzsche's head full grown. There is no point in his writing
where it suddenly appears as a surprising inspiration, although no
published work refers to it by name before its proclamation by Zarathustra." This is what justifies Kaufmann's method—of tracing its
"gradual growth through Nietzsche's notes and books."[35] Kaufmann discusses each of the pertinent works in chronological order,
with a summary description of the different ways Nietzsche conceived the idea of power (for example as an acquisition of control
over others, or as a touchstone to reading many different psycholog-

35. Kaufmann, *Nietzsche*, 179.

ical states). But when he reaches *The Gay Science*, Kaufmann shifts the terms of his analysis, so that a sudden flash of inspiration is used to account for the emergence of the idea of the will to power and *Zarathustra*.

> *The Dawn* might therefore be considered as a final test, a dress re-hearsal, before the will to power is proclaimed as Nietzsche's basic principle. . . . [*The Gay Science*] contains the first tentative consideration of the conception of the eternal recurrence of all events. Then, suddenly, the implication of both the will to power and the eternal recurrence struck Nietzsche's mind at once, like a flash of lightning, and in a fren-zied feeling of inspiration he wrote his *Zarathustra*—the first published work to contain any mention of the will to power by that name.[36]

There is no letter of Nietzsche's in which this inspired moment of "discovery" is recounted. Kaufmann's narrative is an analytical fiction which allows him to interpret what has also been the focus of my attention: the important shift in Nietzsche's thought between *The Gay Science* and *Zarathustra*. The differences in our narratives imply major differences in the way we read Nietzsche. Kaufmann represents Nietzsche working in the free space of meditation, where thought has a life all its own, unsullied by mundane personal experi-ences. Such thoughts will seem the spontaneous effect of autono-mous ideas (like "eternal return" and "the will to power") coming together all at once, and in a flash, to produce *Zarathustra*. Such thoughts are the pure effects of genius. Narrating things this way in-sulates Nietzsche from anything outside, from anything, such as Lou Salomé, other than himself. This perspective helps explain why Kaufmann relegates his recounting of selected motifs of Nietzsche's life to a chapter entitled "Nietzsche's Life as Background of His Thought." The record of Nietzsche's life is useful background, to be served up quickly and separately, so as to focus most attention upon a more important object—Nietzsche's thought qua thought—and a different task, a synthetic overview and analysis of that thought. My biographical reading of Nietzsche has sought to contest that proce-dure. Readers of Kaufmann's study will find Lou Salomé and Paul Rée discussed over a hundred pages apart from the paragraph where Nietzsche's "discovery" of the will to power is recounted. To suggest why Kaufmann's account of Nietzsche's activity of creation has a perverse and ironic relationship to the concept of the will I find Nietzsche "discovering," let us look more closely at the central image of Kaufmann's account.

36. Ibid., 188–89.

Kaufmann describes the way the "implication" of two thoughts —eternal recurrence and the will to power—struck Nietzsche's mind "at once" to generate the frenzied inspiration used in writing *Zarathustra*. To describe how this event happened, Kaufmann uses the simile "like a flash of lightning." The simile implies that this turn in Nietzsche's thought is sudden, fortuitous, and decisive, and that it is a moment where new light and insight appears. But something in this figure should give us pause. Kaufmann clearly sees this turn in Nietzsche's thought to be quite inevitable, even the natural outgrowth of his earlier ideas, and a useful way to overcome the dualism that threatens Nietzsche's system until he comes up with the global account of things the will to power allows him. So why does he describe this event as the sudden coincidence of two thoughts crossing, and why does he use one of the proverbial metaphors and examples of the accidental event—lightning striking? We can get some understanding of this question by following the genealogy of this image as it relates to the composition of *Zarathustra*.

Here are three relevant instances of lightning striking from Nietzsche's text, quoted in the order in which they were written.
From Zarathustra's speech in the Prologue:

> Where is the lightning to lick you with its tongue? Where is the frenzy with which you should be inoculated? Behold, I teach you the overman: he is this lightning, he is this frenzy. . . . Behold, I am a herald of the lightning and a heavy drop from the cloud; but this lightning is called *overman*. ["Prologue," 3, 4]

From a letter to Franz Overbeck after writing *Zarathustra*:

> It is night all around me again, I feel as if the lightning had flashed—I was for a short time completely in my element and in my light. And now it has passed. I think I shall inevitably go to pieces, unless something happens—I have no idea *what*.
> . . . My whole life has crumbled under my gaze: this whole eerie, deliberately secluded secret life, which takes a step every six years, and actually wants nothing but the taking of this step, while everything else, all my human relationships, have to do with a mask of me and I must perpetually be the victim of living a completely hidden life. I have always been exposed to the cruelest coincidences [*grausamsten Zufällen*]—or, rather, it is I who have always turned all coincidence into cruelty. [L, 373; 2/10/83]

In *Ecce Homo* Nietzsche offers a description of the "inspiration" which attended the composition of *Zarathustra*:

One hears, one does not seek; one accepts, one does not ask who gives; like lightning, a thought flashes up, with necessity, without hesitation regarding its form—I never had any choice. [*BWN:EH, Thus Spake Zarathustra*, 3, 756]

In all three of these texts, "lightning striking" is as sudden, decisive, and fortuitous as Kaufmann's narrative suggests. His account is closest to Nietzsche's glorification of writing *Zarathustra* in *Ecce Homo*. But a reflection on the resources and implications of this image as Nietzsche uses it will indicate the ways Kaufmann has idealized it. Because lightning striking is the purest energy in nature, it is not an event that has a structure or form necessary for the protocols of knowledge; its flash is too sudden and too vast for us to be present to it in the mode of conscious control; finally, its effects are too incalculable for us to plan to make use of its happening. If, to use a favorite idea of Nietzsche's, this lightning is part of a game of chance, it is not men but the gods who are playing (with us). Nietzsche draws on these resources of the image when he uses it in the prologue to *Zarathustra*. To overcome himself and his old values, man will have to allow himself to be struck by the lightning of the overman. In his letter Nietzsche shows how he is for a moment "completely in my element and in my light," but how quickly it passes. Two aspects of this creative instant need to be noted. It is not a moment of self-possession, but one of self-expenditure and loss. It is not a moment shaped by a controlling consciousness in the process of meditation, but an instant where Nietzsche becomes a medium of an event which exceeds conscious control ("I never had any choice").

These two ideas are implicit in the central illusion of this event as Nietzsche narrates it: this lightning striking is an inward event, something welling up—as Nietzsche's "inspiration," as Zarathustra's teachings of the overman, as a punctual episode of composition in February 1883—*but it is experienced as an external event*, something breaking over Nietzsche from outside. This helps explain the important shift Nietzsche works near the end of his letter to Overbeck. Alluding to the personal losses and victimization attending the Lou Salomé episode, he first says "I have always been exposed to the cruelest coincidences," as though they were a purely external contingent event; but he immediately revises the words to make himself party to these events: "or, rather, it is I who have always turned all coincidence into cruelty." How can this reversal of agency be so? It is the operation of the unconscious will which, by collaborating with the outside world in ways that are obscure to us, precipitates "events" in our lives which appear as contingent and necessary as lightning striking. In a famous passage of *The Genealogy of Morals* Nietzsche describes the will as so indissociably embedded in both the deed and the doer, that any postulated agent is subordinated to the more primary event—the deed where the will of the doer is discharged. He uses the same image which concerns us here:

> For just as the popular mind separates the lightning from its flash and takes the latter for an *action*, for the operation of a subject called lightning, so popular morality also separates strength from expressions of strength, as if there were a neutral substratum behind the strong man, which was *free* to express strength or not to do so. But there is no such substratum; there is no "being" behind doing, effecting, becoming; "the doer" is merely a fiction added to the deed—the deed is everything. [*BWN:GM*, I, 13, 481]

In both Kaufmann's and Nietzsche's accounts, both the writing of *Zarathustra*, and the idea of the will to power it announces, are deeds which have the character of necessity. But for Kaufmann this "discovery" is the spontaneous act of a free agent, bound only by the necessity of its own genius. This carefully cultivated indwelling genius allows Nietzsche, in a movement similar to the progress of Hegel's *Phenomenology of Mind*, to recuperate all the ideas of his philosophy up to that moment in the concept of "the will to power."[37] By contrast, in writing *Zarathustra*, Nietzsche describes himself as enveloped in and predicated by a flash of lightning. In its single absolute alternation between light and dark, the flash becomes a metaphor for sudden access and equally sudden loss. The lightning striking is produced by the momentary converging necessities of his recent life experience, and an obscure responding will.

When Nietzsche begins to compose *Zarathustra* he is weighted down with clouds of partially interpreted incident and half-articulate emotions. He is also carrying fresh scars. His life in the last months has come to seem like a series of violations—of lightning striking. The Lou Salomé episode—not Salomé in herself, but the experience of her which includes both Nietzsche and Salomé and much else—is an imposition upon Nietzsche's thought. The rethinking of the will it makes necessary did not *have* to happen by some internal principle, a lack or preexistent aporia of Nietzsche's thought. It is doubtful this rethinking would have taken the form it did if Nietzsche had never met Lou Salomé, if she and Rée had not pushed the trinity scheme,

37. Ibid., 178, 202.

[200]

if the quarrel had not happened the way it did, if Elisabeth had not intervened so powerfully, if Rée had not fallen in love with Salomé, and if Salomé had not decided against the living arrangement. This is why this episode is not the aporia of the system, the blind-spot implied by a preexistent philosophic text, but the impositioning of a contingent heterogeneous term, or set of terms, which has a decisive effect on the life lived and the text written. But, as we have seen, this is only half the story. This sequence of events is not absolutely exterior to Nietzsche; he has a collaborative part in shaping each event, both in its happening, and in the way he interprets it. At each stage of its unfolding, the Salomé episode also confronts Nietzsche with avatars of a hidden self, releasing repressed desires, and triggering the operation of an unconscious will. But since neither the events nor Nietzsche's responses to them were iron-clad and inevitable, they are also chance and arbitrary in their happening.

Writing Zarathustra *as a Revision of "Sanctus Januarius"*

Zarathustra is the culmination of much of Nietzsche's writing before 1883, and the seedbed for much of what follows. But I suggest that, most especially in writing Books I and II of *Zarathustra* in the first six months of 1883, Nietzsche is impelled toward a revision of "Sanctus Januarius" in the light of the Lou Salomé experience. His doing so becomes an act of defense, revenge, mourning, and revision. In following this writing practice, we can watch both a gain in conceptual density, as Nietzsche's text articulates a new concept of the will, and a loss of some of the human scale and social finesse of *The Gay Science*. In order to stay within the scope of this book, however, we can only make a beginning on a reading of *Zarathustra* from this vantage point.[38] One should start by noting how very much of the ethos which informs *The Gay Science* is extended in *Zarathustra*. There is the same glorification of risk, and the same aesthetic delight in the contingent as that which exceeds human control and be-

---

38. *Zarathustra* very much needs a reading which will combine detailed comprehensive commentary with a strong interpretation of the text. One starting point is suggested by the biographical perspectives of this study; a whole series of others are suggested by the eight sections of *Ecce Homo* that Nietzsche devoted to *Zarathustra*.

comes a test of our ability to say "yes" to life. But many things have changed also. Thus, a number of commentators have pointed out the way much of Zarathustra's social philosophy—critiques of marriage, chastity, and pity—refers, in a mode of anger and even revenge, to the morality of his sister and the false idealizations of Lou Salomé.[39] In the passage "On Child and Marriage," Zarathustra offers a scathing critique of the way marriage too often becomes a refuge and compromise borne of one's own weakness. His words suggest the way this weak love and his own recent experience in love might be recuperated:

> But even your best love is merely an ecstatic parable and a painful ardor. It is a torch that should light up higher paths for you. Over and beyond yourselves you shall love one day. Thus *learn* first to love. And for that you had to drain the bitter cup of your love. Bitterness lies in the cup of even the best love: thus it arouses longing for the overman; thus it arouses your thirst, creator. [Z, I, 20]

Nietzsche presents Zarathustra as the impassioned creator of a higher human type. Zarathustra is an artist, but one whose practice has none of the joyous ease of art evidenced in *The Gay Science*. Not the ingenious gardener or the deft musician but the sculptor, one ready to "be hard" enough to assault hard stone, becomes the representative artist of *Zarathustra*. In "Upon the Blessed Isles," Zarathustra describes his aesthetic mission:

> O men, in the stone there sleeps an image, the image of my images. Alas, that it must sleep in the hardest, the ugliest stone! Now my hammer rages cruelly against its prison. Pieces of rock rain from the stone: what is that to me? I want to perfect it: for a shadow came to me—the stillest and lightest of all things once came to me. The beauty of the overman came to me as a shadow. [Z, II, 2]

This text offers a repetition and displacement of "Vita Femina." The spontaneous arrival of a moment of beauty—here not the sun on the mountain, nor the woman who is "life," but the shadow of the overman—is not a moment of ecstatic culmination. Instead it justifies a strenuous attack upon man, "the ugliest stone." Now, not a rare and singular coincidence of factors makes possible seeing the ultimate beauties of a work, but the labor, the cruelty, and violence of carving this idea from stone. Between the vision of an idea of

39. Hayman, *Nietzsche*, chap. 10, "Zarathustra."

beauty and its actual production there is a crucial act of will. Of the hard, ugly stone which is man Zarathustra says, "I want to perfect it" (*Vollenden will ich's*).[40]

After the trauma of the Salomé episode, Nietzsche prescribes a goal for himself: to find a way to stand over and above his own experience.[41] He calls this process "self-overcoming." Thus he writes a text that allows him to speak in the voice of a god, Zarathustra, who preaches the "overman." While many passages of the text seem to teach the lessons of that experience, four contiguous sections of Book II seem most intimately connected with it. They are "The Night Song," "The Dancing Song," "The Tomb Song," and "On Self-Overcoming." Zarathustra's three songs are set apart from the text that surrounds them in several ways, which effects a pause in the action and indicates they are a disguised species of life-writing. In these three songs, there are no didactic speeches which speak out of (even the presumption) of a possession of the truth. Here, Zarathustra's own feeling and personal experience are directly engaged and become the focus of attention. Finally, the form of each—a song, with its attendant lyricism—is the conventional locus for a meditation upon love. These sections of *Zarathustra* move through the trajectory of Nietzsche's love experience: from purity of anticipatory desire, to an intimacy that becomes perplexing, to the regret that accompanies loss, to the triumph of an interpretation of the experience of this love's loss which allows it to be affirmed. What these texts offer, however, is *not* an arabesque of a narrative of what Nietzsche lived, but of what Zarathustra *would have* lived if he had stood in Nietzsche's place. This is how Nietzsche sought to say "yes" to the most difficult experience of his life: by reliving *as* Zarathustra his love affair with Lou Salomé.

"The Night Song" is one of the most famous lyrics in *Zarathustra*. Zarathustra is imagined to be alone at night and awake. He feels the pathos of being a god who cannot have the desires, longings, and concomitant pleasures of being a human. Here is the beginning of the song:

Night has come; now all fountains speak more loudly. And my soul too is a fountain.

40. This text echoes Michelangelo's famous words about an uncut stone: "I see an angel in it and I must free her."

41. In a letter to Heinrich von Stein, Nietzsche describes this aim: "What I desire most, then, is a high point from which I can see the tragic problem lying *beneath* me. I would like to *take away* from human existence some of its heartbreaking and cruel character" (L, 342; 12/82).

> Night has come; only now all the songs of lovers awaken. And my
> soul too is the song of a lover.
> Something unstilled, unstillable is within me; it wants to be voiced. A
> craving for love is within me; it speaks the language of love. [Z, II, 9]

The song develops the ironies that emerge from one set of images: it is not the solar god Zarathustra, but the weak humans receiving that light in the darkness of their desire, who know how to "create warmth out of that which shines," and "drink milk and
refreshment out of the udders of light." The god Zarathustra is condemned to stand apart, like a sun moving in its orbit, following its
"inexorable will" in "enmity" against all that shines. But finally Zarathustra's song partially contradicts itself. His desire (to desire) makes
him a kind of lover in his turn—but one consigned to a permanent,
though unwilling, renunciation. As a reliving of Nietzsche's relationship with Salomé, this song is first of all an expression of his love for
her. Nietzsche says in *Ecce Homo* that he composed the song on his
visit to Rome in the spring of 1883; his return there must have
brought back memories of meeting Lou Salomé there one year before. But at the same time this song is a defense against the lowly entanglements of a human love; it is, by the way it covertly invokes the
loftier calling of his work, an alibi constructed against ever again
seeking this all-too-human love.

After his suffering in love, nothing would have been easier than
for Nietzsche to have joined his voice to the chorus of philosophical
condemnations of love and passion. The lyrical longing of "The
Night Song" makes Zarathustra one who desires. In "The Dancing
Song," Zarathustra's affirmation of the value of youth, beauty, and
love becomes still more explicit. The section recounts a small dramatic episode, with a song in the middle. Zarathustra comes with his
followers upon some lovely young girls dancing in the forest, and
encourages them not to be shy but to keep dancing, especially with
that silly fellow Cupid. Zarathustra mocks the seriousness of Cupid
and offers a song as accompaniment. The song describes a series of
scenes and exchanges with two rivals for Zarathustra's love: Wisdom
and Life. By the song's end, Zarathustra has become confused and
entangled. He is overtaken by a chill, and something unknown is
around him, making him question and doubt the value of life.

Because Elisabeth's jealous rivalry with Lou Salomé helped break
up Nietzsche's living experiment, it is appropriate that in the scene
which here throws Zarathustra into despair about the value of life,

Zarathustra must contend with two jealous women who make competing claims on him: Life and Wisdom. To the extent that this scene replays a few elements of the Salomé affair, Life is endowed with Lou's mockery and directness of speech, and Wisdom has Elisabeth's penchant for indignant accusation. Zarathustra occupies Nietzsche's dangerous position in the middle where the fire of these two claimants cross.

Nietzsche's plunge into an open-ended relationship with Lou Salomé assumed the fundamental compatibility between the claims of life and those of philosophy. This belief was expressed poetically in the "Vita Femina" where the woman who is announced to be Life at the end of the aphorism is also the veiled figure of Truth, *Alētheia*. But we have also seen the way Nietzsche's interpretations in the spring of 1882 make his new desire for "life," as expressed in the trinity scheme, a separate, subordinate supplement to his love for wisdom—his "philo sophia," as expressed in his plans for writing *Zarathustra*.

The allegorical scene that unfolds in Zarathustra's song is not just a shadowy repetition of Nietzsche's experience, with Life promising love and sex, and Wisdom demanding attention to work and duty. This text also provides a more general analysis of Nietzsche's problem in 1882: as part of a barter for wisdom, this "seeker after knowledge" has renounced the more direct experience of love he imagines others know and he periodically yearns for. "The Dancing Song" reinterprets the situation of the philosopher and his desire. The central folly of Zarathustra's effort in this scene is his attempt to distinguish Life and Wisdom from both himself and each other, by explaining each to the other, and themselves. Thus when he describes Life to Life, she just laughs and insists that he projects his qualities upon her: "you men call me profound, faithful, eternal, and mysterious. But you men always present us with your own virtues, O you virtuous men!" Next Wisdom accuses him of only wanting and loving "Life." Then Zarathustra tries to settle this confusion by saying how "matters stand among the three of us." But his announced preference for Life is confused when he acknowledges that he is well disposed toward Wisdom because she reminds him so much of Life. "She has her eyes, her laugh, and even her little golden fishing rod: is it my fault that the two look so similar?" Then Life asks "Who is this Wisdom?" Zarathustra describes Wisdom, and his desire for her; she is "changeable and stubborn"; he "thirsts after her and is never satisfied," always wanting to tear away her veils; and "just when she speaks ill of herself she is most seductive." Then finally, Life confounds Zarathustra by rejoining with the words "of whom are you speaking? . . . no doubt of me."

Why does this episode throw Zarathustra into a deep and even suicidal perplexity? Because, just as Nietzsche's experience with Lou Salomé confused his effort to subordinate and separate Salomé from "Sophia," the symmetrical responses of these two-women-who-are-one confutes Zarathustra's effort to separate Life and Wisdom. If Wisdom and Life are rivals who are doubles, who are also always a part of Zarathustra's own act of projection, then several strange facts follow. Because the desire directed toward Life is fundamentally the same as the desire directed toward Wisdom, the effort to separate them from each other and subordinate either one to his desire for the other will fail. It follows that anything said by one of the trio about the others must come under suspicion, because it is just as revelatory of the speaker as of the one about whom he or she speaks. If one takes up residence in this love triangle, and as a seeker after knowledge one must, then one may become party to its imbroglio of desire, its vertiginous ironies, and the paralysis and hatred of life it can threaten.

The depression that overtakes Zarathustra at the end of "The Dancing Song" calls for a therapeutic journey, a journey into Zarathustra's past. So in "The Tomb Song" Zarathustra goes to the lost isle of his youth to recover the past so he can recover from it. There he breaks out of the past that threatens to become a tomb for him. But though "The Tomb Song" is supposed to be about Zarathustra's youth, the moment he starts to speak we find that it also relives the passions of a much more proximate part of Nietzsche's past: Salomé, Rée, and Elisabeth, and most especially the agonies of December and January. Two diametrically opposed feelings are registered. First there is the memory of the rich, erotic, and spiritual promise that lived for a moment in the past: "divine moments . . . divine glances and moments: I have not yet learned any other name. Verily, you have died too soon for me, you fugitives. Yet you did not flee from me, nor did I flee from you: we are equally innocent in our disloyalty." From the vantage point of this emotion, Zarathustra wants to make peace with his past. But he also feels anger, and registers a reproach with his "enemies" for having taken away "the visions and dearest wonders of [his] youth." When Zarathustra tried to affirm "all beings as divine," and asserted a gay wisdom, these enemies "stole my nights from me and sold them into sleepless agony."

Who are these "blessed ones" and these "enemies"? Here, as in

"The Dancing Song," Zarathustra confronts the problem of the double: for the very same persons and spirits who are favorably addressed at the beginning of the song as the visions and apparitions of his youth are also the enemies who receive his curse. The bearers of his joys and the focus of his most lovely memories—"you glance of love, you divine moments"—are also those who "murdered" these memories. And this is why he brings both an evergreen wreath to lay down, and a curse to speak. Expressing metaphorically the "opposing passions" Nietzsche complains of to Overbeck in his Christmas Day letter, these two opposed feelings about the same object threaten Nietzsche's sanity and require overcoming through an alchemical act of writing which will turn "muck" to "gold." But how can this be managed? Certainly not with Christian "forgiveness," which will neither forget nor forgive, and conceals a resentment in its expectations of eventual revenge.[42] Instead Zarathustra's vehement curses echo the reproaches to Salomé and Elisabeth stated earlier in Nietzsche's letters. But here, in Zarathustra's delayed repetition of them, these reproaches are offered in a form and context that will allow their overcoming.

The first accusation concerns the way the "enemies" of Zarathustra/Nietzsche have traduced the wisdom of his "youth," quite explicitly the positions of *The Gay Science*: "'All days shall be holy to me'—thus said the wisdom of my youth once; verily, it was the saying of a gay wisdom. But . . . where has this gay wisdom fled now?" In the letters, Nietzsche speaks of Lou Salomé as a bird of good omen who has blessed his path. But her early indiscretions and later insinuations have turned hoped-for beauty to ugliness. Zarathustra's cognate curse: "Once I craved happy omens from the birds; then you led a monster of an owl across my way, a revolting one. Alas, where did my tender desire flee then?" Nietzsche blamed Salomé for precipitating his break with Elisabeth and his mother and for estranging him from Rée. Zarathustra's accusation: "you changed those near and nearest me into putrid boils . . . [making] those who loved me scream that I was hurting them most." Elisabeth's piety and virtue are condemned in the letters for spoiling Nietzsche's love for Lou Salomé. Zarathustra registers a parallel reproach: "you wounded my virtue in its faith. And whenever I laid down for a sacrifice even what was holiest to me, your 'piety' immediately placed its fatter gifts alongside, and in the fumes of your fat what was holiest

42. See the splendid curse of the Christian against his Roman oppressor cited by Nietzsche from Thomas Aquinas, in *The Genealogy of Morals* (*BWN:GM*, I, 15, 485–88).

to me suffocated." And finally, a double reproach is leveled, so that it falls in different ways upon both Lou and Elisabeth: "And once I wanted to dance as I had never danced before, over all the heavens I wanted to dance. Then you [Elisabeth/Lou] persuaded my dearest singer [Lou/Rée]. And he struck up a horrible dismal tune; alas, he tooted in my ears like a gloomy horn."

In aligning Zarathustra's curses with Nietzsche's reproaches in his letters, I do not intend to reduce fiction to fact, to transport an imaginary effusion to the more precisely specified ground of a real event. That is what I have described above as the "biographical reduction." Instead, my alignment of similar texts allows me to mark a displacement Nietzsche's writing of *Zarathustra* has effected. For when Nietzsche's reproaches are repeated as Zarathustra's "curses," and Nietzsche's joyous hopes for the spring and summer as Zarathustra's "blessings," all these impassioned enunciations appear as so many expressions of will. When Nietzsche rejoiced in the coincident gifts of the summer (*The Gay Science*, Salomé, Elisabeth's) and the promise they offered in the winter (the trinity, Zarathustra), his will seemed singular, harmonious, and self-consciously ready to express itself freely in the achievement of its goals (writing *Zarathustra*, loving Lou). But when the relationship with Lou Salomé fails, the role of Nietzsche's will is transformed. Now the trinity scheme and its failure appear as a psychic knot, a symptom and episode where the will has expressed itself in ways which were devious, conflicted, and multiple; it has operated unconsciously as well as consciously, and has betrayed a certain fatality about the self. This will also seems to have been deflected from its central creative goal. Thus the climatic reproach directed at Lou, Rée, and Elisabeth by Nietzsche in December, the most urgent curse directed at his "enemies" by Zarathustra in "The Tomb Song":

> Murderous singer, tool of malice, most innocent yourself! I stood ready for the best dance, when you murdered my ecstasy with your sounds. Only in the dance do I know how to tell the parable of the highest things: and now my highest parable remained unspoken in my limbs. My highest hope remained unspoken and unredeemed. And all the visions and consolations of my youth died! [Z, II, 11]

This "curse" short-circuits itself in its enunciation. For the "highest hope" Zarathustra mourns for as "unspoken" is spoken in *Zarathustra*. It is this irony which triggers Zarathustra's two questions: "how did I endure it? how did I get over and overcome such wounds?" As with "The Dancing Song" the ironic opposition of the doubles—Life and Wisdom, the blessed ones and enemies,—shows that Zarathustra is implicated in this scene and cannot assume an innocently injured relationship to it. He is entangled by his own will, operating unconsciously. But this is equally true of his surprising compositional victory. Zarathustra can only conclude that there is the obscure force of unforeseen strength which operates in one's life in unexpected ways: "Indeed, in me there is something invulnerable and unburiable, something that explodes rock: that is *my will*. Silent and unchanged it strides through the years." That the ways of this will are both hidden and heroic is implicit in the form of Zarathustra's praise of the self rescued by his will. Zarathustra offers an apostrophe to a self who is absent from himself in some fundamental way: "You are still alive and your old self, most patient one. You have still broken out of every tomb. What in my youth was unredeemed lives on in you; and as life and youth you sit there, full of hope, on yellow ruins of tombs." Nietzsche seemed paralyzed, dizzy, and at a loss. But lightning strikes; the will discharges itself; *Zarathustra* is written. Of this event, Nietzsche writes, "I had no choice." And by this writing, at least while in the element of composition, Nietzsche overcomes the galling conflicts of the Lou Salomé episode. In the imagery of this section, the tomb that threatened permanent death has become a platform for resurrecting old goals.

How is Nietzsche able (as Zarathustra) to represent the "overcoming" of the experiences of 1882? The answer is suggested in a single line of the reproach directed at Lou and Elisabeth: "Murderous singer, tool of malice, most innocent yourself!" For Nietzsche to step above the episode he has just lived, and overcome his own anger, he will need a general interpretation of the will, one which apprehends the way all the parties to the personal disasters of this year—by putting their wills in play in the form of values, desires, and renunciations—have been "innocent." The need to achieve this tougher, less personal, and more farsighted perspective on his recent trials helps explain why "On Self-Overcoming" comes directly after the three songs. Zarathustra's personal meditation suddenly gives way, without any transition, to the assumed public persona of a teacher. This grounds, in some more objective way, the self-overcoming he hopes he has achieved.

Nietzsche's writing *Zarathustra*, in spite of all that seemed to block it, stands as an instance of the very self-overcoming he here describes in three areas: knowledge, ethics, and politics. Self-overcoming is an only partly voluntary process by which a subject seeks to reach a certain end through the use of a focused conscious will, but this very expression of will recoils back upon the person to change him and his destination. One who knows the "will to truth" wants to "*make* all being thinkable." The one who names valuations of "good and evil" seeks to "create the world before which [he or she] can kneel." And he who wills to command finds that very will recoils to command obedience. In each of these cases a more powerful will operates behind the punctual intentional will that thinks it guides the efforts at knowledge, ethics, and command. Nietzsche calls this more comprehensive will "the will to power." It always confounds and exceeds the will's original effort. Thus Life announces of truth: the "will to power walks also on the heels of your will to truth." The icons of good and evil erected on the bark which floats upon the river of becoming are not threatened by time or the river, but by the very thing which created those values: "that will itself, the will to power—the unexhausted procreative will of life." Finally he who rules must "still pay for its commanding. [He] must become the judge, the avenger, and the victim of its own law." In its ironic reversals and nonteleological movement, "self-overcoming" parodies the advance of the (Hegelian) dialectic it supplants.[43]

By valuing the self's self-overcoming, and the will to power that enables the self to overcome itself, Nietzsche befriends the events and actions of the past year. Thus, for example, nothing has hurt him more in 1882 than a series of harsh moral judgments: Elisabeth's judgments of Salomé and himself; Lou's judgments of Nietzsche's crass motives; and Nietzsche's own strident judgments of both women. But with a broader conception of the will which *Zarathustra* postulates, Nietzsche can bracket the content of these moral valuations. He can see all these judgments as false, yet quite affirmatively human in their longing, and best of all, on the way to something better. "With your values and words of good and evil you do violence when you value; and this is your hidden love and the splendor and trembling and overflowing of your soul. But a more violent force and a new overcoming grow out of your values and break egg and eggshell." Zarathustra's account of the will to power is intended to offer a general account of the most fundamental drive behind life. But it is also an interpretation of what has worked through Nietzsche and those close to him in the last year. Zarathustra describes the

---

43. For the way Nietzsche's writing offers a fundamental alternative to the Hegelian dialectic, see the final chapters of Gilles Deleuze, *Nietzsche et la philosophie*.

will to power as a force and process which makes men ready to risk, is shaped by an end which is inevitably overcome, proceeds by contradictory movements, and in its creative action expends itself. This general analysis doubles as a philosophic allegory of the Lou Salomé episode.

> And where men make sacrifices and serve and cast amorous glances, there too is the will to be master. . . .

> And life itself confided this secret to me: "Behold," it said, "I am *that which must always overcome itself.*" Indeed, you call it a will to procreate or a drive to an end, to something higher, farther, more manifold: but all this is one, and one secret.

> "Rather would I perish than forswear this; and verily, where there is perishing [*untergehen*] and a falling of leaves, behold, there life sacrifices itself—for power. That I must be struggle and a becoming and an end and an opposition to ends—alas, whoever guesses what is my will should also guess on what *crooked* paths it must proceed.

> "Whatever I create and however much I love it—soon I must oppose it and my love; thus my will wills it. And you too, lover of knowledge, are only a path and footprint of my will". . . . [Z, II, 12]

For Nietzsche, as he began to write in January 1883, the personal dilemma and the philosophic problem posed by the task of *Zarathustra* were the same: how does one find a vantage from which even *this* experience—the Lou Salomé episode, with its bitter losses and its mockery of cherished values—can be affirmed as something to which one can say an unconditional "Yes"? Our reading of these three songs and "On Self-Overcoming" helps to indicate how. First Nietzsche assumes the mask of a god, repeating human desires from a safe position above human entanglements. Then he repeats and interprets the dizzying confusion of his designs upon Life and Wisdom. He then gives ambivalent expression to his hatred and love in a series of blessings and curses. Finally all these moments—desire, confusion, and ambivalence—issue in the writing of *Zarathustra*. By interpreting life as an expression of the will to power, *Zarathustra* attempts to vindicate an experience it does not comprehend. Now even the losses of this episode in Nietzsche's life have become that which, to paraphrase "Personal Providence," "must not be missing." In this way Nietzsche hopes he has changed the fatality of the "it was" to the affirmation of "thus I willed it" (Z, II, 20).

By writing *Zarathustra*, Nietzsche meets one of the goals of the social adventure of 1882. But this original purpose for experiencing Lou Salomé has been realized in an ironic mode, for this end has changed in Nietzsche's approach to it. It is true that the first two parts of *Zarathustra* give Nietzsche a firm grasp of those concepts of the will to power, the overman and eternal recurrence, which will allow him to conceive the great works of the final six years before he goes mad. But *Zarathustra* also entails a certain loss for him. For to comprehend the human condition at the highest level of moral generality, Nietzsche writes a parody of the New Testament, where the protagonist-god speaks with a new obliqueness and abstractness of statement. At times it also seems that Nietzsche has reinvented the harangue of the Old Testament prophet. His criticism can become so unremitting and ungenerous that it seems prejudiced by the very personal sufferings and resentments Nietzsche warns against and has labored so arduously to "overcome." What has vanished are the precise social horizons of *The Gay Science*, where Nietzsche's narrator, speaking as a contemporary European, could be generously open to social exchange, practice a philosophy unoppressed by the "spirit of gravity," and make subtle, patient discriminations in reading art, cities, peoples, and the moods of his own experience. Lou Salomé, in articles published between 1891 and 1893, seems to have been the first to analyze this fundamental shift in Nietzsche's work. Salomé criticizes *Zarathustra*, and the works that follow it, for engaging in a mytho-prophetic glorification of the will which lapses away from the more radical, rational critique of religion found in the earlier works. While I do not agree with Salomé's sweeping subordination of the later work available to her, it is a valuable antidote to the presumption of a relentless dialectical advance which most ascribe to Nietzsche, and which I have criticized above in my reading of Walter Kaufmann.[44] No less than Freud's institution of psychoanalysis, Nietzsche's movement after 1882 into a global cultural-historical critique may be an equivocal achievement, entailing loss as well as gain.

The crisis and turn in Nietzsche's life and writing in the winter of 1882–1883 also had lasting personal costs. Nietzsche does not again risk a close, passionate friendship. Thus "self-overcoming" can be lonely and difficult. But perhaps Nietzsche had little choice. Writing *Zarathustra* was not the expression of a controlled and unified inten-

44. Salomé's reading of Nietzsche's work may be found in *Friedrich Nietzsche in seinen Werken* (Vienna, 1894). Biddy Martin's forthcoming study will offer the first sympathetic reading of Lou Salomé's interpretation of Nietzsche's life and work available in English. For Binion's treatment of these issues see part II, chap. 5 of *Frau Lou: Nietzsche's Wayward Disciple*.

tion, but a compromise formation which would allow emotional survival. *Zarathustra* gives a useful articulation to the conflicts and oppositions of will, the perishings and expenditures of energy which, under the aegis of the concept of the will to power, Nietzsche makes a concomitant of this and every creative effort. In writing of the will to power he uses one theme and trope repeatedly to characterize what is creative and destructive and surprising about its process: "it is hazard and danger and casting dice for death." To affirm life as an expression of the will to power, and as released from teleological goals or predetermined values, means learning to affirm chance. In doing so, Nietzsche endorses that tragic consciousness which can say "yes" to life even in the midst of loss. This positive valuation is one reason for his embrace of the Dionysian from *The Birth of Tragedy* to the penultimate name in *Ecce Homo*. And an ethos of self-expenditure is expressed in the title of the text which stands over the Salomé episode as the promise of a gay science, and the allure of Zarathustra, and a warning of the year's coming suffering. "Incipit Tragedeia": tragedy begins. The central happening of tragedy is a human loss which appears as chance, that arbitrary fatality tragedy is constructed to express and contain. This is one reason it is appropriate that our reading of Nietzsche will now issue in a reading of *Hamlet*.

Near the beginning of Book III of *Zarathustra* one may read what is perhaps Nietzsche's most ringing tribute to chance. This passage from "Before Sunrise" seems an apt way to close the second movement of this book. It would seem too facile and comprehensive in its "yes-saying," if we did not know how costly it was in the earning, how bittersweet the results:

> This is my blessing: to stand over every single thing as its own heaven, as its round roof, its azure bell, and eternal security. . . . "Over all things stand the heaven Accident [*Zufall*], the heaven Innocence, the heaven Chance, the heaven Prankishness." But chance [*Ohnegefahr*, literally, "without risk or danger"]—that is the most ancient nobility of the world, and this I restored to all things: I delivered them from their bondage under Purpose. . . ."

> O heaven over me, pure and high! . . . you are to me a dance floor for divine accidents [*Zufälle*], . . . a divine table for divine dice and dice players [*Wurfelspieler*]. [Z, III, 4]

A CRITICAL READING
OF THE TRAGIC ALEATORY:
THE CASE OF HAMLET, PRINCE
OF DENMARK

[*Hamlet*] is built up on Hamlet's hesitations over fulfilling the task of revenge that is assigned to him. According to the view which was originated by Goethe and is still the prevailing one today, Hamlet represents the type of man whose power of direct action is paralysed by an excessive development of his intellect. . . . What is it, then, that inhibits him in fulfilling the task set him by his father's ghost? The answer, once, again, is that it is the peculiar nature of the task. Hamlet is able to do anything—except take vengeance on the man who did away with his father and took that father's place with his mother, the man who shows him the repressed wishes of his own childhood realized. Thus the loathing which should drive him on to revenge is replaced in him by self-reproaches, by scruples of conscience, which remind him that he himself is literally no better than the sinner whom he is to punish. Here I have translated into conscious terms what was bound to remain unconscious in Hamlet's mind; and if anyone is inclined to call him a hysteric, I can only accept the fact as one that is implied by my interpretation.

—Freud, *The Interpretation of Dreams*

The metaphysical comfort—with which, I am suggesting even now, every true tragedy leaves us—that life is at bottom of things, despite all the changes of appearances, indestructibly powerful and pleasurable. . . .

[215]

In this sense the Dionysian man resembles Hamlet: both have once looked truly into the essence of things, they have *gained knowledge,* and nausea inhibits action; for their action could not change anything in the eternal nature of things; they feel it to be ridiculous or humiliating that they should be asked to set right a world that is out of joint. Knowledge kills action; action requires the veils of illusion: that is the doctrine of Hamlet, not that cheap wisdom of Jack the Dreamer who reflects too much and, as it were, from an excess of possibilities does not get around to action. Not reflection, no—true knowledge, an insight into the horrible truth, outweighs any motive for action, both in Hamlet and in the Dionysian man.

—Nietzsche, *The Birth of Tragedy*

The Sublimity of Shakespeare's Greatness

If Shakespeare could return to this world and again be one of our company, I suspect that nothing would seem stranger to him about our century than the idolatry directed at one William Shakespeare. Critics of literature, especially those of a traditional cast, are supposed to be used to estimating the extent of a poet's greatness. But somewhere in the Romantic period, critics apparently lost the means to measure the achievement of Shakespeare's art. Or so we are told in two modern essays which make their own attempt to define and measure Shakespearean greatness: George Steiner's "Shakespeare —Four Hundredth," written for the birthday celebration of 1964, and Murray Krieger's brief survey of the critical history of Shakespeare's reception, entitled "Shakespeare and the Critics: Idolatry of the Word."[1] To some extent these two essays cheerfully fall prey to the phenomenon they describe: those who attempt a critical assessment of Shakespeare's art end in idolatrous praise and hyperbole. Because this tendency seems to me not atypical of Shakespeare criticism at large, it is worth taking note of how, in these two essays, rational criticism modulates into a testament to Shakespeare's artistic mastery. Then we will be in a position to plot a path for reading around that mastery.

Both articles note the most striking feature of the history of

1. See Steiner's *Language and Silence: Essays on Language, Literature, and the Inhuman* (New York: Atheneum, 1974), 198–211, and the Krieger article in *Shakespeare: Aspects of Influence*, ed. G. B. Evans (Cambridge: Harvard University Press, 1976), 193–210.

Shakespeare's reception: as Steiner writes, in describing pre-Romantic judgments: For Samuel Johnson, "Shakespeare was a very great writer, at moments unsurpassed. But his achievement was no unique riddle of glory" (199). By quoting passages from Dryden to Johnson, Murray Krieger shows how Shakespeare's "greatness" was not deemed to encompass every artistic virtue; instead he was viewed as the greatest example of an artist ruled by an undisciplined "natural" genius—as opposed to the genius shaped by rules of a more artful decorum, typified by Ben Jonson, and more strictly indebted to the norms of classical antiquity, as understood by contemporary aesthetics. But toward the end of the eighteenth century, Shakespeare's art begins to be associated with the sublime, the limitless, and an attendant sense of mystery. When Coleridge finds that Shakespeare's work displays an organic rather than mechanical form, which helps reconcile its parts into a larger mysterious unity; and when he draws upon a German Romantic exaltation of genius over talent to go with this German aesthetic; he is prepared to insist that Shakespeare's art has *both* the natural genius usually accorded it, and the artistic judgment more often denied it. This opinion overturns an earlier measured sense of Shakespeare's strengths and limits, and projects a mysterious beyond for his art and language, which Krieger then traces down through the New Critics to his own aesthetic theory. The title of Krieger's essay implies that he can stand outside the "idolatry" of Shakespeare's "word," but he finally endorses that idolatry as the precondition of modern critical practice.

George Steiner's essay pursues an answer to the enigma of the incomparable greatness of Shakespeare's art. Steiner finds that greatness growing out of a range of diverse factors: Shakespeare's proximity to medieval conceptions and folk art; the Renaissance discovery of "new Americas" of bold intellectual inquiry; the high quality and social diversity of his audience; the sinew and inventiveness of Elizabethan language; and that language's proximity to the materiality of daily life. But when Steiner exhausts the many ways Shakespeare was "lucky in his times" and asks why he goes so far beyond his contemporaries, he can only respond that Shakespeare has done something more with language. "More than any other human intellect of which we have adequate record, Shakespeare used language in a condition of total possibility." Thus, Steiner explains, Shakespeare engages the polysemous and multivalent array of meanings opened in every word: "in Shakespeare, this alertness, this mastering response to the sum of all potential meanings and values, reaches an intensity far beyond the norm" (206). But Steiner cannot really explain the grounds of this special "mastering response" to meaning, so he offers a reader's testimonial: "To read Shakespeare is to be in contact with a verbal medium of unequalled richness and exactitude" (207). He even entertains the notion that Shakespeare enjoyed a special neurological advantage, "harnessing more fully, more economically than other men, areas of the cortex in which speech functions are thought to be localized" (206). Steiner speculates that this advantage may enable Shakespeare's language to have a special relation to the way the word emerges from a mysterious original human experience into articulate meaning, that is by "reach[ing] back to the . . . obscure primary zone where human language emerges from a 'pre-vocabulary' of biological and somatic stimulus or recognition" (206). Steiner's text has not here given up the effort to explain the enigma of Shakespeare's unique greatness. Instead, that enigma is relocated from the artist (and his age) to his language (or his brain). In the absence of an explanation, Steiner offers a climactic analogy to figure our relationship to the greatness of Shakespeare's language: "We speak as if words were a piano score; Shakespeare's is the full orchestration" (207). The unique powers here claimed for Shakespeare's art, as beyond all other human art in language, prepares for Steiner's gloomy closing assessments: that we are entering a time of semi-literacy where a direct reading apprehension of Shakespeare will become increasingly unusual; that nuclear war may bring *Hamlet* and *Othello* into "partial oblivion"; and finally, that no one will ever "surpass" Shakespeare. This crepuscular ending indirectly assures us that the solar presence of this essay— Shakespeare's art—abides solitary, self-identical, and unrivaled in its Appollonian apartness. Its existence is absolute, above and outside the flux and contingency of its reception.

The estimates of Shakespeare's literary influence offered by Krieger and Steiner are as sweeping and vertiginous as their estimate of his greatness. Krieger maintains that Shakespeare's presence is the crucial factor in the greater liberalism and flexibility of English critical practice, and further, that Shakespeare has been the "shaping power" behind English poetics since Coleridge because it has been impelled to account for the miraculous power of Shakespearean language: "[critics] assume normal habits of semantics and logic to operate in our language, and . . . see Shakespeare as forcing upon language an illogic that opens for us, and yet controls, an untold pattern of semantic possibilities" (205). Steiner's essay opens by expanding Shakespeare's text so that it engulfs every speaker of English with belatedness and indebtedness. By the logic of this remarkable passage, there is little wonder we cannot stand outside Shakespeare's text and estimate its greatness; we are always already inside this text and this artist which/who "speaks" itself through us.

> The words with which we seek to do him homage are his. We look for new celebration and find echo. Shakespeare has his mastering grip on the marrow of our speech. The shapes of life which he created give voice to our inward needs. We catch ourselves crooning desire like street-corner Romeos; . . . Shakespeare is the common house of our feelings. He has seen so exactly, so variously for us; he has struck the note of consciousness over so wide a range of human experience; he found for what he saw and felt such authority of statement—making his words not only a mirror of truth, but its vital, inexhaustible form —that we meet his voice around every corner of our sensibility. Even our cry and our laughter are only partly ours; we find them where he left them, and they bear his stamp. [198]

This extravagant estimate of Shakespeare's greatness and influence makes his art a vast appropriating force, which stamps, possesses, and encloses a significant part of every human effort at expression. As the medium of every effort of expression it becomes the horizon—both the "beyond" and the limit—of any subsequent artistic effort. Because Steiner has situated us all in the not-so-home-like enclosure of this indebtedness, it is no surprise that, by essay's end, he is "certain" that none "will surpass Shakespeare . . . [who is] not only the greatest writer who has ever lived, but who will ever live" (211). By speaking from the vantage point of the Shakespearean text he figures, Steiner is finally enabled to claim a prophetic and eschatological authority—to speak not only of all that men and women have done, but also of all they ever will do.

In praising Shakespeare, in proclaiming their gratitude and debt to him, and in groping to take his measure, critics since the eighteenth century have produced someone above and apart from the mortal who wrote the plays, a new figure named "Shakespeare" with something of an independent history in criticism, which has had no little influence upon our way of reading the plays. It is worth putting this name in quotation marks, to remind the reader that I am now referring to a product of cultural image-making, of which the essays by Krieger and Steiner are vivid instances. What are the dominant attributes of this "Shakespeare"? The course of Shakespeare idolatry, as it is both reported and reenacted in these essays, has effected a certain shift: the peculiar greatness of Shakespeare's art has gone from being the product of a mortal, carrying certain definable

and visible qualities, to being miraculous, undefinably great, and finally invisible to the critic. Shakespeare's influence begins as calcula-
ble, and since some repeat him, and others do not, our debt to him
measurable. But as idolatry grows, he becomes an indispensable element of our being in language; now, his influence is as incalculable
as is our debt to him. With these shifts toward a sublime idea of
Shakespeare's art and influence comes a concomitant shift in the operative concept of the reader/spectator opposite the plays: from
being one who can read, assimilate, and criticize Shakespeare's art
like any other, the reader/spectator comes to be a function of
"Shakespeare" as the defining horizon of our consciousness. Critics
proclaim him a translunar body of the aesthetic firmament, a kind
of DNA for our imaginations; he becomes a fateful necessity and enclosure whose accelerating greatness diminishes us. The reader/
spectator as discrete agent has vanished.[2]

It is not sufficient to insist that a certain bizarre hyperbole is operating here, or to wonder what institutional or ideological ends such
testaments of belief might serve. I am most concerned with how
such an idea and image of "Shakespeare" helps determine in advance a certain interpretation of his text, which I have found working in many modern readings of *Hamlet*. From the vantage of Shakespeare idolatry, Shakespeare's text is a self-complete totality, which is
neither partial in itself nor limited to the meanings discovered in it;
it is a masterpiece of design and structure, which, however, is inter-
animated with a linguistic energy that exceeds any of the topoi,
genres, or structures it engages. This idea of structure makes the
text seem inexhaustible; the text replenishes itself continually, offering some new aspect of its truth to each age. There was, it is presumed, a moment when "Shakespeare," as masterful creating genius, saturated this text with a surplus of intended truths. The idea of
such a presiding genius still haunts the text's readers, furthering the
belief that what is written here is immune, in both its production
and its reception, from the effects of chance and contingency. It is
these interpretive assumptions, as they operate in the most familiar
interpretations of Shakespeare's most famous play, that I wish to
open to critical examination.

By bringing the question of chance to Shakespeare's text, I can
probe and contest the mastery claimed for Shakespeare the way I

2. The metaphor of DNA is not my act of hyperbole. It is taken from an article by
Paul D'Andrea, "'Thou Starre of Poets': Shakespeare as DNA," in *Shakespeare: Aspects
of Influence*, ed. Evans, 163–92.

did with Freud and Nietzsche. But, as noted in the Introduction, I immediately encounter a practical obstacle. There is almost no biographical "life-writing" for Shakespeare, no writing carrying the linguistic traces of a contingent historicity which we could use to read against the mastery of the artistic text. It is not that such life-writing never existed. The sonnets may, for example, have originally been part of a correspondence rife with proposals, promises, and reproaches—perhaps even the times and places of planned assignations. But this broader field of life-writing has become invisible (as life-writing). Shakespeare has almost no personal history for us. This absence has produced the illusion that he, and his text, are beyond history, contingency, and partiality. To investigate the mastery of Shakespeare's text, I will need to adopt a more circuitous strategy. Just as chemists observing chemical reactions before the discovery of nuclear accelerators were able to surmise many facts about nuclear structure, so I shall read chance in *Hamlet* indirectly. I will begin by reading from the vantage point of Hamlet the character, so we can understand how chance obscures and complicates his efforts to avenge his father, and to become heir to the mastery both public legend and personal memory attribute to his father. Next I will take note of a suppression of chance in critical readings of *Hamlet* and of the more general way those readings presume artistic mimesis to operate. Finally I will attempt a textual reading which will allow me to stand outside the frame of Hamlet's desire. Then we can read the series of binding contingent reversals which compose Hamlet's last act.

Once one has analyzed the many ways the institution of literary study removes Shakespeare's text from the effects of an arbitrary and contingent history, then the disappearance of Shakespeare's life-writing no longer appears a gratuitous accident that our reading is calculated to circumvent or repair. Instead, the erasure is an especially striking instance of the claim to a position apart from life made for most art. Erasing history puts the frame around the image, the sculpture on its pedestal, and the written text into the abstract space of the canon of classics. Finally, the erasure of life-writing is a crucial enabling factor in the production of that most purely artistic of all artists, a "Shakespeare" who has the authority to be and represent "everything and no thing," the terms used by Keats (and Borges) to describe Shakespeare's negative capability, his penetration into the essence of life from a sublime and magisterial position above its mundane contingencies.

Chance, Tragedy, and Hamlet

In the first scene of *Hamlet* the appearance of the ghost propels character and spectator into a reading space oriented toward an ominous and contingent future. Bernardo and Marcellus do not simply share their sight of "this apparition" with Horatio. All three collaborate in sketching a context for interpreting the ghost; they link its appearance with two other coincident events: Denmark's sudden and hasty preparations for foreign war and the movement of the stars. This connection gives the ghost a particular meaning: it is an early sign and warning of a violent change in the course of Danish history. Horatio supplements this intepretation by offering a long narrative account of that other decisive, violent, and chance-ridden moment of Danish history, when thirty years earlier King Hamlet appeared in the very same garb and killed Fortinbras in a duel. The interpretation is clinched with a historical analogy: in Rome, "A little ere the mightiest Julius fell" disruption in the body politic was echoed by disturbances in the spirit world ("the sheeted dead / Did squeak and gibber in the Roman streets"), and in the cosmos ("As stars with trains of fire and dews of blood, / Disasters in the sun").[3]

When chance and indeterminacy reach a maximum in human affairs, how might a person affect this "other" force or entity beyond human control or comprehension, which is supposed to play the decisive part in shaping uncertain events? Within its textual network, *Hamlet* carries the traces of the most primitive human mode of influencing this divinely powerful "other"—the institution of human sacrifice. During one of his "mad" ramblings, Hamlet calls Polonius "Jephthah, judge of Israel," and in doing so engages the biblical story of Jephthah and his daughter. The story tells us a lot about the way primitive cultures coped with chance. It is organized around a grim and simple exchange. Facing the uncertainty of a crucial battle, Jephthah vows to give Yahweh a human victim in exchange for victory: "the first person to meet me from the door of my house." The accidental quality of the victim's designation is a way of offering Yahweh choice of the victim, who in this case is Jephthah's daughter,

3. I, i, 117–21. In quoting *Hamlet,* I have used the outstanding new Arden *Hamlet,* ed. Harold Jenkins (London: Methuen, 1982). I am grateful to Methuen & Co. for permission to do so.

and only child. Here chance becomes the moment and contact point for the expression of divine will.[4]

In his writing on tragedy, Northrop Frye recalls the many ways tragedy, no matter how sophisticated (that is, no matter how moral and rational) it labors to be, never loses touch with the tone and movement of ritual sacrifice: its dark tonalities, the sense of a fateful and enigmatic encounter with the beyond, the renovating energy won for the community at the expense of the one who dies.[5] Hamlet, like all protagonists of tragedy, is elevated to an exposed and risky height, an elevation that both glorifies and destroys him. And he is *our* victim—the victim of and for every audience who has watched his story with rapt fascination. Hamlet's relationship to his fate is more complex and complicitous than is the case with Jephthah's daughter. But his selection for special suffering will sometimes appear like hers—chance, arbitrary, and beyond explanation.

If Hamlet's position as victim is determined in part by chance, it is little wonder that *Hamlet* is punctuated with various responses to fortune. The text invokes the traditional allegorical image of fortune, found throughout medieval and Renaissance literature, of a blind woman spinning a wheel. As blind, fortune is stupid and nonrational in her operation (she does not see what she does, her action is the opposite of provident); the wheel, as a spinning object, is determined in its motion by a haphazard materiality; and the wheel—as a circular form which goes successively through opposite positions—is prone to reversal. *Hamlet* comprises widely divergent responses to shifts in human fortune. The same hero who announces that "there's a providence in the fall of a sparrow," requests from the player a speech in which a gruesome description of Hecuba's suffering is followed by this broad condemnation of "fortune":

> *Out, out, thou strumpet Fortune! All you gods*
> *In general synod take away her power,*
> *Break all the spokes and fellies from her wheel,*

4. René Girard makes this point in discussing the random selection of victims in ritual sacrifice. See the "Conclusion" of *Violence and the Sacred* (Baltimore: The Johns Hopkins University Press, 1972), 311–14. Girard goes on to interpret random selection in light of his theory about the ways sacrifice is used to avoid the catastrophe of mimetic rivalry—a random selection prevents that question from becoming the trigger of violence. I have used the translation of *The Jerusalem Bible*, ed. Alexander Jones (Garden City, N.Y.: Doubleday, 1966).

5. Frye, *Anatomy of Criticism: Four Essays* (Princeton: Princeton University Press, 1957), 214–15.

> And bowl the round nave down the hill of heaven
> As low as to the fiends.
>
> [II, ii, 489–93]

The speech Hamlet may have written for inclusion in "The Murder of Gonzalos" offers a radically different response to the sudden shifts of fortune.[6] The Player King evinces a serene resignation to reversals of fortune which appear to him as an inevitable adjunct of time's passing:

> *This world is not for aye, nor 'tis not strange*
> *That even our loves should with our fortunes change,*
> *For 'tis a question left us yet to prove,*
> *Whether love lead fortune or else fortune love. . . .*
>
> [III, ii, 195–98]

These contradictory responses to chance are not a failure of coherence in either text or central character. Rather they seem to be endemic to tragedy. Even in a single moment of the text, response to chance can be contradictory. When Hamlet contemplates the "vicious mole of nature" that can corrupt a man's character, it is described as an effect of fortune; but it draws neither sweeping anger nor mute acceptance. Instead the ambiguous placement of this "defect" is an indicator of the exploratory and multivalent discourse on chance active in tragedy.[7]

In the Introduction I noted how, in representations of the Fall such as Milton's, an event which from a divine vantage point must appear necessary appears chance to the single person. The concept of "original sin" extends this ambiguity forward through human history typologically, so that the "vicious mole" spoken of in Hamlet's famous speech takes us toward the fundamental equivocation about chance that lies at the center of tragic discourse. Here Hamlet vacillates between considering this "mole" a sin, interpretable in the light of a moral calculus of good and evil, and an arbitrary instance of chance, quite apart from the responsibile will of the person it

6. The *Variorum Shakespeare: Hamlet* sketches the debate as to which Hamlet is meant to have written, which focuses on this speech (favored on style and correct length) and later lines spoken by Lucianus, "Thoughts black, hands apt. . ." (favored on content, and by their effect). See *Variorum*, vol. I, ed. Horace H. Furness (Philadelphia: Lippincott, 1905).

7. *Aristotle's Poetics: The Argument*, ed. Gerald F. Else (Leiden: Brill, 1957), for a non-Renaissance perspective upon this "mole."

afflicts. The passage follows a more general reflection about the Danish reputation for drunkenness, which is in turn occasioned by Claudius' noisy late-night revel. Hamlet continues:

> So, oft it chances in particular men,
> That for some vicious mole of nature in them,
> As in their birth, wherein they are not guilty
> (Since nature cannot choose his origin),
> By their o'ergrowth of some complexion,
> Oft breaking down the pales and forts of reason,
> Or by some habit, that too much o'erleavens
> The form of plausive manners—that these men,
> Carrying, I say, the stamp of one defect,
> Being Nature's livery or Fortune's star,
> His virtues else, be they as pure as grace,
> As infinite as man may undergo,
> Shall in the general censure take corruption
> From that particular fault. The dram of evil
> Doth all the noble substance often dout
> To his own scandal.
>
> [I, iv, 23–38]

It is easy enough to interpret this "vicious mole of nature" as a sin for which the person is culpable. We have noted that the context of the passage connects it with drunkenness, which not only is a fault, but must seem all the more so to Hamlet for belonging to Claudius. This flaw is described as the result of an excess of some temperament or habit, for which the possessor is to blame. The slightness of this fault ("the *dram* of evil") tallies well with the Christian idea of the uncanny transforming power of sin. It can corrupt a body otherwise pure. The passage suggests that the flaw spreads through the body like a disease. This analogy engages one of the dominant image clusters of the text, where rottenness and pollution are habitually both physical and spiritual.

But disease may arise through a purely physical process, and this opens to a competing explanation of the misfortune brought by this "vicious mole." For the whole passage makes this fault's presence and effect seem perversely arbitrary. Why? The passage begins by emphasizing the contingency of this condition: "So oft it *chances* in particular men . . ." (my emphasis). The flaw is described as single and minute—something which may infect one who is *almost* perfect ("His virtues else, be they as pure as grace, . . ."). It might come from their birth "wherein they are not guilty (since nature cannot choose his origin)." Also, the defect is described as a "stamp"—thus, ambiguously, the true character, but also something imposed or impressed from without on something which has an intrinsic quality or nature, quite apart from and untainted by this stamp. Finally, this defect is described as "Nature's livery or Fortune's star"—that is, as one early commentator annotates, "being a defect which is either natural or accidental."[8]

A lot is at stake in the contradictory tendencies of this passage. For the more one reads *Hamlet,* and readers of *Hamlet,* the more one becomes caught up in divergent ways of interpreting failure. We all understand the kind of consolation which comes from explaining adversity by blaming the afflicted person: it returns every shift of fortune to the moral calculus of divine punishments and rewards. But disparate interpretations of fortune are etched into the inchoate design of tragedy. When the doctrine of rewards overwhelms the tragic text, we are left with works like Tate's edition of *King Lear,* where Lear and Cordelia are forcibly enjoined to live happily ever after. Although critics have tried to weave a thematic convergence for *Hamlet* on the question of fortune and providence (and these efforts will doubtless continue), no amount of theological ingenuity can make *Hamlet* tally with the orthodox Renaissance position on chance, of which the *locus classicus* is the third book of Sidney's *Arcadia.* There Pamela's wicked Aunt Cecropia tries to draw her into sexual pleasure ["do you enjoy the heaven of your youth"] by arguing for a godless materialist universe of autonomous elements where alterations follow natural causes and "particular accidents" without any single guiding direction. Pamela responds with a short systematic treatise on chance. She argues that all that is couldn't have arisen from chance, since while chance is variable, nature has existed from eternity, is steady and permanent in its causal systems, and can be held in its "perfect" and "beautiful" "cooperating unity" only by the continuous force and presence of divine "wisdom, goodness, and providence." Pamela's position on chance is a Christian version of Aristotle's, who, of course, heavily influenced theologians, Aquinas among them, who developed the Renaissance perspective on chance.[9]

By casting out chance, as something secondary to God, being, and nature, one makes chance an effect of a single person's limits of vision, and therefore illusory. The idea of God, when introduced as

8. This gloss is by Clarendon as cited in the *Variorum,* vol. I, 82.

9. Sir Philip Sidney, *The Countesse of Pembroke's Arcadia* (1590–1593), ed. Ernest A. Baker (London, 1907).

the privileged term in a discursive space, has so much totalizing power that it can "explain" any turn of action, idea, character. This omnipotence is all the more important in a text like *Hamlet*, where the Christian perspective is explicit invoked, has undeniable pertinence, and can serve to construe (parts of) the play. But the traditional Christian marginalization of chance cancels out the crucial locus of tragic action: the person's eccentric personal experience, where single chance determinations have enormous force and meaning.

This insight helps to explain why I am writing Movement Three of this book on chance *as* a close reading of *Hamlet*. It is not that the play makes chance a central conscious concern of its author or main character. Nor does the text seem to organize itself thematically around "chance" in the same way that it may be said to focus on "pollution," "infidelity," "revenge," or "death." Rather, as both character and text become involved with the fact of pollution and the task of revenge, and go through a given trajectory of action, chance becomes a constant secondary question, concern, and impinging reality. And because *Hamlet* makes the personal experience of the main character an almost obsessive concern, it is an especially useful textual network for the study of chance and the person. Thus, in what follows, our first task will be to read *Hamlet* as carefully and effectively as possible. Then, only in a second stage of reading, will we find that we have moved toward an understanding of the way the relationship between chance and experience are coimplicated in the production of tragedy.

The Trajectory of the Action

A large part of *Hamlet* is concerned with Hamlet's working out an interpretation of his world and situation, and his subsequent efforts to have this interpretation prevail in Denmark. This interpretation involves idealizing his father and man, condemning woman, who is allegorized as changeable and unfaithful, believing in the efficacy of revenge, and being dedicated to the practice of "true mimesis" —that is, the use of language which achieves a relationship of adequation between the word and what it represents. I call this the "guiding interpretation" because it guides Hamlet's words and actions through the first three acts of the play.[10] Perhaps a rude and skeptical voice might interrupt at this point: "Isn't this typical! A teacher of literature, because *he* is constantly juggling different interpretations of literature, tells us that Hamlet's activity is focused around an interpretation of his situation, as if Hamlet were as wordy and ingenious as the professors and students who study him! Hamlet's concern is quite simple: avenging the murder of his father." The pragmatic tenor of this interruption helps me focus my point. If Hamlet were *less* of an interpreter and less of a metaphysician, Act I might be the same as it is, but after Hamlet's interview with the ghost, we might substitute the following:

> Act II, scene i: Hamlet enters with drawn sword and stabs the King. The King dies.

For the first three acts of *Hamlet,* the "guiding interpretation" is the warp and woof of the text, and every word and act of the protagonist get their meaning through reference to it. The division of the text into a region of action (or nonaction)—which is judged primary—and a region of ideas, responses, and interpretation—which is called secondary—has organized most thinking about *Hamlet* for two hundred years. We shall see that this belief in the primacy and purity of action (as revenge) is part of the "guiding interpretation" that Hamlet labors to enforce; but this belief is subjected to powerful critique by the larger textual network called *Hamlet.*

There are several things to note about the locus of this guiding interpretation. Hamlet is not the only character who engages elements of this interpretation. Some of its positions are articulated before he appears on stage, and many are repeated after it ceases to guide his action. Hamlet adopts its elements from the world he inhabits, but when he forges them into a particular combination and tries to act on them, this interpretation becomes Hamlet's formative reality. Also, it does *not* undergo development. This statement may be verified by comparing the first soliloquy, "O that this too too sullied flesh would melt, . . ." early in Act I with his dialogue with his mother at the end of Act III. Both scenes repeat the same themes and oppositions, and both take Hamlet through the same circuit of obsessions. These first three acts of the play are marked by nothing

---

10. The best definition of the Nietzschean concept of interpretation of which I am here making use is found in Essay II, 12, of *The Genealogy of Morals.*

so much as the single-mindedness and tenacity of Hamlet's efforts to impose this interpretation on those around him. But although the guiding interpretation does not change or develop in the play, there is a kind of progression in Hamlet's expression of its ideas: from the disguises, wit, "madness," and indirection of the dialogues with Polonius, Rosencrantz and Guildenstern, and Ophelia to the more elaborate forms of representation in Act III: teaching an aesthetic to the Players, delivering his panegyric to Horatio on the special value of their friendship, staging a dramatic performance for Claudius and the court, and offering moral instruction to his mother in her bedchamber. Given the energy and variety of these efforts, it is perhaps a surprise that Hamlet fails. His inability to get the guiding interpretation to hold sway at the Danish court is one reason for his much discussed delay. The interpretation simply does not work. And its failure has less to do with the external opposition it meets with (Claudius' ingenuity, Gertrude's sensuality) or certain mistakes Hamlet makes (like killing Polonius), than with the resistance to this interpretation which emerges from the nonmimetic understructure of language. So somewhere in Act IV the guiding interpretation—as a guide for Hamlet's action—breaks up and drops away. Its failure after Act III reorients everything in Hamlet's situation. This is why Hamlet is so changed upon his return from his sea voyage, and why he is ready to improvise a strange compromise formation—the duel with Laertes—to win a scene where revenge can happen.

What is Hamlet's guiding interpretation? It begins with an identification with the father, as the ideal man, with man as an ideal father. This ideal is the position of mastery, knowledge, and uncompromising strength associated with the victorious warrior; but it is also the place of the most perfect human emotions. Hamlet broods, his father was "so loving to my mother / That he might not beteem the winds of heaven / Visit her face too roughly" (I, ii, 140–42). His father's perfection does not readily admit of pale verbal description, but when he offers Gertrude a "counterfeit presentment of two brothers," Hamlet describes his father as a living catalogue of the most imposing qualities of each god: he had "Hyperion's curls," "the front of Jove himself," "an eye like Mars," and "a station like the herald Mercury / New-lighted on a heaven-kissing hill—." The word "heaven" comes readily to use when Hamlet speaks of his father; but what comes to fruition is "man": he is a "combination and a form" "to give the world assurance of a man" (III, iv, 55–63). And when Horatio calls him "a goodly king," Hamlet deflects the confining tendencies of this epithet, and offers instead the circular purity of this tautology: "He was a man, take him for all in all: I shall not look upon his like again" (I, ii, 186–88). Here "man" means the most perfect man, a paragon among men. It also means the opposite of woman, the locus of Hamlet's disappointments.

The guiding interpretation is organized as a series of oppositions, whose terms observe a rigid hierarchy. If man is steadfast and strong, woman is changeable, weak, compromised, and compromising. Hamlet's anger at woman is most explicitly directed at a mother who so easily shifts her affections from his father to Claudius, and at a lover who suddenly refuses his letters and attentions. But Hamlet goes beyond his response to these two individuals to formulate a much more comprehensive misogyny. If the father makes man the locus of oneness and identity, woman is hateful because she is the carrier of the contagion of uncontrollable change. Rosencrantz and Guildenstern joke that they get neither the best nor worst from capricious fortune, but are in "the middle of her favours . . . her privates." Hamlet gives emphasis to the idea of fortune as a woman and a whore in responding, "In the secret parts of Fortune? O most true, she is a strumpet" (II, ii, 235–36). Woman is changeable for two reasons: she is wanton in following her passions, and she is concerned with appearances and surfaces that are unstable. Thus, in speaking with Ophelia, he accuses all women: "God hath given you one face and you make yourselves another. You jig and amble, and you lisp . . ." Nothing that comes near woman can escape transformation: a woman's "beauty" will "transform honesty from what it is to a bawd"; and "wise men know well enough what monsters you make of them"—cuckolds (III, i. 111–41).

The guiding interpretation leads Hamlet to eschew the theatrical modes of the court and the social compromises they entail: the frivolity of the courtier Osric, the manipulations of Polonius and Rosencrantz and Guildenstern, the smooth deceit of Claudius. To the shifting appearances of the social sphere, Hamlet offers his own idea of what man is and should be. Man has an inner reality of feeling and identity to which he must be true. Although this single inner self cannot be expressed in the languages of dress and social code, Hamlet is determined to affirm his sense of the beyondness of this self. This is the ethos expressed in his masterful reply to his mother when she asks him why his father's death "seems" so "particular," that is, so personal and individual to Hamlet, rather than a general social fact shared by the whole court.

> *Hamlet:* Seems, madam? Nay, it is. I know not "seems."
> 'Tis not alone my inky cloak, good mother,
> Nor customary suits of solemn black,
> Nor windy suspiration of forc'd breath,
> No, nor the fruitful river in the eye,
> Nor the dejected haviour of the visage,
> Together with all forms, moods, shapes of grief,
> That can denote me truly. These indeed seem,
> For they are actions that a man might play;
> But I have that within which passes show,
> These but the trappings and the suits of woe.
>
> [I, ii, 76–86]

What the court shares is the externality of its clothes, gestures, and facial expressions—forms that are predictable, repeatable, and might be feigned. In rejecting this suspect social language, Hamlet has found an indirect way—by negating the inadequate—to describe the indescribable. He solicits the same mysterious interiority of the person when he enjoins Guildenstern to play the recorder. The recorder's music is like the voice, the inner spirituality of the person, which Hamlet accuses Guildenstern of trying to appropriate: "You would play upon me, you would seem to know my stops, you would pluck out the heart of my mystery, you would sound me from my lowest note to the top of my compass" (III, ii, 355–58). The integrity of the single inner self is guarded by being unknowable. This idea of the self is enormously appealing to Hamlet because it affords a basis for living apart from the shifting opportunism of the court and the contagion of woman's love. This is why Hamlet offers Horatio his highest praise—and pledges to link this "man" to his own inmost self, with these words:

> and blest are those
> Whose blood and judgment are so well commeddled
> That they are not a pipe for Fortune's finger
> To sound what stop she please. Give me that man
> That is not passion's slave, and I will wear him
> In my heart's core, ay, in my heart of heart,
> As I do thee.
>
> [III, ii, 68–74]

Notice how Hamlet's language doubles the inwardness of this interiority—"the heart of my mystery," "my heart's core," "in my heart of heart"—in a fashion that confounds clear definition, but makes the self's center seem richly inaccessible. Below, we shall see that this movement of the text will be a crux for guiding (and misguiding) the humanist readings of *Hamlet*.

Hamlet's guiding interpretation gains much of its urgency and character by the way it does something which is far from inevitable: it aligns the oppositions man and woman, interiority and social performance, with a series of oppositions affiliated with each other: mind and body, true and false, good and evil. This whole system of oppositions is Manichean in character, for everything positive is supposed to reside in one term, everything negative in the other. The stark bipolarity of this way of seeing and thinking is habitually evident—as when Hamlet compares his father and uncle, his father and mother, man and woman, or even the exalted and degraded sides of single entities, as in his speech to Rosencrantz and Guildenstern: the earth is a "goodly frame" and a "sterile promontory"; the sky a "brave o'erhanging firmament" and a "pestilent congregation of vapours"; and man is "the beauty of the world, the paragon of animals" and "this quintessence of dust" (II, ii, 298–308). At times these oppositions seem justified by Hamlet's use of a conventional Renaissance form of instruction—as when he offers Gertrude a "counterfeit presentment of two brothers" so that she inevitably must make a moral and rational choice. But Hamlet's way of returning again and again to certain subjects—like these two brothers, or Gertrude's sexuality—gives his way of pressing every encountered term into the poles of these Manichean oppositions a most compulsive cast.

The set of valuations inscribed in the guiding interpretation implies an imperative for a certain use of language in representation. Thus Hamlet insists upon the distinction between a false representation or mimesis, which currently afflicts Denmark, and a true mimesis which once held sway and which he would restore. The centrality of this distinction becomes apparent when one notes that the ghost's revelation about Claudius' crime is merely an example—albeit a quite spectacular one—in a more general lesson in reading reality. The Ghost teaches Hamlet that something can appear one thing and be another. Thus the Ghost introduces his account by saying, "the whole ear of Denmark / Is by a forged process of my death / Rankly abus'd . . . ," Gertrude is called "my most seeming virtuous queen," and Hamlet quickens his hatred for Claudius and summarizes what he has learned from the Ghost with a statement

[233]

that insists upon the fact of false mimesis: "Meet it is I set it down /
That one may smile, and smile, and be a villain" (I, v, 36–38; 46;
107–8).

The distinction between "true" and "false" mimesis is crucial to
the project of the guiding interpretation because only true mimesis
can make that which is "out there"—the object, reality—present to
consciousness in the mode of truth. In his speech to the players,
Hamlet formulates this imperative into an aesthetic praxis which is
intended to guarantee that the singleness of what is (here, "action"
and "nature") is faithfully aligned with language (here, "the word")
so that it is carried to the viewer of the performance:

> Suit the action to the word, the word to the action, with this special ob-
> servance, that you o'erstep not the modesty of nature. For anything so
> o'erdone is from the purpose of playing, whose end, both at the first
> and now, was and is to hold as 'twere the mirror up to nature; to show
> virtue her feature, scorn her own image, and the very age and body of
> the time his form and pressure. [III, ii, 17–24]

Notice that this passage implies that true mimesis is a question of
finding the *single* correct sign for repeating a self-identical object.
This idea is implicit in the chiasmic interplay of "action" and "word,"
the apparently flawless doubling power of the mirror, and in the assumption that virtue and scorn have their *own* proper feature and
image, and time *his* form and pressure. The use of the possessive
pronoun here becomes a marker of the singularity of the object repeated in representation.

Once one is attentive to Hamlet's concern with true and false mimesis, one finds this concern shaping passages that at first seem remote from questions of representation. Thus, in the closet scene,
when Hamlet seeks to express the extremity of Gertrude's infidelity,
he describes her act as one that corrupts the proper and regulating
mimetic relationship between the appearance and fact of virtuous
love:

> Such an act
> That blurs the grace and blush of modesty,
> Calls virtue hypocrite, takes off the rose
> From the fair forehead of an innocent love,
> And sets a blister there, makes marriage vows
> As false as dicers' oaths—O, such a deed
> As from the body of contraction plucks

The very soul, and sweet religion makes
A rhapsody of words.
[III, iv, 40–48]

Here, false mimesis has become a disease which contaminates the
signs of fidelity by mixing them with signs that "blur" the truth by
multiplying uncontrollably—as do a blister or dicers' oaths or any
"rhapsody of words." Hamlet would cure Denmark by restoring a
single true representation of what is.

What are the practical means Hamlet finds to live out the full spirituality of this interpretation—its inwardness, its identification with
the father, and the ethos of "true" mimesis? Hamlet makes a twofold
effort through remembrance and revenge. He imposes a certain demand upon himself and others: to stay continually present to the
memory of his father, the locus of plenitude and identity that undergirds the guiding interpretation. That means resisting all the displacements and transformations of time which Hamlet so fiercely
condemns, and which he makes all the more unbearable by having
the Player King mournfully accept. Hamlet's effort to remember is
expressed in two ways: in the black mourning clothes he wears as an
outward sign of the memory within, and in his complaint against
his mother for forgetting his father so quickly. Hamlet wishes the
"whole kingdom" of Denmark were, as Claudius says but does not
do, "contracted in one brow of woe." But how can one fulfill this demand, made explicit in the Ghost's parting words, "Adieu, adieu,
adieu. Remember me . . ."? These words articulate the problem.
"Adieu" announces a departure and the fact of absence; "remember
me" demands that Hamlet's mind and heart stay present to the
ghost—but *as* memory. Hamlet responds by writing down the
Ghost's words and lesson on a tablet. The Ghost is now deposited as
a visible memory trace. Because it is written, it is permanent; but because it is only writing, and thus only the trace of a prior presence, it
is a present absence, or absent presence. A memory is like a ghost
—the haunting ghost of the father, that is, something once full and
powerful, but now only a trace of its former self. And as a memory
trace, it is deposited in proximity to innumerable other traces that
have been etched in the mind by time and numberless others the future will bring. Hamlet responds to this problem by vowing to "wipe
away all trivial fond records . . . That youth and observation copied
there / And thy commandment all alone shall live / Within the book
and volume of my brain" (I, v, 99–103). How can this be done?
There are two hints in the text of how a person might live out the

impossible logic of this demand for remembrance. Hamlet says to Ophelia, before the performance at court, "What should a man do but be merry? For look you how cheerfully my mother looks and my father died within's two hours." If Hamlet's father died "within's two hours," he died just now. His death is not something to be remembered from the past—it is there, as a living fact of death, continually. And so Hamlet compares his mother unfavorably to Niobe— who mourned so intensely for her dead children that she was turned to a stone which continually dropped tears. Thus Hamlet can only really fulfill the demand of remembrance by freezing time, time as the carrier of new feelings, new thoughts, and new memory traces. That is why he complains so bitterly of time's passing and why the demand for remembrance, as Hamlet lives it, is impossible: it lies in a contradictory relationship to the fact of time and its modulations and displacements.

The guiding interpretation postulates an idea of what revenge is and what it will accomplish. Revenge will be curative because it functions as a culmination of every element of the guiding interpretation. The same act of revenge that will remember and honor the father will also allow Hamlet to assume the self's true identity as his father's son and legitimate heir. This act will affirm a whole system of valuations: the father will be exalted as an embodiment of spirit, truth, and goodness while revenge destroys Claudius as the embodiment of body, falsehood, evil, and the compromising performative transactions of the social sphere. There are several ways in which this act of revenge is conceptualized as a form of true mimesis—the repetition of a prior identity. By acting, Hamlet seeks to model himself upon a certain version of his father—the father as valiant warrior whose creative act of will (the duel with Fortinbras) has shaped modern Danish history. And the whole play is stamped with a nostalgia for the soldier's simple and unreflected relation with acts of violence. Thus Hamlet admires young Fortinbras marching to war, just as Fortinbras orders a soldier's funeral for the dead Hamlet.

Revenge is to be the act that imitates a father capable of action. It will realize the self, in its uniqueness and inwardness, because action is supposed to be an outward expression of will, and will a focused expression of the self's identity. Here the relationship between action and will, and will and identity is fundamentally mimetic: action becomes the representation of the self's identity—the true way one writes oneself in the world. But, within the frame of the guiding interpretation, revenge will also have an external social function. Hamlet's revenge is an imitation and doubling of the crime which has polluted the social body. Thus the "Mouse-trap play" has a double structure—the dumb show represents the crime, with the poisoner kissing the crown he seeks, while the subsequent play represents the same crime, only doubled as revenge, with the nephew killing the king. In revenge Hamlet seeks far more than blood for blood. All his forms of imitation and representation—of the father, the self, and the polluting crime—appear as pathways to the truth Hamlet's guiding interpretation is shaped to seek and find. Hamlet's project is everywhere mediated by this metaphysical desire: he desires the position of truthfulness he finds in the image of his father. Little wonder that Hamlet cannot "sweep" to his revenge, "as swift as meditation or the thoughts of love" (I, v, 29–30). Little wonder that the text submits his efforts to hesitation, displacements, and surprising compromise formations.

Almost the moment Hamlet begins to apply the guiding interpretation, it founders, and his efforts undergo strange displacements. This happens because of a twofold impediment. First, the guiding interpretation is out of phase with Denmark's social sphere—its terms, goals, exchanges, compromises and mediations. Second, although his interpretation exalts a sublime and absent male and renounces woman, Hamlet's desire for the woman *subsists,* and continues to operate in all his words and actions.[11] In other words, the guiding interpretation is blind to the economy of desire within which it operates. Revenge will work not to reject but to reappropriate woman, as the object of desire. But this object is woven into the social network, and it is therefore accessible only through the turnings and languages of that network. This is the pragmatic reason why Hamlet does not simply affirm the guiding interpretation with one sudden symbolic act—killing Claudius. A sudden revenge only seems to be consistent with the guiding interpretation. Thus although Hamlet reproaches himself for not sweeping to his revenge, his larger strategy—to the extent that we can divine one—is shaped to make the complex metaphysics of the guiding interpretation hold sway in Denmark. This goal entails several moves: a disruption of the social framework so Claudius may be drawn into exposing himself; the reeducation of Gertrude so she is weaned of her attachment to Claudius; and the murder of his uncle, so Hamlet may avenge his father and repossess the throne. This "program" for action, never stated in the text, but implicit in Hamlet's behavior, is undertaken in a social sphere organized on principles hostile, at nearly every point,

11. This insight is the major contribution of the psychoanalytic reading of the text.

to those Hamlet seeks to advance—thus, the tortuous complexity of his task. The fundamental antinomy between Hamlet's project and the social matrix he inhabits helps to account for some of the ironies that attend his initial application of his interpretation: Hamlet is the character who most insistently espouses truthfulness and steadfastness, but from the beginning of Act II, he is also the character who habitually uses disguise and indirection, and is perceived by all as changed and constantly changing.

What does Hamlet do to and in this social reality? First, it must be noted that in the social world of the court, where the play of appearances takes precedence over interior realities, Hamlet is a masterful actor. Thus Ophelia calls Hamlet, "the glass of fashion and the mold of form," and we see glimpses of his social grace in his easy banter with Horatio, in the finesse with which he directs conversation with Rosencrantz and Guildenstern, and in his open and generous welcome to the players. But the obsessions and judgments of the guiding interpretation have disrupted Hamlet's concourse with this social world. This is dramatically evident at several moments in the play when Hamlet responds as if the social world has caused a rupture in the self; he responds with behavior which ruptures that social world. We see this response in its most moderate form in his first colloquy with his old friends Rosencrantz and Guildenstern. Hamlet gradually draws them into the confession that they "were sent for." This fact triggers Hamlet's anger. If his old school friends are little better than spies, then the social sphere is corrupt in itself and hostile toward him. Here is a confirmation of the stark moral oppositions of the guiding interpretation, which Hamlet here uses to organize his speech on the cosmos and man. The content of this speech expresses his sense of having been violated, but the form of his response precipitates a rupture of the circuit of communication integral to the social sphere. Thus Hamlet's use of antithesis engenders ambiguity about what he is saying: "What a piece of work is man, how noble in reason, how infinite in faculties . . . and yet, to me, what is this quintessence of dust?" (II, ii, 303–8). But the ambiguity is considerably deepened by the strange way he introduces his speech:

Hamlet: I will tell you why [you were sent for] . . . I have of late, but wherefore I know not, lost all my mirth, forgone all custom of exercises; and indeed it goes so heavily with my disposition that this goodly frame the earth seems to me a sterile promontory, this most excellent canopy the air. . . .[II, ii, 293–300]

[238]

These lines give Hamlet's speech a problematic status. Is the speech an explanation? At first it seems that Hamlet might be explaining why he has felt melancholy of late. But its context in the exchange, the strangely remote way he describes himself ("I have of late. . . ."), and the way he is aware that Rosencrantz and Guildenstern and the King and Queen are all aware of his behavior—all this gives a stagey, self-conscious cast to these pronouncements. Apparently this speech is an illustration of Hamlet's disposition, through a performance at one remove, for those who may not have been there earlier. But this casts suspicion upon both Hamlet's "disposition" and his expressed opinions. For how genuine are feelings that can be repeated at one remove from their original locus, and how genuine are the ideas enunciated in this staged performance? The performative irony of Hamlet's language moves his auditors—Rosencrantz and Guildenstern—and those hearing the play into a position where it is impossible, any longer, to make clear adjudications about intended meaning. Here language is not a medium of communication guided in its usage by a communally accepted network of meanings and carrying intended meanings from an earnest speaker to an attentive auditor; nor is the language Hamlet uses simply nonsense. Instead Hamlet has begun to use language as a way to rupture the social world, with which he no longer wants to communicate.

What is the meaning of Hamlet's attack on the Danish court? Our first sight of Hamlet is of someone framed by a social sphere he detests. He resists this world with his silence, his black mourning clothes, and his clipped ironical replies. He makes himself an uncompromising reminder of death for those who would rather forget it and live life's everyday concerns and pleasures. Claudius' speeches introduce us to the wisdom of this sphere—its overt advocacy of moderation, compromise, and deft diplomacy. Claudius takes extremes of grief, anger, or joy (Hamlet's, Fortinbras', Gertrude's) and modulates them into the more restrained expressions of a shared social experience. We get closer to the functional ethos of this social sphere in the scenes of the underplot, where Laertes offers advice to Ophelia, and Polonius advises both his children. There emerges a fundamental critique of the demand for self-identity Hamlet makes of himself and others. It is not just that this torrent of advice is shaped by concerns of prudent self-interest and the whole economic project of maximizing one's worth through society's exchanges. Nor that Polonius sees Hamlet's avowals of love as hollow ploys to trick his daughter into bed. Rather, the advice in this scene offers a whole different account of how the self functions in society. Instead of action's being a faithful repetition of the self and its will, social facts and forces—such as Hamlet's being a prince—mean that he may not be able to be faithful to Ophelia. Laertes warns, "Perhaps he loves you now, / And no soil nor cautel doth besmirch / The virtue of his will; . . . [but] his will is not his own. . . . He may not . . . Carve for himself [in matters of marriage], for on his choice depends / The sanity and health of this whole state" (I, iii, 14–21). Then Laertes gives another way in which the self may be divided from its principles: shifts of mood and passion can, in an errant moment, stir the self out of the guidance of virtue. Therefore he warns Ophelia to stay "Out of the shot and danger of desire. / The chariest maid is prodigal enough / If she unmask her beauty to the moon" (I, iii, 35–37).

When Polonius enters to prate his farewell advice to Laertes, he does not assume there is a private interiority that must be either hidden or faithfully expressed—but that social life is an intricate and calculated game of disclosure and concealment which the mature, successful man must learn to play well. When Polonius says "give thy thoughts no tongue, nor any unproportioned thought his act," he is calling for a careful manipulation of appearances. Hamlet would no doubt call this form of self-representation false, but for Polonius and others it is a way of being one cannot avoid. It is simply a necessary and constitutive part of social reality.

Now we are in a better position to understand the logic of Hamlet's theatrical use of language. It functions as a compromise formation: on one hand, he uses language to place himself in a social world; but he speaks in ways—as if in half-soliloquy—that make his language a medium for expressing ideas and feelings incompatible with that social world. Usually this works very well—as when he taunts Polonius as having "one fair daughter" by singing several lines of a ballad. Hamlet gives vent to private meanings he can enjoy, while the old man is confused. When Hamlet wins certitude of Claudius' guilt, by the way the King breaks up the performance of the Mouse-trap play, Hamlet displaces his giddy excitement, the vertigo of looking at the *fact* of fratricide, by modulating into poetry and ballads. But sometimes dialogue is risky for Hamlet, as when it leads him to the core of his obsessions. This is nowhere more evident than in his dialogue with Ophelia—a scene which has disturbed attentive readers of *Hamlet* for centuries.

It is important to note what triggers Hamlet's tirade against Ophelia. His opening greeting to her, while she reads her prayer book, is most gentle: "Nymph, in thy orisons / Be all my sins remember'd." And to Ophelia's question—"How does your honour for this many a day?"—Hamlet's reply is cordial, "I humbly thank you, well" (III, i, 86–87). But when Ophelia seeks to return the love letters he has sent her, his tone changes completely. Why? As a sign of a complete break in relations the return of love letters is perhaps always one of the most galling events of love. But for Hamlet the gesture also confirms his most bitter suspicions of woman's infidelity and elicits from him, in their subsequent dialogue, the whole complex of the guiding interpretation: woman as corrupted by lust; human loyalties as ephemeral; life subjected to a sweeping moral condemnation; the breakdown of language as a medium of truthful exchange (of his old love-vows, Hamlet says, "You should not have believed me. . . believe none of us"); and social intercourse as no longer possible ("Get thee to a nunnery. . . we will have no mo marriage").

These ideas are in themselves harsh enough. But I suspect that the scandal to readers caused by Hamlet's tirade is more the result of how these ideas have suffused and transformed the forms of his language, so that his ways of addressing Ophelia violate every convention of humane social exchange. Hamlet's language seems haphazard enough, but each utterance has the effect of disorienting Ophelia by overturning what she expects: a personal conversation between two people who share mutual regard. To the letters he responds with a surprising denial, "No, not I. / I never gave you aught"; follows with laughter and insinuating questions, "Are you honest?," "Are you fair?," and then turns these questions into a riddle (about "honesty" not having commerce with "beauty") whose solution turns on "the power of beauty" to "transform honesty from what it is to a bawd." This riddle does several things to displace the dialogue out of personal conversation: as a puzzling question it is a taunt to the auditor; it puts the speaker at a safe distance behind his answer; and it abstracts Ophelia's beauty and honesty into general qualities. Then Hamlet offers a bait to wrench the conversation back into the sphere of sincere feeling: "I did love you once." He immediately ironizes this statement by submitting it to reversal: "I loved you not." This functions to disrupt the speaking subject as the locus of any steadily held position or meaning. Hamlet follows by lashing out with curses and warnings, "Get thee to a nunnery. Why, wouldst thou be a breeder of sinners. . . . If thou dost marry, I'll give thee this plague for thy dowry. . . ." But, as if to disperse the personal involvement with Ophelia his anger might imply, he intersperses the curses with a self-condemnation: "I could accuse me of such things that it were better my mother had not borne me. . . . What should such fellows as I do crawling between earth and heaven?"

Hamlet's part of this exchange climaxes with an important shift in the form of address: from the personal "thou" to the "you," which is directed not at Ophelia, but at Woman, all individual women considered as an abstract entity: "I have heard of your paintings well enough. God hath given you one face and you make yourselves another. You jig and amble, and you lisp, you nickname God's creatures, and make your wantonness your ignorance" (III, i, 144–48). Absorbing Ophelia into the category Woman is the culminating step in this exchange: Ophelia has ceased to be there as a sentient person capable of response; she exists only as an index of the general figure of Woman: woman as fickle, changeable, unfaithful. Hamlet at the close of this scene is talking to this abstract figure. But if Ophelia is not present as a person for Hamlet, her final words reflect a symmetrical insight—at this moment, when Hamlet is in the brace of his *obsessions,* he is not "all there." She addresses a plea for help, not to Hamlet, but to "you sweet heavens," and upon his departure she delivers her eloquent tribute to the memory of one who is "gone"; "O, what a noble mind is here o'erthrown! . . ."

At moments like this the extremity of Hamlet's passion not only ruptures social relations—it also takes him beyond a shared social reality and the self-control that shared reality implies. He seems close to being overcome by what one might call the abysmal literality of his desire, and the compulsion to repeat the obsessional forms his imagination gives this desire. At one point Hamlet does seem to lose control. In the closet scene, he gives Gertrude a moral lesson by confronting her with "the counterfeit presentment of two brothers," and the image of her sin: choosing Claudius after knowing King Hamlet, and giving way to her lust. As he begins, Hamlet seems to be in full rhetorical control of his lesson. But as he circles around what appears to him the scandal of Gertrude's lust, he gives way to the full purity of his rage, and there seems to be no appeal Gertrude can make to stop the tirade. Hamlet's words are finally interrupted by Gertrude:

> . . . And reason panders will.
>
> *Queen:*   O Hamlet, speak no more.
> Thou turn'st my eyes into my very soul. . . .
> *Hamlet:*   Nay, but to live
> In the rank sweat of an enseamed bed,
> Stew'd in corruption, honeying and making love
> Over the nasty sty!

Queen:	O speak to me no more
	These words like daggers enter in my ears.
	No more, sweet Hamlet.
Hamlet:	A murderer and a villain,
	A slave. . . .
Queen:	No more. . . .

Enter GHOST

[III, iv, 87–103]

Hamlet then addresses the Ghost, and the Queen declares of Hamlet, "Alas, he's mad." There is a certain irony in the timing of this judgment. It is before, not after, the entrance of the Ghost that Hamlet seems completely unable to heed her appeal to end his tirade, repeated four times with the words "no more." The Ghost's role is equivocal. The Ghost is a figure that certifies the truth of Hamlet's guiding interpretation, and thus is linked in the play to Hamlet's private passion. This is marked by the fact that Hamlet is the only character who speaks with the Ghost. But here the Ghost does not function as a spur to passion. He is a counselor who arrives here to help Hamlet externalize and objectify his passion so that it can serve some socially useful end: first, to focus his anger at Claudius into action (his "almost blunted purpose") and, second, to protect his mother from the extremity of "amazement" and pain that Hamlet's tirade has triggered.

In spite of this moment of extremity, Hamlet is usually willing to modulate his passion into some containing form and submit the guiding interpretation to the counterpressures of the social sphere. Thus his bitter speech to Rosencrantz and Guildenstern upon the cosmos and man is followed by the arrival of the players, who provide Hamlet a means of acting out, at one remove, the scenes that circle through his imagination. By giving the play, Hamlet shows he is willing to take the Ghost and put its authority, and the authority of its charge against Claudius, in doubt. In this way Hamlet wins independent social verification for his strong suspicions of Claudius' guilt.

Although Hamlet stops short of succumbing to his obsessions, we do get vivid examples in this text of characters who act out their passion and desire in all of its unmediated literality. Thus it would be difficult to imagine a more zealous participant in a blood feud than the Pyrrhus who stalks Priam. He is "head to foot. . . horridly tricked / With blood of fathers, mothers, daughters, sons." And Lucianus, the avenging nephew in "The Murder of Gonzago" has completely assimilated himself to the passions and protocols of re-

[243]

venge. Hamlet is interested in these fictional avengers because of the absolute singleness of purpose they demonstrate, though he never chooses to emulate it. But in this play it is above all Ophelia who becomes so overladen with desire that she loses any apparent critical distance between herself and the passions she feels, these passions and the social or linguistic forms which give them an acceptable collective embodiment. Ophelia's behavior engenders this irony. It is Ophelia, not Hamlet, who acts out the ethos of true mimesis he propounds: as a child who loses her father, she lives the kind of excess of sorrow Hamlet expects of himself; as a lover, she is openly desiring; and as a woman, she shows the kind of passive fidelity Hamlet demands of Gertrude. And she does these things without restraint, reserve, or any regard for mediating social forms. This shocking directness—a scandal for her auditors both inside and outside the play—is the result of an absence of the self-consciousness that a social matrix engenders, by enjoining each of its members to see themselves as others see them. Without this double awareness Ophelia seems mad. As Claudius comments, "poor Ophelia / Divided from herself and her fair judgment, / Without the which we are pictures, or mere beasts" (IV, v, 84–86). Without a double self, a personal self and a social self, that is, without self-consciousness, a person becomes a flat representation—a "picture." Ophelia's madness achieves an effect of the simplicity and literality that Hamlet's guiding interpretation had exalted, but that prove to be a bad joke and dead end for her.

By the last act Hamlet seems to have recognized that there is something problematic about the self's direct expressions of passion. Laertes' gesture at Ophelia's funeral—leaping into her grave, to catch "her once more in mine arms"—is the most literal possible expression of love for the dead. But it is also a scandal. For in embracing a corpse, Laertes refuses the mourning process of separation and acquiescence in death that the funeral as a social form exists to solemnize. When Hamlet challenges Laertes in his use of this histrionic gesture and the hyperbolic expressions of loss which follow, he is angry with Laertes not for his sorrow but for his naive efforts to give it literal expression: "What is he whose grief / Bears such an emphasis, whose phrase of sorrow / Conjures the wand'ring stars" (V, i, 247–49). Hamlet makes those efforts seem ludicrous by his willingness to compete in demonstrations of love: will Laertes "weep," "fight," "fast," or "eat a crocodile?" Hamlet proclaims he will match every feat. Laertes' gesture expresses the presentness of his love; Hamlet simply says "I loved Ophelia." By using the past tense,

Hamlet accepts Ophelia's death, and takes her corpse not as the body of a present person, but as a sign, or emblem, of one who is gone. In this way Hamlet accedes to a very different idea of social reality and language than that which the guiding interpretation projected. This difference will have important consequences for the shape of the revenge Hamlet fashions, and which is fashioned for him.

It has been the work of the foregoing analysis to illuminate the basic nature of Hamlet's conflict—a conflict which I do not find mysterious, tortured, or perverse. Hamlet's most personal passions are organized by a guiding interpretation that makes it imperative for him to engage a social sphere whose principles of operation are inimical to that interpretation. One result of and response to this impasse is to suspend the self's attachments, negate every social position, and make irony and skepticism one's most fundamental stance. It is this side of Hamlet's behavior that has been most exhaustively explored by critics and this is what the popular mind associates with Hamlet —his tendency toward reflection, irony, seeing too many sides of one question. All this brings delay. A suspension of the personal position is implicit in many of Hamlet's most characteristic uses of language: the displacement of voice into ballads and poetry does not just conceal response, it also disperses personal response into language of ambiguous tendency; Hamlet's almost pervasive use of antithesis immobilizes the subject between two equally compelling positions—as the life and death of "To be or not to be," or the "angel" and "dust" of the speech on man; and Hamlet uses a curious form of negation to both forbid and describe Gertrude's submission to Claudius' seduction:

> Queen: What shall I do?
> Hamlet: Not this, by no means, that I bid you do:
>   Let the bloat King tempt you again to his bed,
>   Pinch wanton on your cheek, call you his mouse. . . .
>   [III, iv, 182–85]

For critics such as Goethe this suspension or displacement of the self is just a symptom of a disease of the will and a "soul unfit for the performance" of the "great action" laid upon it. But the language Hamlet uses in his position of hesitation, doubt, and equivocation pushes him to perspectives beyond the metaphysics of self, will, and identity that Goethe assumes that the guiding interpretation was designed to serve. One of these is the perspectivism Hamlet asserts in his first dialogue with Rosencrantz and Guildenstern—reality does not inhere in a thing, but in the position from which it is viewed: "there is nothing either good or bad but thinking makes it so. . . I could be bounded in a nutshell and count myself a king of infinite space—were it not that I have bad dreams" (II, ii, 249–56). Here Hamlet is asserting the piquancy of his private perspective, but later this same insight operates in a more objective way, when he regrets his anger at Laertes by the graveside. He tells Horatio, "For by the image of my cause I see / The portraiture of his" (V, ii, 77–78). Perhaps in another time and place, Hamlet could have been playing Laertes' part, Laertes Hamlet's.

In Hamlet's graveside meditations, death makes the person too shadowy, mobile, and abstract to sustain any form. With the body's dissolution, one also loses the unified vessal and image of the self. Thus the skull Hamlet holds in his hand was once the head of an individual man or woman, but as Hamlet entertains a series of possibilities—it might have been a politician, a courtier, a lady, a lawyer—as he goes through a rich rhetorical elaboration, the skull becomes something quite abstract, the skull of no man and everyman, the emblem of death itself. And this has happened partly because of the series of surmises that organizes this meditation, and partly because of the physical effect of death—as the face becomes a skull, the individual is dissolved into an anonymous object. As life submits to the force of death, death ceases to be that which can be represented as "belonging" to a living individual.

Hamlet's graveside meditations on death carry his suspension of the personal position to its logical limit. But already in this scene there are signs of another response to death. Hamlet assumes the carefree mockery of a determined moralist, until the gravedigger identifies one skull as that of Yorick, the King's jester. Hamlet's eloquence pauses with one word, "This?" Hamlet feels anger: "my gorge rises at it. . ." Then he expresses his memory of Yorick in a way which balances Hamlet's personal sense of loss against the general ironizing force of death. Irony is expressed by asking Yorick, as if this skull could listen, "where" all his jests are "now." But the series that Hamlet develops within the frame of this question helps to make his speech a tribute to and celebration of Yorick and the joyous social life of laughter he advanced: "Where be your gibes now, your gambols, your songs, your flashes of merriment, that were wont to set the table on a roar?" (V, i, 183–85). Implicit in the sympathy these lines express for Yorick is Hamlet's movement beyond an ironic suspension of self. This becomes explicit a few lines later when the funeral party enters and Hamlet sees Laertes leap into Ophelia's grave. By following Laertes into it and grappling with him, Hamlet shows himself ready to assert his own personal position, with its eccentric, perhaps accidental, but nonetheless genuine emotional investments. In this moment of abandon, rivalry, and involvement he is capable of what must seem, to every reader, an entirely novel simplicity of statement: "I loved Ophelia." Hamlet has moved beyond the impasse created by the conflict between the guiding interpretation and the social sphere. He also eschews the ironic stance and suspension of self the impasse engendered. Hamlet's readiness to stake himself evidences the change in character nearly every critic of this text has noticed.

Hamlet's Change

How and why does Hamlet change? To establish a frame for responding to this question, we must look back to earlier scenes in the drama, and trace the way he begins to find indirect means to express his desire. To start with, he takes two actors—the player and Fortinbras—as models, and though he misinterprets their ways of acting, his emulation of their performances takes him in a practical and concrete movement toward a new relationship to language and to the systems of representation he employs to act. It is only after he changes his idea of language, away from the ethos of "true" mimesis, that Hamlet can touch or affect the social sphere he inhabits. Then he can, in Act V, enter a field of uncertain events prepared to assume a position—a body, a trajectory of effort, and the desire that effort expresses—within the play-space of the duel. What will happen there will be neither inaction, nor simple action, but a compromise formation that permits Hamlet to arrive at a space and time where the revenge he has been given as his life-task may be attempted or allowed to happen in full exposure to chance.

Why does Hamlet turn toward the player and Fortinbras, and take them as models for action? For Hamlet, both are completely engaged in their action, but seem to enjoy a serene relation to it, what one almost might call an aesthetic distance from it. This is explicit with the player, who is an actor in artistic drama, and such distance also seems implicit in Fortinbras' attachment to the principle of honor. Perhaps the actions of these actors are possible because they are fictional—with the actor's self-consciousness of the fictional grounds of his act disengaging him from the act, so he *can* act, easily. This detachment allows the player and Fortinbras to avoid forms of paralysis that have dogged Hamlet: they are not assimilated to the hyperbolic intensities of desire, as Ophelia is in her madness, or Hamlet is during his tirades; nor do they need to suspend the self and its attachments behind the shield of a philosophic irony. Finally, both the player and Fortinbras have found forms of action fully compatible with the social sphere they inhabit.

Hamlet's adoption of these two models engages him in a certain contradictory movement. In the two soliloquies in which he responds to the player and Fortinbras, Hamlet interprets their activity in terms of the metaphysical categories and affirmations of the guiding interpretation. But the most important effect of his taking them as models of action is that he is carried into a fictional nonmimetic use of language which allows him to negate the guiding interpretation. The first of these soliloquies comes near the end of Act II, after the player's speech on Pyrrhus' murder of Priam, and after Hamlet has sent the players off with Polonius. It begins "O what a rogue and peasant slave am I!" The second soliloquy comes just before Hamlet's departure for England in Act IV, and after his brief interview with the captain of Fortinbras' troops. In both these speeches Hamlet interrogates his own failure to act. One finds three common activities:

(1) *The elaboration of a searing self-criticism based on the mimetic assumptions of the guiding interpretation.* Hamlet calls himself a "dull and muddy-mettled rascal" for not avenging the wrong done the King, his father. And why doesn't he?—because no one "plucks off my beard and blows in my face," or "calls me villain." In other words, Hamlet lacks the spirituality, the inwardness and imagination, to carry through his revenge because the offense to himself does not come to him in the most stupid physical form. This self-criticism becomes more explicit in the rhetorical question about "man" that he develops in the second soliloquy:

> How all occasions do inform against me,
> And spur my dull revenge. What is man
> If his chief good and market of his time
> Be but to sleep and feed? A beast, no more.
> Sure he that made us with such large discourse,
> Looking before and after, gave us not
> That capability and godlike reason
> To fust in us unus'd.
>
> [IV, iv, 32–39]

And this general perspective is at work when Hamlet insists that he carry through a simple and manly act of revenge. What does he demand of himself?—a direct, nonproblematic relationship between the words of his command ("This thing's to do") and the act which would win a true mimetic relationship between the crime (the murder of his father) and its revenge (the murder of his uncle). In order to carry out this mimesis, he must use words in an economical proportion to action. There must be no excess of words. Thus when Hamlet starts ranting about Claudius with an obsessive profusion of epithets, he stops, and reproaches himself for showing a whore's readiness with words and incapacity for action:

> Why, what an ass am I! This is most brave,
> That I, the son of a dear father murder'd
> Prompted to my revenge my heaven and hell,
> Must like a whole unpack my heart with words
> And fall a-cursing like a very drab,
> A scullion!
>
> *[II, ii, 578–83]*

(2) *The choice of a model capable of "true" mimetic action.* Each of these soliloquies is triggered by Hamlet's admiration for one who demonstrates a true mimetic relationship between his act and the idea that action expresses. Thus the player forces all the forms of body and soul to his idea or "conceit"; and Fortinbras is a "delicate and tender prince" who risks all, finding quarrel even "in a straw," for the sake of his guiding idea—his "honor." It is the very slightness of the motives for these actions which makes these comparisons invidious for Hamlet. Hamlet castigates himself by imaging how the player would act had he "the motive and the cue for passion" Hamlet has: he would make a "horrid speech" that would "make mad the guilty, and appall the free. . ."

(3) *The formulation of a new resolve or purpose.* Hamlet's most famous soliloquy, "To be or not to be," also touches on the question of action and inaction, but ends in doubt. These two soliloquies lead Hamlet to formulate a new resolve or purpose. After watching the players' speech, Hamlet asks the troop to perform "The Murder of Gonzago," supplemented with "some dozen or sixteen lines" of his own composition. In this way Hamlet plans to trap his uncle—not through direct action, but through a calculated representation of "something like the murder of my father / Before mine uncle." At the end of the second soliloquy Hamlet makes a more general resolve: "O, from this time forth / My thoughts be bloody or be noth-

ing worth!" Later in the play, we learn that he has been as good as his word. When a vague uneasiness disturbs his sleep at sea, and he looks into the deadly commission Claudius has sent with Rosencrantz and Guildenstern, Hamlet swiftly forges the new orders that seal his "friends'" fate. The "mouse-trap" play and the forged letter both emerge from soliloquies where Hamlet reproaches himself with using too many words and failing to act. But these two pieces of artifice evade this simplistic distinction between words and action, for they are words that act and actions in the shape of words.

Hamlet's appropriation of the player and Fortinbras as models is built around a basic error. Hamlet would imitate these actors because their actions so effectively imitate their ideas. But his own words make it perfectly evident that neither acts according to the principles of true mimesis—that is, a proportional univocal relation between word and action, their action and some prompting event. Instead with each actor there is a *disproportion* between the action and the cause or idea toward which that action is directed. Thus Hamlet is astonished that the player acts but "in a fiction" and "a dream of passion," fitting all the forms of face and eyes to a "conceit," for what?—"for nothing! For Hecuba!" And, in a similar vein, Fortinbras exposes his own life to "fortune, death, and danger," for what?—for an "eggshell," that is, something with nothing in it, something as abstract as "honor" or the "fantasy and trick of fame" for which 20,000 men follow Fortinbras to "their graves like beds." And Hamlet's self-accusation is organized around the irony of antithetical disproportions: he has everything prodding him toward action, and does "nothing," they have "nothing" guiding them to act, yet they act with remarkable clarity, purpose, and force.

Hamlet's efforts to act in the wake of these models is marked by a double irony. The first register of irony comes from his misunderstanding of these actors. Instead of seeing the willful, rhetorical, and performative use of language that lies behind their ability to act, Hamlet finds something else to emulate. With the player he finds a comprehensive histrionic projection of feeling that echoes the intensities of his own largely concealed passions. In the production Hamlet devises, a melodramatic directness of language and action is intended to shock Claudius out of the pose of innocence. But this play, in being crude, tendentious, and all too transparent in its manipulations, has tendencies Hamlet apparently fails to grasp: first, it completely lacks those qualities of restraint and discretion he called for in his speech to the players; it also fails wretchedly in producing a plausible representation of the "real" Danish court with which

Shakespeare presents us. Thus if we compare Gertrude's language and bearing with those of the Player Queen, or the Player King with either Claudius or King Hamlet, can anyone feel that Hamlet and his art have "held the mirror up to nature," or shown the age its "form and pressure"? Finally this play is performed to expose Claudius as guilty, but it just as surely exposes Hamlet as intent on revenge.

With Fortinbras, Hamlet's most overt response is a conscious admiration of that in his action which makes it spiritual and romantic: its extravagance, its singleness of purpose, its invitation to uncertainty, and its willingness to risk and lose all. But Hamlet's explicit admiration is mightily qualified by the more sensible analysis of war that can be woven from his words: this, like all wars, will involve enormous waste of precious human life, for nothing more tangible than honor; the combatants wage war out of a perverse imitative rivalry, where each will match the other's effort—as in garrisoning and invading "a little patch of ground / That hath in it no profit but the name"; so this behavior provokes an ironic perspective on human societies. Hamlet tells the captain, "This is the impostume of much wealth and peace / That inward breaks, and shows no cause / Why the man dies." Thus war is not waged within any logical economy of loss and gain; rather it expresses a human will to waste and expend itself. . . . in death.

The ironies that emerge from Hamlet's way of misunderstanding his models and misapplying their methods are doubled by another register of irony: none of his failures of apprehension really matter. To the extent that these models carry him further into a scene of representation and language use, Hamlet begins, unbeknownst to himself, a process that has been going on since the beginning of Act II: an undoing of the power of the guiding interpretation. And the unraveling of the guiding interpretation is linked with the two characteristics of his trajectory which have occupied and preoccupied Hamlet and his critics since the beginning, in the form of two vexing questions: why does he delay in carrying through his revenge? and why is he so changed upon his return to Denmark? I think the answers to these two questions and an explanation of the failure of the guiding interpretation are of a piece. They all arise from the rude discrepancy Hamlet encounters—but never really understands—between the guiding interpretation he seeks to act on and the social sphere in which every action is subject to the displacements of language. The guiding interpretation supposes that Hamlet can constitute himself as an authentic self by being faithful to his father, renouncing woman, and carrying out a swift revenge that will repeat, counterbalance, and erase the crime it imitates. But this presupposes a certain idea of language and mimesis—that Hamlet's words and actions can be a faithful instrument of representation. We have seen, however, how this program for immediate action founders when it enters the social sphere. In conference with spies like Rosencrantz and Guildenstern, "acting" does not mean a direct kind of doing, but performing with most subtle feints and motions. Here a faithful representation of self could prove fatal. Irony becomes a habitual companion and a necessary disguise. In dialogue with Ophelia or Gertrude the suppressed desire for woman reasserts itself and carries its life into the turns of gesture and language. Hamlet has fallen into the labyrinths of representation as the only scene for his desire and he finds himself compelled to use a language system that is not "faithful," immediate, or organized according to the canons of true mimesis. He changes as he loses his grasp on his initial certitudes. All appearances become suspect. The Ghost-as-father had authorized the guiding interpretation: now it is a doubtful trace—perhaps the devil—which must be subjected to test.

Hamlet-and-language is a conjunction worth pausing before. Hamlet, among all the heroes of tragedy, is the most deft, rhetorical, and witty user of language—at times more a jester and a clown than a tragic protagonist.[12] But he is a troubled player with language. He cannot control the wave of rhetoric he seems to ride so easily. And his complex encounter with language has enormous consequences. Delay is the result of a series of displacements: the act of revenge is displaced into the manipulation and restructuring of the social sphere that harbors the object of desire; this restructuring requires a deft use of language which in its nonmimetic character begins to shift, subvert, and ironize the mimetic assumptions of personal identity, will, and action that undergird the guiding interpretation and justify the initial task—the act of revenge. Hamlet's use of language creates a drag upon his attempt to act decisively, because the metaphysical presuppositions of the guiding interpretation—the real father, the self-identical subject, the idea of faithful, mimetic revenge as efficacious action, and woman as a figure of corrupting instability —all these presuppositions are subjected to displacement and deconstruction by Hamlet's own use of language. Language, apparently an instrument in the hands of the agent, has circled back to

12. Jacques Lacan makes this point about Hamlet, extracted from the seminars, and published in the form of an essay in *Yale French Studies*, edited by Shoshana Felman: "Desire and the Interpretation of Desire in *Hamlet*," no. 55/56 (1977), 11–52.

paralyze action and change the character of the would-be avenger. Little wonder that Hamlet founders and delays—and by his return to Denmark has decisively changed his relationship to the act of revenge.

This discussion allows us to put Hamlet's appropriation of the player and Fortinbras as models for action in clearer focus. They are exemplary for him because they act vividly and have a detached and aesthetic relationship to their action. And this is so precisely because, through the mediation of the "nothing" of Hecuba, and honor, their relationship to action is nonmimetic—nonproportional, arbitrary, nonnecessary and metaphoric. A nonmimetic operational conception of language turns out to be decisive for Hamlet and the revenge he finally participates in. This is why language becomes a question and problem in this play, and why, in the eddies of the action, Hamlet and others give remarkably detailed expression to those nonmimetic qualities of language that make it a corrosive medium for representing any fixed truth or meaning.[13] Here are several of those qualities discovered and named by Hamlet.

Language habitually falls away from the speaking subject and its intention(s) and control. Before the "mouse-trap" play, Hamlet carries on a brief exchange with Claudius. The King asks, "How fares our cousin Hamlet?" and Hamlet answers in an ambiguous way which taunts the King for giving Hamlet the promise but not the substance of advancement at court: "Excellent, i' faith, of the chameleon's dish. I eat the air, promise-crammed. You cannot feed capons so." Claudius deflects this response as inappropriate: "I have nothing with this answer, Hamlet. These words are not mine." Hamlet rejoins: "No, nor mine now" (III, ii, 92–97). This exchange pivots on the question of possession: to whom (or what) do these words belong—to the speaker who speaks them?, or to the referent they are shaped to describe? Claudius does not just reject proper possession of these words because they are metaphorical, or threaten dangerous rivalry. He also seems to mean that these words do not correctly represent things at the Danish court. Thus when Hamlet complains to Rosencrantz that he, Hamlet, "lack(s) advancement," Rosencrantz replies —"How can that be, when you have the voice of the King himself for your succession in Denmark?" (III, ii, 332–33). Hamlet's reluctance to believe Claudius' "voice" echoes his refusal, in this brief exchange, to take responsible possession of words he has spoken—

13. For the nonmimetic qualities of language, see chap. 1 of Part I of Saussure's *Course in General Linguistics* (New York: McGraw Hill, 1966), 65–71.

they are not "mine now," he tells Claudius. These words are adrift between speaker and referent, beginning intention and received meaning, and in this in-between position, language can be faint and unnourishing—as insubstantial as the air, of which spoken words are made, and as shifting as the color of the chameleon.

From the position of language, the referent appears as "nothing"; therefore the proliferation of meaning in language is deviant, uncertain, and impure. In *Hamlet*, the Clown is a gravedigger, and the tragic hero Hamlet likes to clown. So while the Clown digs Ophelia's grave, he and Hamlet joust with words. Their exchange turns on a question—who possesses the grave, the gravedigger who makes it or the tenant who will fill it?—and unfolds around several meanings of the word "lie": to recline, to be placed in, and to tell an untruth.

Hamlet:	I will speak to this fellow.—Whose grave's this, sirrah?
Gravedigger:	Mine, sir.
	[Sings] O a pit of clay for to be made—
Hamlet:	I think it be thine indeed, for thou liest in't.
Gravedigger:	You lie out on't, sir, and therefore 'tis not yours. For my part, I do not lie in't, yet it is mine.
Hamlet:	Thou dost lie in't, to be in't and say 'tis thine.
	'Tis for the dead, not for the quick: therefore thou liest.
Gravedigger:	'Tis a quick lie, sir, 'twill away again from me to you.

[V, i, 115–25]

In this exchange, the referent is the grave—that is, a gap or hole in the earth, something which is nothing. This absence can belong to no one—neither he who stood near it (Hamlet), nor he who stands in it (the Clown), nor even she who will lie in it always—Ophelia— for being dead she can possess nothing. This grave—as the referent which is nothing—gives the lie to successive efforts to establish through words the fact of proximity and possession. Thus Hamlet seems quite confident he has won the contest of wits when he denies the gravedigger's claim on the grave, in favor of the dead. He concludes "therefore thou liest." But the Clown wins the palm in this debate by explicating a more general irony about the effort to name truth: the inaccessibility of the referent to language, and the multiple meanings of the word "lie," means that every speaker, while living in speech, must be engulfed in error. Thus the Clown says, about this word "lie" and the position of lying—"'Tis a quick lie, sir," that is a living and mobile lie, which will not rest. It swiftly moves "away again from me to you"—from "me," the person your enunciation names, to "you," the speaker of words that must habitually lie.

The uncertain relation of the sign and referent makes language the locus for innuendo and nuance, the suggestive and the desire-laden. A gentleman of the court is worried with the way Ophelia is speaking. He tells the queen of a kind of language that is scandalous for the way it becomes a screen for each auditor's projective desire.

> [Ophelia] speaks things in doubt
> That carry but half sense. Her speech is nothing,
> Yet the unshaped use of it doth move
> The hearers to collection. They aim at it,
> And botch the words up fit to their own thoughts,
> Which, as her winks and nods and gestures yield them,
> Indeed would make one think there might be thought,
> Though nothing sure, yet much unhappily.
>
> [IV, v, 6–13]

Ophelia's language does not trigger desire merely because her madness makes her speech daringly revealing. It also dramatizes a more general quality of language: it is the nothingness in Ophelia's speech that begins a drift of multiple meanings. And this starts a play of meaning which is alluring to the auditor, and encourages a projective, desire-laden production of meaning.[14]

But since language does not re-present reality, it can displace or transform it. Before his departure for England, Hamlet never really relinquishes his explicit allegiance to the idea of virtue his father's memory engages, and the code of true mimesis this involves. In the closet scene with Gertrude, Hamlet invokes this virtue, its purity of being, the authority that commands its repetition, and a shunning of its vicious opposite, vice. But in the same scene Hamlet promotes a practical pathway to virtue which is predicated upon a fundamentally different version of reality and language. For in abjuring Gertrude not to return to Claudius' bed, Hamlet explains that custom, here operating like language, does not just repeat or embody a preexistent virtue and reality—it can almost transform that reality.

> But go not to my uncle's bed.
> Assume a virtue if you have it not.
> That monster, custom, who all sense doth eat

14. Jacques Lacan finds this (fascinating, castrating) drift of the signifier to be productive of human desire.

> Of habits evil, is angel yet in this,
> That to the use of actions fair and good
> He likewise gives a frock or livery
> That aptly is put on. Refrain tonight,
> And that shall lend a kind of easiness
> To the next abstinence, the next more easy;
> For use almost can change the stamp of nature,
> And either lodge the devil or throw him out
> With wondrous potency.
>
> [III, iv, 161–72]

Custom is a "monster" that consumes sense and meaning, because like language it is based upon an arbitrary and habitual usage which becomes a recurrent social practice. Custom, like the sign of systems of language or the clothes one wears, is assumed to have a secondary relation to a prior reality—here, the virtuous act, or the naked body. And in this speech Hamlet repeatedly urges Gertrude to "put on," to assume, to cover her body and self with a covering, the appearance, the "habits" of virtue. But Hamlet's use of this clothes metaphor subtly puts in question the presumed priority of a self-identical virtue. For where does custom get the "wonderous potency" to almost change the stamp of nature? Like language, custom operates slowly, steadily, pervasively, and it does so by shifting our experience of what we know of a thing—its outer appearance. Language is powerful precisely because it slides between being an extrinsic mark and the token of actuality. It operates like "the stamp of nature," thus ambiguously that mark or label which is imposed from without upon the body of nature, but also the true property or quality of nature.

What does Hamlet discover in these asides upon language? First, that language does not involve a simple repetition of that which is, but takes its user on a detour into a relationship with "nothing." This is not the bleak or melodramatic encounter with the "nothing" of nihilism or existentialism—the mere afterimage of too much gazing upon God. Instead this "nothing" becomes folded into Hamlet's experience as a more complex negative moment of any production of meaning and interpretation in language. And in the corners of this text where language becomes an explicit question, it engages the same problems that trouble Plato in *The Cratylus* and *The Sophist*. There Plato sees that language is the philosopher's only pathway to truth, but he distrusts language because, lacking the plenitude of being of ideal forms and the truth-in-itself, language can lie, it can name that which is not (like the unicorn), or be misused by masterful rhetoricians like the sophists.

Plato's philosophical inquiry into mimesis and language is compatible with Hamlet's practical ruminations on the subject. For both, language becomes something ghostly and indefinite, a trace of reality that is neither an absence nor a simple presence, but productive of our experience of both. As such, language may not cooperate so readily in our projects of representation—like suiting the "word" to the "action," or holding a clean repeating mirror up to nature. Instead, in the social encounters Hamlet knows, language can be as shifting as the color of the chameleon, as dispossessed and dispossessing as the gap in the earth called a grave. But the nothingness that these meditations find and name as an aspect of language need not lead to paralysis. Quite the contrary. It is through forming an alliance with this negating power of language that the fictional projection of a new interpretation can be ventured. Then the player can enact Hecuba's sorrow, Fortinbras can invade Poland, and perhaps Gertrude could be schooled away from Claudius' bed. This play shows Hamlet learning a practical fact: only through a subtle and inventive use of language can one translate something personal—a fiction or a dream of passion—into a collective social reality—something bearing the name of action.[15]

These four related properties of language involve Hamlet in a basic shift away from the mimetic assumptions of the guiding interpretation. Thus he incorporates a nonmimetic, nonproportional ratio into the treatment he meditates for Gertrude when he will meet her in her bedchamber. To offer effective moral instruction and draw her away from the King's party, Hamlet plans to show a calculated cruelty so his words reflect the rage he feels, but his actions do not. This requires a division between words and deeds that will echo a division in the acting self:

> I will speak daggers to her, but use none.
> My tongue and soul in this be hypocrites:
> How in my words somever she be shent,
> To give them seals never my soul consent.
>
> [III, ii, 387–90]

15. In Movement One we found an analogous juncture in the trajectory of Freud's thought and career in the 1890s. His interpretation of the *non vixit* dream is something of and about language; at the same time this piece of writing enables Freud to realign his relationship to Fliess (and the father), and institute psychoanalysis.

This division of the self does not lead Hamlet to paralysis. For at the same time that his encounter with language blocks the kind of mimetic action he contemplated, and breaks up the guiding interpretation, it also becomes the condition of the possibility of the kind of action he does take. This is true in two senses: first, most concretely, Hamlet's initial movements toward revenge happen through a highly rhetorical self-conscious use of language: in the "mouse-trap" play, in the lesson given Gertrude in her closet, and in the forged letter that sends Rosencrantz and Guildenstern to their fate. And, in a larger frame, Hamlet's encounter with language is concomitant with his taking the player and Fortinbras as model actors: both developments introduce Hamlet to the process of negating the facticity of "what is" and producing fictions through a manipulation of language operated upon nonmimetic principles.

There is no particular point in Hamlet's life-story where he is suddenly aware of his new relationship to language, and the way it transforms the project of revenge. But there is a point in the text that marks a decisive break with the guiding interpretation, the authority of the father, and efforts at true mimesis. It comes when Hamlet becomes a shipboard forger of the King's writing. The importance of this moment is dramatized by the way Hamlet presents it in his narrative. Here he assumes all the trappings of the hero of romance: on a sea voyage, in the middle of the night, suspicion and a providential curiosity lead him to look into the King's dispatch only to discover a plot on his life. With Odyssean cunning he turns this instrument back on his would-be destroyers, and the next day is rescued accidentally, by pirates. This moment offers a temptation to Hamlet and his auditors: to see Hamlet enveloped in an aura of will, courage, and purpose which enables him, like every true hero, to master himself, others, and every situation, no matter how precarious.[16] But such a perspective would only obscure what is actually unfolding.

This shipboard scene is not a "scene" in an ordinary sense. Instead it is a species of life-writing by which an incident becomes an event represented, interpreted, and turned to use. Here a character's nar-

16. Helen Gardner has pointed out how Hamlet's remorseless removal of Rosencrantz and Guildenstern makes this passage of *Hamlet* a moment of pure revenge drama in a larger play (*The Tragedy of Hamlet*) that has a very different tendency. See "Hamlet and the Tragedy of Revenge," in *Shakespeare: Modern Essays in Criticism*, ed. Leonard F. Dean (Oxford: Oxford University Press, 1957), 218–26. This narrated episode also carries Hamlet the closest he ever gets to being like the successful, and surviving, avenger of his father that we have in two of the sources of *Hamlet*: Saxo Grammaticus' *Amleth*, and Belleforest's *The Hystorie of Hamblet, Prince of Denmarke*.

ration in a play seems to serve the same purpose that life-writing does for Freud and Nietzsche. Freud's written interpretation of the *non vixit* dream allows him to assume the authority to "father" psychoanalysis, and Nietzache's "overcoming" of the Lou Salomé episode (by writing *Zarathustra*) allows him to secure the conceptual perspective for his subsequent critique of culture. So here, the character Hamlet offers an interpretation of a contingent moment decisive to his future—he did not have to look into the royal commission, but did so "rashly"—and describes the action by which he for the first time assumes effective authority, and begins the struggle in earnest with Claudius which will lead to the avenging of King Hamlet. As with Freud and Nietzsche, once contingent events are embedded in life-writing they take on the aura of necessity. Here Hamlet's rash looking, his "indiscretion," serves him so well that he is quite sure, in narrating these events, that "there's a divinity that shapes our ends, / Rough-hew them how we will."

If we look carefully at this scene, Hamlet does not turn to action according to the protocols laid down by the guiding interpretation. There, fidelity to the memory of the father meant effacing other memory traces and all "trivial fond records" from "the book and volume of my brain" so the Ghost's "commandments" could live as all that was written there. This would lead to the simple destruction of the usurping King and "father," Claudius, and his replacement upon the throne with Hamlet. But in this "scene," Hamlet challenges authority with writing. With the subtle displacing powers of language, Hamlet exercises an interpretive leeway, and modifies the world he inhabits. This involves him in a subversion of a false father and imitation of a true one which is both indirect and ingenious. Hamlet shapes his response to the particular form in which he confronts royal and paternal authority: a commission sent to England, imitating the "fair" calligraphy of the royal scribes, the grand style of his uncle, and sealed with the official seal of the King. Script, style, and signet are supposed to function as the unique marks of a single source of power. They are also what allows a king or father to *be* powerful—by extending his personal will over space and time in the form of authentic script. But Hamlet forges the writing of his uncle—the script of his scribes, and the style of his speech—so as to turn the capital sentence against Rosencrantz and Guildenstern, and he lends the stamp of authenticity to this act of forgery by sealing the letter with his father's signet which was "the model of that Danish seal." In doing so Hamlet exploits certain related qualities of language and writing—the arbitrary relation and consequent distance between signifier and signified, the iterability of the sign, the absolute invisibility of differences between repeated forms of the same sign. Thus in this scene, authority is not naturally vested in one person—like a father or a king—and then transmitted through controlled mimetic representation and delegation—in the person of a son or the King's messenger. Instead authority is the effect of a violent and discontinuous leap from one agent to another, modeled upon metaphoric substitution—as when Hamlet substitutes Rosencrantz and Guildenstern for himself, and turns the writing and signet of his uncle and father to his own uses. This has certain ironic effects. For the very moment when Hamlet is apparently learning to be his father's son through resolute action is the same moment he puts in question the identity of identity, the priority of paternity, and the authority of identity, paternity, and authority.

Out of the passing of the guiding interpretation there arises a compromise formation—play as sport—that allows Hamlet's relationship to his adversaries and the act of revenge to take on an entirely new tone and character. I call play a "compromise formation" because it has emerged as a form which offers a compromise solution to the several pressures Hamlet has felt, from inside and outside himself, throughout the play: most narrowly, the task of revenge, his ambition to emulate his father, his desire to win his mother back from Claudius. But more broadly, play allows Hamlet to do other things: to avoid being enthralled by the hyperbolic literality of his desire (as Ophelia is); to go beyond a skeptical and paralyzing suspension of the self in irony; and to imitate the player and Fortinbras by being both caught up in and disengaged from the act he performs. Within the arena of play, which culminates in the duel, revenge will not be the result of a consciously focused deed but the effect of an incalculable manifold of events.

How does Hamlet get to the point where he can collaborate in designing this compromise formation? First, he adopts a new kind of passivity about his position at court and role as avenger. Earlier he had complained "Oh cursed spite, that ever I was born to set it right." But in the closet scene, Hamlet expresses his acceptance of the necessities of his role—however perverse or arbitrary it may feel—with this graceful cadence of speech: "heaven hath pleas'd it so, / To punish me with this and this with me, / That I must be their scourge and minister" (III, iv, 175–77). The passivity of this acceptance of the external constraints or "givens" of one's situation lies outside the opposition action/inaction that organized the early part of the play. And this passivity is a precondition for the activity we call "play." Hamlet is being gamely passive when he shows a willingness to accompany Rosencrantz and Guildenstern to England even before the death of Polonius, and when he accepts the challenge to fight Laertes as the champion of the King, his mortal enemy.

By accepting his position and role, Hamlet is suddenly able to develop that in his situation which is productive of genuine aesthetic pleasure: a relationship of rivalry with his adversaries that demands tactical manipulation and brings an arresting suspense. Thus Hamlet tells his mother that "'tis most sweet / When in one line two crafts directly meet." In going off with Rosencrantz and Guildenstern, who, he says "I will trust as I would adders fanged," he will dig one deeper than their plots, for, as he says, with the aesthetic detachment integral to the pleasure of play, "'Tis the sport to have the enginer / Hoist with his own petard." The same zest for rivalry is apparent after the sea voyage: in the laconic letter with which Hamlet announces his return to Denmark, but shrouds that return in a mystery calculated to disturb Claudius; in his leaping into Ophelia's grave; in his accepting the wager to duel with Laertes. It does not really matter that these rivalries will partake of the fictive character of opponents in sport. Hamlet plunges in anyway, even though Rosencrantz and Guildenstern are the King's pawns, or he sees in Laertes "the image of [his own] cause." Within the arena of play marked out in collaboration with his adversaries, the arbitrarily invented rules of the duel have become the real parameters of a life-wager Hamlet has determined to let run its course.

Play engenders interest and anxiety for player and spectator precisely to the degree that the victor is uncertain, that things can go either way. This radical contingency in play emerges from the collision of innumerable forces and elements interacting in a manner which is incalculable. This is why the outcome of play is not predictable, and its results defy sure retrospective cause-effect analysis. But this lacuna in the midst of play is not just fascinating, it is also disturbing. Little wonder that Hamlet, like most other players, represses this radical contingency by seeking consolation in false explanations. When he has "won" the first round of his contest with Claudius, by sending Rosencrantz and Guildenstern to their deaths, Hamlet names a reason for his success. Given what he has said to Gertrude of how he will trust these "friends," the sleeplessness and suspicion that lead Hamlet to finger the "grand commission" do not seem surprising to me. But Hamlet discovers in this a wonderful "rashness" that should teach us "There's a divinity that shapes our ends / Rough-hew them how we will—," that is, there is a God ouside this perimeter of play, who sees and knows things beyond our limited vision and has reasons for things that happen, and reasons for these reasons. It is this God Hamlet refers to when he feels uneasy before the duel, but decides to fight anyway, with the words "There is a special providence in the fall of a sparrow." The Christian vista of a universe saturated with purposiveness is the only way to be sure that what is about to happen will have some legitimate reason for happening. But this verbal gesture of Hamlet's tends to mask the fact that here, on entering the chance-laden arena of play, at least for Hamlet "seeing before" (*pro-vident*), seeing what will happen before it happens, is precisely what he cannot do. This is why there is a false bravado in saying, of the time before Claudius knows of the fate of Rosencrantz and Guildenstern, "the interim is mine." If this interval of time offers Hamlet opportunities, it extends equal opportunity to Claudius. For time in play and exposed to chance is precisely time and space—an interim—none can control or possess.

Below, after examining the readings of a spectrum of critics, I will be able to develop a broader context for Hamlet's sudden appeal to a Christian way of circumscribing the uncertainty of chance. But the gesture is an example of a more general tendency. Once a contingent moment is isolated and interpreted, it becomes framed by a system of meaning that makes its contingency fade. And this is a problem for my own discussion of the duel as a contingent scene of play. Once I have said the word "play," it becomes tempting to see Hamlet, and the reader who identifies with him, as a subject unified in its will and pleasure within what Johan Huizinga calls "the magic circle of play." At first this duel does seem to obey the criteria laid down in *Homo Ludens* for play: unfolding in a limited space and time, proceeding according to fixed, collectively accepted rules, play affords participants and spectators a heightened reality apart.[17] And Hamlet's acceptance of a limited sphere for his effort *does* offer a welcome relief. Here, for the first time in the text, Hamlet can befriend his own will—whatever its complex deficiencies—and discharge its energies with a free forgetful consciousness.

But on closer inspection this scene offers only a simulacrum of the form of play Huizinga celebrates. For here there are no codes of fairness or intrinsic limits that Claudius or Laertes will observe in advancing their ends; and Gertrude, in her desire to drink from the cup that was to touch Hamlet's lips, cannot be kept outside a play-space that has no secure boundaries; and Hamlet, no matter how

17. For a definition of "play" see the first 27 pages of Johan Huizinga, *Homo Ludens: A Study of the Play-Element in Culture* (Boston: Beacon, 1950).

Horatio and Fortinbras exalt him at the play's end, has entered a contaminating arena where there can be no clear distinction between winner and loser, player and judge, participant and spectator. None dominate a space traversed by a chance that cannot be controlled. The failure of agency becomes most evident in the way the lust for control—the inevitable desire of play—expresses itself in this scene. To Claudius' plan to give Laertes an unbated sword to kill Hamlet, Laertes adds the poison that will make the slightest scratch from his sword's tip deadly. And to this extra precaution, Claudius adds the poison cup from which Hamlet will drink if his body escapes the poison sword tip. In the scene that ensues, it is this plethora of precautions designed to prevent backfire which backfire. Laertes quickly gives this turn of events a moral interpretation: "as a woodcock to mine own springe, Osric. / I am justly killed with mine own treachery. . . . The foul practice / Hath turned itself on me." But I urge a suspicion of this godly, just, and logical irony. Does it explain Hamlet's death? or Gertrude's? Instead the scene of the duel appears as an arena where chance is mixed into action so the duel's issue appears as an event; in this scene, instruments that are designed, like poisoned tips and drinks, to be shaped toward a certain end (the death of Hamlet) begin to turn and move in a way which is incalculable and tropological. They move like the language of Hamlet's play which may "trap" Claudius, but does so "trapically"—that is, "tropically"—so it also divulges Hamlet's intentions; or like the commission to execute Hamlet, whose forged revisions turn on its carriers. In this space, each turn of events generates effects of meaning beyond the control of any supervising intention or rational process. This is so because each of the interested parties to this scene—whether characters, Shakespeare, or his readers—finds himself in Hamlet's situation: playing a game where no amount of morality, intelligence, or will can prevent the outcome from being a product of human desire and . . . chance.

The Critics and the Annulment of Chance

Up to this point I have interpreted *Hamlet* from the vantage of its fictional protagonist. It is from this position that the question and problem of chance, the person, and language have come to the fore. But why then has most of the criticism of the last three hundred years—criticism which has also usually oriented itself around Hamlet—minimized the import of what we have found so much of in the drama, the virulent force of chance and the constitutive role of language? I will pursue this question by undertaking a very selective analysis of *Hamlet* criticism. My goal is to isolate a profile of one important manner in which critics have responded to *Hamlet*. Then I will demonstrate the way this cluster of responses is authorized and undergirded by a broader metaphysics: the mimetic system by which the artist is presumed to produce an artwork that represents a reality, truth, or idea to which the critic helps the reader/spectator have access.

The most influential interpretations of *Hamlet* over the last three hundred years involve one or some combination of the following three positions: (1) the critic insists there is a necessity to *identify* with Hamlet, though it may be risky to do so; (2) the critic passes a *judgment* on Hamlet; and (3) the critic demonstrates that Hamlet's "case" provides a *lesson* for the reader.

Identification with Hamlet. Among all art forms, drama is presumed to be most likely to bring its spectators together into a community of common experience. But *Hamlet* not only tells the story of a shattered social network (the Danish court); by the *way* it encourages an unruly proliferation of interpretations, it becomes a scandal to the desire for a shared experience of art. So when critics step forward to offer their readings, they often do so with an apology and warning that there will be something inevitably personal about their responses to *Hamlet*. Upon beginning his well-known essay "The World of Hamlet," Maynard Mack tells us somewhat mournfully: "I know too well, if I may echo a sentiment of Mr. E. M. W. Tillyard's, that no one is likely to accept another man's reading of *Hamlet*."[18] Harry Levin begins *The Question of Hamlet* by comparing the text to "Hamlet's ink-blot test"—the clouds Hamlet asks Polonius to designate after the mouse-trap play. *Hamlet*, Levin tells us, "has clouded our mental horizons with its peculiar sense of obscurity or of anxiety, and has inspired its interpreters to discern an unending succession of shapes."[19]

Why does this text provoke a response which is so anxious and personal? Perhaps because of the reader/spectator's identification with the main character. William Hazlitt has written the most eloquent testament to the inevitability of this identification.

18. Maynard Mack, "The World of Hamlet," reprinted in *The Tragedy of Hamlet*, ed. Edward Hubler (New York: New American Library, 1963), 235.
19. Harry Levin, *The Question of Hamlet* (Oxford: Oxford University Press, 1959), 3.

Hamlet is a name; his speeches and sayings but the idle coinage of the poet's brain. What then, are they not real? They are as real as our thoughts. Their reality is in the reader's mind. It is *we* who are Hamlet. This play has a prophetic truth, which is above that of history. Whoever has become thoughtful and melancholy through his own mishaps or those of others; whoever has borne about with him the clouded brow of reflection, and thought himself "too much i' th' sun"; . . . whoever has known "the pangs of despised love, the insolence of office". . . . whose powers of action have been eaten up by thought, he to whom the universe seems infinite, and himself nothing; whose bitterness of soul makes him careless of consequences, and who goes to a play as his best resource to shove off, to a second remove, the evils of life by a mock representation of them—this is the true Hamlet. [*Characters of Shakespeare's Plays* (1817)][20]

In Hazlitt's account, identification emerges from both a philosophic idealism—words produce "reality" in a "reader's mind"—and the particular qualities of Hamlet's experience. But, most interesting, the urgent rhythms of Hazlitt's prose enact the very identification his language describes. With *Hamlet,* the process by which a reader/spectator engages in an imaginary identification with a character is evidently more intense than usual—more fascinating, more mysterious, and more fraught with the likelihood of interpretive blindness. The mystery that *Hamlet* allows us to encounter is the same that enthralls Narcissus by the water: the self sees itself as other, in the other, as an image.

Why has this text become a mirror, the site for a compelling but risky self-consciousness? Is it, as Hazlitt maintains, that Hamlet shows us the pathos of our own desire and disappointments? Or is it because Hamlet is so heroically principled, inward, and spiritual? Or that with others he possesses the cool irony and instant wit we would all like to have? Or that alone he blends weakness with mastery, emotional resonance, and vulnerability in a way most imagine themselves to do? All of this is to say that Hamlet has triggered in many readers exactly those qualities of admiration, wonder, idealization—with a pointed sense of being fatefully implicated—that the Ghost provokes in Hamlet. And the theories critics evolve seem no less eccentric and rigidly metaphysical than the guiding interpretation Hamlet formulates to modify his world.

Hamlet judged. Identification with Hamlet has unleashed something discreditable in the critic. The best way to restore order, and

20. Excerpted in the Norton Critical Edition of *Hamlet,* ed. Cyrus Hoy (New York: Norton, 1963), 164.

the critic's authority, is to engage in an activity which is apparently more elevated and less private: judgment. Critics condemn Hamlet for his failure to act swiftly in avenging his father, and for his cruelty to Ophelia. Both are connected with the more general charge of being "unmanly." Judgment comes in the form of a character assessment that seeks to explain Hamlet's deficiencies. Goethe finds Hamlet suffering from "the effects of a great action laid upon a soul unfit for the performance of it."[21] Coleridge attributes this failure to an "over-meditative" mind, that fails to sustain a due balance between "outward objects" and "inward thoughts."[22] Schlegel turns this perspective toward a much more caustic judgment: "In the resolutions which [Hamlet] so often embraces and always leaves unexecuted, his weakness is too apparent: . . . he has a natural inclination for crooked ways; he is a hypocrite towards himself; his far-fetched scruples are often mere pretexts to cover his want of determination . . ."[23] Harsh judgment of Hamlet reaches one of its possible extremes when G. Wilson Knight describes Hamlet as something of a morally righteous Dracula, who, having known death, returns to haunt and poison the life of the court. Hamlet is compared unfavorably with Claudius, whom Knight describes as "human."[24]

One may examine the grounds for these judgments by asking, "Why does Hamlet delay?" This oldest of critical questions must seem tedious and fruitless on "hearsay evidence," and may seem all the more so upon reading the arguments marshaled around this question. There are many modern critics who have maintained that the whole debate is simply misguided and beside the point.[25] But the efforts to shift interpretation away from this question altogether, or exonerate Hamlet in some way (as Helen Gardner does) all founder upon the way Hamlet makes such a fuss about the question, and condemns himself openly for delay.[26] In our reading of the play, we have seen that Hamlet's judgment against himself is

---

21. Goethe, *Wilhelm Meister's Apprenticeship* (1795), trans. Thomas Carlyle, Book IV, chap. 13, excerpted by Hoy, 153.
22. Coleridge, "Notes on the Tragedies: *Hamlet*," in *Coleridge's Shakespeare Criticism*, ed. Thomas M. Raysor (Cambridge, Mass., 1930), excerpted by Hoy, 163.
23. Schlegel, *Lectures on Dramatic Art and Literature* (1808), trans. John Black (London, 1846), 404–6, excerpted by Hoy, 155.
24. G. Wilson Knight, "The Embassy of Death: An Essay on *Hamlet*," from *The Wheel of Fire* (London: Methuen, 1930).
25. Jenkins, in his extensive introduction to the Arden *Hamlet*, reviews the arguments Elmer Stoll and others use to minimize the centrality of delay as an aspect of the drama. See Arden *Hamlet*, 136–40. For another version of the same argument see Norman Holland, *The Shakespearean Imagination* (New York: Macmillan, 1964).
26. See Gardner, "Hamlet and the Tragedy of Revenge."

linked with a desire to attain authentic selfhood by imitating a father presumed to have the power to translate personal identity into will and then into action. Perhaps the chorus of anger and disapproval which runs through the history of *Hamlet* criticism and culminates in a judgment against Hamlet is like his judgment against himself, part of a complex disappointment that his situation has not been met with a single decisive manly act. This judgment wards off what identification with Hamlet implies—that the reader/spectator is implicated in the way Hamlet's desire to act in a simple, vivid instant gets displaced and delayed into the forked pathways of representation, social mediation, and chance event. Thus, judgment of Hamlet and identification with him are affiliated responses; sometimes judgment seems to be a defense against an identification that lingers latent within judgment. Critics have pointed to the way Coleridge's Hamlet resembles Coleridge, and the elegant metaphor Goethe makes to describe Hamlet's fate—"There is an oak-tree planted in a costly jar . . . in its bosom; the roots expand, the jar is shivered"—seems much more apt for describing the tragic course of Werther's love for Lotte than Hamlet's career of desire, intrigue, and revenge.[27]

Why do critics respond to Hamlet in these ways? First, let us note the simplest thing about Hamlet: he is the hero of the play. The spectator identifies with the hero, because, in addition to skill, craft, and strength, he is in possession of an aura of invincibility. Whatever his trials along the way, the hero finally prevails; to *be a hero* he must finally overcome the vagaries of chance and master destiny. And, in fact, Hamlet is just this kind of hero in the romance sources. Of course, Shakespeare's Hamlet is more complex and less "heroic." But paradoxically, identification with Hamlet, as Shakespeare presents him, becomes all the more inviting by reasons of his spirituality and wit and weakness. Nonetheless, the audience still demands that he prevail. When things go wrong with the hero, how does the reader/spectator respond? Perhaps with the pity and fear which Aristotle described and which are the symptoms and aftereffects of identification. But also with disappointment, anger, and a quite understandable desire to separate oneself from the "loser." The result is a judgment which rationalizes failure: "Hamlet failed because . . ." What is being assumed is the existence of a rational order—whether natural or divine, knowable or unknowable—which intersects with and shapes the lives of human beings in decisive ways. This order

---

27. Despite its aptness for Werther, the metaphor is to be found in *Wilhelm Meister's Apprenticeship*, as excerpted by Hoy, 153.

subordinates chance to the functioning of its own processes. It also authorizes the judgment the critic makes in its name. This rational explanation and judgment of Hamlet's failure is an implicit part of a vast portion of *Hamlet* criticism. It punishes Hamlet for failing to satisfy the desire behind the identification he triggered.

The lesson of Hamlet's case. Critics have read Hamlet's story as one of failure and loss. In extended readings of the play, critics often work to convert this sense of loss into a lesson learned. The belief that one has learned something helps to heal the wound caused by any attachment felt for Hamlet; it realizes that sense of superiority implicit in the act of judgment; and it recuperates failure and loss in the form of an improving "truth" or ethos. These interpretive efforts are directed most intently at the final scene of the play. Perhaps this is inevitable, as there is a long tradition in the West of evaluating the spiritual disposition of a person by the way he meets his end. And every artwork seems to receive a decisive turn of meaning in its final moment. But *this* last scene becomes a special problem for the critics who would take the moral and interpretive sum of Hamlet's life. We can verify this assertion by looking at what is done with this scene by three modern readers of the play—Maynard Mack, Harry Levin, and Harold Rosenberg.

These critics develop very different readings of *Hamlet,* but they share two important assumptions. First, they assume that in entering the last scene, Hamlet has left behind the indecision and equivocation of the first four acts and is in possession of a coherent self, ready for action. Second, all three critics assume that the self's identity is defined through action. Thus, writing of *Oedipus Rex,* in view of *Hamlet,* Rosenberg asserts, that for the hero "the action is the point of knowing, in that it partakes of creating, and makes itself responsible for, that which it brings to light."[28] The self comes into the light of its truth through action. But how is this expectation to be met by the final scene of *Hamlet?* True, after a play full of waiting, there is plenty of action. But this "action" is puzzling to interpret, for it is detached from the overall dramatic situation by the artifice of the game, and from the control of any intending agent by the intervention of chance. Samuel Johnson apprehends this clearly when he writes: "Hamlet is . . . rather an instrument than an agent. . . . [Claudius'] death is at last effected by an incident which Hamlet has no part in producing. The catastrophe is not very happily produced; the exchange of weapons is rather an expedient of necessity, than a

28. Harold Rosenberg, *Act and the Actor: Making the Self* (New York: New American Library, 1970), 59.

stroke of art."[29] In the last scene things happen in play and by chance, but they cannot be ignored, for what happens is all too final and decisive. And all three of these critics engage in interesting interpretive work in order to convert Hamlet's dubious end into a kind of knowledge.

Maynard Mack concludes "The World of Hamlet" with an eloquent catalogue of what Hamlet has "learned," lessons Mack clearly invites us to learn too: "[Hamlet] has now learned, and accepted the boundaries in which human action, human judgment, are enclosed . . . [he] had been encroaching on the role of providence . . . [and] sought to play at God." Hamlet has been proud—the Christian sin *par excellence.* And to support a religious interpretation of the text Mack alludes to Hamlet's words about providence and a divinity shaping our ends and tells us Hamlet "has been religious all through the play." But, most interesting, Mack stops short of the explicitly Christian interpretation of *Hamlet* his language seems to solicit. And it is significant that he says nothing about the strange way Hamlet dies. Instead Hamlet's end is given value, in an oblique fashion, by the way Mack celebrates Hamlet's final epiphany, as expressed in the graveyard scene. Mack does not emphasize what is caustic, comic, or irreverent about Hamlet's role. Instead he summarizes his wide-ranging thematic reading of the text with these words: "[Hamlet] confronts, recognizes and accepts the condition of being man . . . the haunting mystery of life . . . holding in its inscrutable folds . . . the mystery of evil . . . the mystery of reality . . . the mystery of human limitation."[30] By this account, Hamlet has become the locus of a kind of negative knowledge—the humbling knowledge of one's ignorance. And this interpretation allows Mack to take the blank of Hamlet's death and encircle it with a ring of mystery, so it becomes a token of divine truth—a truth that is all the more sublime and powerful for being indecipherable.

Harry Levin closes *The Question of Hamlet* with a complex effort to come to terms with the haphazard way Hamlet dies. After a detailed discussion of the duel scene, Levin ends his book with a three-paragraph finale written in a lyrical style and directed by an authoritative and ethical "we." Each statement is made in an indefinite mode of reference that allows Levin's assertions to float between the character Hamlet, the text of *Hamlet,* tragedy in general, and human life. From the vantage point of these enunciations, Levin hesitates be-

29. From Samuel Johnson, ed., *The Plays of William Shakespeare* (London, 1765), VIII, 311.
30. Mack, 253–55.

tween two ways of understanding Hamlet's end: the last scene may be the work of providence or "an encounter with sheer contingency," "the finger of the deity or the determination of chance." Then Levin seems to make his choice: tragedy is a "forewarning" against chance, "lest our blessings be turned to curses . . . it . . . indicate[s] limits which we may overstep at our peril." The next sentence takes Levin toward a consistently ethical judgment of Hamlet's end:

Marry

> Vengeance is [tragedy's] most habitual theme because the revenger is called upon to take into his own hands what might better be left to providence, however we define it; and if the revenge gets out of hand and goes amiss, as it is almost bound to do, if the mistaken purposes fall upon their inventors' heads, then that reversal is an ironic commentary upon the ways of human destiny.[31]

Here is the most traditional way of interpreting the turn of fortune's wheel—as a divine corrective directed at human pride and presumption. But Levin's *way* of saying this has consequences. He embeds the crucial clause in the conditional and passive voice ("Vengeance . . . might better be left to providence"), and he appends a modifying phrase that blurs the meaning of "providence" ("however we define it"). This puts Levin at some remove from the very thing he is saying: Hamlet's death is a judgment (by God) for exceeding human limits in carrying out his own vengeance. Clearly Levin does not want to commit himself or his reading to a belief in God. Instead he assumes a neutrality before the many ways men have sought some "principle of arrangement in the universe." He takes the alternatives offered by Seneca, Hardy, Kierkegaard, and Dante, and entertains them with a certain generous pluralism. *Hamlet,* by his reading, leaves us free to believe what we wish.

But Levin has nonetheless found a specific vantage point on the nagging question of Hamlet's fate. How? By locating himself in the place of Shakespeare's art, which "conveys us beyond the man-made sphere of poetic justice toward the ever-receding horizons of cosmic irony."[32] What does this mean? "Irony" is the title of the last essay in *The Question of Hamlet.* It registers the climactic "truth" of Shakespeare's art. This irony cannot solve a mystery as intractable as Levin names, "the incalculable contradictions between the personal life and the nature of things." "Yet," Levin continues, "it can teach

31. Levin, 104.
32. Ibid. 105.

us to live with them; and that is no mean achievement." "Irony" as used by Levin, like the "mystery" Mack solicits, is a way of having things two ways: Shakespeare's art teaches us to know without knowing, to glimpse the principles of human fate without our comprehending them. Levin's reading of *Hamlet* suggests that human fates are patterned, without being caught wrong with a vulgar and feeble explanation of the cosmos. Hamlet's death—as dubious and chance-ridden as it may appear—confirms this pattern, at the same time that it registers a "cosmic irony" that makes knowledge of that pattern something beyond an ever-receding horizon.

Mack and Levin have taken everything in Hamlet's life which is doubtful and problematic—including its failures—and through the alchemical processes of their critical art have made his life-story a spiritual exemplum and bridge. But, strange to say, readers of a much more skeptical cast manage the same trick. For Harold Rosenberg the text solicits an entirely different ratio of belief and doubt, but Hamlet's case is no less capable of teaching lessons. Rosenberg attributes Hamlet's delay to his protracted search for an "act of true color" that could realize authentic selfhood. For Rosenberg Hamlet is the failed existential hero of the modern historical moment, exemplary because, like the leader of the proletariat, he is betrayed by the particular historical role he is given. "On the stage which is the world the plot is written by nobody and no one can denote himself truly" (Rosenberg, 102).

When Freud takes up *Hamlet* in *The Interpretation of Dreams*, he seems to be inaugurating a fundamental break with the directions of traditional *Hamlet* criticism. But, in fact, he simply does a psychoanalytic variation on the tripart response we have been examining. For by explaining the special power of *Oedipus Rex* and *Hamlet* to move spectators through an appeal to the universal fact of Oedipal desire, Freud does not only explain identification, he makes it all the more iron-clad. Thus he writes of Oedipus what is equally true of Hamlet: "His destiny moves us only because it might have been ours. It is the fate of all of us, perhaps, to direct our first sexual impulse towards our mother and our first hatred and our first murderous wish against our father" (*ID*, 262). Freud judges Hamlet by turning him into a "case" of hysteria, which may be analyzed with serene, sympathetic clinical detachment. Psychoanalysis can learn from Hamlet, and use him to teach, because Hamlet, in delaying the revenge, and Shakespeare, in representing this delay, and all previous critics of the play, in refusing to understand this delay, are assimilated to a universal psychoanalytic subject which Freud elucidates through his two-part discussion of *Oedipus Rex* and *Hamlet*.[33]

I will be in a better position to assess the productions of these critics if I return to this book's general perspectives on chance and art. Tragedy confronts its reader/spectator with a scandal: life being given its weave and shape, in its most crucial moments, by the work of chance. And from the point of view of the person, chance appears arbitrary and violent—violent *because* it seems arbitrary. But another stratum of the tragic text tries to annul the power of chance by recuperating chance as a subordinate part of "nature," identity, and the moral design of either the drama, the artist, or God. Most critics of *Hamlet* labor to serve this second recuperative function of tragedy. This is particularly apparent if one examines their way of reading the last scene.

The position of the duel at the end of the text puts chance in play at the climax of the action. Here, as in all sporting events, objects and persons are set in motion so events appear uncontrollable, and things could go either way. Coleridge is particularly alert to this aspect of *Hamlet*. Speaking of Hamlet's fortunate capture by pirates (an accidental exchange in the confusion of battle), Coleridge makes this general comment: *Hamlet* is "almost the only play of Shakespeare, in which mere accidents, independent of all will, form an essential part of the plot."[34] Chance is also active and "essential" in the last scene when Gertrude drinks from the goblet intended for Hamlet, and when Hamlet and Laertes exchange rapiers (another accidental exchange in the confusion of a contest). Uncontrollable exchange, arbitrary reversal, the turns of chance—these accidents are disturbing to the critics: Coleridge calls them "mere" accidents, and Johnson dubs the exchange of weapons "an expedient" rather than "a stroke of art." Why? Perhaps these chance events are not controlled by any higher interpretive design. Perhaps the very way Hamlet fails and succeeds in the duel—accidentally—is symptomatic of a broader failure to control, whether it is the shape of events, by any moral design, or the form of the plot, by the strokes of Shakespeare's pen.

It is not only readers of *Hamlet,* but all the main characters in the play who respond with swift urgency to chance as it is released, like a violent contagion, by the duel. In dying Hamlet describes these

33. Freud connects *Oedipus Rex* and *Hamlet* in both his early letter to Fliess, where he announces the "Oedipus complex," and in the related passage from *The Interpretation of Dreams: Origins*, 10/15/97, and *I.D.*, 260–66.

34. Coleridge, "Notes on the Tragedies: *Hamlet*," Act IV, scene vi, excerpted by Hoy, 162.

events as "this chance," and says he would respond with his own account if he had time: "You that look pale and tremble at this chance,
/ That are but mutes or audience to this act, / Had I but time . . . I
could tell you— / But let it be" (V, ii, 339–43). Hamlet must die and
his language lapse into ellipsis, but in his closing moments he im-
provises two responses to the uncertainty produced by these chance-
charged deaths: he enjoins Horatio to tell his "story," so as to protect his reputation from the vagaries of other interpretations—with
"things standing thus unknown," most likely a "wounded name"; he
gives his "dying voice" to the election of Fortinbras, so as to spare
the kingdom the violence which would ensue from a throne standing open. What has come to pass is cause, as Horatio says, for woe
and wonder. The new arrivals from Poland and England register
their shock:

> *Fortinbras:* Where is this sight? . . .
>   This quarry cries on havoc . . .
> *Ambassador:* The sight is dismal . . .

And in promising a full account of events to his astonished auditors,
Horatio offers a cursory description that gives emphasis to the part
chance has played in all that has happened:

> So shall you hear
> Of carnal, bloody, and unnatural acts,
> Of accidental judgments, casual slaughters,
> Of deaths put on by cunning and forc'd cause,
> And, in this upshot, purposes mistook
> Fall 'n on th' inventors' heads.
>   [V, ii, 385–90]

The last scene offers a shocking spectacle. Hamlet is now a corpse,
a sight that is always a scandal to human culture: a living person become an object. He/It must be covered over, and this is managed,
with a generous euphemism appropriate to the moment, by giving
Hamlet a soldier's funeral—not because he was a brave soldier, but
because he might have been one. But it is not the simple fact of
death that has, in Horatio's words, made men's minds wild. Hamlet's
life-story carries a more virulent germ. This death, this failure, and
this loss are scandalous because they appear as nothing so much as
the effect of chance. Chance, like the corpse, must be contained,
controlled, and covered over, "lest more mischance / On plots and

errors happen" (V, ii, 399–400). And this must be done by burying it in both the narrative and the transfer of power Horatio has urged be "presently performed." Horatio's promise of a restorative narrative helps to explain the function of the critical response to *Hamlet* I have arranged under the headings "identification," "judgment," and a "lesson." In telling and retelling Hamlet's story, critics have followed in Horatio's path—they have told a story as he might have told it, and they have done it for much the same reason—to annul that about chance which is dangerous and disturbing to human life.

A judgment against chance is apparent in the critical readings we have been examining. Mack, Levin, and Rosenberg offer markedly different interpretations of *Hamlet,* yet they seem as one in treating the chance active in the text as inimical to the value and truth they seek for the self. Mack eludes chance by means of the passages he selects for close reading. In focusing on the graveyard scene, he bypasses almost any comment on the final duel and draws Hamlet's death into a purely contemplative space, where it is assimilated to the advance of "providence." A reader's bewilderment at Hamlet's fate is recuperated as a sanctifying sense of life's "mystery." Harry Levin balances "sheer contingency" against "providential" design so as to stand at the fulcrum of a cosmic irony, where he can savor the truth beyond human reason laid bare by Shakespeare's art. Harold Rosenberg makes a demand of Hamlet which echoes the demand Hamlet makes of himself, through the guiding interpretation: to find an action that expresses an essential constant self, such that neither action nor self is contaminated by chance. When chance plays all too much part in Hamlet's end, Rosenberg sees evidence of Hamlet's failure: "The triumph of the plot over the hero . . . is exposed in the accidental character of Hamlet's revenge in the course of the 'foolery' of the fencing match."[35]

Of all readings of *Hamlet,* psychoanalysis seems to manage the most sweeping annulment of chance. Thus in his discussion of *Oedipus Rex,* Freud does not just demonstrate the necessity of those actions of the hero the Oedipus story had made appear coincidental—killing his father and sleeping with his mother. Freud insists these supposed coincidences are a necessary and universal aspect of psychic life. Given this premise, there is little wonder that followers like Ernest Jones will divine an aptness and fatality in the smallest detail of Hamlet's life-trajectory. Since Hamlet's delay in revenge is said to arise from a conflict between envy and admiration for Claudius,

35. Rosenberg, 101.

Hamlet, Jones tells us, "cannot kill [Claudius] without also killing himself." Jones continues: "The course of alternate action and inaction that he embarks on, and the provocations he gives to his suspicious uncle, can lead to no other end than to his own ruin and, incidentally, to that of his uncle."[36] By this account Claudius is not really "other" than Hamlet. Claudius and all the other characters and terms of the drama are like a dream text which emanates from the psychic space of the protagonist (behind whom stands the author, dreaming). But for both Jones, in construing the hidden but iron-clad logic of Hamlet's death, and Jacques Lacan, in attributing Hamlet's accession to the symbolic in the graveyard scene [with Ophelia a version of *O phallos*], Hamlet becomes a type whose history allegorizes a developmental progression—whether through the Oedipus complex or into the Symbolic of language—one cannot choose not to follow.[37]

In the four interpretations of *Hamlet* I am here critiquing, it is quite impossible to imagine the course of the action, and the space of the drama, as open to anything other than what happens. By contrast, in the interpretation of Hamlet's life-trajectory I have developed above, Hamlet's encounter with language displaces him out of the interpretation of his world that guided him through the first three acts of the play. The particular quality of that encounter, and Hamlet's collaboration with his adversaries, lead to the compromise formation of the duel scene, where Hamlet can arrive and attempt his revenge. To me this sequence of events seems not the result of a "free" expression of a liberated will, nor the evidence of a valuable mystery, nor the converging point of cosmic ironies, nor a moment where historical plot wins out over individual action, nor the fulfillment of a preordained Oedipal scenario. Instead Hamlet exercises a limited interpretive leeway in shaping the life-situation he inherits. The severe limits of his control make the issue uncertain. It also makes the forms of his response, at least in part, his own achievements (and failures). By accepting a duel with Laertes and embracing its attendant risks and chances, Hamlet overcomes the judgment against a contingent fate and situation which was embedded in his rage, skepticism, and indecision. The zest and pleasure Hamlet shows in making his final rendezvous with chance make him a Nie-

36. Ernest Jones, *Hamlet and Oedipus* (New York: W. W. Norton, 1949), 100.
37. Lacan, "Desire and the Interpretation of Desire," 20. That Hamlet is undertaking and undertaken by a movement from the "imaginary" to the "symbolic" makes Lacan's reading of *Hamlet* parallel at many points with his reading of Poe's "The Purloined Letter."

tzschean tragic hero: one who sees the chance that lies as the absurd grounding condition of his life, but is able nonetheless to affirm life's value.

The Mimetic System

Throughout the foregoing discussion of critical responses to *Hamlet,* an annulment of chance seemed to arise from the conscious choices, shades of temperament, and the ideological commitments of diverse readers. But in the background of these discrete reading acts and powerfully engaged in them, there is a larger system for interpreting art, and the interpretation of art, which puts out of play what is chance about the production of meaning in and around *Hamlet.* I must risk a short description of its broad outlines. Only in this way can I hope to make my reading of *Hamlet* more than the proffering of yet another theme (in this case "chance"), released from the silence of artistic form by the critic, so as to decipher the author's presumed message about the nature of reality.

In *Hegel's Concept of Experience* Heidegger demonstrates that the Western idea of truth operates by establishing a mimetic relationship between language and that which is: in order for consciousness to be present to being in the mode of truth, that which is (being, reality) must be repeated by language.[38] Language is the middle term which brings that which is into the presence of consciousness. Art, as one system for apprehending reality, translates this formulation in the following way. The artist uses language to make an artwork that will bring reality into presence for human consciousness (his or her own, the reader's, the spectator's). There is an unspoken assumption about language in both these systems: language is, or can be, or should be, transparent to that which it represents. It is this transparence of language which allows artist, artwork, and reality to be open to one another in a truth-full way. These three terms (artist, artwork, reality) are, with language, complementary elements in this mimetic system. But since, as in the history of *Hamlet* criticism, critics often give more weight to one term than to another , they also function as alternatives. So here is a brief sketch of the mimetic system, through a discussion of its three pillars and the critical perspective that gives each a special priority in its ways of reading *Hamlet.*[39]

38. Heidegger, *Hegel's Concept of Experience* (New York: Harper & Row, 1970).

39. M. H. Abrams offers a more wide-ranging discussion of the different ways aesthetic systems can conceive their goals and procedures in the first chapter of *The Mirror and the Lamp* (New York: Oxford University Press, 1953), 3–29.

The reality represented. The critics of *Hamlet* we have been reading seem quite confident that Shakespeare's text represents some idea, truth, or message about the order of things. Their hermeneutical labors are directed at scanning the text for this fragment of truth—the theme—so they can present it to the reader. *Hamlet,* through their narratives, brings us insight into the mysteries of "evil . . . reality . . . human limitation" (Mack), or the "irony" of "the incalculable contradictions between the personal life and the nature of things" (Levin), or the futility of that effort of will which must fail to be an "act of 'true color'" (Rosenberg). The themes these critics uncover seem, by implication, to be the residue of authorial design. By contrast, the illuminating truth Freud finds hidden in this text—Oedipal desire—has been deposited by the artist's unconscious. This makes it not less, but all the more, a generative theme of the work, and a telling representation of that which is.

The artwork which represents. Another group of critics is less sure than "thematic" critics that the reality *Hamlet* embodies can be focused into thematic statement. These "formalist" critics purify critical discourse of any assertions about authorial design or intention; instead they focus on the language of the artwork, the style and imagery of the language, the structure of the plot, its participation in a genre such as tragedy, and so on. Aristotle is often the mentor and patron saint of these critics. But though they are anxious to be faithful to the text's full complexity and desist from reducing its many facets of form to a single vulgarly explicit message, still, these critics always seem to come around to tendering some meaning for the forms they delineate. This is so because formalist criticism still operates within the mimetic system I am describing. The form of the artwork is shown to re-present some aspect of reality, though the "reality" represented will be less likely to have the specificity of reference, or ethical utility, of the "reality" described by thematic critics. Nor does the "form" ascribed to the artwork have to have the clarity of structure Francis Fergusson ascribes to *Hamlet* in his discussion of the play.[40] Thus Stephen Booth, in his article "On the Value of *Hamlet,*" demonstrates how the artwork operates as a kind of antiform, and "self-consuming artifact," that carries through a series of formal displacements which discredit all attempts to fix the thematic meaning of the text.[41] Here, apparently, we have moved

40. See Francis Fergusson, *The Idea of a Theatre* (Princeton: Princeton University Press, 1947).

41. Stephen Booth, "On the Value of *Hamlet,*" *Reinterpretations of Elizabethan Drama,* Selected Papers from the English Institute, ed. Norman Rabkin (New York: Columbia University Press, 1969), 137–76.

beyond a mimetic correlation of form and meaning, artwork and represented reality. But a closer look reveals something different. Booth ends his article with an extended celebration of Shakespeare's creation for being a form elastic and subtle enough to "contain" the mobility and multiplicity of meanings Booth would have us "value."

> . . . an alliteration of subjects . . . gives shape and identity, nonphysical substance, to the play that contains the situation. Such a container allows Shakespeare to replace *conclusion* with *inclusion*; it provides a particular and temporary context that overcomes the intellectual terror ordinarily inherent in looking at an action in all the value systems it invades. Such a container . . . makes its audience capable of contemplating more truth than the mind should be able to bear. . . . Truth is bigger than any one system for knowing it, and *Hamlet* is bigger than any of the frames of reference it inhabits. Hamlet allows us to comprehend—hold on to—all the contradictions it contains.[42]

According to Booth's account, *Hamlet* seems to carry us beyond the usual ways form is aligned with meaning. But this artwork is still a form. It still has the capacity to contain, enclose, and thereby be present to the (infinitely complex) truth it represents. This argument expands the range of representation, but the structure of mimesis remains intact.

The artist who represents. Notice that at one point in Stephen Booth's panegyric to the text of *Hamlet,* there is a furtive reference to the artist: "Such a container allows Shakespeare to replace *conclusion* with *inclusion*." This is an index of a general fact about *Hamlet* criticism. Appeals to the reality represented by the text and to the formal qualities of the artwork are corollary with and often rest upon a certain concept of the artist. The artist is conceptualized as a godlike creator whose genius gives him the power to create art which has the truth and authority of nature. Of course this is one conventional concept of the artist. (Kant develops it in *The Critique of Judgment.*) But it is worth looking at Shakespeare's special relationship to this *topos.*[43] For some reason Shakespeare is the one artist whose artworks have garnered authority analogous to that we ascribe to nature. Shakespeare was not called a "natural genius" in the eighteenth century simply because he had failed to observe the rules for classi-

---

42. Ibid., 174–75.
43. For a discussion and an unsettling of this idea as developed by Kant, see Jacques Derrida, "Economimesis," and Richard Klein, "Kant's Sunshine," in the special issue of *Diacritics* entitled "The Ghost of Theology: Readings of Kant and Hegel," 11 (Summer, 1981).

cal drama the court of Charles II brought from France after the Restoration. Nor, in order to register the highest possible estimation of his art, does one have to say what Dumas said: "After God, Shakespeare created most." Reading Shakespeare, and most especially reading his critics, one is tempted to believe that lurking behind this text I read, there is a locus of omniscience and control, a kind of guarantee of Truth: if not God, then the best thing after that—Shakespeare.

The acts of identification, judgment, and instruction orchestrated by critics around Hamlet have essentialized Hamlet into a rigid nature, existing apart from the contingencies which mark his experience. The mimetic system I have been describing achieves an analogous effect for the whole text by managing a suppression of chance. Because the system focuses the meaning of the artwork into a thematic statement about the artist's "design," the reality represented is filtered of contingency, so it seems immune to time and change (first exclusion); placed in a frame, on a pedestal, surrounded with white margins, the artwork appears radically separate, fixed in form, and purified of history (second exclusion); and this thematic "design" is presumed to be embedded in this fixed form by an artist whose god-like powers of representation have translated this chance-ridden life into art (third exclusion). This triple exclusion of chance is the powerful illusion the mimetic system is contrived to effect.

By investigating the shape and effects of this mimetic system, I hope to upset the authority it gains by being invisible, and therefore seeming "natural"; I do not mean to imply there is a simple and sweeping alternative to it. For all systems of thought and most forms of expression seem predicated upon some notion of representation. Thus, the moment I try to determine what is, and think what is by putting it in language, at that moment I am caught up in mimesis and repetition. Most criticism of *Hamlet* has chosen to become involved with the text in a manner that offers a striking resemblance to the guiding interpretation Hamlet shapes to respond to his situation. Critics reading this text, like Hamlet reading his world, are confronted by a dubious situation, where truth and virtue are confounded with vice and error. Little wonder that they too are seized by a desire for certitude and true representations. Both Hamlet and his critics respond with Manichean oppositions, harsh judgments, and the will to simplify life into belief. Thus, for example, a textual editor determining the proper text for *Hamlet*, no less than Hamlet settling upon his course of action, becomes concerned with establishing legitimacy and authority. And in carrying through these tasks

[279]

both Hamlet and the critic affirm an ultimate faith in a ghostly figure of a father (King Hamlet, Shakespeare) presumed to be all-powerful. But in the first section of this movement I have tried to show how Hamlet overcomes this quest for mastery. We shall try to follow him in this.

How can I contest the annulment of chance effected by the readings of *Hamlet* I have been discussing? How can I do in *this* reading something analogous with what Hamlet manages in Act V, scene ii—face toward chance as an active, potentially determining force? I can begin by complicating our understanding of represented reality, the artwork, and the artist with these three ideas: (1) One "reality" attested to by tragedy—chance as it traverses the life of a single person—is obscure to the person and confounds general representation; (2) the artwork may appear to be, but is not decisively cut off from the "world" which produces and transmits it; (3) Shakespeare's "godlike" powers are, paradoxically, the effect of his indebtedness to others and his invisibility.

The first idea of this triad is the central theme of Movement One of this book. In Freud's accounts of the way the particularity of the person rests upon an interpretive response to the primal scenes of life, chance enters the life of the person as language. There chance takes the form of "singular repetition," a relation between self and other, inside and outside, which constitutes the person at the same time it broaches the person as a fixed identity. Nietzsche's text indicates the way this relation is fundamentally tropological and cannot be present to consciousness in the mode of truth. Thus chance, as singular repetition, must appear arbitrary and enigmatic to the person. In tragedy, chance appears as the violent possibility of sudden death and loss. In this movement, I have all the time been on the way to demonstrating how *Hamlet* both obscures and articulates the relation between the person, chance, and language.

One of the main aesthetic stays against chance is the idea of the artwork's pure separateness and autonomy. The "institution of literature" fosters this idea in a number of different ways: it has labored to produce an authoritative text for *Hamlet*; it organizes typography so the text is in boldface, the variants in italics, and the footnotes in small print; it elevates *Hamlet* to a special place in the canon of texts taught, performed, and read; and it crowns this text with epithets such as the "greatest artwork ever made," the "most-debated of all artworks," etc.[44] But the very critics, performers, and teachers who

44. For examples of the way typography gives a special privilege to the text "proper," even if they are no less certain than the variants relegated to the smallest notes, one may consult the *Variorum Hamlet* edited by Horace H. Furness or the Ar-

oversee this process also compromise the integrity and mastery of *Hamlet*. First, the play as written is so long that almost all directors have abridged the text they honor with performance. Then *Hamlet* comes to us in three texts—the first and second quartos and the first folio. Textual editors may agree on the "higher authority" of the second quarto, but there are places in the text when they must resort to the other two so as to overcome the deficiencies of the second quarto.[45] The text thereby produced is an imperfect hybrid of uncertain origin and authority. We can never finally know what words or lines of *Hamlet* we have gotten "wrong." Last, the very scholars who insist that this play is "incomparably" great burrow away at the specialness this implies by comparing Hamlet to all the literature and thought of the Renaissance. This research compromises *Hamlet's* autonomy by showing how the text's ideas are a weave of commonplaces, how the story comes from Saxo and Belleforest, and how many of its precise formulations are indebted to contemporary Christianity, Nashe, Montaigne, and others.[46] All of this is to say that *Hamlet* is traversed by historical contingencies—accidents of transmission and accidents of influence—that Shakespeare could affect but not completely control. We may dramatize this point by indicating the final factor that challenges this test's autonomy. Much of *Hamlet* evidently came to Shakespeare through an "Ur-Hamlet," a ghostly text, apparently written by Thomas Kyd, which haunts Shakespeare's text with rights of paternity, and puts in question the origin, uniqueness, and originality of *Hamlet*. The Ur-Hamlet hollows *Hamlet* out from within, with a (possible) resemblance that threatens to turn the "original" into a (partial) repetition and copy.[47]

And how do these signs of "indebtedness" affect Shakespeare's position as the most godlike and powerful of all artists? First we should note that "indebtedness" is the delicate term critics often use for Shakespeare's borrowings, even when, as with "his" description of Cleopatra on her barge, we are so close to Plutarch's text that if the passage were encountered in a contemporary student's paper, it

---

den *Hamlet* edited by Harold Jenkins. To read the "main" text in large bold print allows us to forget what every note recalls: there is a most uncertain authority for many of the best known and best loved lines of Shakespeare.

45. In his long and complex discussion of the tangled textual situation of *Hamlet*, Harold Jenkins makes a strong case for the higher authority of the second quarto, but also justifies occasional use of the first folio, and even the "bad" first quarto. See pages 1–82 of his introduction to the Arden *Hamlet*.

46. See ibid., 81--112. Also see the sources in the Norton Critical Edition of *Hamlet*, ed. Hoy, 107–45.

47. Jenkins, 45–47.

would be labeled plagiarism. Critics miss the point when they shield Shakespeare's originality with euphemisms or elaborate accounts of the very different way Renaissance writers repeat their precursors. For strange to say, Shakespeare's many-faceted indebtedness seems to have as one of its effects Shakespeare's much-vaunted "universality." By letting so much of everything into his text, Shakespeare has something for all times and all peoples. (God is everywhere.) And the authority of Shakespeare as the Artist/God is enhanced by something else—his invisibility. Because of his invisibility, that in Shakespeare's plays which may have resulted from a response to life which was arbitrary, stupid, or obsessive—in other words, personal— simply disappears back into the text. Now, psychoanalytic critics may complain: "But after all, Shakespeare was human too; he had a mother and a father—where else but from his own life and psyche could all this creative energy come?" As an abstract proposition, this idea seems irrefutable. But because they know almost nothing about Shakespeare as a person, the only recourse of these critics is a circular mode of reading. Out of certain patterns in Shakespeare's texts they read a psychological profile of the author, which they then use to interpret Shakespeare's texts. But even if they were right about Shakespeare as a person, no one would know. Thus, for example, Shakespeare's texts do seem more than commonly concerned with certain themes—for instance, sexual infidelity. But who can say? Shakespeare's silence and invisibility finally defeat the efforts of these critics. They always seem to sketch a Shakespeare after their own hearts, resembling themselves; the Shakespearean text becomes the mirror, the critic Narcissus. Shakespeare is the ghostly (spiritual and invisible) father who haunts the text. This leads to a final insight. One of the few things we know about Shakespeare is that he played the Ghost in productions of *Hamlet*. By taking this fact, and a hint from Borges' vignette on Shakespeare, we should perhaps try to think Shakespeare's mastery and invisibility in relation to his vocation. Shakespeare was an actor—thus a person of little social prominence; but he was also one who habitually displaced self and identity into a role on the stage. By writing as an actor, he could produce artworks which accrue enormous authority to themselves precisely because they cannot usefully be viewed the way we view almost all other human productions—as a response to confining personal and historical contingencies.[48] Thus Shakespeare uses the aesthetic al-

48. See Jorge Luis Borges, "Everything and Nothing," a parable from *Labyrinths*, ed. Donald A. Yates and James E. Irby (New York: New Directions, 1962), 248–49. See below in the epilogue.

chemy of compositional and linguistic displacements to translate (other people's) lead into (his own) gold. With Shakespeare one may put in question, but I do not pretend one may entirely elude, the metaphysical determination of art as the locus of beauty and value.

The Textuality of Hamlet, *or Denouement as Singular Repetition*

The *Hamlet* criticism I have been discussing operates according to three interrelated assumptions: that the person (or "man") is central, privileged, and separate from the social discourses that would define him; that language is a neutral and transparent instrument for naming that which is; and that in the artistic representations of the person which tragedy effects and criticism describes, chance is a dissonant factor which must be suppressed so as to avoid two kinds of loss—the suffering that accompanies the violence of the accidental, and the incomprehensibility that shadows every event described as chance. In this configuration the suppression of the alterity of chance and language establishes the individual person as the locus of uniqueness, value, knowledge, sympathy and control. This idea of the person is the interpretive assertion at the core of humanism, in both its Renaissance and contemporary forms. To the extent that tragedy offers a coherent collective view of one person's suffering, tragedy offers (partial) assent to this fiction. But the text of *Hamlet* also allows us to see this fictional presumption of human separateness and centrality as a fiction that is inscribed within a larger textual field of alternative possibilities.

The textual (re-)reading of *Hamlet* with which I will close this movement does not reverse or annul the force of the reading of *Hamlet* developed in the first part. There I entered into complicity with the privileging of Hamlet's position that the form of the drama effects and a long tradition of "character criticism" has solidified. By reading from Hamlet's personal vantage point, over the trajectory of the action, with special attention to everything within the horizon of Hamlet's consciousness, I could describe Hamlet's guiding interpretation, the encounter with language that displaces that interpretation, and the ethos of sport which moves him toward an active engagement with chance in the final scene. But having carried through an analysis of the principles which guide much of *Hamlet* criticism, I am in a position to resituate my initial reading of *Hamlet* so it is overtaken by the opaqueness and otherness of chance and language. This means modifying the disposition with which we read. We need to suspend the desire to read a deep and redeeming truth in Hamlet's "fate." Only by doing this can we terminate the melodrama of empathic identification, judgment, and lesson-making which is rooted in the desire to elude contingency—a tendency I criticized in others, but could not entirely avoid myself. If we can suspend for a while the old anxiety about human loss, assume a more neutral curiosity before this text, and displace the mimetic assumptions that underpin traditional readings, we can gain access to the particular way Hamlet's story, with its chance-ridden end, is inscribed within a larger textual matrix of interpretations and potential interpretations.

We may begin to explore this matrix by noting one of the implicit effects of the guiding interpretation: its moral symmetries give Hamlet a sense of separateness from Gertrude, Ophelia, Claudius, and others whom he so vigorously condemns. In this way he may experience himself as singular and unique, and thus the (potentially) legitimate heir to his father's fullness of being. Even when Hamlet is hardest upon himself, he is so in soliloquy—a form of speech which confirms his isolation and separateness. But just as the guiding interpretation is disrupted the moment Hamlet tries to act upon it, the course of the action is continually compromising his separateness. Thus Hamlet seeks to carry out an act of purification by washing away sin with the blood of the sinner. But whenever he acts, he is touched by the other from which he would stay stiffly and virtuously apart, and becomes caught up in impurity. Above we noted how Hamlet is guilty of the very vacillation of which he accuses others and how his own dramaturgy violates the codes of mimesis, restraint, and discretion he promotes. And when Hamlet comes upon Claudius at prayer, the spectator is confronted with a curious reversal of positions. Throughout the play Hamlet has appropriated moral authority to himself, by representing Claudius as the deviously active murderer of his own brother. But in this scene it is Claudius who acts the way Hamlet has: he is steeped in an indecisive meditation and concerned with matters of cosmic reach. And now Hamlet is the dangerous agent who sneaks up on his prey with murderous thoughts while his would-be victim is unaware. How does this reversal happen? Revenge as a project undercuts the self-righteous separateness and singularity of the avenger, by getting him to repeat not only the crime but the very manner of his rival. Within *Hamlet* there is a textual emblem of the way the act of revenge Hamlet plots is structured by the logic of singular repetition. In the performance Hamlet and Claudius have just watched, the dumb show and the play repeat each other *while* they represent the same act of murder. But the slight displacement from the dumb show, where the criminal murders for ambition (he kisses the crown), to the play, where Lucianus is nephew to the victim, splits the act. The singular self-defining act (of revenge) Hamlet plans is seen as nearly identical with, really just a version of the criminal act he reviles, but is compelled to repeat.

This text not only implicates Hamlet in the positions of his rivals; we also witness a symmetrical reversal. Just as Hamlet is beginning to throw off the terms of the guiding interpretation, Hamlet's rivals, Claudius and Laertes, begin to use its terms to define their own situations. At prayer, Claudius condemns himself for being unable to achieve a true mimetic relation between "words" and "thoughts," so that his prayers could reach heaven where "the action lies [before God] / In his true nature" (III, iii, 61–62). Just as Hamlet feels rage at the way the marriage celebration of his mother and uncle mocks his father's death, so Laertes is angered when he returns to Denmark to find the burial ceremonies given his father and sister failing to be adequate to their greatness and virtue. Laertes describes Ophelia as a paragon: her "worth . . . stood challenger on mount of all the age / For her perfections." La Morde is described as a paragon by Claudius, and Osric's speech to Hamlet heaping extravagant praise upon Laertes, which Hamlet picks up and completes in the spirit of banter, ends offering a stunning parodic repetition of Hamlet's praise of King Hamlet as the locus of an incomparable self-identical virtue:

> *Osric:*   . . . Laertes [is] . . . an absolute gentleman, full of most excellent differences . . . he is the card or calendar of gentry . . .
>
> *Hamlet:*   . . . I know to divide him inventorially would dozy th'arithmetic of memory. . . . I take him to be a soul of great article and his infusion of such dearth and rareness as, to make true diction of him, his semblable is his mirror and who else would trace him his umbrage, nothing more. [V, ii, 106–20]

Of course many of the parallels between Laertes and Hamlet may be ascribed to the tasks they come to share at the drama's end—avenging their fathers' deaths. But Laertes as avenger is not Ham-

[285]

let's double; he is a double for the Hamlet of the first three acts, when Hamlet is operating in the brace of the guiding interpretation. Thus, when Claudius becomes Laertes' accomplice, the King primes Laertes for action by using nearly the same language and rhetoric that Hamlet has used against Claudius. He suggests that Laertes may be demonstrating the same false feeling that so galled Hamlet: "Laertes, was your father dear to you? / Or are you like the painting of a sorrow, / A face without a heart?" And as if to mime Hamlet in soliloquy, or the speech of the Player King, Claudius warns that love is passion begun by time, that time qualifies it, and that the violent expression of passion can easily become a substitute for action (IV, vii, 106–25).

What does this reversal of positions and transposition of languages mean? Critics have usually interpreted reversal in terms of some ethical truth or read it under the sign of irony. But I do not think we should be in a hurry to do so. Since reversal is endemic to a vast amount of tragedy and is a pervasive aspect of *Hamlet,* a lot is at stake in how one reads reversal. In the introductory essay to the new Arden edition of *Hamlet,* Harold Jenkins develops a good deal of his interpretation around the compromising consequences of Hamlet's becoming the murderer of another father: "The hero charged with a deed of vengeance now also incurs vengeance. The situation of revenge is revealed as one in which the same man may act both parts; and the paradox of man's dual nature, compound of nobility and baseness, god and beast, repeatedly placed before us in the words of the play and represented in its action in the contrasting brother kings, is also exemplified in the hero's dual role."[49] For Jenkins, reversal is a ready consequence of the double valence of human nature, which we have seen as derived from the moral polarities of the guiding interpretation, but which Jenkins sees as the central expressed intention of both play and author. Then what unfolds in the action, at the play's end, will represent a certain justice: "The hero who is both punisher and punished finally kills the King only on receiving from Laertes his own death-wound."[50] Jenkins does not quite say that he literally accepts the Christian idea of man as compounded of good and evil, or that the providential design working through events reflects this fact. But his interpretation everywhere implies it. Hamlet can in this way become a compelling representative of the complex situation of entanglement this leaves "us" all in:

49. Jenkins, 144.
50. Ibid.

"Instead of the hero of concealed but unswerving purpose, celebrated for his courage and virtue, we have a hero who in seeking to
right a wrong commits one, whose aspirations and achievements are
matched by failures and offences, and in whom potentialities for
good and evil hauntingly coexist. And this is what transforms the
single-minded revenger into the complex representative of us all."[51]

The ethical coherence of Jenkins' view of reversal arises in part
from the way he organizes his analysis around Hamlet and his relationship to Laertes. By contrast, Thomas Van Laan demonstrates
that every level and region of the text, from its thematic leitmotifs to
whole strands of the action, "dramatizes" the way "the individual's
own self-seeking gesture, through a reflex action, becomes itself the
weapon that destroys him."[52] By this account "reversal" seems less
guided and moral in its action, and more "ironic" in its effects. Van
Laan considers the attempts of readers who assimilate the pattern of
"ironic reversal" to the idea of divine providence. Hamlet is the first
of these when he reflects upon his narrow escape at sea: "There's a
divinity that shapes our ends, / Rough-hew them how we will." And
certainly Hamlet proves himself a most accomplished moralistic interpreter of reversal when he handles skulls at graveside, meditates
the fate of ladies and lawyers, and tells Horatio, "Here's fine revolu-
tion and we had the trick to see't" (V, i, 89). But Van Laan points
out that in two other renderings of "ironic reversal," Hamlet gives its
operation quite a different tenor. When Hamlet describes the ape
who tries to imitate birds and falls, the tone of the anecdote "stresses
the sardonically humorous aspects" of ironic reversal. And when
Hamlet tells Gertrude he is ready to take on Rosencrantz and Guildenstern, he insists upon the special aesthetic pleasure which accrues
to finding a way to have plots and purposes displaced so they fall on
their inventors' heads: "For 'tis the sport to have the enginer / Hoist
with his own petard" (III, iv, 208–9). Van Laan concludes with a
judgment against the ethical reading of reversal which is entirely
compatible with the way I construed the final scene earlier: "Since
the victims of ironic reversal in this play range from the guilty
through the neutral to the innocent, the conclusion must be that the
universe of *Hamlet* negates all human activity, whether vicious or
not."[53]

But if a Christian God does not control "ironic reversal" in *Hamlet*,

51. Ibid., 146.
52. Thomas Van Laan, *The Idiom of Drama* (Ithaca: Cornell University Press, 1970),
201.
53. Ibid., 203.

who or what does? Van Laan's use of the metaphor of "universe" suggests what is never explicitly stated. "Ironic reversal" may seem to be a moment of discontinuity, exposure, and uncertainty. It may suggest a universe that is, as Van Laan says, a "negation of the Christian world" and "essentially malevolent."[54] But because the artwork is still a "universe"—and thus autonomous, *uni*fied, and as spiritually elevating as the stars—it assumes an artist-creator who has the freedom to construct a universe that will be determining for his characters, and informing for us. Van Laan's discussion makes it clear that it is Shakespeare who constructs "the universe of *Hamlet*" so "ironic reversal" is the seed, the central theme, principle of plot, and end in terms of which the whole drama follows its trajectory.[55] Thus though Van Laan's position contests the moral meanings Jenkins puts forward, both critics make reversal a controlled element of rhetorical design. Jenkins is more like the "thematic" critics discussed above in postulating a universal ethical message in Hamlet's participation in reversal. (For God is ultimately the rhetorician.) Van Laan is more like the formalist critics in emphasizing the autonomous organization of meaning effected by the artwork. (Shakespeare is the rhetorician.) Both assume the pattern of reversal unfolds in view of Shakespeare's artistic intention.

Reversal is the central figure of human destiny in the tragic text. Why does it provoke special fascination? Roland Barthes's discussion of reversal in *Sur Racine,* and an essay upon the "Fait Divers" can deepen our understanding. Reversal fascinates for several related reasons: it disrupts the accustomed patterns of coherence based upon causation; its happening is experienced as arbitrary and chance—a coincidence causing wonder; the change reversal brings is exciting, sweeping, and violent; for the spectator of a sudden (depressive) reversal of fortune, there is pity, fear, and (perhaps) a certain sadistic pleasure. And with reversal there is always this overpowering illusion: that behind this event there is a controlling agent who effects a reversal with a particular meaning—irony. Why is this supposed to be so? Because, in its form, reversal is so perfectly symmetrical, even artificial. So when one is confronted with reversal, one's deepest interpretive reflex is to presume some controlling agency has brought it about. This is the pervasive popular prejudice.[56] But

54. Ibid., 204.
55. Ibid., 194–96.
56. See Roland Barthes, *On Racine,* trans. Richard Howard (New York: Hill and Wang, 1964), 41–45; and Barthes, *Critical Essays,* trans. Richard Howard (Evanston: Northwestern University Press, 1972), 191–92.

perhaps reversal is not stamped upon events from the outside by some agent. Perhaps it is inherent as a possibility in any system or continuum—such as society, history, or language—where terms get their character from their relationship to other terms in the same system. Then reversal is not an eruption from without, but something always already latent in the system, like the potential shifts graphed by catastrophe theory.[57] When *Hamlet* opens, Denmark has just been overtaken by a sudden change, or turn of events—a catastrophe. And no one feels the arbitrariness of Claudius' elevation to the position occupied by King Hamlet—upon the throne, in Gertrude's arms—more keenly than Hamlet. Given the way power and pleasure inhere in such positions, it is little wonder that throughout *Hamlet,* Claudius and Hamlet strive to enhance their authority by naturalizing what is perhaps always somewhat arbitrary—a given position or role in the social-historical continuum. They seek to establish a single necessary connection between themselves and this asserted position. Each does so through an elaborate interpretation: Claudius, by assuming all the public signs of kingship, through his regal airs and expert statecraft . . . and by concealing the crime which emptied the position he now occupies. Hamlet legitimizes the act of revenge he plans with the guiding interpretation he elaborates in collaboration with the Ghost. It is designed to establish his privileged relation to the father—the true and legitimate source of the authority Hamlet and Claudius are contesting.

In the meditations upon reversal which lace this text, and the interpretive measures characters take to shape them, reversal is expressed with certain tropes: antithesis, negation, and chiasmus. In the long speech Claudius gives to his court in the second scene of the drama, the new King uses stately antithetical rhythms of language to describe and contain the reversal which has just overtaken the court. He intends that the reversal precipitated by his crime will help institute an enduring political order; this would make it the final reversal. By contrast the Player King describes reversal as swift and violent and ever open to new reversals. He tells his Queen, *"Grief joys, joy grieves, on slender accident. . . . For 'tis a question left us yet to prove, / Whether love lead fortune or else fortune love"* (III, ii, 194–98). The chiasmic pattern by which two words—grief and joy, love and fortune—are repeated in reversed order calls special attention to the uncontrollability of reversal. Many of the reversals in *Hamlet*

57. For a general discussion see *Catastrophe Theory,* by Alexander Woodcock and Monte Davis (New York: Dutton, 1978).

turn upon the way a sign can trigger uncontrollable turns of meaning. Thus in telling Claudius the name of his play Hamlet puns upon the word trope and trap:

> *Claudius:* What do you call the play?
> *Hamlet:* The *Mousetrap*—marry, how tropically!

(The Second Quarto has "how trapically.") In staging the play, Hamlet hopes to catch Claudius in the coils of a trap constructed of tropes that turn in unexpected ways. This becomes the model for those later instruments in the play whose capacity to turn brings sudden violent reversal: the commission carried to England, and the poisoned rapier carried by Laertes into the final duel.

Of course no character fully controls the instruments he marshals. In producing the play that exposes Claudius's guilt, Hamlet discloses his suspicions of Claudius. Hamlet repeatedly uses tropes of reversal to challenge the authority of others. When he enters his mother's closet, Gertrude reproaches him for his offense to Claudius in staging the play:

> *Queen*: Hamlet, thou hast thy father much offended.
> *Hamlet*: Mother, you have my father much offended.
> *Queen*: Come, come, you answer with an idle tongue.
> *Hamlet*: Go, go, you question with a wicked tongue.
> [III, iv, 8–11]

In this exchange Gertrude is determined to make herself a stern locus of parental authority, capable of delivering a moral rebuke. Hamlet overthrows this determination by showing how every word she uses to assert her moral authority can be inverted so as to be used against her. His rhetorical move is possible because of shifters like "thou," antithetical terms like "question" and "answer," and the way the position of "father" can be interpreted as one which is natural and genetic (as Hamlet does) or as social role (as Gertrude does). When Rosencrantz and Guildenstern accuse Hamlet of being ambitious, this triggers a contest as to how insubstantial ambition can be made to seem. They attribute Hamlet's "bad dreams" to ambition. And if ambition is a "shadow of a dream," and a dream but a shadow, then "ambition" is, as Rosencrantz and Guildenstern say, "of so airy and light a quality that it is but a shadow's shadow." Hamlet concludes the debate by giving a paradoxical turn to the argument. If the great occupy the position of ambition—a "shadow's shadow,"—then the lowly must be the "body" of which the great become shadows. "Then are our beggars bodies, and our monarchs and outstretched heroes the beggars' shadows" (II, ii, 263–64). The vertigo which comes of compounding insubstantiality allows Hamlet to parody the discriminations of Medieval logicians on the way to reversing the accustomed hierarchy of great and small. But this paradoxical translogical conclusion—which uses reversal to put in question the stability of any position—leads to another reversal. For Hamlet immediately asks pointed questions which draw Rosencrantz and Guildenstern into confessing they were "sent for" by the King and thus are acting as his agents. Thus in this scene, Hamlet has won a reversal of positions: those who have brought the accusation (of ambition) are found guilty (of ambition).

The reversibility of human positions in this text makes any kind of affirmation hopelessly entangled with its opposite. Thus, when in the closet scene, Hamlet convinces Gertrude to mend her ways, he delivers his final advice in a strange way. Since he sees her current life as a perverse reversal of her former life, he tells her not what to do, but what not to do: "Not this, by no means, that I bid you do: / Let the bloat King tempt you again to bed" (III, iv, 183–84). If sin has resulted from reversal, virtue consists in reversing reversal. We have seen how revenge catches Hamlet in the same tangle of opposites. Since the punishment repeats the crime it resembles, Hamlet begins to imitate the images of his rivals at the very moment they begin to resemble in speech his own earlier interpretive formulations. Late in the play Hamlet seems to develop a partial awareness of this strange reversibility of positions. He regrets grappling with Laertes in Ophelia's grave, for, as he says to Horatio of Laertes, "by the image of my cause I see / The portraiture of his." And in accepting the duel he fights on behalf of his enemy Claudius, calls his rival Laertes, "brother," and tells him "I'll be your foil, Laertes," that is, "I'll be the ground to figure your greatness." Hamlet says this, although he intends exactly the reverse.

Reading Hamlet's participation in reversal from the point of view of tropes of reversal allows us to read the double valence of his situation. As a "character" he is an illusionistic version of a person confined to a belief in his own singularity. As such, Hamlet enters the final duel intent upon asserting the singularity of his claims, his desire, and his role as avenger. When this action gets caught up in reversal and so much of the energy summoned to effect a certain end recoils to destroy Hamlet, Gertrude, and others, the irony of the situation, as with every other reversal of fortune in this play, is a byproduct of the single person's assertion of singularity. It is not necessary to postulate a providential or artistic design depositing this irony in the text, as a contrived effect or conscious judgment of the action. Hamlet's task (revenge), his descent (from King Hamlet), and his desire (for Gertrude and Ophelia) describe the singular shape of a life which cannot avoid being traversed by repetition of the crime avenged or of the father's ghostly will. To the extent that Hamlet is embedded in a text that is constructed in terms of this fact, he is allowed to speak words that articulate an interpretation of his position in excess of any he could really inhabit or be conscious of as character and person. Thus just before the duel, Hamlet explains his readiness to meet Laertes, in spite of evil feelings from his own heart that foreshadow danger. He tells Horatio he will "defy augury"; he declares "there is special providence in the fall of a sparrow." Then he describes the moment of death in this way: "If it be now, 'tis not to come; if it be not to come, it will be now; if it be not now, yet it will come" (V, ii, 216–18). The first two lines describe one situation —death now—in four clauses arranged in a chiasmic pattern (now/ come/come/now). The last line describes an alternate situation— death later—but through a negation and one more chiasmus (*not* now/come). The last line utilizes all the words already used in this syllogistic formula; this has the effect of making life and death converge. These lines place Hamlet's life-situation in what is, strictly speaking, an (impossible) nonplace: within reversal and singular repetition. For in the oscillation of these two moments (now and later), life and death—the most vivid opposition the person knows— suddenly appear as reverse images of each other. Now two moments appear as one, and the difference between life and death a matter of indifference. This passage embeds Hamlet's most vivid effort at self-reflection in the obscure matrix of the person's life: the double (non-present) "moment" of singular repetition.

Throughout this story, Hamlet asserts the singularity of his task, his fate, his appointed role. All these are singular because they are unusual, but also because they are particular to this single "person," Hamlet, Prince of Denmark. To an extent, this is the way every person—in order to feel like one person—experiences his or her life. But in this text Hamlet's singularity "leans upon" and rises out of his uncle's cruel murder of his father and the report of this crime, which is singular because it happened in one time and place, and because it carries a scandalous, unheard-of horror, to which Hamlet is compelled to respond. At a textual level this crime functions as the origin, the "primal scene" of the character Hamlet's singularity. But if one traces how this crime is woven into the action and the text, its status becomes complex and multivalent.

So let us start with the simplest and most stupid aspect of the crime's coming to Hamlet's knowledge. Why is the report of the Ghost's appearance brought to him? Why do the two guards of the watch, Marcellus and Barnardo, and their friend Horatio, consider it their duty to take their account not to Claudius, their recently crowned King, but to Hamlet? Are they asserting the priority of the father-son relation to the brother-brother relationship? Why do they keep this report from Claudius even before Hamlet enjoins them to do so? They must be aware of a rivalry between nephew and uncle which is already going on; in taking their report to Hamlet they have aligned themselves with his party.

It is difficult to imagine what Claudius and the Ghost might have said to one another if circumstances had conspired to bring them together. Of course, we have seen how Hamlet and the Ghost—given their ruling passions—are uniquely well fitted for each other, a fact reflected in what Hamlet makes of Horatio's report. Horatio describes the "apparition" as "a figure like your father," and Hamlet at first seems to accept this uncertainty by swearing to speak to it if "it assume my noble father's person." The Ghost comes as an appearance or likeness; what "it" is remains in doubt. But the moment Horatio and the others leave the stage, Hamlet fixes both the Ghost's identity and the meaning of its appearance: he says, "My father's spirit—in arms! All is not well. / I doubt some foul play." And when Hamlet sees the Ghost and decides to speak with it, he names it: "I'll call thee Hamlet, / King, father, royal Dane" (I, iv, 44–45). Finally, upon hearing the Ghost identify the murderer, Hamlet cries, "O my prophetic soul! My uncle!" (I, v, 41). For Hamlet this Ghost is less objectively determined than another person, and less fugitive than a private fantasy. As a trace which eludes the opposition presence/absence, the Ghost in its disclosure obeys the logic of the traumatic event: it can have singular self-defining force in this text only because it repeats what rested latent, already half-known and half-desired, in Hamlet. And when the Ghost appears, Hamlet can take him as an external expression and likeness of the interpretation of reality he was already well on the way to formulating.

There is one aspect of the Ghost's representation which helps the crime to function as an origin: its instantaneousness. The Ghost tells Hamlet of the way Claudius poisoned him while he was sleeping in his "orchard": the "cursed hebenon" poured in his ear coursed through his body *"swift as quicksilver,"* "and with a *sudden* vigour it doth posset / And curd . . . / The thin and wholesome blood . . . / And a *most instant* tetter bark'd about. . . . Thus was I . . . / Of life, of crown, of queen *at once* dispatch'd" (I, v, 62–75; my emphasis). The representation of the crime as instantaneous helps to create a certain impression: that this crime is uncalled for, unprepared for, and had no clear reason for happening. It is pure sin and excess, imposed from without upon a world innocent of the evil of this crime until the act occurs. This idea of the crime justifies the sense of shock and scandal that the Ghost evinces and Hamlet immediately echoes. The disease metaphors which lace the text, and which are so favored by Hamlet, imply the existence of a natural healthful body before the disease.

It is not just the suddenness of the crime that allows it to function as the instantaneous origin and seed of the revenge fiction; it appears as the arbitrary cause of all that follows. When Claudius alludes to his crime in prayer, he offers a two-line explanation of his act: he despairs of receiving heavenly absolution because he is still possessed "of those effects for which I did the murder— / My crown, mine own ambition, and my queen" (III, iii, 54–55). But because there is no narrative elaboration of the reasons behind these reasons, the crime appears to the spectator as the single enigmatic origin of the action.

The biblical allusions engaged by the murder do not explain the crime, though they disperse its singularity. Since King Hamlet is murdered in his orchard and Claudius is described as a serpent, the crime repeats the first sin, the serpent's temptation in Eden; and since, as Claudius says, the crime has "the primal eldest curse upon't — / A brother's murder," it repeats the first murder, Cain's murder of Abel (III, iii, 37–38). But once we have noticed its relationship to these archetypal crimes, then this crime can no longer be viewed as singular or original. Instead, it is part of the fatality of Christian history: an unending chain of sins, illustrated by the echoes of biblical typology, which human beings are condemned to repeat. And if one attends to the way these two archetypal transgressions are represented by the Western tradition, their originality is put in question in another way. Thus although Milton follows Christian doctrine in clearing Adam and Eve of any sin until they eat the apple, his narrative takes the moment of sin and disobedience upon a regress backward in time. In order to think the possibility of the serpent's temptation of Eve, one must suppose a desire to rival God and challenge his law, before the serpent's temptation. And to account for the serpent's opposition to God, the Christian tradition supposes a whole series of events: Satan's rivalry with Christ, a war in heaven, and the fall of Satan and his allies, long before man's "original" Fall.[58] In a parallel fashion Cain's murder is not an uncalled-for accidental origin; it is a response to the special favor God extends to Abel, by accepting Abel's sacrifice and rejecting Cain's (Gen. 4:3–5). These examples and the text of *Hamlet* might lead one to wonder: can one ever locate a pure "time before" rivalry and division?

The Ghost and Hamlet conspire to imagine this crime as nonhistorical, outside of time, and gratuitous. In this way the crime authorizes the extremity of their indignation and the task of revenge as a way to cleanse Denmark of sin. But everything we have noted about this crime embeds its singularity in a network of repetitions: the rivalry that precedes the ghostly account of the crime; Hamlet's uncanny foreknowledge of it; its impossible instantaneity; its intertextual repetition of (non-)original biblical crimes. If we become almost perversely literal and take this text as the fragmentary chronical of a real kingdom, we can speculate that Claudius's murder of his brother would be embedded in a series of conditions, causes, and desires hidden from us. Was Claudius' act an expression of fraternal rivalry which had festered for years? Was it a response to the arbitrary fate of being a less favored brother?[59] How did Claudius feel when his brother married the woman he may have always desired, had the son he would have liked, and defeated old Fortinbras, to become the legendary hero of Denmark? I do not ask these questions, or make these surmises, with a view to finding a "correct" answer. Rather I use them to suggest that the singularity of the crime, and of Hamlet's position as it is projected by the crime, is an effect of an artificial *coupure*, which cuts us (and the Ghost? and Hamlet?) off from seeing the matrix of repetitions within which the singularity of the person-as-person is inscribed.

There is a strange coincidental element of this text which allows the reader to glimpse the play of repetitions within which the life of the person appears as singular. Near the beginning of the play Horatio tells of the dual in which, thirty years earlier, King Hamlet defeated Fortinbras of Norway. In Act V the gravedigger tells us

58. Here I am depending especially upon Milton's interpretations of that tradition in *Paradise Lost*.

59. Shakespeare often chronicles the arbitrary disadvantage which accrues to the second son. See, for example, the hostile rivalry between Frederick and Duke Senior in *As You Like It* and between Antonio and Prospero in *The Tempest*.

that upon this very day he was given his job as gravedigger and Prince Hamlet was born. The whole central portion of this drama is focused upon the unfolding of one person's single trajectory of life: Prince Hamlet's effort to find an adequate (and effective) revenge for King Hamlet's murder. When the moment arrives, Hamlet enters the duel to wager life in a moment as brief as a single thrust of his rapier. Thus he reflects to Horatio "And a man's life is no more than to say 'one'." Perhaps this moment has the same double character as the magnificent pearl or "union" that Claudius drops into Hamlet's goblet at the beginning of the duel. As each pearl is supposed to be unique in its shape, the greatest and most perfect pearls were called "unions." But as Claudius uses the pearl as a vehicle and lure for the poison he adds to Hamlet's drink, the union also becomes the single vanishing point where the unique life of a person is fixed and dissolved in death. Thus this moment of immediacy and self-summoning self-presence, of which Hamlet can say things like "the interim is mine" and "the readiness is all," and accept a "fate" he supposes will be unique and singular, this climactic moment of life and drama, also turns out to be a repetition in reverse of that moment thirty years earlier when Hamlet's father killed Fortinbras' father. But now, under very different circumstances, a Hamlet is defeated, a Fortinbras ascends the throne, and the gravedigger—the only person perhaps capable of reflecting on these symmetries—is silent.

Of course the participants in this final scene can be only dimly aware of the relationship of this duel to an earlier duel. Instead they keep their attention focused upon their singular trajectories of effort and intention. But this does not prevent them from repeating the earlier moment, now in a pattern of chiasmic reversal. For the spectator who becomes aware of this pattern, there is a certain interpretive temptation: by posing the question "what does this coincidence mean?" the reader can readily move, through a logic I analyzed above, from converting chance into a sign to supposing a controlling design behind every incident of the text and the life it represents. One will presume, that by contriving this coincidence, Shakespeare must be "saying" something about the nature of reality. He might, for example, be calling attention to the *contrast* between these two duels and the epoch each embodies: the age when adherence to chivalric codes of honor could endow a duel with the resonance and value of sacred ritual, and a later, more "fallen" historical period, when the duel becomes the setting for the most egregious and chaotic forms of self-assertion. Through this contrast, Shake-

[296]

speare is supposed to offer an ironic critique of the positions of those caught in the latter. This is the kind of perspective upon *Hamlet* developed by Francis Fergusson and Sigurd Burckhardt, under the influence of the "modernist" understanding of Western civilization T. S. Eliot had so much part in formulating.[60] But this perspective ignores something *Hamlet* demonstrates with compelling clarity: we always know a past, supposed to be golden, through the (desire-laden) legends produced in a present always presumed to belong to an age of iron. This contrast seems to hold now just as it did in the England of Shakespeare's time and the Denmark of Hamlet's (fictional) epoch. And besides, isn't the idea of historical decline and fall always shot through with one's point of view? Thus the reader of this text gets to hear of King Hamlet's duel with old Fortinbras only through an account which sounds like Denmark's official legend. Wouldn't Claudius have told it quite differently? And surely the Fortinbras who is plotting his revenge at the play's beginning would have told it in still another way. The second duel will be no less subject to the influence of historical bias. For if young Fortinbras inaugurates a long and fruitful reign in Denmark, won't his successors think of the day he won his throne in a way strangely, and perhaps only obliquely related to the feelings stirred by Hamlet's death in those spectators of his life and death, both inside and outside the text, who have been invited by the form of Shakespeare's fiction to feel with him?

All of this is to say that, instead of taking the final scene of this text as a fixed datum with a single meaning, we should assume that there are incompatible alternative realities and interpretations suspended *in potentia* in the "same" matrix of events. Then we will not need to interpret the text as a dialectical progression which embeds and subsumes the truth and value of an earlier duel (as loss) within the later duel. Then the "irony" produced by the resemblance of these two duels is not the intended effect of the artist as a presiding deity. Instead it is the effect of reading this coincidence from a position this text both favors and puts in question: the vantage point of Hamlet's interests and desires. The symmetrical appearance of these two duels is not evidence of an overarching order; the coherence

60. See Fergusson, *The Idea of a Theatre*; Sigurd Burckhardt, *Shakespearean Meanings* (Princeton: Princeton University Press, 1968); and T. S. Eliot in his many essays upon Dante, Donne, and others. This perspective has been brought to my attention, with particular vividness and force by my colleague Richard Fly. See his forthcoming article "Accommodating Death: The Ending of *Hamlet*." For an inventive meditation upon the centrality of chance to *Hamlet*, see Tom Stoppard's play, *Rosencrantz and Guildenstern Are Dead*.

arises out of the process of weaving a life (as Hamlet does), a text (as Shakespeare does), a reading experience (as we do). And in these weavings, these acts of interpretation, each will encounter these two duels as alien doubles or displaced repetitions which, like a symptom or an uncanny eruption from the unconscious, cannot be comprehended by the person, as a single person, in the mode of consciousness. As a sign, and as chance, the climactic duel sustains its otherness to the person. The person's life unfolds in singular repetition as a singular repetition. Like the likeness of two terms that founds the single moment of beauty, the repetition of the fathers' duel in the sons' duel stamps Hamlet's life-trajectory with a shape which must seem both arbitrary and inevitable, natural and a contrivance of art.

EPILOGUE

MASTERY AS EFFECT OF
A TEXTUAL LABYRINTH

And yet, and yet . . . Denying temporal succession, denying the self, denying the astronomical universe, are apparent desperations and secret consolations. Our destiny . . . is not frightful by being unreal; it is frightful because it is irreversible and iron-clad. Time is the substance I am made of. Time is a river which sweeps me along, but I am the river; it is a tiger which destroys me, but I am the tiger; it is a fire which consumes me, but I am the fire. The world, unfortunately is real; I, unfortunately, am Borges.

Borges, "A New Refutation of Time," *Labyrinths*

Twentieth-century readers are indebted to the Argentine writer Jorge Luis Borges for one of the most compelling images of an all-comprehending text which exceeds comprehension, a labyrinthine text which puts mastery under erasure. A quick reading of one of his fictions can offer a template for aligning and reseeing the three conceptual narratives of this book. Then we can sharpen our focus of the (revised) image of the master-text we have all the time been on the way to constructing. In one of the stories from *Labyrinths,* "The Garden of Forking Paths," Borges tells the story of a German spy of Chinese extraction named Hai Feng. Being pursued by a relentless English policeman named Madden, he has only a few hours to generate a sign which will communicate to his German superiors the French city where a new English artillery park has been built. To achieve this objective, he finds the name of a person who happens to share the same name as this city—"Albert"—, journeys to his house in the suburbs, and after an hour's conversation kills him. A few moments later, Madden arrives and arrests Hai Feng. This story of the

[299]

last few hours of Hai Feng's freedom receives its drama from the series of uncanny coincidences which befall him. The English countryside he walks through reminds him of the legendary labyrinth said to have been constructed by his ancestor Ts'ui Pên. The music playing in the garden of the man he has marked out for murder is Chinese. Finally, this man, Stephen Albert, is a Sinologist who has spent his life deciphering the very labyrinth, named "The Garden of Forking Paths," invented by Ts'ui Pên. In the short time they have before Madden's arrival, Albert explains the logic of the labyrinth to Hai Feng. "The Garden of Forking Paths" is not a physical place, but refers to the vast inchoate mass of narratives assembled into a book of that title. A passage from that point in the story at which Albert reveals the secret structure of "The Garden of Forking Paths" can serve as a fictional commentary on those episodes of the person's encounter with chance I have recounted in this book.

"In all fictional works, each time a man is confronted with several alternatives, he chooses one and eliminates the others; in the fiction of Ts'ui Pên, he chooses—simultaneously—all of them. *He creates,* in this way, diverse futures, diverse times which themselves also proliferate and fork. Here, then, is the explanation of the novel's contradictions. Fang, let us say, has a secret; a stranger calls at his door; Fang resolves to kill him. Naturally, there are several possible outcomes; Fang can kill the intruder, the intruder can kill Fang, they both can escape, they both can die, and so forth. In the work of Ts'ui Pên, all possible outcomes occur; each one is the point of departure for other forkings. Sometimes, the paths of this labyrinth converge: for example, you arrive at this house, but in one of the possible pasts you are my enemy, in another, my friend."

. . . He read with slow precision two versions of the same epic chapter. In the first, an army marches to a battle across a lonely mountain; the horror of the rocks and shadows makes the men undervalue their lives and they gain an easy victory. In the second, the same army traverses a palace where a great festival is taking place; the resplendent battle seems to them a continuation of the celebration and they win the victory. . . . I remember the last words, repeated in each version like a secret commandment: *Thus fought the heroes, tranquil their admirable hearts, violent their swords, resigned to kill and to die.* From that moment on, I felt about me and within my dark body an invisible, intangible swarming. Not the swarming of the divergent, parallel and finally coalescent armies, but a more inaccessible, more intimate agitation that they in some manner prefigured.[1]

1. "The Garden of Forking Paths," trans. Donald A. Yates, in *Labyrinths: Selected Short Stories & Other Writings* (New York: New Directions, 1962), 26, 27.

This text sets up a series of echoes between Hai Feng's situation and the examples used by Stephen Albert to illustrate the labyrinth: Feng too is an "intruder" upon a murderous mission; he is the agent of one of two "coalscent armies"; and the last words of the double narrative (*Thus fought the heroes . . .*) become his own "secret commandment." These uncanny repetitions create the story's "intimate agitation." It comes of a tension between two orders of his being: a foreground, where Feng feels both the singularity of his own person and the immediacy and the necessity of his task; and a background of textual traces and echoes and suppressed memories (of ancestors and homelands) which seem to undergird his very person, but also threaten to dissolve all differences of place, time, and person into an undifferentiated textual labyrinth. In this labyrinth Stephen Albert can become a double of a long-dead ancestor and their two gardens one garden in a space outside time. This background is not only "inaccessible" to consciousness because its possibilities are infinite in number; a person must repress its proliferating repetitions to be any one at all. But there are moments when, standing in the midst of the self's single role, the labyrinth of (our) other selves suddenly impinges, and one feels what is chance and arbitrary about the one person one is. This is the characteristic climax of a Borges fiction: a single person (a spy, a librarian, Borges himself) tells a story that gradually implicates him (and the reader) as one defined by a textual labyrinth of which he cannot become fully conscious. In these stories, the moment of shock, surprise, and chance can be described as a humiliating revision of number. A position which seemed singular and unique is suddenly seen to be inscribed in a field of infinite repetitions. It is this boundary position that produces the intimate agitation the story records, and that Borges clearly hopes to provoke in its reader.

From the distance afforded by Borges' text, we can bring into focus the *mise en scène* of the person, chance, and mastery found in this fiction, and also operating in my three conceptual narratives. The readings I have ventured in these narratives are a way of releasing the historicity of the "protagonist's" interpretive act/event from under the sway of a text, understood as a metaphysical noncontingent locus of truth and authority. In all three narratives, the deconstruction of a metaphysical notion of mastery issues in an account of how the *effect* of mastery has been produced. In each narrative there is a moment when the protagonist projects himself into the position of supposed mastery: Freud claims he has "fathered" psychoanalysis in heroic isolation; saying an artistic "yes" to that life that is a woman (and Lou Salomé), Nietzsche (will) speak(s) to men as the god Zara-thustra; in passionate loyalty to the memory of his father, Hamlet would sweep to his revenge "as fast as meditation, or the thoughts of love." This moment of mastery is essentially wishful and fantasmatic. It is almost immediately countered by the emergence of limits which seem necessary, material, arbitrary. They can not be erased, but in-stead are something that must become part of the itinerary: the pri-mal scene of rivalry where claims to priority will be specious; the eruption of an unconscious will, which is multiple, heterogeneous, uncontrollable; that "drag" of a resistant social and linguistic me-dium that obviates a swift revenge.

By rereading these three texts in relation to the life-writing of two people and one character, I have reconceived moments of imagined mastery as emerging as the effect of interpretations which have three distinct but related elements: a collaboration with an other, a turn into the labyrinths of language, and the perception of a decisive coincidence. In these collaborative, language-bound interpretive ef-forts, what catalyzes interpretation is the perception of a chance con-vergence which has meaning precisely for "me." Freud reads his friend Fliess as the Caesar to whom he will play Brutus; Nietzsche reads Lou Salomé as the woman who personifies the life to which he would say "yes"; and Hamlet gropes toward revenge by collaborat-ing a performance with the players, modeling his action upon two effective actors, and becoming a forger. Let me specify more pre-cisely how chance catalyzes interpretation. No less than for Borges' spy Hai Feng, these moments arrive when the protagonists of my three narratives are immersed in work with language—dream inter-pretation, revising *The Gay Science* and planning *Zarathustra,* produc-ing a play, forging a letter, and arranging the duel. It is then that they hear the "intangible swarming sensation" produced by a laby-rinth of explicit and incipient coincidences. Each protagonist finds a useful way to negotiate uncanny repetitions. While interpreting the *non vixit* dream, Freud conjures up the primal scene of his rivalry with his nephew John, where he plays the role of Brutus; "strange to say," he really did play that role once as a child of fourteen, and it seems he is preparing to do so again. In meditating about his new passion for Lou Salomé, Nietzsche discovers those "dear coinci-dences" of sensibility and work and love, by which a poem like "On Pain" can be written in a voice for which he has been waiting his whole life. And just before he enters the duel scene and repeats in reverse the duel in which his father defeated old Fortinbras, Hamlet tells Horatio of those vague misgivings which bode some (possible) misfortune. In grappling with this chance, the person is pushed to the limit of consciousness, and is forced to linger before the fact of his failure to control his future. In this situation, the observation of a coincidence plays a decisive role in the interpretive movement by which the person becomes ready to release himself into a future of a certain shape. This gesture of assumed fatality engenders part of the romance of chance. Something has happened about which it is nearly impossible to believe it is "simply" chance; you have an "uncanny" intimation that you have been here before, that you are "not alone at the helm," that there is "a divinity that shapes our ends," or a "personal providence" which creates an analogous illusion.[2]

This book has tried to grasp the full strangeness of those turnings the person experiences as chance. They are not one, but always both of two opposed possibilities: a function of the life-position of a single person, and yet also something "other" which exceeds that position; an act chosen by the interpretation of chance, and a binding contingency with the character of an event; an intrapsychic fantasy, and the etched memory of the actual; the outside in, and the inside out; art and history; a singular repetition. When chance appears before the person in this double (dis-)guise, the differences (of time, of person, of historical moment) which found identity can converge to a point. They coincide as coincidence. The person is in so many places that he can no longer know precisely where he is. We do not inhabit but become a "garden of forking paths." This is the site of uncontrol, before which the subject knows a kind of interpretive agoraphobia. A dream interpretation has reached its point of contact with the unknown. Friends and lovers are condemned to take divergent roads. Ingenious devices return upon their inventors' heads. Lightning strikes.

The contingency of these acts/events still signify something, but perhaps it is something repressed that we would rather not hear, some scene or act or anger we find ourselves compelled to repeat. For example, like the simple scene that repeats itself in three widely spaced narratives of this book—two people are in rivalry to take possession of one person or thing. Perhaps the two are Freud and his nephew John, or Nietzsche and Rée, or Hamlet and Laertes . . . and the object both want to control is the body of psychoanalysis, or is a woman whose name could be Lou Salomé or Ophelia or Pauline, or is to be left indeterminate. There is something deathly about the

2. Freud's essay "The Uncanny"; André Breton, *Nadja*, trans. Richard Howard (New York: Grove Press, 1960); Hamlet, V, ii, 10; *GS*, 277.

return of this scene. What is at issue in the scene and reiterates itself throughout this text is a strife for mastery and absolute possession, and the encounter with the limits to mastery. But by writing of, and within, and outside life-writing, each attempt of interpretation produces a text: *The Interpretation of Dreams; Zarathustra*; Shakespeare's tragedy and Hamlet's last act. By instituting psychoanalysis, teaching a philosophy, and achieving (a) performance, each of these texts does something in the "world." And though the single separateness of this making is an illusion dependent upon the forgetting of an other (Fliess, or Salomé, or one's father's very different duel), the pathway through a labyrinth of life and language experienced as chance still achieves effects of mastery which can never be won outright.

INDEX

Abrams, M. H., 276
Aristotle, 227, 267, 277
Art: as a suppression of chance, 26, 279
Austin, J. L., 98
Authority:
    of Freud's writings, 39–40
    See also Mastery

Barthes, Roland, 288
Binion, Rudolph, 119–20, 159
Biographical reading, 27
    chance a term within, 16
    criticism's excision of, 156, 197
    of "life-writing," 29
    as monumental history, 157–58
    as a reduction, 156
    risks of/skepticism about, 28, 156
Booth, Stephen, 277–78
Borges, Jorge Luis, 142
    "The Garden of Forking Paths,"
        299–302
    on Shakespeare, 282
Burckhardt, Jacob, 121

Chance:
    Christian marginalization of, 227–28
    definition of, 16, 20
    as enigma to read, 19, 302–3
    etymology of, 21–22
    and falling, 20–21
    as idea in *Hamlet*, 223–27
    knowledge as response to, 19–20
    mastery through suppression of,
        22–23
    neither determined nor "free," 54
    Nietzsche raising the question of, 17,
        131–32

as operator of my readings, 28
and sacrifice, 223–24
scandal of, in *Hamlet*, 272–74
and Shakespeare's text, 221–22,
    280–81
and text and experience, relation
    described, 16–17
urgent to the person, 18–19
Western marginalization of, 17–18
Christianity: marginalization of chance,
    227–28
Coincidence. *See* Chance
Coleridge, Samuel Taylor, 218–19, 266,
    272
Contingency. *See* Chance
Corngold, Stanley, 128–30, 151–52

Decartes: rewritten by Nietzsche, 135–37
Deconstruction: literary readings a subset
    of, 13–14
Deconstructive reading, of Nietzsche,
    125–27
de Lauretis, Teresa, 22
Deleuze, Gilles, 124
de Man, Paul, 125–26, 129, 151
Derrida, Jacques:
    on chance, 21n
    deconstructive reading of Nietzsche,
        125–27
    on experience, 17n

Eagleton, Terry, 14–15
Experience, 16–17

Fergusson, Francis, 277, 297
Fliess, Wilhelm:
    Freud's editors' discomfort with,
        79–81

Library of Congress Cataloging-in-Publication Data

Warner, William Beatty.
  Chance and the text of experience.

  Includes index.
  1. Shakespeare, William, 1564–1616. Hamlet. 2. Psychoanalysis and
literature. 3. Freud, Sigmund, 1856–1939. 4. Nietzsche, Friedrich Wilhelm,
1844–1900. I. Title.
PR2807.W28   1986   822.3'3   86–6276
ISBN 0-8014-1754-6 (alk. paper)